ESSENTIAL

Teacher Knowledge

CORE CONCEPTS IN ENGLISH LANGUAGE TEACHING

Contents

Text and discourse

B BACKGROUND TO LANGUAGE TEACHING METHODOLOGY 81

C TEACHING LANGUAGE AND LANGUAGE SKILLS 101

Introduction

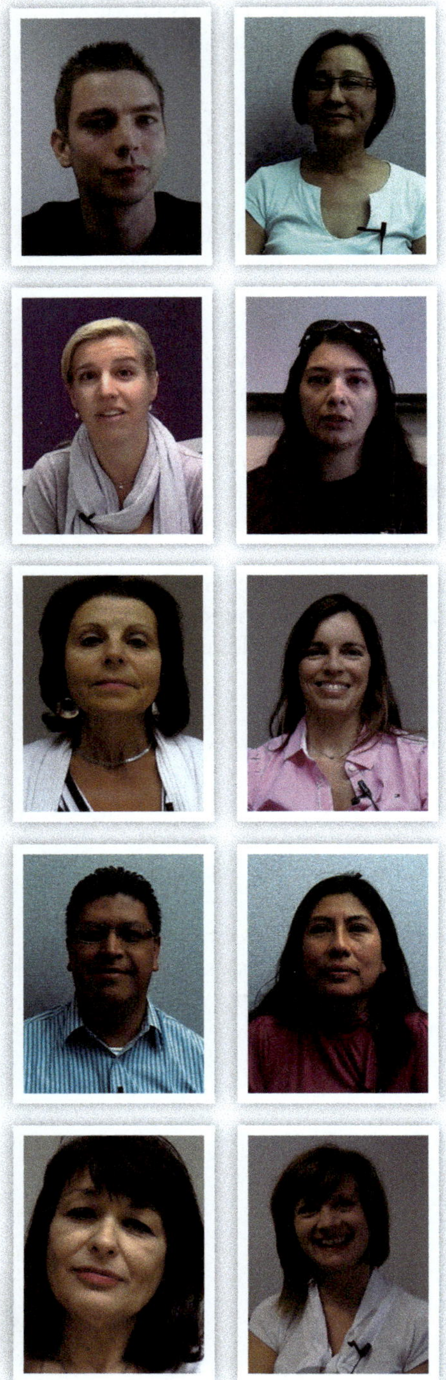

Welcome to *Essential Teacher Knowledge* (*ETK*). This book is written for people around the world who teach (or are going to teach) English. We have designed it to be useful to teachers of adults, teenagers and young learners – whether they are teaching general English or CLIL.

ETK is especially useful (but not only) for teachers who have English as a second language.

1 What is in *Essential Teacher Knowledge*?

- *ETK* has 110 units about the English language and about how to teach it. The units describe practical classroom ideas as well as the ideas (the theory) behind them.
- There is an accompanying DVD. You can watch examples of teachers at work, and you can hear teachers from around the world talking about how they do things.
- We have divided *ETK* into separate sections so that it is easier to use. For example, if you want to improve your knowledge of English grammar, vocabulary, pronunciation or text and discourse (the 'nuts and bolts' of the language), then you can look at the units in Section A. If, however, you are thinking of teaching CLIL (content and language integrated learning), then you will be more interested in Section G. Teachers who work (or will work) with young learners will find Section F especially relevant.
- However, many of the topics that we deal with are important in more than one area. Topics such as planning matter whether you teach adults, teenagers or children. As a result, there are units on planning in general (Units 79 and 80); there is a unit (100), on using topics and themes for planning young learner lessons; and we discuss planning for CLIL in Unit 109.
- Most of the unit topics in Section D (Managing learning and teaching) are just as relevant for teaching children and teenagers as they are for teaching adults. They will be just as interesting for CLIL teachers as they are for anyone else!
- When you are reading *ETK* you will often see technical terms written like this: PAIRWORK. This means that you can find the word in the **Glossdex** (pages 257–287). The **Glossdex** entry for *pairwork* looks like this (the numbers are the unit numbers in which pairwork is mentioned):

  pair, pairwork when two students work together →22, 26, 39, 42, 46, 56, 58, **67**, 79, 86, 89, 93, 102, 107, 109
- We give references to help you move around the book. For example, in Unit 43 (on motivation) you will find this: extensive reading →**54**. This means that if you go to Unit 54, you will find more information about extensive reading.
- If you see DVD12, it means that you can look at Teaching Techniques track 12 on the DVD to see examples of teaching.
- If you see T10, it means that you can go to track 10 in the audio section of our website (*www.pearsonELT.com/ETK*) to hear an audio clip.

2 How to use *Essential Teacher Knowledge*

You can use the units in *ETK* in any way you choose, of course. However, we have some suggestions about how the book can be most effective.

- You can choose the section that is most relevant to you and read the units in that section.
- You can look at the Contents list and choose the units that sound interesting to you.
- You can follow the references between the units (such as extensive reading →**54**, mentioned above).
- You can look at the **Glossdex** and search for topics that interest you. For example, if you are interested in pairwork, you can follow up all the unit references that you find there to learn a lot about the use of pairwork in a variety of different contexts.

- You can watch the film clips on the DVD in any sequence that you want. However, it may be helpful if you wait until you find references to the DVD (such as DVD12) in the units and then watch the video excerpts. They will make more sense because you can read about the techniques and procedures which they show.

3 The lives of teachers

In Section A we look at how the English language works.

- Language (grammar, vocabulary, pronunciation and text and discourse) is contextualised in short stories about a variety of teachers from around the world.
- We also discuss various topics (such as homework, discipline, teacher burnout, etc.) in connection with the stories about teachers' lives.

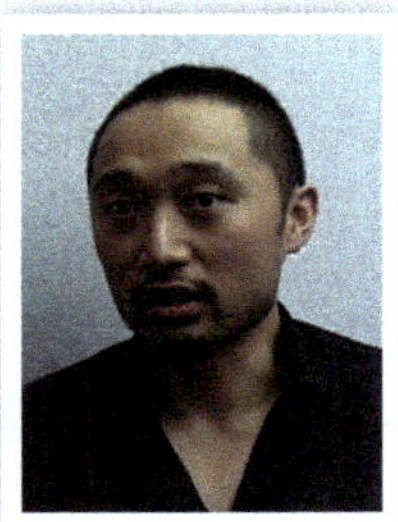

4 Practical teaching ideas

Section C (Teaching language and language skills) contains many different examples of practical techniques and activities. But this is not the only place where such ideas can be found.

- In Units 7 and 17 we discuss different grammar teaching ideas.
- In Unit 22 we look at ideas for meeting and remembering words.
- In Units 28 and 29 we show ideas for teaching pronunciation.
- In Units 93–99 we look at classroom activities for young learners.
- In Unit 108 we look at activities for CLIL learners

5 Teachers' voices

In the Teachers' Voices section of the DVD you will find clips of teachers from around the world talking about their teaching experiences and what they do in the classroom. Here is a list of the teachers and the topics they talk about. You can listen to many more teachers' voices on our website: *www.pearsonELT.com/ETK*

1 Graciela Barreto (Uruguay) Managing young learners
2 Magdalena Custodio Espinar (Spain) Teaching young learners
3 Victor Chen (Taiwan) Helping students to progress
4 Melinda Madrassy (Hungary) Using puppets
5 Marija Andraka (Croatia) Young learners and grammar
6 Magdalena Custodio Espinar (Spain) Teaching CLIL using two languages
7 Liliana Burga (Peru) Groupwork and pairwork with teenagers
8 Ann Masako Mayeda (Japan) Creating motivation through student choice
9 Nino Chelidze (Georgia) Teaching adults
10 Oğuzhan Kalkan (Turkey) Using (and adding to) coursebooks
11 Bianca Hofmann (German) Using vocabulary tests to motivate students
12 Deniz Atesok (Turkey) Teaching mixed ability/differentiation
13 Jeannette Jimenez Pachas (Peru) Correcting during accuracy and fluency
14 German Gomez (Guatemala) Using dialogues to teach grammar
15 Katie Malik (Poland) Exposing students to different accents
16 Kamelija Simonovska (Macedonia) A vocabulary activity
17 Nino Chelidze (Georgia) Using dictionaries after reading
18 Monika Czyrska (Poland) Student project work with PowerPoint
19 Alex Field (UK) An end-of-lesson vocabulary game
20 Vivian Hagos Ibrahim (Eritrea) An end-of-lesson vocabulary activity
21 Diana Karan (Canada) Using exit cards to check learning

6 Revise, research, reflect

You will find exercises and questions for each unit of *ETK* on our website: *www.pearsonELT.com/ETK*

Essential Teacher Knowledge and the TKT (Teaching Knowledge Test)

Because *Essential Teacher Knowledge* is for *anyone* who wants to know about language teaching, it has not been written just for people who are taking the various elements of the TKT test. However, if you want to take the TKT, this book will help you to prepare for success in the test – whichever paper or module you are interested in.

The following chart gives details of the papers and modules of the TKT and shows which units in *Essential Teacher Knowledge* are relevant for them. However, the book is organised a little differently from the actual TKT syllabus so that, for example, a topic like 'managing learners' (which is in the TKT Young learners module) is in a different section in *Essential Teacher Knowledge* because it covers issues (for example, discipline) which do not just apply to young learners.

Readers can also consult the **Glossdex** on pages 257–287 to look for references to (and explanations of) TKT terms. The **Glossdex** contains the most important and useful technical words used by the TKT test writers – as well as others that are important for teaching English success. Readers who want the official TKT exam-based glossaries can download them from the Cambridge ESOL website:
www.cambridgeesol.org/exam-preparation/index.html#tkt

TKT Test/Module	**TKT section/ part number**	**Topic**	**Unit number(s) in *Essential Teacher Knowledge***
TKT Modules 1, 2 and 3	1 Describing language and language skills	Grammar: parts of speech	1
		Vocabulary: types of meaning	18
		Vocabulary: word formation	19
		Vocabulary: word groupings	20
		Pronunciation: symbols from the International Phonemic Alphabet (IPA)/phonemes	23
		Pronunciation: stress	26
		Pronunciation: intonation	27
		Pronunciation: connected speech (language)	25
		Functions	30
		Language skills: reading, listening speaking, writing and sub-skills	51–62
		Features of spoken and written texts	31
		Features of spoken and written texts: accuracy and fluency	73, 92
	2 Background to language learning	Motivation	43
		Exposure to language and focus on form (acquisition and learning)	35, 36
		The role of error	37
		Differences in age	38, 39, 40
		Differences in the context of learning	41
		Learner characteristics	40
		Maturity and past learning experiences	40
	3 Background to language teaching	Introductory activities	70
		Common ways of presenting/introducing language	44, 45, 46
		Production tasks (practice)	47–50
		Common comprehension tasks (language skills)	41–62
		Assessment types and tasks	88, 89, 101, 110
Knowledge about language	1 Lexis	Types of meaning; sense relations	18
		Word formation	19
		Lexical units: collocation, lexical phrases/chunks	20
		Register	33
	2 Phonology	Phonemes	23
		Word stress and sentence stress; contrastive stress	26
		Intonation and what it means	27

TKT Test/Module	TKT section/ part number	Topic	Unit number(s) in *Essential Teacher Knowledge*
	3 Grammar	The role of context in grammar	5
		Word class in grammatical structure	1
		Different types of noun	12
		Determiners	13, 14
		Adjectives	15
		Noun phrase structures	15, 16, 17
		Verb types	4
		Verb patterns	10
		Verb mode (declarative, negative, etc.)	17
		Modality	8
		Time and tense	5
		Aspect	6
		Hypotheticality (conditionals)	2
		Adverbials	11
		The passive	1, 32, 33
		Reported speech	10, 103
		Sentences and clauses	2
	4 Discourse	Coherence	34
		Anaphoric reference, etc.	34
		Lexical cohesion	34
		Register	33
		Written and spoken English	31
		Genre	32
Young learners	1 Knowledge of young learners and principles of teaching young learners	Children's characteristics as language learners	91
		Developing children's learning strategies through language learning and communication	92, 93–99, 107
		Developing children's cognitive and communication strategies through language learning	92, 93–99, 107
	2 Planning and preparing young learners lessons	Lesson plans and what goes into them	79, 80, 100, 109, Appendix C
		Providing support and challenge when selecting and using coursebooks and supplementary materials	81, 82, 83, 106
		Additional resources	82, 83, 106
	3 Teaching young learners	Scaffolding children's understanding; teacher language and strategies	65, 68, 69, 74, 91, 97, 102, 107
		Using practice activities to consolidate children's language learning	93–99
		Managing young learners	70, 71
	4 Assessing young learner learning	Purpose and focus of different kinds of test	88, 89, 101, 110
Content and Language Integrated Learning	1 Knowledge of CLIL and principles of CLIL	Aims and rationale for CLIL	102
		Language across the curriculum	103
		Communication skills across the curriculum	103, 104
		Learning skills across the curriculum	107
	2 Lesson preparation	Planning a lesson or a series of lessons	79, 80, 109, Appendix C
		Language demands of subject content and tasks	109
		Resources: visual organisers and multi-media	106, 105
	3 Lesson delivery	Classroom language	107
		Scaffolding content and language learning	65, 69, 74, 91, 97, 102, 107
		Methods to help learners develop learning strategies	107
	4 Assessment	Focusing on content and language	109
		Types of assessment	88, 89, 110
		Support strategies	
Practical		Making a lesson plan	79, 80, 100, 109, Appendix C
		Teaching a lesson	44–75

(present simple)
I work

Section A: Language

Section A looks at four main area of language: **Grammar** (Units 1–17), **Vocabulary** (Units 18–22), **Pronunciation** (Units 23–29) and **Text and discourse** (Units 30–34).

Almost all of the units in Section A start with shorts texts and dialogues about the lives of teachers around the world. These show examples of the language that the unit is focusing on. In the grammar units this includes the elements of the sentence, parts of speech, sentences and questions, verbs (and adverbs), and the noun phrase (including articles, quantifiers, adjectives and post-modification). In the vocabulary section we look at word meaning, on how words 'get together' (collocation and lexical phrases/chunks) and at metaphor, idioms and proverbs. In the pronunciation section we focus on the phonemic alphabet, on how and where (in the mouth) we make sounds, on what happens when sounds are used together, on how we stress words and phrases and on how we use pitch change for different intonation. Finally, in the section on text and discourse we look at differences between speaking and writing, and on how we compose texts (written and spoken) that actually make sense.

Five units within this section give classroom teaching ideas. These are ideas for helping students learn about verb tense and aspect (Unit 7), various elements of the noun phrase (Unit 17), ways of remembering words (Unit 22), sounds (Unit 28) and stress and intonation (Unit 29).

Many of the units in Section A also contain short discussions of issues such as homework, teacher burnout, what it feels like to be corrected, the difference (if any) between native-speaker and non-native-speaker teachers, etc.

Grammar

1 What's in a sentence?
2 How we use clauses
3 Asking questions
4 Introducing verbs
5 Verb tenses (form and meaning)
6 Aspect
7 Teaching verbs (and adverbs)
8 Auxiliaries and modals
9 Multi-word and phrasal verbs
10 Verb complementation
11 Introducing adverbs
12 Introducing nouns
13 Articles
14 Quantifiers
15 Introducing adjectives
16 What comes after nouns?
17 Teaching the noun phrase

Lexis and vocabulary

18 What words mean
19 How words are formed
20 Collocation and lexical phrases
21 Metaphor, idiom, proverb and cliché
22 Meeting and remembering words

Pronunciation

23 The phonemic alphabet
24 Where sounds are made
25 Sounds in combination
26 Stress
27 Intonation
28 Teaching sounds
29 Teaching stress and intonation

Text and discourse

30 Language functions
31 Written and spoken English
32 Genre
33 Register
34 Cohesion and coherence

1

What's in a sentence?

The mobile phone

Manuela is a teacher. She lives in Buenos Aires, Argentina. Last week she was presented with a 'Teacher of the Year' award by the director of her school. The prize was some money and some flowers.

Manuela teaches teenagers at a large secondary school and at the weekends she gives private English classes. She is married to a man she met when she was skiing in Bariloche. Bariloche is a famous ski resort in Argentina.

Yesterday was Manuela's wedding anniversary. In the morning her husband gave her a beautiful necklace. She was very happy. She cried! She gave him a new mobile phone. He thanked her enthusiastically, even though he had bought himself the same phone the previous day. He wonders when he will tell her, but he thinks today is not the right time.

Parts of speech

- In the story about Manuela there are quite a few NOUNS, such as *Manuela*, *Buenos Aires*, *Bariloche*, *teacher*, *school*, *husband* and *award*. Nouns are the names of people, places or things. We look at nouns in →**12**.
- There are also PRONOUNS (which take the place of nouns), such as *she*, *he* and *her*. We look at pronouns in →**12**.
- The ADJECTIVES in the text include *famous*, *beautiful* and *happy*. Adjectives describe nouns. We look at adjectives in →**15**.
- The text above also has a number of VERBS (which describe actions, states and events), such as *is*, *lives*, *was awarded*, *teaches*, *gave*, *had bought*, etc. We look at verbs in →**4**.
- The word *enthusiastically* is an ADVERB (it describes the verb); there are ADVERBIAL PHRASES in the text, too, such as *last week* and *in the morning*. We look at adverbs in →**11**.
- There are two ARTICLES in the text: the INDEFINITE ARTICLE *a* and the DEFINITE ARTICLE *the*. The word *some* is a QUANTIFIER (it tells us 'how much'). We look at articles in →**13** and quantifiers in →**14**.
- PREPOSITIONS, such as *in* and *of*, show how other words are connected. We look at PREPOSITIONAL PHRASES in →**16**.
- The CONJUNCTIONS *and* and *but* connect SENTENCES and clauses.

Sentence elements

How do we know where to put the parts of speech to make a sentence? What are the ELEMENTS OF A SENTENCE and what order should they go in?

- Sentences consist of some or all of the following: a SUBJECT (*She*) + a verb (*teaches*), an OBJECT (*teenagers*) and an adverb or an adverbial phrase (*at a large secondary school*).
- Sometimes sentences have more than one object. In the sentence *Her husband gave her a beautiful necklace*, *a beautiful necklace* is the DIRECT OBJECT (it is the thing that was given) and *her* is the INDIRECT OBJECT (she was the one who benefited from the action).
- Some sentences do not have an object. Instead they have a subject (*she*), a verb (*was*) and a COMPLEMENT (*happy*).
- Sometimes we only use a subject and a verb (*She cried*) →4.
- Sometimes we make more complicated sentences by joining together a number of CLAUSES. *She is married to a man / She met the man when she was skiing / She was skiing in Bariloche* becomes *She is married to a man she met when she was skiing in Bariloche.* We look at clauses in →2.

Getting things in the right order

The basic sentence elements (subject, verb, object, complement) are the spaces into which we place words. But we have to be careful which words we put into these spaces. For example, we can put pronouns (*she*, *he*, *they*, etc.) or NOUN PHRASES (*the young woman*, *the director*, *her husband*, etc.) into the subject space, but the sentence would not work if we put an adjective or an adverb there. For example, we cannot say ~~*Previous is a teacher*~~ or ~~*Seriously is a student*~~. Similarly, we cannot put nouns or adjectives where verbs go, etc.

The sentence elements have to be arranged in correct sequences. For example, we can say *Manuela is a teacher* (SVC), or we can change the order to make a question: *Is Manuela a teacher?* (VSC). But we cannot say ~~*Is a teacher Manuela*~~ because we do not use the sequence VCS.

However, sometimes we re-arrange the order of the SVO elements and put the (indirect) object in the subject position. This is because we want to focus on who 'receives' the action (or because we don't know who did the action). For example, instead of using the ACTIVE VOICE and saying *The director of her school (1) presented her (2) with a 'Teacher of the Year' award*, we can use the PASSIVE VOICE: *She (2) was presented with a 'Teacher of the Year' award by the director of her school (1)*. We look at an activity to teach the passive voice in →7.

Teaching ideas: word order

We often get students to reorder words to make sentences. This makes them think carefully about syntax (the correct sequence of sentence elements). For example, we can say:

Put the following words in order to make correct sentences:
a) *Manuela's / was / wedding anniversary / yesterday*
b) *a / at / Buenos Aires / teenagers / in / large / Manuela / secondary school / teaches*
c) *bus / by / go / I / school / to / usually*

We can also ask the students to put in punctuation, such as CAPITAL LETTERS, FULL STOPS (periods), QUESTION MARKS, INVERTED COMMAS (quotation marks), etc. →31

An enjoyable variation is to have the students hold the words on cards above their heads (so they can't see their own words). The other members of the class have to tell them where to stand to make a correct sentence DVD1.

2

How we use clauses

Hiro's lesson

(1) As soon as the lesson is over, Hiro walks back to the teachers' room. (2) He's happy and he wants to tell his friend Akiko about it. (3) Although Akiko is a geography teacher (and Hiro is an English teacher), they always tell each other about their lessons and talk about their students.

(4) Hiro is happy because his students particularly enjoyed the lesson which he taught after the first break.

(5) After school Hiro is going to go straight home so that he'll have time for some music. (6) He's going to play the guitar he bought two weeks ago. (7) If he hadn't trained to be a teacher, Hiro would have studied music.

Main clauses and subordinate clauses

All the sentences in the text about Hiro have more than one CLAUSE in them. A clause has a subject and a verb – and so all sentences (such as *He is happy*) have at least one clause. But there's more to it than that!

- Sentence 2 has two MAIN CLAUSES: *He's happy. He wants to tell his friend Akiko about it.* Main clauses can exist on their own and are often joined by CONJUNCTIONS like *and*, *but*, *or*, *so*, etc.
- Sentence 1 has a main clause (*Hiro walks back to the teachers' room*) and a SUBORDINATE CLAUSE (*as soon as the lesson is over*). Subordinate clauses only exist if there is a main clause that they can attach themselves to; we don't usually use them on their own.
- Sentence 4 has two main clauses (*Hiro is happy* and *his students particularly enjoyed the lesson*) and one subordinate clause (*which he taught after the first break*).

Clause functions and meanings

Clauses can have different functions and meanings. For example, sentence 1 has a TIME CLAUSE (*as soon as the lesson is over*). Sentence 3 has a CONCESSIVE CLAUSE (*although Akiko is a geography teacher*). We use concessive clauses when we want to say that there is a 'weakness' in the idea of the main clause. Sentence 4 has a REASON CLAUSE (*because his students particularly enjoyed the lesson*) and sentence 5 has a PURPOSE CLAUSE (*so that he'll have time for some music*).

Relative clauses

In sentence 4 the clause *which he taught after the first break* is a **RELATIVE CLAUSE**, introduced by a relative pronoun (*which*). We use the **RELATIVE PRONOUNS** *which* and *that* for things and *who* or *that* for people (*She's the woman* ***who*** *married a prince*), *where* for places (*That's the house* ***where*** *she met him*) and *whose* for possession (*She's the woman* ***whose*** *children go to the same school as mine*). Relative clauses can be **DEFINING** (as in sentence 4 where the clause tells us which lesson is being talked about) or **NON-DEFINING** as in sentences like *He likes his school, which is in the centre of town*. In that last sentence (notice the use of the comma) we know which school is being talked about; we are just giving additional information.

Note that in sentence 6 we don't have to use a relative pronoun because the noun being described (*the guitar)* is the object of the clause (*he bought the guitar*). We call these clauses **CONTACT CLAUSES** or **REDUCED RELATIVE CLAUSES**.

Conditional clauses

Sentence 7 in the text about Hiro's lesson is a **CONDITIONAL SENTENCE** which contains the **CONDITIONAL CLAUSE** *If he hadn't trained to be a teacher* and the consequence *Hiro would have studied music*. We use conditional sentences to say a) what will or will probably happen (*If he wears sunscreen, he won't get sunburned*), b) what might (but is less likely to) happen (*If he won a lot of money, he would buy a new house*) or c) what definitely won't happen because it is in the past (*If he hadn't trained to be a teacher, he would have studied music*). These are often called **FIRST CONDITIONAL** (a), **SECOND CONDITIONAL** (b) and **THIRD CONDITIONAL** (c). We use the past tense for the second conditional and the **PAST PERFECT** tense for the third conditional to show that the meaning is **HYPOTHETICAL**, because it will always be 'unreal'. Some people also talk about the **ZERO CONDITIONAL** to refer to things which are always true (*If you heat water, it boils*).

Note that the clauses can go in different sequences (*He won't get sunburned if he wears sunscreen / If he wears sunscreen, he won't get sunburned*) and that we can use other future-meaning verbs and auxiliaries instead of *will* and *would*, etc. For example, *If I go to the beach, I'm going to wear sunscreen; I couldn't have done it if you hadn't helped me*.

We use *unless* to mean 'if not': *Unless he wears sunscreen he will get sunburned.*

We can make **MIXED CONDITIONALS** by using/mixing different verb tenses in sentences like *I won't call you unless I've finished.*

Teaching ideas: conditional clauses

Many teachers use stories with 'consequences' to teach conditionals. For example, we could tell the students a story →45 about a man in a bar (*If he has another drink, he will stay in the bar. If he stays in the bar, he will get home late. If he gets home late, his wife will leave him, etc.*) to produce 'tragic' stories. We can talk about the 'superpower' qualities that teachers would like to have, such as being able to fly or being able to see through walls (*If I could fly, I would visit all the cities in the world in one day*). Others talk about stories in the past; they say what would have happened if things had been different (*If he hadn't gone swimming, he wouldn't have been attacked by a shark*).

3

Asking questions

Private lesson

Manuela is giving an online lesson to her private student, Carmen.

Manuela: Let's start with some conversation practice.
Carmen: OK. I'd like that.
Manuela: Where did you go at the weekend, Carmen?
Carmen: I went to Recoleta Park.
Manuela: Did your boyfriend go with you?
Carmen: No, he didn't. He couldn't make it.
Manuela: So who went with you?
Carmen: My sister.
Manuela: Your boyfriend's an engineer, isn't he?
Carmen: Yes, he is. He designs bridges.
Manuela: He designs bridges?
Carmen: Yes.
Manuela: What's he working on at the moment?
Carmen: They're constructing a new bridge in Mendoza.
Manuela: When's he coming back?
Carmen: When's he coming back? I'm not sure. Sometimes it seems like he's never at home!
Manuela: Don't worry! I'm sure it'll work out in the end.
Carmen: Yes, I know. And I'm really pleased for him – that his work is going so well.
Manuela: That's great, Carmen. Anyway, shall we do some vocabulary work now?

Saying *yes*, saying *no*

- In Manuela and Carmen's conversation, Carmen uses a number of AFFIRMATIVE SENTENCES (*I'd like that. I went to Recoleta Park. They're constructing a new bridge in Mendoza*) and ANSWERS (*Yes. Yes, he is*). Affirmative sentences say 'yes' or show agreement. They are the opposite of NEGATIVE SENTENCES.
- Carmen also uses a negative answer (*No, he didn't*) and sentences (*He couldn't make it. I'm not sure*). Negative answers and sentences say 'no' and we usually make them by adding *not* to the verb. In spoken English (and INFORMAL written English) we often use the CONTRACTED FORM *n't* with the verb (*don't*, *can't*, *isn't*, *won't*, etc.).
- We can also give affirmative sentences a negative CONNOTATION by using negative ADVERBS such as *never*, *seldom*, *nowhere*, etc. (*he's never at home*). In most varieties of English we don't usually use two negatives in the same sentence; we don't say ~~*He isn't never at home*~~. However, this 'double negative' is used in *some* varieties of spoken English; it just isn't acceptable in educated English – or in most English exams!
- We use negative verbs in many commands or suggestions (***Don't*** *worry*!).

Different types of questions

In Manuela's online conversation with her private student (Carmen) there are a number of different types of question:

- *Did your boyfriend go with you?* and *Shall we do some vocabulary work now?* are examples of YES/NO QUESTIONS – also called CLOSED QUESTIONS. Notice that the order of affirmative sentences – subject-verb – (e.g. *We (1) shall (2) do some vocabulary work*) is reversed when we make a question (*Shall (2) we (1) do some vocabulary work?*). We use *do, did,* etc. to make questions when there is no other AUXILIARY VERB available.
- We call questions like *Where did you go at the weekend?* and *When's he coming back?* WH- QUESTIONS. They are also called OPEN QUESTIONS. Open questions start with *what, when, how, why, how often, who,* etc. They are called open questions because the answer is unpredictable – and will be more than *yes* or *no*. In questions like this we use *do* or *did* if there is no other auxiliary.
- SUBJECT QUESTIONS like *Who went with you?* don't need an auxiliary verb because they are asking about the subject of the verb (***My sister** went with me*). However, OBJECT QUESTIONS like *Where did you go at the weekend?* need the auxiliary (*do*) because they are asking about the object of the verb (*I went to **Recoleta Park***).
- Although we usually make questions by putting the verb before the subject (*Did your boyfriend go with you?*), we can also make questions, in spoken English, by saying an affirmative sentence with questioning INTONATION (*He designs bridges?*). In spoken English we can often make just one word into a question (***Coffee?** Yes, please. **Sugar?** No, thanks*). We look at intonation in →27.
- In spoken English we can make a sentence into a question by adding a QUESTION TAG (*Your boyfriend's an engineer, isn't he?*). If the verb in the sentence is affirmative (*Your boyfriend's an engineer*), the question tag is usually negative (***isn't** he?*). But if the verb in the sentence is negative, the tag is usually in the affirmative (***is** he?*). When we use tag questions to confirm something we think we know (or if we want the listener to agree with us), we often use a falling intonation tune on the tag. If we don't know the answer to our question – or if we are worried about it – we use a rising intonation tune on the tag. Some people use the word *right* as a general tag word in sentences like *You're a teacher, **right**?* This is when they want their guess (*I think you are teacher*) confirmed →27.
- Sometimes, like Carmen, we use echo questions (*When's he coming back?*) to help the conversation along.

Learning English by telephone and *Skype*

Many teachers, like Manuela, have private students who learn either on the telephone (popular in France) or by using telephone/video computer software such as *Skype*. They can share a virtual 'board', too; both of them can see the same thing on their computer screens. Even if they are physically distant from each other, the lesson is not unlike a typical face-to-face one.

There are many other ways in which people can make contact with others via the INTERNET. We look at these VIRTUAL LEARNING ENVIRONMENTS (VLEs) in →87.

4

Introducing verbs

Ratih's lesson

Yesterday was the first day of the new semester, so Ratih arrived at school two hours before her first lesson. After she had had some breakfast, she left home very early because the traffic in Jakarta (where she lives) can be very bad indeed. And yesterday it rained so it was even worse than usual!

In her first lesson (for beginners), Ratih asked the students to do various things. 'Open your books,' she said, and later, 'Go to the door. Open the door. Close the door. Sit down.' She wanted her students to learn simple English verbs (like *go* and *open*) and nouns (like *book* and *door*). It was a happy lesson and many of the students laughed – which Ratih thinks is a good thing. She believes that when students are happy and engaged (involved) in what they are doing, they may learn better than if they are bored and inactive.

Ratih enjoys teaching and she is always looking for ways to improve what she does. Later she is going to look into the possibility of doing a postgraduate course in Australia next year. Right now, however, she has to plan next week's lessons. She has to work out how to teach the future to her class of elementary students.

Types of verb

- The verbs in the story about Ratih describe ACTIONS (***had had*** *some breakfast*, ***open*** *your books*, *the students* ***laughed***, *she has to* ***plan***, etc.), STATES (*Yesterday* ***was*** *the first day of the semester*, *the traffic* ***can be*** *bad*), STATES OF MIND (*she* ***believes*** *that when students are happy*) and EVENTS (*it* ***rained***). We discuss simple verbs (for states) and continuous verbs (for actions) in →6.
- *Open*, *believes* and *rained* are LEXICAL VERBS (sometimes called MAIN VERBS or FULL VERBS). These are verbs which express a whole range of meanings. We can use them on their own in sentences.
- Verbs like *had*, *can*, *are*, *may* and *is* are AUXILIARY VERBS. Their function is often grammatical and they help, or interact with, lexical verbs.

- *Can* and *may* are MODAL AUXILIARY VERBS. We look at auxiliary and modal auxiliary verbs in →8.
- *Laughed* and *sit down* are INTRANSITIVE verbs – that means they do not need or take an OBJECT. *Enjoys* and *plan* are TRANSITIVE verbs – they do take an object. Notice, however, that *open* (*Open your books*) is transitive in the story about Ratih, but *open* (like a number of other verbs) can also be intransitive in sentences like *The door opened*. In the same way, some LINKING VERBS like *get* and *taste* can be transitive (*He got a letter in the post*, *She tasted the soup*) and intransitive (*He got upset*, *It tasted delicious*).
- *Sit down*, *look into* and *work out* are called MULTI-WORD VERBS because they are made up of more than one word. *Look into* and *work out* are PHRASAL VERBS because although we may understand the individual words (*look* and *into*, *work* and *out*) that does not mean we understand the complete verb (*look into*, *work out*). In other words, they have IDIOMATIC meaning →21 (unlike *sit down* which is far easier to understand). We look at phrasal verbs in more detail in →9.

How verbs are made

- All verbs have a BASE FORM, that is the INFINITIVE without *to*. In the text about Ratih's lesson, verbs like *go* and *open* are in their base (simplest) form. Ratih uses these base forms to make IMPERATIVE sentences (*Go to the door*, *Open the door*, etc.). Other base form infinitives in the story about Ratih include *learn*, *improve*, *look* and *plan*.
- We change the base form of verbs to show agreement, TENSE →5 and ASPECT →6. We do this by adding or changing MORPHEMES. Morphemes are the smallest units of grammatical meaning – they are smaller than words. For example, when the text about Ratih says *she think**s** it is a good thing* and *she believe**s** that when students are happy and engaged* …, we have added the 's' morpheme to the base form of the verb. This is necessary when we use the present simple with *he*, *she* or *it*.
- We add the *-ed* morpheme to all REGULAR VERBS when we talk about the past →6, e.g. *rain**ed***, *ask**ed***, *laugh**ed***, *want**ed***.
- We call verbs that do not add *-ed* in the past IRREGULAR VERBS. For example, the past tense of *go* is *went* (not ~~*goed*~~!) and the past participle is *gone*. *Left* in the story about Ratih is the past form of the verb *leave*.
- We add the *-ing* morpheme to the base form of the verb for PRESENT PARTICIPLES (*She is always look**ing** for ways to improve what she does*).

Verbs in combination

Many verbs 'trigger' the grammar of the verbs that follow them →10. For example, the verb *enjoy* is always followed by a present participle (*Ratih enjoys teaching*); it is never followed by *to* + *infinitive* (we cannot say *She enjoys* ~~*to teach*~~). *Ask* is often followed by object + *to* + infinitive (*Ratih asked the students to do various things*). Knowing a verb means knowing what behaviour it triggers.

Total physical response

Ratih's lesson is an example of TOTAL PHYSICAL RESPONSE (TPR) →45, a 1970s method described by James Asher, in which students first respond to and then give commands. The idea is that we learn by doing things. This is especially appropriate for students who respond well to more KINAESTHETIC ACTIVITIES (those that involve physical movement and activity). Most experts suggest that TPR is especially useful for lower-level students.

5 Verb tenses (form and meaning)

Correcting homework isn't always his favourite task!

Arnulfo seems to spend his whole day criss-crossing the busy streets of Mexico City. He teaches in three different places. But not today. Today is Sunday so he is having a well-earned rest.

Yesterday wasn't so relaxed, though. He corrected homework for three hours. Correcting homework isn't always his favourite task, but he had to do it – and when he did, he was pleased with his students' efforts. They will be disappointed (and demotivated) if he does not hand it back on Monday.

After he had finished correcting, he went to the cinema with his wife. They saw an English film about a writer's community in an English village. A young woman returns to the village after some years away. She causes a lot of trouble because all the men fall in love with her, and she has to decide which one to choose. It was a very funny movie.

Tonight Arnulfo's parents are coming over for dinner. Then he has one day's teaching before he and his wife go on holiday. They leave Mexico early in the morning and fly to Boston. If they can, they are going to visit New York, too. He will have a lot to tell his students when he gets home.

How verbs show time

We change or add to the BASE FORM of the verb →4 to show whether we are talking about the PAST, the PRESENT or the FUTURE. There are many examples of this in the text about Arnulfo.

- The verbs *seems*, *teaches* and *is having* in the first paragraph all refer to the present. Notice that the PRESENT CONTINUOUS form →6 (*is having*) refers to what is happening now, but *seems* and *teaches* refer to things that are more generally true most of the time.
- *Wasn't*, *corrected* and *had to* in the second paragraph all refer to past time, and *had finished correcting* refers to a time before the past (*he went*).
- *Are coming over*, *go on holiday*, *leave*, *are going to visit*, *will have* and *gets* in the fourth paragraph all refer to the future.
- Verbs are not the only ways of showing time. ADVERBIALS such as *today* (paragraph 1), *yesterday* and *on Monday* (paragraph 2), *after* (paragraph 3), *tonight* and *in the morning* (paragraph 4) also say what time we are talking about. This is very important when we realise that the same verb form can refer to many different times.

One form, many meanings

One of the features of English verb forms is that they can mean many different things – they can refer to different times. This is not special to verbs, as we shall see when we introduce words and their meanings in →18. There are many examples of this in the text about Arnulfo.

- *Arnulfo* ***seems*** (a present STATE) and *he* ***teaches*** (a present routine) in paragraph 1 both refer to the present and use the PRESENT SIMPLE form →6.
- *A young woman* ***returns*** *to the village* and *she* ***causes*** *a lot of trouble* in paragraph 3 use the same verb form (present simple) but they are telling a story. We often use the present simple in this way, even when it refers to the past.
- *He and his wife* ***go*** *on holiday* and *they* ***leave*** *Mexico* (paragraph 4) refer to the future, yet they are using the same present simple form.
- *He* ***is having*** *a well-earned rest* (paragraph 1) uses the PRESENT CONTINUOUS →6 and refers to the present. However, *Arnulfo's parents* ***are coming over*** *to dinner* (paragraph 4) refers to the future.
- It is because one verb can mean so many different things that CONTEXT and the use of time adverbials is so important.

One meaning, many forms

The future is talked about in the text about Arnulfo. But this is done using a number of different forms.

- *Will* is often referred to as the 'neutral' future when it refers to things that are inevitable in the future. Examples are *his students* ***will*** *be disappointed* (paragraph 2) and *he* ***will*** *have a lot to tell his students* (paragraph 4). *Will* is a MODAL AUXILIARY VERB →8.
- The present simple is often used to describe fixed schedules, e.g. *he and his wife* ***go*** *on holiday*, *they* ***leave*** *Mexico* (paragraph 4).
- *Going to* + INFINITIVE is often used to describe plans and intentions, e.g. *they* ***are going to visit*** *New York* (paragraph 4).
- The present continuous is often used to describe future arrangements – things that are almost definitely going to happen or things that have already been decided on – e.g. *Arnulfo's parents* ***are coming over*** *for dinner*.

As we can see, there is no one-to-one connection between TENSE (for example the present simple in the sentence *They* ***leave*** *Mexico*) and time (Arnulfo and his wife's future). In the same way, a CONDITIONAL sentence →2 like *If I had a million pounds I would buy a house*, includes the past tense of *have* (*had*) but refers to present time.

We suggest ways of teaching the verb phrase in →7.

The homework issue

Homework works! It is good for learners, even though doing it - and correcting it - can sometimes seem like a lot of work. Teachers have to decide how much homework to give and when to give it.

One of the most important things about homework is that the students should hand it in on time - and the teacher should give it back quickly, too! If not, the students will start to think, next time, that they don't have to do it.

We look at homework in more detail in →76.

6

Aspect

You'll never burn out!

Hiro is standing in the kitchen. He's drinking a glass of water. He is breathing heavily.

Hiro has been jogging because his friend Akiko told him he was unfit. 'You haven't taken any exercise for weeks,' she said. 'You've been getting up late, rushing to school and then going out at weekends, playing music. It's not good for you.'

It was true! He had been working very hard and he hadn't been getting enough sleep. Last week, for example, he was teaching a lesson on the present perfect and his students just weren't interested. They were looking bored and he couldn't find a way of motivating them. When he left the class he just felt exhausted.

'When this semester ends, I will have been a teacher for ten years,' he told Akiko in the staff room after that lesson. 'It feels like a long time. I don't want to get teacher "burnout" like some of the older teachers.'

'Don't be silly, Hiro,' Akiko told him. 'You'll never suffer from burnout. You're a great teacher. We all have lessons which don't work sometimes, but that doesn't happen often with you! You do need to do something to make yourself feel better!' and that's when she told him to take more exercise.

What is aspect?

Whereas TENSE refers to the form of the verbs we use →5, and TIME is about *when* we are referring to, ASPECT refers to the way a speaker wants you to understand the situation which they are talking about. For example, the sentences *I teach*, *I am teaching*, *I have taught* and *I have been teaching* all refer to the present, but in each case the speaker's attitude to the teaching (whether it is habitual, whether it is continuing, whether it finished in the past, or whether it is in the past but has present relevance, etc.) is different.

Simple and continuous

In the story about Hiro there are number of CONTINUOUS and SIMPLE verb forms.

- *It **feels** like a long time* (paragraph 4) and *we all **have** lessons which **don't work*** (paragraph 5) are examples of the PRESENT SIMPLE. We use the present simple a) to talk about facts that are true and will be true for some time; b) to describe repeated actions or habits; and c) for storytelling and future reference →5. We use the base form of the verb (+ the 's' MORPHEME for the third person singular →4) to make the present simple.
- *He **left** the room* (paragraph 3) and *she **told** him* (paragraph 5) are examples of the PAST SIMPLE. They described completed actions. *They **weren't** interested* (paragraph 4) describes a past state. We form the past simple by adding the *-ed* morpheme in one of its realisations to regular verbs. IRREGULAR VERBS have their own forms, such as *take–took* →4.

- *Hiro is standing in the kitchen* and the next two sentences in paragraph 1 are example of the PRESENT CONTINUOUS (also called the PRESENT PROGRESSIVE). They describe an action that is still ongoing (that hasn't finished) at the time of speaking. They emphasise the action rather than the result of it. We can also use the present continuous for future reference →5. To make continuous verb forms we use the AUXILIARY VERB *to be* + PRESENT PARTICIPLE (BASE FORM + *-ing*).
- *He was teaching a lesson* and *they were looking bored* (Paragraph 3) are examples of the PAST CONTINUOUS and describe an action that was ongoing at the actual moment in time that the speaker is referring to.
- Verbs like *feels* (*it feels like a long time* – paragraph 4) are often called STATIVE VERBS because they refer to a state of mind (other verbs like this include *believe*, *hate*, *love* and *think*). We almost always use simple forms (rather than continuous forms) with verbs like this when we are referring to the state itself (*I* ***believe*** *in miracles*). However, some stative verbs *can* be used with continuous forms when we wish to emphasise the ongoing and active nature of that state (e.g. *I'm thinking – please don't interrupt me*).

Perfect verbs

In the story about Hiro there are a number of PERFECT VERBS.

- *You haven't taken any exercise for weeks* and *you've been getting up late* (paragraph 2) are both examples of the PRESENT PERFECT – simple and continuous. The present perfect suggests something which started in the past and which a) is still true, or b) still has present 'consequences', or c) still isn't finished. We use *have* + PAST PARTICIPLE to form the present perfect.
- *He had been working very hard* and *he hadn't been getting enough sleep* (paragraph 3) are both examples of the PAST PERFECT. Past perfect verbs describe things that started before the past, but still have 'relevance' in the past moment that we are describing. We use *had* + past participle to make past perfect verbs.
- *I will have been a teacher for ten years* (paragraph 4) is an example of the FUTURE PERFECT. We use *will have* + past participle to make this verb form.
- Speakers of American English often use the past simple instead of the present perfect: *Did you see him yet?* (American English) versus *Have you seen him yet?* (British English). However, in some varieties of American English the present perfect is used in the same ways as in British English, especially in more formal or writing-like situations.

Burnout

Many teachers feel tired and demotivated at times. They feel they have had enough of teaching. This is sometimes called BURNOUT. It is often a temporary condition (fortunately not a permanent one). We look at teacher development (including how to avoid or deal with burnout) in →78.

7

Teaching verbs (and adverbs)

Teaching ideas

In this unit we look at a few ideas for teaching (and practising) some verb tenses – and adverbs. There are many other teaching suggestions in →44–64.

Teaching the present continuous and present simple

- Students can pretend to be police officers on surveillance duty – or spies – to practise the PRESENT CONTINUOUS. They say what people are doing in sentences like *A man is walking into the shop. He's carrying a bag*, etc.
- We can contrast people's work and holiday lives with the PRESENT SIMPLE and CONTINUOUS in sentences like *He usually gets up at six thirty, but it's ten o'clock now and he's lying in bed reading a book.*
- We can get our students to listen to sounds and tell them to describe what they think is happening.
- We can talk about someone's daily routine to teach and practise the PRESENT SIMPLE, e.g. *She gets up at six o'clock. She goes to work by car*, etc. →44. Students can talk about their own lives and routines.
- We can also use mime games to practise the present continuous (*Are you playing the guitar? Are you reading a book?*).

Teaching the present perfect

- To practise the PRESENT PERFECT SIMPLE the students can mime looking happy, exhausted, sad, amused, etc., and the other students have to ask them questions with *just*, such as *Why are you sad? Have you just said goodbye to your girlfriend?* etc.
- If we want to introduce the PRESENT PERFECT CONTINUOUS, we can show the students a series of pictures and they have to say what the people have been doing, for example *He's been jogging, she's been shopping, he's been taking an exam, she's been giving a speech.*

Teaching the future

- The students can pretend to go to a fortune teller and ask questions such as *Will I be rich? Will I get married?*
- Students can speculate about what they are going to do at a time in the future, in sentences such as *When I leave school I'm going to travel round the world.*
- Students can make New Year's resolutions, saying what they are going to do and what they are not going to do in the next 12 months (*I'm going to give up eating chocolate. I'm not going to stay up late every evening*, etc.).

Teaching the past simple

- We can tell STORIES with the PAST SIMPLE. For example, we can ask our students to describe their week (*On Monday I went to the cinema. On Tuesday I had a coffee with my brother*, etc.).
- BEGINNER students can be given cards →86 with either the BASE FORM of a verb or its PAST TENSE FORM. They have to find the student with the matching card (e.g. *run – ran* or *go – went*). They then make sentences with the past tense verb.

Teaching the past continuous and the past simple

Many teachers (and students) enjoy playing the game **'ALIBI'** to practise the **PAST CONTINUOUS** and the past simple. The class imagines that a crime was committed at 10 pm last night. Four students go out of the room and agree on a story about what they were doing last night at this time. The students then come back into the class, one by one, and the other students question them by asking *What were you doing at 10 o'clock? What were you eating? What happened then?* etc. The student whose story is different from the others (because he or she can't remember all the details) is the 'criminal'. We look at more **GAMES** in **→49**.

Teaching the past perfect

We can give our students a story which uses past simple and past perfect verb forms. They have to circle the verbs and then say which action happened first.

> When Shelley got home she realised that someone (or something) had been in her flat.
> She was sure that she had locked the door that morning.
> She noticed that someone had left muddy footprints on the carpet, etc.

Teaching *used to*

- We can compare our present lives with the lives of our grandparents or great grandparents to teach **USED TO**.

> We send emails, but they used to write letters.
> We pay for many things by credit card, but they used to pay for everything in cash.

- We can talk about our own lives in sentences like *I used to live in London, but now I am living in Shanghai*.

Teaching the passive

- We can use various industrial, scientific and other processes to teach and practise the **PASSIVE**. For example, we can talk about how chocolate is made with sentences like *Cocoa beans are harvested. The beans are dried. The beans are shipped to a factory. The beans are roasted*, etc.
- We can discuss historical works of art, inventions, discoveries and conquests in sentences like *The Mona Lisa was painted by Leonardo da Vinci*, *Mexico was invaded by the Spanish in 1519*, *Penicillin was discovered by Alexander Fleming*, etc.

Teaching adverbs

- We can play a speaking game in which two students are selected. The class give them each an occupation (*doctor*, *policeman*, *shopkeeper*, etc.) a location (*at the cinema*, *at a restaurant*, *on a bus*, etc.) and a topic (perhaps this will be something the students have been studying recently). The teacher then gives each speaker a piece of paper with an adverb or adverbial phrase on it (e.g. *angrily*, *quietly*, *in a worried way*, etc.). The two students then start speaking and the rest of the class have to try to guess which adverbs they were given.
- We can give the students scripts of scenes from plays, short dialogues, etc. They have to write adverbs and adverbial phrases to describe how the speakers should act. They then act out the scene or dialogue using those adverbs as a guide.

8

Auxiliaries and modals

Your English might get better!

This is a transcript of a moment in Ratih's class yesterday:

Cutar: I'm sorry I'm late.
Ratih: Do you have your homework with you?
Cutar: No, sorry. I couldn't do it.
Ratih: Why not?
Cutar: I was helping my father at the restaurant. I didn't get home till late.
Ratih: You must have been very tired.
Cutar: No, I felt fine. I slept for hours. Why?
Ratih: But you said ...
Cutar: Oh, yes. I mean I was very tired. That's why I didn't do my homework. May I sit down?
Ratih: Oh, all right. But you must try to get here on time, OK?
Cutar: Yes, teacher. I will. I promise.
Kemala: *Buk Guru, kapan kita ujian?* (Teacher, when are we going to have our test?)
Ratih: You should really try to speak English, you know.
Kemala: It's difficult.
Ratih: Yes, but if you use English more often, your English might suddenly start to improve! You really ought to try it!

Auxiliaries and modal auxiliaries

- In the excerpt from Ratih's lesson Cutar and Ratih use the AUXILIARY VERBS →4 *be* (*I'm sorry **I'm** late, I **was** very tired*) and *do* (***Do** you have your homework? I **didn't** do my homework*). In a sentence such as ***Have** you done your homework? have* is an auxiliary verb.
- *There are a number of* MODAL AUXILIARY VERBS in the transcript above: *can* (*I **couldn't** do it*), *must* (*you **must** try to get here on time*), *should* (*You **should** really try to speak English*) and *might* (*your English **might** suddenly start to improve*). We use them to express our attitude or certainty about what we are saying.
- *Ought to* (*you really* **ought to** *try it*), *need to* and *used to* are often called SEMI-MODAL AUXILIARY VERBS because although they have two words, they behave like ordinary modal auxiliaries.
- *Do* and *have* are special because they can be either auxiliary verbs (see above) or LEXICAL VERBS →4 as in sentences like *I **have** too much homework!* and *She **did** the New York Marathon.*

What modal auxiliaries mean

- We often use modal auxiliary verbs to talk about certainty, possibility and probability in sentences such as *Your English **might** start to improve* and *You **must** have been tired.*
- We use modal auxiliaries to talk about obligation – about getting things done – in sentences such as *You must get here on time* and *You should really try to speak English.*
- Modal verbs can express more than one meaning. For example, *can* is used for many different meanings including ability (*I **can** speak Spanish*) and permission (*You **can** stay for 15 minutes*). We can use *might* to express probability (*You **might** be right*) or to make a suggestion (*You **might** want to think carefully before you speak!*).

- Modals appear in many common lexical phrases (***Can*** *I help you?* ***Will*** *you be long? You* ***must have been*** *really worried, That* ***can't have been*** *much fun*, etc.).

How modal verbs behave

- Modal verbs are a closed class (they don't change) and they don't take the third person *-s* when used in the present (*He/She* ***can*** *play the guitar).*
- Modal verbs are almost always followed by an infinitive verb without *to* (*You* ***must*** *get here on time*).
- Modal verbs do not have an infinitive form and so they have to be replaced by SEMI-MODALS (*You need to* ***be able to*** (not *can*) *swim*) or other verbs (*I'm going to* ***have to*** (not *must*) *go now*) when an infinitive is required.

Modal verbs and modality

When we use modal verbs we are expressing our attitude to/certainty about what we are saying. Compare, for example, *It is true* with *It might be true*. But we can express modality in other ways, too. For example, we can use verbs like *appear* and *seem* to say that we are not sure if we are correct (*They* ***appear*** *to be running late, He* ***seems*** *to be clever*), or *tend* to say what we think is generally true (*People in the UK* ***tend*** *to eat their biggest meals in the evening*). We can also use phrases like *It is likely that* or *It appears that* (***It is likely that*** *the President will do badly in the mid-term elections*).

Using the students' language – their L1

In the conversation above, Ratih wants her student, Kemala, to use English rather than Indonesian (Kemala's mother tongue). Teachers have different views about this. Some think you should never use the students' L1 in an English class; others think that it is a good thing – at the right time and at appropriate moments, and depending on the students' level. We discuss the use of L1 in →77.

Teaching ideas: modal verbs

Many teachers introduce modals of obligation and permission by talking about rules and regulations in different countries, e.g. *You have to stay at school until you are 16, You don't have to go to school after you are 16.*

Some teachers invent stories (or dialogues) about children talking to their parents (***Must*** *I tidy my room now?*), about people in galleries or libraries (*I'm sorry sir, but you* ***can't*** *take pictures in here*) or about work-regulated regulations (*Protective clothing* ***must*** *be worn at all times*). The situation will depend on the age of the students.

Note: *must* and *have to* are similar. We often use *must* when the speaker creates the obligation (*I* ***must*** *take more exercise*) or in official signs (*Hard hats* ***must*** *be worn*). We use the more INFORMAL *have to* for ordinary regulations (*You* ***have to*** *be careful in this job*). *Have to* is more common in American English. We use *mustn't* to say that something is not allowed (*You* ***mustn't*** *smoke in here*), but *don't have to* and *don't need to/needn't* mean that something is not obligatory (*You* ***don't have to*** *wear a tie).*

We often get students to try to guess what things in pictures are (*That* ***might/must*** *be a musical instrument, but I can't be sure*) or to speculate about the past (*The pyramids* ***might have been*** *built by creatures from outer space*).

9

Multi-word and phrasal verbs

War!

When Arnulfo walked into his 3 o'clock lesson, it looked as if war had broken out! The children were running around the classroom, and one of them, a big boy called Rogelio, was running after Pancho, the class 'clown'. Music was playing from a CD player on Marcela's desk. Arnulfo turned it off immediately. Then he stood in front of the class and told them all to be quiet. Gradually the noise died down. Arnulfo can do that: he has a natural teacher 'presence' and his students generally look up to him. But not Pancho, the boy Rogelio had been chasing. Pancho took off, running out of the classroom and into the corridor. What should Arnulfo do? He couldn't leave the class on their own. But at that moment a student from the teacher training course that the school organised walked past the door. Arnulfo asked her to look after the class while he set off to find Pancho.

What are multi-word verbs?

There are many MULTI-WORD VERBS in English (***get into*** *a car*, ***get off*** *a train*, ***turn on/ turn off*** *the light*). Multi-word verbs have a particle – an ADVERB or a PREPOSITION (and sometimes both) – which is added to a main verb.

PHRASAL VERBS are multi-word verbs which have IDIOMATIC MEANING →21 (the meaning of the phrasal verb is not the same as the meaning of the two or three individual words in it). They are little LEXICAL CHUNKS →20. Phrasal verbs in the story about Arnulfo's lesson include *break out* (*war had* ***broken out***), *look up to* (*his students* ***look up to*** *him*) and *look after* (*He asked her to* ***look after*** *the class*).

Four types of phrasal verb

In the story about Arnulfo's lesson there are four categories of phrasal verb. They all have slightly different grammar.

- *Break out* (= start), *take off* (= leave in a hurry), *die down* (= gradually go quiet) and *set off* (= start a journey) are INTRANSITIVE PHRASAL VERBS. This means that they can stand alone; they don't take an object.
- *Look after* is a TRANSITIVE INSEPARABLE PHRASAL VERB since a) it always takes an object (so it is transitive), and b) the object has to come after the complete phrasal verb (you can't separate the verb and the preposition). Another example of a transitive inseparable phrasal verb is *run into* (= meet by chance) in sentences like *I* ***ran into*** *my friend at the newsagent's*.
- *Turn off* is a TRANSITIVE SEPARABLE PHRASAL VERB because a) it takes an object, and b) you can put the object *either* between the verb and the particle (adverb) *or* after the particle. For example, *He* ***turned*** *the CD player* ***off*** / *He* ***turned off*** *the CD player*. But – and this is a big but – if the object is an object pronoun, it must come between the verb and the particle. We say *He* ***turned*** *it* ***off***, but we can't say ~~*He turned off it*~~. Another verb like *turn off* is *look up* (= tried to find) in the sentence *He* ***looked*** *the word* ***up*** *in the dictionary* / *He* ***looked up*** *the word in the dictionary* / *He* ***looked*** *it* ***up***.

- *Look up to* is a TWO-PARTICLE TRANSITIVE (INSEPARABLE) PHRASAL VERB because a) it takes an object, but b) the object (*him* in the story about Arnulfo) must come after both the particles. With two-particle phrasal verbs the first particle is an adverb and the second is a preposition. Another example of a phrasal verb like this is *run out of* (= to have nothing left) in sentences like *We* ***ran out of*** *petrol on the way home.*

Teaching ideas: phrasal verbs

- Some teachers introduce phrasal verbs one by one, just as they do with other lexical items.
- Some teachers introduce a collection of phrasal verbs with a) the same verb (e.g. ***run*** *after* = chase, ***run*** *into* = meet, ***run*** *off* = leave/disappear, ***run*** *over* = hit someone with a car, ***run*** *out of* = have nothing left) or b) the same particle (e.g. *pick* ***up*** *Arabic* = learn without effort, *take* ***up*** *rowing*= start to do, *look* ***up*** *a word* = search for, *run* ***up*** a bill = spend more and more, etc.).
- Some teachers introduce a collection of phrasal verbs in a story or situation (like, for example, the story about Arnulfo at the beginning of this unit).
- Some teachers point out phrasal verbs when they occur in TEXTS or when they come up in lessons.

There is no best way! Teaching a collection of phrasal verbs *may* work. If that is so, then perhaps teaching them by particle might be a good idea. But teaching phrasal verbs in memorable situations and stories is also good - and it is also useful to get the students to look for phrasal verbs in their own reading and bring them to class. We need to encourage LEARNER AUTONOMY →43 by getting our students to think about the best way to learn phrasal verbs for *them*. DVD2

When war breaks out!

All teachers sometimes find themselves in difficult situations! Classes can sometimes seem to get out of control. When this happens, we need to behave sensibly! The golden rule is to attack (deal with) the problem, not the student. However, it is much better, of course, if such problems never occur, and that is why organisation and preparation are so important. In other words, we need to try to prevent problems - but also know how to deal with them when they do occur →71.

10

Verb complementation

Substitute lesson

In the evening, Manuela's new mobile phone rang. It was the same model of phone as her husband's – the phone that she remembered giving him for their wedding anniversary. He had suggested that it wasn't fair that he had a beautiful new phone and she didn't. So he bought one for her. He was so thoughtful.

She picked up the phone. It was Oriel, a colleague at her school. He said that he had a dentist's appointment the next day and he asked her if she would teach his morning lesson. She didn't want to do it because she hadn't finished preparing her lessons for next week. But that didn't stop Oriel! First of all he told her that he hated going to the dentist. ('I know,' she said, 'I don't enjoy having my teeth done either.') And then he said he had forgotten to arrange cover for his class. He kept on saying things like 'You must help me!' and so, even though she didn't intend to say yes, she finally agreed to teach his lesson.

Verb + verb

When we use one VERB after another, we have to be careful about the grammar we use. For example, the MODAL AUXILIARY VERB *must* (like the other modal verbs →8) is always followed by an INFINITIVE without *to* (*You must **help** me!*). We can't say ~~*You must to help me*~~. There are a number of other examples of verb + verb patterns in the story about Manuela:

- *Finish* (*she hadn't **finished** preparing …*), *enjoy* (*I don't **enjoy** having …*) and *keep on* (*he **kept on** saying …*) are three of the verbs which are followed by the *-ing* PARTICIPLE. We have to use the *-ing* form of the second verb with these three verbs. Other verbs like this include *admit*, *consider*, *dislike*, *imagine*, *miss* and PHRASAL VERBS →9 such as *carry on*, *give up* and *put off*.
- *Agree* (*she finally **agreed** to teach his lesson*) and *want* (*she **didn't want** to do it*) are usually followed by *to* + infinitive. Other verbs like *agree* and *want* include *appear*, *attempt*, *decide*, *hope*, *offer*, *promise* and *refuse*.
- *Hate* (*he **hated** going to the dentist*) and *intend* (*she **didn't intend** to say …*) can be followed by either the *-ing* form or *to* + infinitive without too much change in meaning (*I **hate to go** to the dentist*, *She didn't **intend saying** yes*). Other verbs like *hate* include *begin*, *love* and *start*.
- *Remember* (*she **remembered** giving him …*) can be followed by *-ing* or by *to* + infinitive but the meaning changes. *She **remembered giving** him a phone* = she gave him a phone and she has a memory of doing it, but *she **remembered to give** him a phone* = that was her intention and she didn't forget to do it. Compare *I tried **to open** the window but it was stuck* (I couldn't open it) with *I tried **opening** the window, but the room was still too hot* (I opened it). Notice that although *forget* is usually followed by *to* + infinitive (*He had **forgotten to arrange** cover for his class*), *never forget* (= remember) can also be followed by *-ing* (*I'll never **forget seeing** her for the first time*).
- *Suggest* (*he had **suggested that** it wasn't fair …*) is one of many verbs that can be followed by *that* + SENTENCE. Other verbs like this include *agree* (*he **agreed that** he would go*) and *promise* (*I **promise that** I will help you*).

Reporting what people say

We can report what other people say by quoting DIRECT SPEECH (e.g. *'I know,' she said* and *'You must help me!'* or by using INDIRECT SPEECH (REPORTED SPEECH).

- Oriel's actual words on the phone were *'I have a dentist's appointment tomorrow'*, *'I have forgotten to arrange cover for my class'* and *'I hate going to the dentist'*. If Manuela's husband had been in the room, Manuela could have reported the conversation as it happened like this: *He **says** he has a dentist's appointment tomorrow. He **says** he has forgotten to arrange cover for his class. He **says** he hates going to the dentist* – using *says* in the PRESENT SIMPLE.
- However, because the story is in the past, we have reported Oriel's words in the past, too, and so we write *He **said*** – and then all the other verbs move 'one tense back', e.g. *He said he **had** a dentist's appointment. He said he **hated** going to the dentist.* Notice that *I* (***I** have a dentist's appointment*) becomes *he* (*He said that **he** had a dentist's appointment*) and *tomorrow* becomes *the next day*.
- Oriel said *Will you teach my lesson tomorrow?* and this is reported later as *He asked if she would teach his lesson the next day*. Notice the subject/verb word-order change *Will you teach* becomes *… if she would teach …*
- *Ask* and *tell* are followed by object + *to* + infinitive when we report commands (*She told **her students to be** quiet. He asked **her to wait***).
- We can also use REPORTING VERBS, such as *suggest* (*He **suggested** that they meet later*) and *promise* (*He **promised** to be there on time)*.

Other ways of reporting conversations

In informal conversation people often report (direct) speech with *be like* (***He's like** 'I have a dentist's appointment tomorrow'.*) and *go*, especially in British English (***He goes** 'I have a dentist's appointment tomorrow'*). We don't usually teach this, but students at higher levels need to know about it.

Substitution can be fun

Many teachers enjoy teaching other teachers' classes because they can use their 'best' lesson - and students often like having something different! If you want someone to be a SUBSTITUTE TEACHER for you, however, you should always give them suggestions (but not orders!) about what they can do.

11

Introducing adverbs

Drama in Istanbul!

Yesterday Isil asked her students to do some drama. She uses drama with her students about once every two or three weeks. She often gives them short extracts from plays and they have to decide things about the scene – who the speakers are, how they feel, how they say their lines, etc. Then they prepare their scenes in pairs and groups.

Her students were working happily and productively, though some of them were working more slowly than the others. One of her students called her over in a loud voice. 'Miss,' he said enthusiastically, 'I like doing drama very much.' Her students often tell her things like that!

Later, when they had practised their scenes, the students stood up in pairs and small groups and acted them out in front of the rest of the class. It was truly enjoyable.

Late that evening as she sat on the ferry taking her back over the Bosphorus to the other side of Istanbul, Isil wondered whether she could plan a workshop about drama for an international teachers' conference that she wants to go to. She has never spoken at a conference before, but she could possibly practise on her colleagues at school.

What is an adverb?

- ADVERBS modify verbs – they say how, when or where a verb happens. In the story about Isil, the one-word adverbs are *yesterday*, *happily*, *productively*, *enthusiastically*, *later*, *truly* and *never*.
- We can also make ADVERBIAL PHRASES (where two or more words act as a phrase and behave like one-word adverbs), such as *once every two or three weeks*, *in front of the rest of the class*, *back over the Bosphorus* and *at a conference*.
- ADVERBS OF MANNER describe how something is done (*Her students were working* ***happily*** *and* ***productively****, called her over* ***in a loud voice***).
- ADVERBS OF PLACE describe where something is done (*acted out their scenes* ***in front of the class****, sat* ***on the ferry***).
- ADVERBS OF TIME say when something is done (***Yesterday*** *Isil asked her students,* ***later****, when they had practised their scenes*).
- FREQUENCY ADVERBS say how often something is done (*She* ***often*** *gives them … , she has* ***never*** *spoken at a conference, she uses drama with her students* ***once every two or three weeks***).
- ADVERBS OF CERTAINTY say how sure it is that something is done (*she could* ***possibly*** *practice*).
- ADVERBS OF DEGREE say how much something is done (*I like doing drama* ***very much***).
- Some words, like *late*, can be both adverbs and adjectives. We look at this in more detail in →15.

How to make one-word adverbs

- We can make one-word adverbs by adding *-ly* to ADJECTIVES, (*productive* → *productive**ly***).
- If the adjective ends in *-y*, we change the *y* to *i* and add *-ly* (*happy* → *happ**ily***).
- When the adjective ends in *-ic*, we usually (but not always) add *-ally* (*enthusiastic* → *enthusiastic**ally***).
- When adjectives end in *-e*, we sometimes (but not always) take off the final *-e* (*true* → ***truly***), but if the adjective ends in *-le* we always take off the *-e* and add *-y* (*possible* → *possib**ly***).
- When we want to compare the way people do things, we usually add *more* (*some of them were working* ***more slowly*** *than others*).

Where we put adverbs

- We can put some adverbs at the beginning of a sentence (***Yesterday*** *Isil asked her students* ...), in the middle (*She* ***often*** *gives them short extracts* ...) or at the end (... *she could possibly practise* ... ***at school***).
- We don't usually put an adverb between a verb and its object. We say *I like doing drama* ***very much***, not ~~*I like very much doing drama*~~.
- Adverbs of place and manner usually go at the end of sentences, not in the middle (*Her students were working* ***happily*** *and* ***enthusiastically***, *she could plan* ... ***for an international teachers' conference***).
- Adverbs of time do not usually go in the middle of sentences.
- Frequency adverbs often go in the middle of sentences (*She* ***often*** *gives them, she had* ***never*** *spoken*), immediately before the LEXICAL VERB (but after the AUXILIARY VERB).
- We can sometimes put *usually*, *normally*, *often*, *frequently*, *sometimes* and *occasionally* at the beginning of sentences (***Occasionally*** *Isil goes on holiday to Bodrum*), but we don't usually do this with *always*, *ever*, *never*, *rarely* or *seldom*.

Teaching ideas: adverbs

- We often teach frequency adverbs by showing graphs of how often people do things and then getting the students to make sentences like *She often goes to the cinema on Fridays*.
- We can practise adverbs of manner by showing our students a short playscript. They have to decide how the speakers should say their lines (angrily, sadly, happily, etc.). When students act or take a role in a roleplay, we can secretly give them an adverb (for example *passionately, in a bored manner, enthusiastically*) and the other students have to guess what the adverb is.

We look at an example of adverb teaching in →7.

Using drama in the classroom

Drama is a very good way to get students to repeat the same phrases over and over again (in performance and in the rehearsal stage). We can also use drama to train students to speak and act really well, using good STRESS →26 and INTONATION →27 so that their English sounds wonderful. It can be enormously motivating. We look at using drama in →64.

12

Introducing nouns

Milk in coffee?

On her way home from the language institute in Rio de Janeiro, Brazil, where she teaches, Roberta stopped off at the supermarket. The Hunt family were coming over for dinner and she needed to get some things which she had forgotten to buy earlier. She bought sugar and some milk, in case any of her guests liked milk with their coffee. She didn't know them well, and anyway they were English. (They had only just moved out to Rio where Sarah Hunt was the new academic director at a bilingual school. Roberta had first met Sarah in the changing-room at her gym.) 'Do the English like milk with their coffee?' Roberta asked herself.

When she got home she checked the mail. There was a postcard from her mother and a letter from her daughter's school. But there was no news about the teachers' conference which she wanted to go to. She had written to the organisers weeks ago, but so far they had not sent her a reply. That disappointed her. Perhaps there would be an email later.

A few minutes later, Francisco got in from his weekly game of football and they started to prepare the meal.

In the end, the dinner went very well. The Hunts seemed happy. And the milk? Sarah Hunt had milk with her coffee, but her husband didn't, and their teenage daughter didn't have any coffee at all.

Different kinds of noun

In the story about Roberta and Francisco's dinner party, the words *Roberta*, *dinner*, *things*, *sugar*, *milk*, *coffee*, *mail*, *postcard*, *letter*, *conference*, *reply*, *email*, *meal* and *daughter* are all NOUNS. But not all of them (or the other nouns in the story) behave in the same way.

- *Roberta*, *Francisco*, *Rio* and *Sarah* are all PROPER NOUNS. They give the name of a place, person or thing. Proper nouns start with a CAPITAL LETTER.
- *Supermarket*, *dinner*, *postcard*, *school*, *conference*, *game* and *daughter* are all COUNTABLE NOUNS (sometimes called COUNT NOUNS). This means that we can talk about them in the SINGULAR (*a supermarket*, *a dinner*, *a postcard*, etc.) but we can also make them PLURAL – and we can count them (*two supermarkets*, *three dinners*, *four postcards*, etc.). We can use these nouns with singular or plural verbs.
- *Sugar*, *milk*, *coffee* and *mail* are all UNCOUNTABLE NOUNS (sometimes called NON-COUNT NOUNS). We can't make them plural or talk about 'one' of them. We use

uncountable nouns with singular verbs (*the milk **is** cold, coffee **tastes** lovely*). Notice that although *mail* is an uncountable noun, *email* is a countable noun – we can say *I got fifty-six emails today!* But we have to be careful about this. Roberta bought some *sugar* (uncountable) but after dinner Sarah Hunt had two *sugars* in her coffee (countable). This is because when we say *two sugars* we are talking about things (spoonfuls of sugar, not the sugary mass). In other words, the same word can sometimes be either countable or uncountable, depending on the exact meaning that it has.

- *Family* is a COLLECTIVE NOUN. It describes a collection of things. We can say *The family **are** coming to dinner* if we are talking about the individual members of the family or *The family **is** coming to dinner* if we are talking about the family as a unit. (In American English singular verbs are normally used with collective nouns.)
- *Supermarket*, *postcard* and *football* are all COMPOUND NOUNS. In other words, two nouns (e.g. *post* and *card*) are joined together to make a new noun (*postcard*). Sometimes with compound words, we separate the words (*bilingual school*, *language institute*) and sometimes we use a HYPHEN (*changing-room*) so that there is no ambiguity – the room itself is not changing.
- *News* is a PLURAL NOUN, but we always use it with a singular verb (*The news **is** terrible*).
- *The English* is an example of an ADJECTIVE which turns into a collective noun when we put the definite article in front of it and use it to talk about people or things in general (*the rich*, *the poor*, etc.).

Pronouns

In the story about Roberta and Francisco's dinner party there are a number of PERSONAL PRONOUNS:

- *She*, *they* and *he* are SUBJECT PRONOUNS in phrases like ***she** teaches English*, ***they** were English* and ***they** started to prepare the meal*. Other subject pronouns are *I*, *you*, *it* and *we*.
- *Them* and *her* are OBJECT PRONOUNS in phrases like *she didn't know **them** well* and *they had not sent **her** a reply*. Other object pronouns are *me*, *you*, *him*, *it and us*.
- *Her*, *his and their* are POSSESSIVE ADJECTIVES because they pre-modify nouns by saying whose it is/they are. There are no POSSESSIVE PRONOUNS in the story. *Mine*, *yours*, *hers*, *his*, *its*, *ours* and *theirs* are possessive pronouns, used in sentences like *The idea was **mine**. That house is **ours***.
- *Herself* in *Roberta asked **herself*** is a REFLEXIVE PRONOUN. Other reflexive pronouns are *myself*, *yourself*, *himself*, *itself*, *ourselves*, *yourselves* and *themselves*. We generally use reflexive pronouns in English when we want to emphasise that we did something ourselves (*I cut **myself**, Did you write this composition **yourself**?*).
- *Where* and *which* are RELATIVE PRONOUNS which introduce RELATIVE CLAUSES →2. Other relative pronouns are *whose*, *where*, *that* and *whom*. However, *that* in ***That** disappointed her* is one of four DEMONSTRATIVE PRONOUNS (*this*, *that*, *these* and *those*). We use them to identify which 'thing' we are talking about.

We suggest teaching ideas for nouns in →17.

The pronoun gender problem

English has no gender-neutral pronoun! We have to say things like *If a teacher doesn't plan his or her lessons, he or she may have problems*. Some writers use *they* instead, e.g. *If a teacher doesn't plan **their** lessons, **they** may have problems*, but that is not a very good solution. A better way of doing it may be to say *If **teachers** don't plan **their** lessons, **they** may have problems*.

13

Articles

Steve's big idea

When he was at university Steve had an idea. Actually he had a lot of ideas (that's what a university is for!), but the idea that changed his life for ever was the one about teaching.

The idea came to him when he was listening to the radio (Steve likes radio programmes). An interviewer was asking the Prime Minister about his policies for the unemployed. 'We live at a time,' the Prime Minister said, 'when people can't just expect to get a job automatically. Work does not come to people. People will have to go looking for work.'

Steve wondered where he could look when he had finished university. Then he remembered a friend of his. The friend had done a teacher training course and now he was a teacher of English in China. Wow, Steve thought, I've always wanted to see the Great Wall of China. I've dreamed of seeing Sugarloaf Mountain in Rio de Janeiro. I've imagined standing in front of the Kremlin in Red Square in Moscow. That's it. I'm a native speaker of English. Surely I can get a job like my friend!

What are articles?

In the story about Steve there are two (or maybe three!) types of article, the INDEFINITE ARTICLE *a* (*he was **a** teacher of English*) and the DEFINITE ARTICLE *the* (*he was listening to **the** radio*). Some people also talk about a ZERO ARTICLE – which means the times when we don't need to use an article at all (*People will have to go looking for **work***).

Using the indefinite article

We use *a* before a word which starts with a CONSONANT (*a teacher*, *a native speaker*) or a VOWEL which sounds like a consonant (***a** university*). We use *an* before a word that starts with a vowel-like sound (***an** idea*, ***an** interviewer*).

We use *a* and *an* before singular COUNTABLE NOUNS which refer to something in general, rather than something specific (*Steve had **an** idea …*) or when we want to talk about 'one of a kind' (***An** interviewer was asking … I'm **a** native speaker … that's what **a** university is for*).

We use *a* or *an* before certain professions (*He was **a** teacher of English*) and before some QUANTIFIERS →14 (*He had **a** lot of ideas*).

Using the definite article

- We use *the* when we are describing something specific (***the** idea that changed his life*) or before a noun that has already been mentioned (so people know which specific noun we are talking about), e.g. *Then he remembered **a** friend of his. **The** friend had done a teacher training course.*
- We use *the* when we assume that people will know what 'thing' we are talking about, e.g. ***the** radio.*
- We use *the* when what we are talking about is unique (there is only one of them), e.g. ***the** Prime Minister.*
- We use *the* to talk about a group of people who are clearly plural, e.g. ***the** unemployed* →12.
- We use *the* in some proper names (***the** Great Wall of China*, ***the** Kremlin*) but not in others (*Sugar Loaf Mountain*, *Red Square*).

No article / zero article

We don't generally use *a* or *the* when we talk about general (rather than specific) things:

- We don't use *a* or *the* when we talk about abstract concepts and/or uncountable nouns in general, e.g. ***Work** does not come to people*, *… when he had finished **university**.*
- We don't use *a* or *the* when we talk about plural nouns in general, e.g. *Steve likes **radio programmes**.*
- We don't use *a* or *the* when we talk about institutions in general, e.g. *Steve was at **university*** or about meals, e.g. *Steve had **lunch** at one o'clock.*

However, if we then refer to any of these things specifically, we would use *the*, e.g. ***The** work I did last week … **the** university where Steve did his first degree … **the** radio programme I listened to last night.*

Native speaker or non-native speaker?

Some people think that the best language teachers are **NATIVE SPEAKERS** (people who acquired the language as a first or **HOME LANGUAGE**). But this issue is complicated for a number of reasons: What is a native speaker? For example, if you have a German mother and an English father and at home they speak to you in German and English, but you were born (and went to Spanish-speaking schools) in Madrid, are you a native speaker of Spanish?

Native speakers of English may not be good models of International English (if the (regional) variety of English they speak is not understood by everybody). Some native speakers are really good language teachers; others are not!

Non-native speakers of the language they teach are good examples for their students. They can say (to their students) 'If I learnt English, so can you!' and they may understand their students' learning problems better than someone from 'outside' their students' language. Some are fantastic teachers; some are not!

However, native speakers can be good language models, too, and students may be interested in how they speak and the cultural information they bring.

Most people now agree that the most important question is not 'native speaker or non-native speaker?'; instead the two tests are 'Does the teacher speak English that is good enough?' and 'Does the teacher know how to teach?'

14

Quantifiers

Surprise!

Because she was correcting homework and planning lessons, Brittany went to bed late – and then she overslept!

She had a quick shower but she didn't have any time to put on her makeup. Luckily, she doesn't wear much anyway, but she had wanted to put on some lipstick at least. Too bad! She made herself a coffee and checked the mail. But nobody, it seemed, had remembered her birthday – except for John and Clare whom she had invited for dinner later in the day.

At school, none of her colleagues seemed to have remembered that it was her birthday either and that made her miserable, but at least the children in her second grade class were in a happy mood. It cheered her up, and so every time one of them did something good or gave her a correct answer, she gave them a gold star. They loved that. Luckily, she had enough stars so everyone went home with at least one!

When she got home, Brittany was still tired, so she lay down to have a bit of rest but she didn't get much sleep because her parents rang her from the UK to wish her a happy birthday. At least somebody had remembered! When she finished the call there was no time left for sleeping. She had to get dinner ready.

A few minutes later the doorbell rang. She opened the door. There were a lot of people outside. All of them were wearing party hats! A few of them were carrying plates of food. Most of them were colleagues from her school, but there were many others, too. And then they started to sing 'Happy Birthday ...'.

What are quantifiers?

QUANTIFIERS are words which tell people how many things (or how much of a thing) we are talking about. In the story about Brittany, the quantifiers are *a bit*, *a few*, *enough*, *a lot of*, *all*, *any*, *many*, *most*, *no*, *none* and *some*.

Quantifiers, nouns, sentences and questions

- *A bit of* (***a bit of** a rest*) is a less FORMAL way of saying *a little* (*I'll have just **a little** rest*).
- We use *a few* (***a few** minutes later*, ***a few** of them were carrying*) with COUNTABLE NOUNS. When we use *few* (without *a*) with countable nouns, it has a negative meaning (***Few** of them were happy*).
- We use *a lot of* (*there were **a lot of** people outside*) with both countable and UNCOUNTABLE NOUNS. *Lots of* is more informal and is normally used in conversation or speaking-like writing (*I've been to **lots of** parties!*).
- *All* is used with countable and uncountable nouns (***all** of them were wearing*).
- *Any* (*she didn't have **any** time*) is used in NEGATIVE SENTENCES and in QUESTIONS (*Did she have **any** time?*). But we sometimes use it in AFFIRMATIVE SENTENCES such as *I'll read **any** books* (I like them all). In this case, *any* is stressed.

- *Enough* (*she had **enough** stars*) is used with uncountable and countable nouns.
- *Every* (***every** time*) is used with singular nouns (***every** day*, ***every** week*, etc.).
- We use *many* with countable nouns (***many** others*). We often use *many* in negative statements and questions, such as *There aren't **many** people here. How **many** people went to his lecture?* In affirmative sentences we often use *a lot of* with *quite* in sentences like ***Quite a lot of** people left early.*
- *Much* (*she didn't get **much** sleep*) is often used in negative sentences. We also use *much* in questions, especially with *How* (***How much** do you want?*).
- We use *no* (*there was **no** time left*) with plural countable nouns and uncountable nouns.
- *Some* (*she had wanted to put on **some** lipstick*) is used with countable and uncountable nouns and has a positive meaning in sentences like ***Some** people are nicer than others!* It can have a negative meaning, too (*I don't like **some** people*), but usually with countable nouns only. We also use *some* in OFFERS and REQUESTS such as *Would you like **some** tea? Could I have **some** sugar, please?*

Quantifiers plus!

- Many of the quantifiers in the story about Brittany are used with *of* + PRONOUN in phrases such as ***Most of them** were colleagues* and ***a few of them** were carrying*. This is a common way of talking about specific things. We can also use a quantifier + *of* + pronoun/*the* + noun in phrases such as *none of her colleagues*.
- *Many* and *much* are often used with *so … that …* in sentences such as *There were **so** many people **that** they didn't fit in the house* and *She ate **so** much chocolate **that** she felt sick.*
- *Nobody* (paragraph 2) and *somebody* (*at least **somebody** had remembered*) are not strictly quantifiers, but we make a number of words with *any*, *every*, *some* and *no* + *body*, *thing*, *place*, *where* (*anybody*, *everybody*, *nobody*, *something*, *anything*, *everywhere*, *somewhere*, *nowhere*, etc.). These words occur with singular verbs – we say *everybody **was** late* (not ~~*everybody were late*~~).

Praise, medals and rewards

Teachers often think about how to give their students 'medals' when they do something well. But what should we give them? Gold stars (like Brittany) or PRAISE (*Well done! Fantastic! You are so clever!* etc.)?

Praising students too much – and for no particular reason – probably doesn't work. It may even have a negative effect. But not praising them isn't the answer. We know that YOUNG LEARNERS →91–101 want and benefit from teacher praise. Older students (including ADULT LEARNERS) want this, too! We look at appropriate praise and teacher FEEDBACK in →72.

15

Introducing adjectives

The spicier the better

Hiro and Sam are in a restaurant.

Hiro: I'm sorry I got here late, Sam.
Sam: That's OK. We said we would have a late dinner.
Hiro: I had to go and see my father in hospital, remember?
Sam: Oh yes, I forgot. How is he?
Hiro: He seemed well and happy. He was better than yesterday, anyway, more cheerful. He should make a good recovery.
Sam: That's great. You must be happy about that.
Hiro: When I got there he was sitting up in bed wearing a large, new, red and green silk jacket that my sister had given him. She likes you, by the way.
Sam: Who? Your sister? Me?
Hiro: Yes, she says you're really good-looking.
Sam: She does?
Hiro: Hey, come on, don't look so uncomfortable.
Sam: It's just that, well ...
Hiro: Forget I said anything.
Sam: Anyway, this is your first time in a real Mexican restaurant – a Japanese-Mexican restaurant – so what are you going to eat?
Hiro: I want to try some of those world-famous jalapeno peppers.
Sam: It's not jalapeno, Hiro, it's jalapeño.
Hiro: Are you saying my pronunciation is bad?
Sam: Hey, don't get mad at me. It's just that I worked in a Mexican restaurant once.
Hiro: OK, OK.
Sam: Here, try one of mine. But be careful. They are very spicy.
Hiro: I don't care about that. The spicier the better.
Sam: Sure?
Hiro: Yes, of course. Let's see. May I? Wow that is the hottest, spiciest, most delicious taste I have ever ... water! Water!

What are adjectives?

ADJECTIVES describe NOUNS. The adjectives in the conversation between Hiro and Sam include *better*, *careful*, *cheerful*, *delicious*, *first*, *good-looking*, *great*, *green*, *happy*, *hot*, *late*, *mad*, *Mexican*, *new*, *red*, *spicy*, *uncomfortable*, *well* and *world-famous*.

Some words can be both adjectives and ADVERBS. In the sentence *We said we would have a **late** dinner*, *late* is an adjective because it is describing the dinner. But in the phrase *I got here **late***, it is an adverb because it is describing the verb (*got here*). When Hiro describes his father in the phrase *He seemed **well** and happy*, *well* is an adjective. But in sentences like *She plays the clarinet **well***, *well* is an adverb because it is modifying a verb.

Making adjectives

- Adjectives can be single words (*a **late** dinner*, *a **good** recovery*, *a **Mexican** restaurant*, *they are very **spicy***) or made up of two words such as *good-looking* (adjective + PARTICIPLE) and *world-famous* (noun + adjective). Other combinations include adjective/noun + PREPOSITION (***rolled-up*** *sleeves, a* ***cast-off*** *jacket*) and noun + participle (*a* ***life-changing*** *event*). Two-word adjectives are normally joined by a HYPHEN (-) →12.

- Many adjectives can be changed or made with AFFIXES →19 such as *un* (*comfortable* → ***un****comfortable*), *dis* (*agreeable* → ***dis****agreeable*), *less* (*clue****less***) and *ful* (*care****ful***).
- *You must be* ***happy about*** *that* is an example of the kind of adjective that is always followed by a specific preposition (*about*), whereas *mad* (= angry) in *Don't get* ***mad at*** *me*! can be followed by *at* or *about* (*I was* ***mad about*** *what he said*).
- *Better*, *more cheerful* and *spicier* are examples of COMPARATIVE ADJECTIVES. With short adjectives we add *-er* for the comparative form (*nice* → *nicer*, *young* → *younger*). If the adjective ends in *y*, we change the *y* to *i* (*spicy* → *spicier*, *noisy* → *noisier*). If the adjective ends in VOWEL + CONSONANT, we double the last consonant (*wet* → *wetter*, *thin* → *thinner*).
- If the adjective is longer, we usually say *more* + adjective (*more cheerful*, *more expensive*), though some words can be said in both ways (*clever* → *cleverer*, *more clever*). Some words have comparative forms that are irregular (*good* → *better*).
- *Hottest*, *spiciest* and *most delicious* are examples of SUPERLATIVE ADJECTIVES. We give short adjectives a superlative form by adding *-est* (*nicest*, *youngest*) and, if necessary, we change the spelling in the same way as for comparative forms. With longer adjectives we add *most*. There are also irregular superlative forms like *good* → *best*.

How adjectives work

- When we use more than one adjective before a noun, we separate them with commas (*that is the hottest, spiciest, most delicious taste …*).
- When we use more than one adjective after verbs like *be* and *seem*, we usually put *and* before the last adjective (*He seemed well* ***and*** *happy*). We use *and* when two colours are describing the same thing (*a large, new, red* ***and*** *green jacket*).
- When we have a sequence of adjectives, we usually put general qualities (such as *big*) before adjectives which describe the specific type (such as *red*). GENERAL ADJECTIVES usually appear in the sequence size (*big*), physical properties (*heavy*), age (*new*, *young*) and shape (*square*). SPECIFIC ADJECTIVES appear in the sequence colour (*red*), origin (*Japanese*), material (*silk*) and purpose/use (*musical*). This means we say *a large, new, red and green silk jacket* rather than ~~*a red and green silk, new, large, jacket*~~.
- We can use comparative form adjectives in the pattern *the … the better* (***the*** *spicier* ***the better***), and sometimes we repeat comparative adjectives to emphasise the adjectival quality (*It was getting* ***hotter and hotter***).
- Superlative adjective forms are often used in phrases such as *the most … I have ever seen/tasted*, etc. (*the* ***most*** *delicious taste* ***I have ever*** *experienced*).
- We can use adjectives with the DEFINITE ARTICLE →13 *to make general nouns* (*e.g. the blind, the rich, etc.*).

Do you like being corrected?

Hiro was not very pleased when Sam corrected his pronunciation. Most of us don't particularly like it when people tell us we are wrong.

The language classroom is no different, and yet we frequently have to tell students when they make mistakes and help them to CORRECT themselves (or correct them ourselves). That is why the way we do it is so important →73.

16

What comes after nouns?

Social networks

Going into the small room at the end of the corridor, Roberta sat down in front of the computer. It was the computer she had bought when her old one's hard disk had started to go wrong. Her new computer was a laptop with a lot of extra features and she needed it for her online work with her students. Roberta had started to worry that her students would be bored unless she used modern technology in her teaching.

She turned on the switch at the back of her computer. She looked at all the email messages waiting for her answer, but she ignored them. Then she looked at the homework posted on a special site she had created for her students, but she didn't feel like correcting it. Instead she went to her favourite social network site and looked at all the news about her friends. She sent messages to her favourite people and she had many online conversations about teaching and other things. She posted some new messages on her own web page and then watched a film clip on a video site which her friend had told her about.

By now it was late and she realised that she had spent too much time talking to her friends online. She was very tired. She would have to do all her work in the morning.

Before and after

In the PHRASE *the small room at the end of the corridor* (in sentence 1 of the story about Roberta) we describe the NOUN *room* with an ADJECTIVE before it (*small*) and a phrase after it (*at the end of the corridor*).

Nouns in the story such as *computer*, *laptop*, *work*, *switch*, *messages*, *homework*, *site* and *conversations* are also described by phrases or CLAUSES which come *after* them, e.g. *conversations* ***about teaching***.

Describing nouns

- Many of the nouns are described with PREPOSITIONAL PHRASES – a PREPOSITION + a group of words – in phrases such as *a laptop* ***with a lot of new features***, *her online work* ***with her students***, *the switch* ***at the back of her computer***, *all the news* ***about her friends***, *some new messages* ***on her own web page*** and *a film clip* ***on a video site***.
- Three of the nouns are described with RELATIVE CLAUSES →2 in the phrases *the computer* ***she had bought***, *a special site* ***she had created for her students***, *a video site* ***which her friend had told her about***.
- Two nouns are described by PARTICIPLE PHRASES: a PRESENT PARTICIPLE (*the email messages* ***waiting for her answer***) and a PAST PARTICIPLE (*the homework* ***posted on a special site***).

Participles (and gerunds)

Present participles and GERUNDS are both formed with the BASE FORM of the verb + *-ing*. But how do we know which is which?

- Where the *-ing* form is part of a verb or behaves like a verb, it is a participle, for example in phrases such as ***going** into the small room* or *she is **talking** to her friends*. But if the *-ing* form can be replaced by a **NOUN** – and is being used like a noun – it is a gerund, for example in phrases such as ***teaching** is a wonderful occupation* or ***listening** to music* is one of my favourite things.
- Participles can also be verb-like adjectives (e.g. *a **crying** baby, a **loving** husband*). But we have to be careful! When Roberta worries that her students will be bored, she is using a past participle (*bored*) as an adjective. Students often mix up the two participles and say things like *I am boring* (= that's my character) when they mean to say *I am bored* (= that's how I feel).

Technophile or technophobe?

Some teachers use nothing more in class than a **BOARD** and a book. Others use computers, **INTERACTIVE WHITEBOARDS** (**IWBS**) or more mobile technology, such as **SMART PHONES**, **TABLET COMPUTERS** and various forms of e-reader. In some countries, access to the **INTERNET** is free for all and many children are taught using computers and online resources rather than using books, etc. But in other countries there are fewer possibilities.

Good teaching is about how teachers and students relate to (and interact with) each other - and about how teachers can help students get and remember knowledge. Technology - from old-fashioned boards to modern internet resources - can help, but it's not *what* we use that matters, but *how* we use it.

However, in the modern world, it is important for teachers to keep up with new developments in educational technology so that they can take advantage of new and exciting possibilities if they are appropriate.

We look at classroom resources in →85–87.

Teaching ideas: post-modification

Post-modification is about the words that come after the noun. Pre-modification is about words that come before the noun. We can help students to recognise both of these by getting them to underline examples in any **TEXT** they come across.

We can have them reorder phrases to make whole sentences, e.g.

a) *Looked at the watch / on his wrist / The man / waiting at the station*
b) *in a pink floral dress / in his hand / The woman / walked towards a man / with a big suitcase*

We can give students a sentence and get them to underline the nouns. They then have to add post-modification using prepositional phrases, relative clauses, participle phrases, etc.

We can put objects all over the classroom and get the students to move them around using no pre-modification (so they can't use colour adjectives, etc.). For example, *Put the box with the flowers on it next to the book about history.*

17

Teaching the noun phrase

Countable nouns	Uncountable nouns
banana	milk

Elements of the noun phrase

A NOUN PHRASE can be a) just one NOUN such as *love*, b) a noun with something in front of it – such as an ADJECTIVE – to describe it, such as *romantic love*, or c) a phrase in which the noun has, for example, ARTICLES, QUANTIFIERS and adjectives before it and extra description after it, e.g. *The extraordinarily strong love which he suddenly felt*. Noun phrases are based on the noun at the heart of the phrase (in this case *love*).

In this unit we look at ideas for teaching some of the elements of the noun phrase, and activities to help students to make longer noun phrases.

1 Countable and uncountable nouns (1)

We can show our ELEMENTARY students a picture of a shopping basket. They first have to match words such as *milk*, *sugar*, *bananas*, *juice*, *hamburger*, etc. with the items in the basket. Next, they listen to an audio in which someone is talking about their shopping. They have to decide whether they are COUNTABLE NOUNS or UNCOUNTABLE NOUNS →12 and put them in the correct place in the chart on the left.

Finally, they use the words to talk about what they like to eat and how it is made.

2 Countable and uncountable nouns (2)

We can ask ELEMENTARY students to say what Maggie is going to get at the market. They have to choose whether to say *a* (COUNTABLE) or *some* (UNCOUNTABLE). For example, they can say *She's going to buy an apple* or *She's going to buy some flour*.

3 Articles

We can ask INTERMEDIATE students whether they can put *a(n)* or *the* in the following sentences – or whether they can leave out ARTICLES altogether →13.

1 ___ war never solves anything.
2 ___ First World War was one of the worst in history.
3 It was ___ day like ___ any other day, but then the soldiers came, etc.

We can use similar gapped sentences with items such as RELATIVE PRONOUNS →12 in sentences like *He's the man ___ I met.*

4 Possessive pronouns

We can create a lost property office and fill it with a range of objects. We can then show elementary students different people. The students have to guess who has lost what using POSSESSIVE PRONOUNS →12, saying *I think it's hers*, *I think it's theirs*, etc.

5 Prepositions

We can get our LOWER-INTERMEDIATE students to learn and practise PREPOSITIONS →16 by showing them a picture of an adventure trail/obstacle course. They have to match the following sentences with the activities shown in the picture:

a) Climb ___ the net.	**d)** Run ___ the trees.
b) Crawl ___ the tunnel.	**e)** Slide ___ the skyline.
c) Jump ___ the wall.	**f)** Walk ___ the wire.

and then complete the sentences with the correct preposition from this list:

along down off over through (x2) up

The students can then design their own adventure trail.

6 Comparative adjectives

- In the following DISCOVERY activity →46, elementary students see these adjectives and their comparative forms:

quicker → quicker	lovely → lovelier	bad → worse
fast → faster	thin → thinner	comfortable → more comfortable
nice → nicer	big → bigger	expensive → more expensive
noisy → noisier	good → better	

  We then ask them how we make short adjectives comparative (add *er*), what happens if they end in *y* (we change it to *i*), what happens when one-syllable adjectives end in VOWEL + CONSONANT (they double the consonant), and what we do if the adjective is long (we add *more*), etc. →15.

- When we want our students to practise COMPARATIVE ADJECTIVES, we can ask them to write down words within a certain category (methods of transport, for example) on separate pieces of paper. They put the pieces of paper into a hat (or bowl). A student then takes out two pieces of paper and compares the things that they have selected. If the words are *truck* and *bicycle*, they make a sentence such as *Trucks are usually bigger than bicycles*.

Making noun phrases

1 Adjective order

- We can ask INTERMEDIATE students to think of their favourite object. They have to write down as many adjectives as they can think of to describe it – including size, colour, price, where it comes from, what it is used for, etc.
- The students now have to describe their objects using at least three of their adjectives before the noun. Can they get the adjective order correct? →15

2 Pictures to make an information gap

We can show pairs of students two different pictures to create an INFORMATION GAP →50. They have to find differences between the two pictures in order to practise such things as PREPOSITIONS (A: *In my picture the girl is sitting opposite the boy*. B: *My picture is different. The girl is standing in front of the boy*) or clothes vocabulary (A: *In my picture she is wearing trousers*. B: *In my picture she is wearing a skirt*).

Student A

Student B

3 The never-ending sentence

We can give the students a sentence. In pairs or groups, they have to expand it by using as many words and phrases as possible. For example, the sentence *The man kissed the lady's hand* might be transformed into *The good-looking old Spanish man with grey hair and a luxurious grey beard gently and affectionately kissed the beautiful tall lady's outstretched hand which she had held up to him …*

4 Definitions from the dictionary

- We can play a version of the GAME 'Call my bluff'. In teams, the students have to write three DICTIONARY definitions for a difficult word or phrase →82. One of the definitions is true but the other two must be false. Students in Team A read their definitions. Team B must decide which is the true one.
- With more advanced students, we can play a 'random definition' game. Without looking at the dictionary, a student from Team A gives a page number, column number and word number (e.g. the sixth word). A student from Team B finds the word and reads out the definition. Can the Team A student identify the word?

18

What words mean

Irina and the principal

Irina was fast asleep when the alarm went off. She opened her eyes with difficulty. Her head was throbbing – she had a headache; but she still had to get ready to teach at her school. After she had finished breakfast, she put on her coat and headed to the bus stop. When she got to the staffroom, she found that all the other teachers were having a meeting about Svatislav Melaschenko, the new head of the school. They were unhappy about him because (Vladimir said) his new power had gone to his head. He wouldn't listen any more. He had become very pig-headed. Should they go and talk to him about it, they wondered. In the end, Vladimir tossed a coin – heads or tails (heads = we go to see him, tails = we forget about it) – and it was heads. They decided that they would all go and see him during the lunch break. Irina didn't want to be part of this so she tried to keep her head down, but in spite of this she somehow found herself at the head of the little procession as they marched down the corridor towards Mr Melaschenko's office.

What does *head* mean?

In the text about Irina the word *head* has many different meanings (we call two words which have the same spelling and pronunciation, but mean different things, HOMONYMS).

- In *her **head** was throbbing*, *head* refers to the top part of a body, the part that is supported by the neck. In the third sentence of the story (*the new **head***), *head* means the principal of a school. In the last sentence (*at the **head** of the little procession), head* means at the front. In all of these cases *head* is a NOUN →12.
- In the second sentence of the story (*... and **headed** to the bus stop*), *head* means to go towards. It is a VERB →4.
- *Head* also appears in various IDIOMATIC phrases →21 (*power had **gone to his head*** = made him feel more important than necessary, ***heads** or tails* = what we say when we toss a coin, *trying to **keep her head down*** = she didn't want people to notice her).

How *head* is related to other words

- Sometimes *head* can join with other words (*headache*, *head teacher*, *headword*, *headband*) to make new **COMPOUND** words →12.
- There are words which have an opposite meaning to *head* (e.g. *tails* in the expression *heads or tails*). We call words with opposite meanings **ANTONYMS**.
- In the phrase *headed to the bus stop* (sentence 2 in the story above) we could use *proceeded* instead of *headed* because *proceed* is a **SYNONYM** – it means more or less the same as *head*. But as with many other synonyms, it doesn't mean *exactly* the same. And what is a synonym (or an antonym) for one meaning of a word may not be a synonym for another. Synonyms (S) and antonyms (A) for *rich* in the sentence *The food was really rich* (S = *filling*, A = *light*) are not the same as for *The president was fantastically rich* (S = *well-off*, A = *poor*).
- Irina's principal is described as *pig-headed*. This means the same as *stubborn* or *strong-willed*, but it has a more negative **CONNOTATION**. A connotation is an idea or feeling that a word suggests, which is more than just its meaning.
- Another kind of relationship is between words that are a *part* of something. So, for example, *ears*, *eyes*, *brows* and *chins* are parts of a *head*. We call *head* a **SUPERORDINATE** and say that *ear* is a **HYPONYM** of *head*. *Eye*, *ear*, *brow* and *chin* are called **CO-HYPONYMS** because they are all at the same level in a hierarchy of meaning – as this diagram shows:

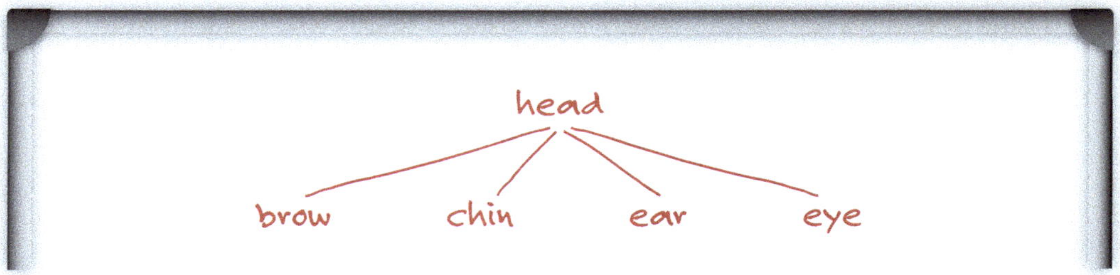

- We also have relationships between words that are a *type* of something (e.g. *bicycles*, *buses*, *cars*, *trains*, *trucks*, etc. are types of *vehicle*).

Teaching ideas: word meaning

The examples of the word *head* tell us a lot about how we can **ELICIT** and teach vocabulary.

- The most important thing to decide is which meaning or meanings of a word to introduce and what level to do it at. For example, **BEGINNER** or **ELEMENTARY** students need to know the meaning of *head* (= the thing on top of your neck), but probably won't need to recognise or use *head of a procession* until they are **UPPER-INTERMEDIATE** level or above. We decide which words to teach on the basis of **FREQUENCY** (how common a word is), how useful it is (for students at that particular level), and how appropriate it is for the students: the word *stethoscope*, for example, is a frequent and useful word for beginner students of English for nursing, but may not be so useful for general English students at beginner level.
- We shouldn't just teach individual words. Words occur as **COLLOCATIONS** (like *fast asleep* in the story about Irina) and in **IDIOMATIC** phrases and **LEXICAL CHUNKS**, such as *heads or tails*, *keep your head down*, *I can't make head or tail of it* (= I can't understand it at all), *It's doing my head in* (= **INFORMAL** British English for 'I am confused and angry about it') and *Let's put our heads together on this* (= let's collaborate to find a solution). So we should teach collocations, phrases and lexical chunks, too, starting with those that are the most frequent, useful and appropriate. We discuss words which often occur together in →20.
- It is often helpful to teach words together with other words that they are related to. We don't usually teach *empty* without teaching *full*, for example.

19

How words are formed

A problem solved

Brittany is sitting in a diner having brunch. She calls it 'brunching' (which her British friends think is funny) and she likes to do it at the weekend after a long week's 'lessoning' (another of her made-up words which she uses instead of *teaching*). So today she slept late, inputted some lesson plans on her computer, got on her bike and came to the diner.

Her mobile phone rings. She retrieves it from her handbag (Brittany still likes using words like *handbag* instead of the American *purse*) and presses the green button with her long thumbnail. She lifts the phone to her ear. It is Amelie's mother. Amelie is a child in Brittany's class.

At first, when Amelie joined her class, Brittany thought the girl was really intelligent, but as the weeks went by she began to think that she had overestimated her ability. And then, gradually, she became aware of the girl's unhappiness.

She tried to find out what the problem was but it was impossible to get Amelie to talk to her – at first. But in the end she discovered that Tracy, another girl in the class, was the ringleader of a gang of girls who had been bullying Amelie. Brittany's head teacher wanted to exclude Tracy, but Brittany disagreed. She worked with Tracy, Amelie and the whole class and now the situation has improved.

That's why Amelie's mother has rung. She wants to say thank you.

Making words from different bits and pieces

Brittany notices Amelie's *unhappiness*. This WORD is made up of three different elements. The ROOT WORD (similar to the BASE FORM of the VERB →4) is the ADJECTIVE *happy*. We can add the SUFFIX *-ness* (changing the *-y* to *-i*) to make the NOUN (***happiness***) and we can add the PREFIX *un-* to give it a negative meaning (***un**happiness*). There are various ways in which we can manipulate root words:

- AFFIXES are small elements of meaning that we can add to the beginnings (prefixes) and endings (suffixes) of root words. Prefixes in the story about Brittany and Amelie include ***re**trieves*, ***over**estimated*, ***un**happiness*, ***im**possible*, ***dis**covered*, ***ex**clude* and ***dis**agreed*. There are two suffixes in the story, *unhappi**ness*** and *situa**tion***.
- We add the *-s* MORPHEME (as an affix) to make INFLECTIONS in words like *ring**s***, *retrieve**s*** and *lift**s***. We add the *-ed* morpheme to inflect base forms of verbs in words like *join**ed***, *discover**ed***, *disagree**d*** and *improve**d***.
- We use the term WORD FAMILY to talk about the different words that are created with a root word – through affixation, etc. When Brittany worried that she had overestimated Amelie's ability, *ability* is part of a family that includes *able*, *ably*, *enable*, *disable*, etc.
- We can join two words together to make new COMPOUND WORDS, such as *weekend*, *handbag*, *ringleader* and *head teacher*. We discuss COMPOUND NOUNS (and whether they are separate or have a HYPHEN, etc.) in →12.
- We can mix two words together and create a new BLEND in words like *brunch* (= *breakfast* + *lunch*).

- We can shorten words and just use one part of them, e.g. *phone* instead of *telephone* or *mobile phone*, *bike* instead of *bicycle*.
- Some people change a word's grammatical class. Brittany talks about *brunching* and *lessoning* – and these may be her own special words – but nouns like *input* are now regularly used as verbs in sentences like *She* ***inputted*** *some lesson plans on her computer*.

Teaching ideas: word formation

We can get our students to complete charts with word families (xxxxxx means there is no form), e.g.

Adjective	Adverb	Noun	Verb
able unable	ably	ability inability disability	enable disable
intelligent unintelligent	intelligently unintelligently	intelligence	xxxxxx

We can ask them to change the form of a word and rewrite a sentence to include it, e.g.

She spoke about motivation. INTELLIGENT

She spoke intelligently about motivation

We can get the students to **NOTICE** what kinds of ending different grammar words have. For example the endings *-ion*, *-ence*, *-ness*, etc. are usually nouns; *-able*, *-ic* and *-y* are often adjectives, *-ly* often comes at the end of adverbs.

We can get our students to make up their own words (like Brittany) using prefixes and suffixes and then use them to tell a story.

American and British English

British English and American English are usually very similar, but some things have different names, e.g. *cellphone* (American) – *mobile phone* (British), *purse* (American) – *handbag* (British) *candy* (American) – *sweet* (British).

Other varieties of English have their own words, too. For example, Australians may talk about *this arvo* (British = *this afternoon*) and Irish speakers may enjoy good *craic* (British English = *fun*).

Bullying

Many children are bullied (or bully) at school. It is something that happens. But it shouldn't. It is harmful for both the bullied and the bully. Many children who bully have been bullied in their turn, and many children who are bullied – face to face or through cyber-bullying (using mobile phones and the **INTERNET** for example) – become extremely unhappy. Both their schoolwork and their development can suffer.

Teachers and schools need to have a clear policy on bullying so that children understand that it is unacceptable, and why. They need to know that if they are being bullied, they should talk about it to someone.

Children who are being bullied need to know who they can talk to. They must be sure that they can say what is going on without suffering any consequences. If they cannot talk to an adult, they should tell their friends what is going on.

Teachers should talk to children who bully others and help them understand why it is wrong –this is always better than just punishment (which can seem like just another form of bullying).

Teachers should involve the whole class in discussions about why bullying is wrong and how to stop it.

20

Collocation and lexical phrases

Nervous in Alexandria

Hassan was in a bad mood. He hadn't slept a wink all night. In fact, he'd been sleeping badly ever since the director of the school had announced that he was coming to observe Hassan's lessons. It was amazing how much it made him nervous. He was absolutely convinced that he could teach, but the problem was that when people watched him, he sometimes forgot what he was doing.

Oh well. He looked out at the grey sea. The sun had not yet risen above the buildings of Alexandria behind him. I'd better get a move on, he thought. He hadn't finished preparing his lesson.

When he got back to the flat his mother, who is English, was already up. 'Would you like a cup of coffee?' she said.

'Don't worry. I'll get it myself,' he replied in an aggressive tone of voice, without thinking. His mother looked as if she would burst into tears, and he was instantly sorry.

'It's because of this observation,' he explained.

'I'm sure you'll be OK,' she told him.

'Yes, it'll be fine,' he replied, but he didn't feel as calm about it as he sounded.

Words alone, words together

Hassan is *absolutely convinced* that he can teach. Of course, we can use the word *convinced* by itself (*he was convinced that he could teach*), but we often use the COLLOCATION *absolutely convinced* when we want to make it sound stronger. Collocations are words which are frequently used together. There are quite a few examples of collocations in Hassan's story:

- *Hassan was in a* ***bad mood*** – *mood* collocates with other ADJECTIVES →15, too (*a* ***good*** *mood, a* ***foul*** *mood, a* ***black*** *mood*).
- *Hassan had been* ***sleeping badly*** – *sleep* also collocates with other ADVERBS →11 (*sleep* ***well****, sleep* ***soundly/deeply****, sleep* ***peacefully****, sleep* ***late***).
- *Hassan's mother nearly* ***burst into tears*** – *tears* also collocates with other VERBS →4 apart from *burst into*, such as ***break down in*** *tears*, ***be moved to*** *tears*, ***bring tears to somebody's eyes***, ***be reduced to*** *tears*, *(his)* ***eyes filled with*** *tears*, *tears* ***ran/rolled down his face***, etc.

Lexical phrases, lexical chunks

Poor Hassan *hadn't slept a wink* all night. Unlike *sleep + badly*, *not sleep a wink* is not a collocation, it is a LEXICAL PHRASE – often referred to as a LEXICAL CHUNK. In a lexical phrase, two or more words join together and *together* act as if they are one unit of meaning. Phrasal verbs like ***run out of** petrol* are lexical phrases, too. There are several lexical phrases in the story about Hassan:

- When Hassan thinks *I'd better get a move on*, he is using a FIXED LEXICAL PHRASE. You can't change any of the words in the phrase. People often use this phrase when they need to leave.
- When Hassan says *I'll get it myself!* he is using a SEMI-FIXED LEXICAL PHRASE. We can change the verb in the phrase and say, for example, *I'll do/make it myself*.
- Hassan's mother asks *Would you like a cup of coffee?* The phrase *would you like a ...* is a lexical chunk which acts as a 'stem' to which you can add different words and phrases (*cup of coffee*, *drink*, *lift*, etc.). We can also change the chunk by saying *Would you like some/any ...?*
- Some lexical phrases, such as ***it was amazing how much** it made him nervous*, act as SENTENCE FRAMES.

Why collocations and chunks matter

If we want to know a word, we need to know what other words go with it. Teachers should show students which words 'live with each other', and offer activities like matching activities →48 and dictionary research →46 to help them to come across them. They need to know, for example, that we say *make the bed* and not *organise* or *tidy the bed*!

All languages have lexical chunks, and if we want to speak a language fluently, we need to be able to use these chunks as if they were one word. Fluent speakers never pause or hesitate in the middle of a lexical chunk – they don't say *I'd* (pause) *better get* (pause) *a move on*. They just say the words as one continuous phrase. That is why these chunks are so important.

Teachers should draw their students' attention to lexical phrases when they occur. They should help them say phrases like *See you later* as if they were one word (we look at how words sound together in →25). The same is true for some grammar-like phrases such as *Have you ever been to ...?* in questions like *Have you ever been to Egypt?*

Being observed

Most teachers are nervous when somebody – a director of studies, principal, colleague, etc. – comes to watch them teach. But observation is a great opportunity for people to learn from each other. You can always see something new when you watch somebody else's lesson; and you can always learn something about yourself when someone watches you and you have a good conversation afterwards. It is worth remembering that directors of study and principals have all been observed in their time.

It is important for the observer and the teacher to discuss *when* an observation will take place – instead of the observer just announcing the time – and both teacher and observer should know *why* it is happening. If the teacher is involved in when and why the observation is going to happen, he or she will feel a lot better about it!

When teachers in a school watch each other (PEER OBSERVATION →78), the observers can tell the other teachers – in teacher meetings – about the exciting and interesting things they saw in their colleagues' lessons. That way, good lesson ideas are passed around the school.

21

Metaphor, idiom, proverb and cliché

The fairy godmother

Today Nicole thinks her classroom is full of glittering jewels. Her students are laughing and playing like a swarm of summer bees or spring lambs playing on a hillside. How unlike her own schooldays!

Nicole didn't get on well at school and she dropped out on her sixteenth birthday. It nearly broke her mother's heart, but her father was furious ('saw red' is how her sister described it) and shouted with rage. He was always boiling with rage about something or other. She couldn't stand it.

Nicole left home. For the next few years she did lots of poorly paid jobs in and around Toronto, the city where she was born. She had a horrible boyfriend, a real wolf in sheep's clothing; he seemed to care for her but he didn't really. She was miserable and unhappy. Her life hit rock bottom.

And then one day Nicole bumped into her fairy godmother, the only teacher from her old school she had ever liked. And so, to cut a long story short, this teacher, Mavis Saavedra, took an interest in Nicole. She helped her get back on her feet and persuaded her to go back to school, and then to teacher training college.

Now Nicole is snowed under with work – preparing lessons, marking, making things, no sleep, being a primary teacher. But, as Mavis always says, every cloud has a silver lining. And it's true: Nicole is doing a job she loves. 'I'm over the moon!' she likes to say and Mavis tells her off for speaking in clichés.

Describing one thing as something else

When we use words to mean exactly (and only) what they mean, our conversation does not sound very exciting. But when we use more 'colourful' language, things are more interesting!

- Sometimes we describe something as if it was something else and has the same qualities as that something else. This is what happens when Nicole thinks of her children as *glittering jewels*. They aren't literally jewels, of course, but in her mind Nicole sees them as if they were. We call this kind of description a METAPHOR.

- When we compare one thing with something else and we want to be sure that our reader/listener understands the comparison, we can say things like *Her students are like a swarm of summer bees or spring lambs playing on a hillside*. We call this kind of a connection a **SIMILE**.
- Many metaphors end up being **IDIOMS** if people use them a lot and they become a normal part of the language. An idiom is a phrase like *drop out of school*. We know what all the individual words mean, but unless we know that *drop out of* means 'to leave a school or university before you reach the end of your course', we will not understand the whole phrase. Many **PHRASAL VERBS →9** such as *tell off* (= Mavis criticises Nicole), *run out of* (petrol), *run up* (a large bill), etc. have the same kind of idiomatic meaning.
- Some idioms, such as *every cloud has a silver lining* (= there is always something good even when the news is bad), become **PROVERBS**. These are phrases that a particular society uses to give advice or to say things that are generally true.
- We call metaphorical/idiomatic phrases like *I'm over the moon* **CLICHÉS** because we are bored with them – we think people use them too much.

More about metaphors

- Many cultures use *colours* to describe feelings. In the text above, Nicole's father *saw red* and this means he became very angry, but in other cultures *red* has a different meaning. If British people call someone *yellow*, it means he or she is a coward, but for people from other cultures the colour refers to spirituality or enlightenment!
- Nicole nearly *broke her mother's heart* (= made her very unhappy). We can also say things like *her heart wasn't really in it* (= she wasn't very keen on it) or talk about *a change of heart* (= changing the way we think). Most parts of the body, such as *mouth*, *eye*, *foot*, *nose*, etc. can be used in metaphorical phrases.
- Nicole is *snowed under* (= she has far too much work). We use many other weather metaphors, such as *storm out* (= to leave very quickly and in anger) or cooking metaphors – Nicole's father was always *boiling with rage about something* (= always very angry).

Teaching ideas: idiom and metaphor

Many idioms are very 'culture-specific'. Nicole's boyfriend was *a wolf in sheep's clothing*; this animal idiom is understood in Britain and the United States to indicate someone who appears harmless but is really dangerous. However, *she thinks she's the cat's whiskers* (= she thinks she is the best) is more common in Britain than in America – but it isn't *very* common in Britain. We should not spend too much time teaching idioms that are not common – even though it might be great fun!

So what can we do?

- We can draw our students' attention to idioms and metaphors when they occur. Recognition is more important here than production, and over-using culturally inappropriate idioms in a foreign language is not a good idea.
- We can get our students to **RESEARCH →46** a common area of metaphorical language (like the body) by looking up words in their dictionaries and listing some metaphorical phrases. Perhaps they can draw a metaphor **WORD MAP →22**.
- We can make sure that students learn metaphors as **LEXICAL CHUNKS →20**.
- We can tell our students to bring 'new' metaphors they find to class.
- We can give the students some metaphorical phrases (or phrasal verbs, etc.). They then have to use four of them in a story.

22

Meeting and remembering words

How do students *remember* words?

It is important to teach new words to students and to introduce them in TEXTS and activities. But how can we help our students to remember new words after they have learnt them? How can we try to ensure that the words are 'there' (available to them) when they want them? There are four possible ways:

Arousal and affect: the 'cuddle factor' (A&A)

Students are far more likely to remember words if they have an AFFECTIVE meeting with them (that is, if their feelings are engaged). A class once told their teacher that they remembered the new word *cuddle* because they liked the meaning of the word and how it sounded. If we can provoke the same kind of 'cuddle factor' with other words, our students are much more likely to remember them than if they are not emotionally engaged when they first meet them.

Cognitive engagement: working it out (CE)

Students are far more likely to remember words if they have to do some work with them – that is, if they have to use their brains to solve puzzles using the words or put them into categories.

Retrieval and use (R&U)

Students will remember words when we encourage them to go and get them – to dig them up from wherever in their brains they are hidden. When we encourage them to use language, especially in COMMUNICATIVE ACTIVITIES, they have to retrieve words in this way, and the more they do so, the more these words will become a permanent part of their language 'store'.

Repetition of encounter: meeting words again and again (RofE)

If students only meet a new word once or twice, they are unlikely to remember it. They need to meet it again and again. And it helps if they keep meeting the new word over a period of time. Just seeing a word three times in one lesson is not enough. Students need to meet the word repeatedly over a period of time – and with gaps in between their meetings to let things settle.

Examples of word-remembering activities

In the following examples we will say which of the four characteristics (above) the activities encourage.

Poetry spaces (A&A, CE)

We can read and show the students a poem with the same words or phrases blanked out each time they occur. The students have to try to guess what the words and phrases are. If the students are engaged and like the activity (and the poem), they will remember the words. We look at more POETRY activities in →63.

Desert island words (A&A, RofE)

At the end of a period of study, the students can look at a list of the words and phrases they have studied. They can then be asked which five words they would take with them to a desert island and why. Another idea is to decide which words they will put in the *fridge* (they'll keep them for later), the *dustbin* (they don't need the words) or their *suitcase* (because they want to use them now).

Categorising words (CE)

We can make our students think about words by categorising them. For example, we can ask them to be *word detectives* and look through all the words they have studied over the last few weeks and put them in different categories, such as transport, words which express emotions, verbs which describe work, etc.

We can ask the students to categorise words with similar meanings in order of how strong they are. For example, we can ask them to look at a list of words and then place them on a love–hate cline:

dislike don't like enjoy hate like love

Negative |____| Positive

Odd one out (CE, RofE)

We can give the students groups of words and ask them to decide which is the odd one out, for example *aeroplane*, *bicycle*, *bus*, *car*, *train* (the answer is *bicycle* because it uses human not mechanical power). A variation is to give the students any one of the words and they have to prove that it is the odd one out.

Word map 1 (R&U) DVD3

We can put a word map like the one shown in diagram 1 below on the board. In pairs or groups, the students have to expand the diagram as far as they can. Diagram 2 shows how they might start.

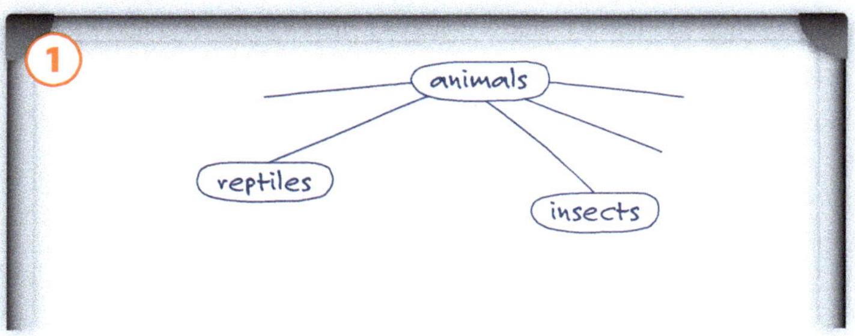

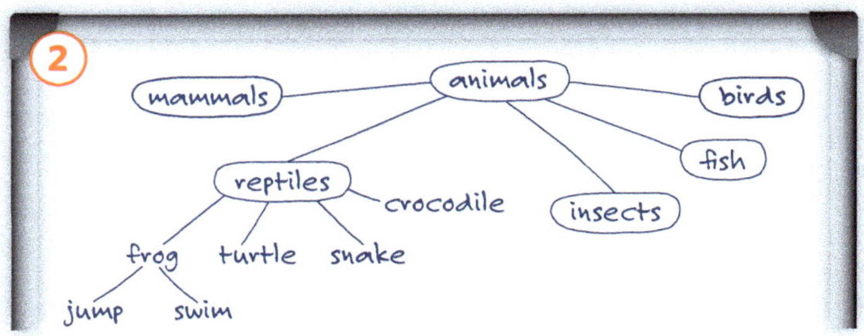

Word map 2 (CE)

We can choose a word and get the students to fill in a word map diagram like this:

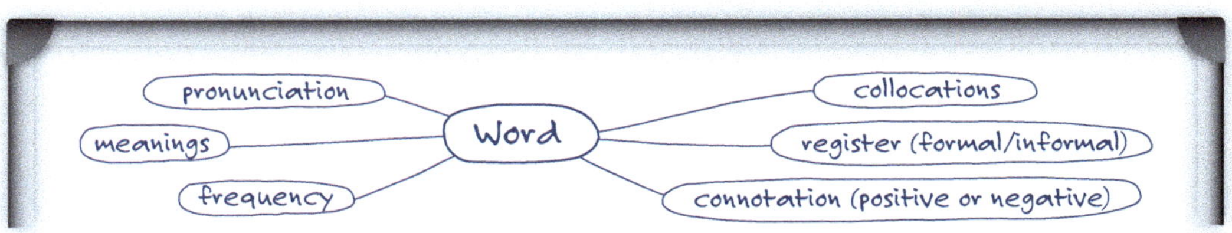

For more on CONNOTATION and FREQUENCY, see →82.

Storytelling (R&U)

We can give students at any level (except complete BEGINNERS) a list of ten words (or any other number). They have to use five of them (or another number you choose) in a story. They prepare the stories in GROUPS →67. One member of each group then goes to another group to tell the story. Then a member from that other group goes to another group to tell the story. Soon all the stories have been told three, four or even five times. Each time the storytelling gets a little bit better.

There are many more teaching ideas for GENERAL ENGLISH in →44–64, for YOUNG LEARNERS in →91–101 and for CLIL in →102–110.

23

The phonemic alphabet

Beijing, Thursday afternoon

T1 Although she was feeling tired after her last lesson and she had a bad cough, English teacher Shengmei didn't go home immediately. She sat in the teachers' room going through her lessons for tomorrow. Then she called her cousin Xiaobing and suggested that they have an early dinner. Xiaobing said yes and so they agreed to meet up in a restaurant four blocks from the famous Lao She Teahouse. When Shengmei got to the restaurant, she couldn't see Xiaobing anywhere, but in the end she found her at a table right at the back. She rushed over to her and when they had ordered their meal, she told Xiaobing her exciting news.

Sounds and spelling

Some students of English find English spelling difficult – and they find it especially difficult to know how to say words when they see them written. This is not surprising when we think of the number of different ways that we can pronounce the *ou* spelling – as shown in the story about Shengmei. In *although*, *ou* has the same sound as in ***so***. *Ou* has the same sound as *off* in the word *cough*, whereas in *through*, *ou* sounds like ***true***. In *cousin*, *ou* has the same sound as ***sun*** and *ou* in *found* sounds like ***how***. Clearly, then, alphabetic spelling is inadequate when it comes to telling us what words sound like. We need a different writing system to show all the different sounds and we call this the PHONEMIC ALPHABET.

The phonemic alphabet

When we write in English, we have the 26 letters of the written alphabet to choose from. But the combination of these letters, and the different spellings we have, give us many more sounds (or PHONEMES), as listed in the phonemic chart on the next page. This allows us to write the word *cough* as /kɒf/ in PHONEMIC TRANSCRIPTION. *Although* is /ɔːlˈðəʊ/, *through* is /θruː/and *cousin* is /ˈkʌzən/, etc.

Consonants				Vowels and diphthongs			
p	professor	b	board	ɪ	written	e	tense
t	teacher	d	dictionary	æ	language	ɒ	cough
k	classroom	g	game	ʌ	luck	ʊ	look
f	phoneme	v	verb	ə	about	i	happy
θ	theme	ð	together	iː	teach	ɑː	after
s	student	z	teachers	ɔː	taught	uː	boot
ʃ	ship	ʒ	genre	ɜː	learner	ɒː	dog (Am)
h	house	x	loch	eɪ	play	aɪ	buy
tʃ	research	dʒ	language	ɔɪ	toy	əʊ	go (Br)
m	motivation	n	noun	oʊ	go (Am)	aʊ	sound
ŋ	song	w	word	ɪə	hear	eə	pairwork
l	learner	r	ring	ʊə	pure	uə	actual
j	you			iə	peculiar		

Should students learn the phonemic alphabet?

Many teachers think that phonemic symbols are useful for teaching. Others, however, disagree.

Yes

- It helps them when they consult DICTIONARIES (if there is no audio available).
- It is really useful when teachers want to point out pronunciation problems – they can point to a phonemic symbol and the students will know which sound they are talking about.
- It helps students focus on specific 'problem' areas – especially when they have sounds that are particularly difficult for them.
- Teachers can do activities, exercises and games using phonemic symbols.

No

- It just confuses them – it's one more thing they have to learn, and it's one thing too much.
- Modern online dictionaries and many mobile devices have audio so students don't need phonemic symbols – they can just listen to the audio.

Using phonemic symbols in teaching

- In many classrooms there is a PHONEMIC CHART. Teachers or students can point to the symbols to make words DVD4.
- Students can play NOUGHTS AND CROSSES (also called TIC-TAC-TOE) where they have to say correctly a word which includes the sound in each square they have chosen so that they can draw a straight line of three *0s* or *Xs* horizontally, diagonally or vertically.
- Some teachers give their students words written in phonemic script. They have to try to work out what the words and phrases are before they hear the phrases on the audio or the teacher says them. Notice that in the example below, the symbol ˈ shows the MAIN STRESS →26.

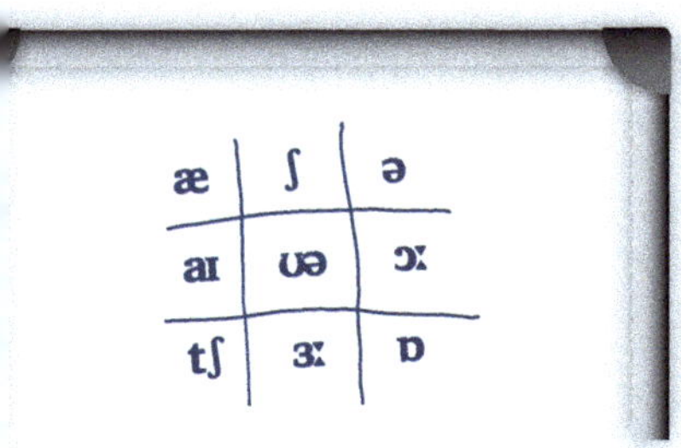

T2 Write the following words and phrases using the normal alphabet. Then listen to the audio to see if you were correct.

a) /kɒf/
b) /ˈælfəbet/
c) /ˈrestərɒnt/
d) /ə bæd ˈkɒf/
e) /ðə ˈtiːtʃəz ruːm/
f) /hɜːr ekˈsaɪtɪŋ njuːz/

We discuss how to demonstrate sounds in →24.

24

Where sounds are made

Diagram

T3 Last week Begoña put up a new picture in her Madrid classroom. It is a diagram of a human head and it shows all the different parts of the mouth. Begoña uses it to explain how to make different sounds in English – especially when they are different from the sounds that her students use in their own language (Spanish). Some students find the diagram useful, but others still have problems saying difficult sounds.

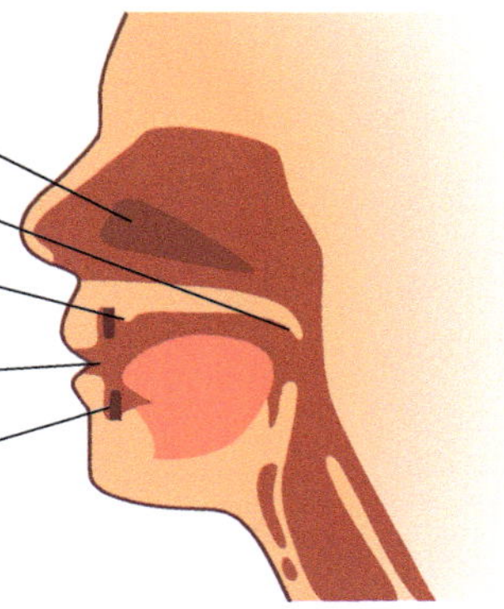

Making consonants

Begoña wants to be able to show how sounds are made when parts of the mouth and lips come together and air from the lungs has to pass through them and past them. This is how different consonants are made:

- /p/ and /b/ in words like ***top*** and ***bit*** are BILABIAL PLOSIVE consonants. To make these sounds we close both our lips (that's why they are called BILABIAL), and then air comes up from the throat, pushing the lips apart in a little explosion (that's what *plosive* means).
- /t/ and /d/ in words like ***tin*** and ***dog*** are ALVEOLAR PLOSIVES because the tongue is stuck to the ALVEOLAR RIDGE until the air pushes them apart.
- /k/ and /g/ in words like ***can't*** and ***dog*** are VELAR PLOSIVES because the back of the tongue and the SOFT PALATE (VELUM) are stuck together until the air pushes them apart.
- /f/ and /v/ in words like ***ferry*** and ***very*** are LABIODENTAL FRICATIVES. The top teeth touch the bottom lip (that's why they are called *labiodental*) and air is forced between them – but there's no explosion; the sound is caused by air friction (that's why they are called FRICATIVES).
- /s/ and /z/ in words like ***students*** and ***teachers*** are called ALVEOLAR FRICATIVES.
- /θ/ and /ð/ in words like ***maths*** and ***this*** are DENTAL FRICATIVES (the tongue is touching the top teeth).
- /ʃ/ and /ʒ/ in words like ***sure*** and ***pleasure*** are called PALATO-ALVEOLAR FRICATIVES.
- /tʃ/ and /dʒ/ in words like ***church*** and ***judge*** are called PALATO-ALVEOLAR AFFRICATES. AFFRICATES start like a plosive and end like a fricative.
- /l/ in words like *Liverpool* and *language* is a LATERAL. The tongue closes the airflow at the alveolar ridge, but air flows out around the side of the tongue.

- /j/ and /w/ in words like ***university*** and ***world*** are called APPROXIMANTS because they are almost more like vowels than consonants.
- /m/, /n/ and /ŋ/ in words like ***must***, ***not*** and ***sing*** are NASAL CONSONANTS because the air comes through the nose. /m/ is a bilabial consonant, /n/ is an ALVEOLAR NASAL and /ŋ/ is a VELAR NASAL.

What vocal cords are for

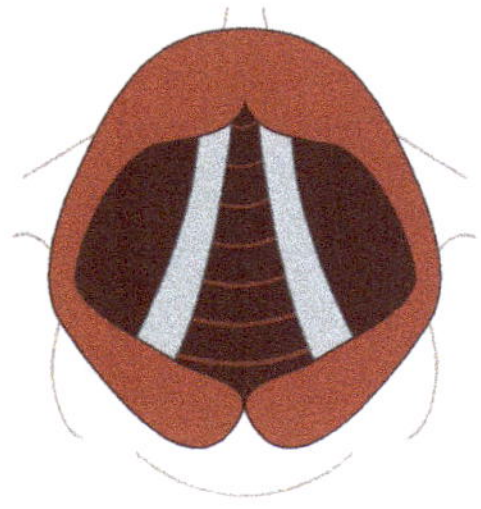

Vocal cords open (seen from above) for voiceless sounds.

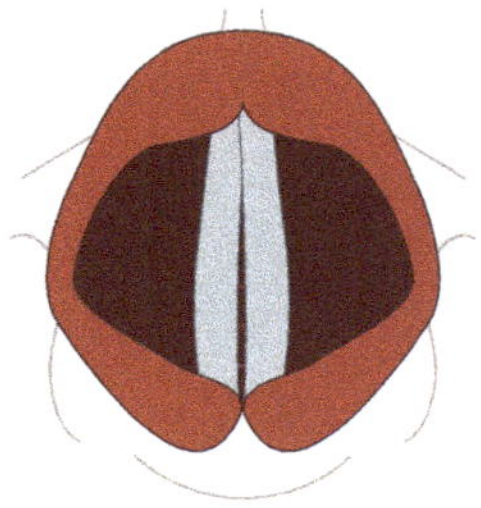

Vocal cords closed (seen from above) for voiced sounds.

If you could look down inside someone's throat, you would see the two VOCAL CORDS (sometime called VOCAL FOLDS) behind the larynx – the Adam's apple. When they are relaxed, they are apart – and so air from the lungs can come up the throat and out through the mouth without us using our voice. That's why sounds like /p/, /t/, /f/, /s/, /ʃ/, /θ/ /tʃ/ and /k/ are called VOICELESS consonants.

However, when we close our vocal cords together, the air coming up from the lungs pushes them apart and together and apart again in a rapid movement, so that they vibrate – and we are using our voice. That why we call consonants like /b/, /d/, /v/, /z/, /ʒ/, /dʒ/, /ð/ and /g/ VOICED consonants. Note that all vowels are voiced.

Making vowels

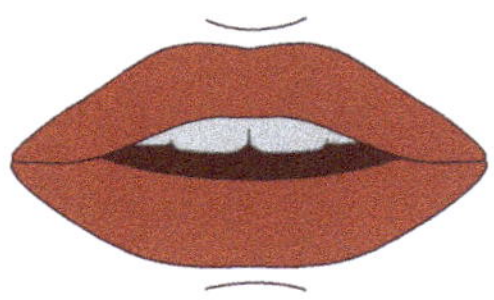

rounded

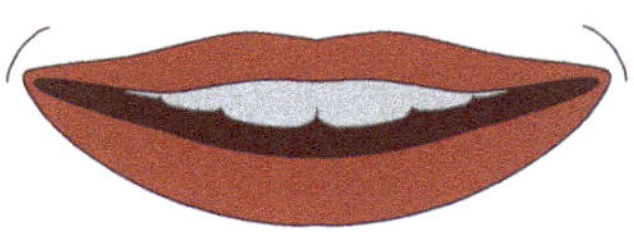

stretched

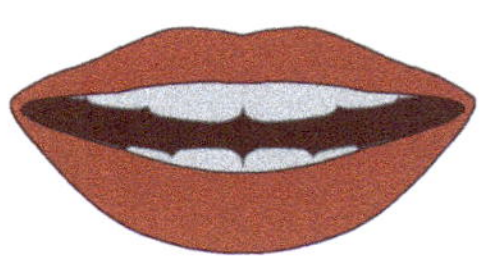

neutral

Lip positions

When we make vowels, no parts of the mouth and throat touch each other, though the shape of the mouth is important. The tongue changes shape in the mouth, the shape of the lips changes and the lower jaw moves.

- When we say CLOSE VOWELS, the tongue is raised and is near the front of the mouth in sounds like /iː/ ***sheep*** (the lips are stretched) and /ɪ/ ***ship*** (the lips are spread loosely); with /ʊ/ ***book***, the tongue is further back in the mouth and the lips are rounded; with /uː/ ***food***, the tongue is at the back of the mouth and the lips are rounded.
- In MID VOWELS like /e/ ***egg***, /ə/ ***photograph***, /ɜː/ ***word*** and /ɔː/ ***horse***, the tongue is neither high nor low in the mouth.
- In OPEN VOWELS like /æ/ ***hat***, /ʌ/ ***hut***, /ɑː/ ***heart*** and /ɒ/ ***hot***, the tongue is low.

Making diphthongs

DIPHTHONGS start with one vowel and end with another.

- We call /ɪə/ ***hear***, /eə/ ***pairwork*** and /ʊə/ ***pure*** CENTRING DIPHTHONGS because the end sound is /ə/, which is a centre vowel.
- We call /eɪ/ ***play***, /aɪ/ ***buy***, /ɔɪ/ ***toy***, /əʊ/ ***go*** and /aʊ/ ***found*** CLOSING DIPHTHONGS because the end vowels /ɪ/ or /ʊ/ are close vowels.

Show, explain or listen?

Begoña knows that we can show people how some sounds are made, though for others it is more difficult. For example, in sounds like /f/ and /v/ we can demonstrate (or use a diagram to explain) how the teeth and the lips make contact. We can demonstrate the position of the lips (ROUNDED, STRETCHED or NEUTRAL), too. The most important thing is for the students to be able to hear and distinguish the sounds so that they can produce them themselves.

We look at teaching sounds in →28.

25

Sounds in combination

A bit nervous

T4 Steve has got his first teaching job at a school in Dubai. He is talking to his friend, Sean in a London café.

Sean: I saw Ana at the concert last night.
Steve: Was it a good concert?
Sean: Yes. But she doesn't know about Dubai.
Steve: You told her?
Sean: No, of course not. That's your job.
Steve: Yeah. I should have told her.
Sean: Yes, you should. You still can. When are you flying to Dubai?
Steve: Next week.
Sean: Are you looking forward to it?
Steve: Yes, I am. I wouldn't have applied for the job otherwise. But I don't know quite what to expect. I'm a bit nervous.
Sean: You are?
Steve: Yes. First teaching job. New country. New culture.
Sean: Where are you going to live?
Steve: I'll probably get an apartment near the school.
Sean: Sounds fantastic.
Steve: I hope so. Look I have to go.
Sean: Call Ana, OK?
Steve: All right.

Sounds alone, sounds together

Because we use parts of our mouth to make sounds →24, things often change when one sound follows another. For example, if we say the word *looking* on its own, it ends with the sound /ŋ/. This is a VELAR PLOSIVE and happens at the back of the mouth. But when Sean says *Are you looking forward to it?* in the conversation above, /ŋ/ changes to /n/ in /lʊkɪnfɔːwəd/. This is because it would be too much effort for Sean to change from a consonant at the back of the mouth /ŋ/ to one at the front /f/ – a LABIODENTAL FRICATIVE – and so he uses /n/ (a consonant nearer the front of the mouth) instead. In connected speech we make a lot of sound changes like that. Here are some of the more important ones.

- We often contract AUXILIARY VERBS in speech. For example, Steve doesn't actually say *I should have told her*. Instead he uses the CONTRACTION *I should've told her*, in which /hæv/ becomes /əv/. In the same way, when Sean asks *Where are you going to live?* he doesn't say /weə ɑ: ju: gəʊɪŋ tə lɪv/. Instead /weə ɑ:/ becomes /weərə/ and he says /weərəju:gəʊɪŋtəlɪv/.
- We often leave out sounds like /t/ and /d/ at the end of words when sounds are connected in phrases like *next week*. Steve says /nekswi:k/. We lose the final /d/ in phrases like *we stopped for a coffee*. We call this ELISION.
- The SCHWA (/ə/) often disappears in connected speech in UNSTRESSED SYLLABLES →26. Instead of saying /prɒbəbli/, Steve says /prɒbli/ in *I'll probably get an apartment*. Sometimes, instead of saying a word like /sekrəteri/ (*secretary*) people say /sektri/.
- The final sound of *looking* in the phrase *looking forward to it* is an example of ASSIMILATION – where a sound changes because we want to get ready for the next sound that is coming. When Steve asks *Was it a good concert?* the /d/ at the end of /gʊd/ becomes /g/: /ə gʊgkɒnsət/. Also /t/ changes to /p/ in *apartment* /əpɑ:pmənt/.
- When Sean says *I saw Ana* and *Call Ana, OK?* He puts in the LINKING SOUND /r/ to make the change from one vowel to another easier, e.g. /sɔ:rænə/ and /kɔ:lænərəʊkeɪ/. The same thing happens between *where* and *are* in *Where are you going to live?*
- When Steve says *Yes, I am*, he includes the linking sound /j/ between the vowels /aɪjæm/.
- When Sean says *You are?* he uses a linking /w/ between the vowels /u:/ and /ɑ:/ to say /ju:wɑ:/.
- When someone says *Would you like* /mɔ:raɪs/? they could be saying *more ice* or *more rice* This is an example of JUNCTURE. However, we normally understand what is being said because of the context.

Do students have to learn sounds together?

Does it matter if speakers of English as a second language don't use contractions and other features of connected speech? No, of course it doesn't. They will still be understood.

Does it matter if students don't understand contracted English and other features of connected speech? Yes, of course it does.

The most important thing is that students should *hear* natural speech where these features occur - and we can make students aware of what they are hearing.

It may be difficult (and a waste of time) to try to get students of English to *use* assimilation, juncture and elision as effectively as some NATIVE SPEAKERS. What we need to do, therefore, is to choose what connected speech we *can* and *should* teach. For example, we will teach contractions such as *I do**n't** know*, *she**'s** not coming*, *you should**'ve** told me*. We will focus on assimilations like the way the sound /d/ changes to /t/ for the -*ed* past tense ending (*walked* - /wɔ:kt/) or to /ɪd/ (*waited* - /weɪtɪd/), on the elision of past tense endings with following sounds (e.g /wɒtʃ ti:vi:/) for /wɒtʃt ti:vi:/ and the different sounds for plural endings (/ʃɪps/, /dɒgz/, /wɒtʃɪz/).

We *can* make sure that some features, such as assimilation and linking, are used in phrases the students are studying (e.g. *Yes, I am*) because we can then get them to say the phrases correctly.

Teaching ideas: contractions

Many teachers use physical gestures to show how contractions are made. For example, we can say that one hand = *I*, and the other = *am*. When we join them together, we say *I'm*. We can also use finger contractions DVD5.

You should have told her.

You should've told her.

26

Stress

Controversy!

T5 Nicole is talking to her friend Katazyna.

Nicole:	Robert gave me a lovely present.
Katazyna:	Wow. I would never have expected that of Roger.
Nicole:	No, not Roger! Robert gave me a present.
Katazyna:	Oh I see. What was it?
Nicole:	It was one of those clickers.
Katazyna:	A clicker? What's that?
Nicole:	You are so old-fashioned sometimes! Don't you know anything?
Katazyna:	Well, I may be old-fashioned. Archaic even! But I am dependable!
Nicole:	If you say so.
Katazyna:	Yes, I do say so! But I still don't understand. What is a clicker?
Nicole:	It's one of those remote-controlled things, so I can change the slides in my *PowerPoint* presentation.
Katazyna:	Presentation? You're going to present?
Nicole:	Yes. To the teachers. To you! Next Wednesday!
Katazyna:	What's it about?
Nicole:	Reading comprehension – about the vocabulary controversy. Should we teach new vocabulary before students read or after?
Katazyna:	Don't you mean controversy?
Nicole:	Honestly! You're impossible sometimes!

All words have a stressed syllable

In every English word one SYLLABLE is stressed (we use more breath and the voice is louder). In the first line of Nicole and Katazyna's conversation, *Robert* has two syllables, and the stress is on the first syllable: *RObert*. The stress is on the first syllable in *PREsent*, too. When one syllable in a word is stressed it means that the other syllables are UNSTRESSED. Unstressed syllables often have the SCHWA sound /ə/ in words like /dɪˈpendəbəl/ (*dependable*) and /əˈbaʊt/ (*about*).

Word stress does not always happen in the way we expect, but here are some guidelines:

- In two-syllable NOUNS and ADJECTIVES the first syllable is usually stressed in words like *LOVely*, *PREsent*, *CLIckers*, *TEAchers*, *WEDnesday*.
- In two-syllable VERBS the stress is on the second syllable in words like *presENT*.
- In COMPOUND NOUNS we usually stress the first word, e.g. *POWerPoint*, but in compound adjectives we often stress the second adjective, e.g. *old-FASHioned*.
- In words ending in *-ic* we often place the MAIN STRESS on the *penultimate* syllable (the one before the end) as in *archAic* (which means old and no longer used). We usually stress the penultimate syllable, too, in words ending in *-sion* and *-tion*, such as *compreHENsion* and *presenTAtion*
- We usually stress the *pre-penultimate* syllable (three syllables from the end) in words which end in *-al* or *-able*, such as *dePENdable* (meaning you can always trust me to do the right thing). We also, usually, stress the pre-penultimate syllable in words which end in *-cy*, *-ty*, *-phy* and *-gy*, such as *deMOcracy* and *phoTOgraphy*.

- We do not stress PREFIXES or SUFFIXES →19 in words like *imPOSSible*.
- People often disagree about where to stress some words, like *controversy* (Nicole puts the stress on the first syllable, Katazyna prefers the second) and *television*. Different VARIETIES OF ENGLISH use stress differently, too. For example, British English speakers usually say *adVERtisement*, but American English speakers often say *advertTISEment*.

Showing stress

There are many ways of showing word stress.

In dictionaries →82 stress is often shown like this: /ˌ**prezən'teɪʃən**/. Notice that the main stress is on the syllable /'**teɪ**/, but the word also has a secondary stress on /ˌ**pre**/.

- We can use squares or circles above the words like this: de■pendable depe●ndable.
- We can underline the stressed syllable like this: de<u>pen</u>dable.
- We can use gestures to show stress, too.
- We look at teaching stress and INTONATION in →29.

All phrases have a main stressed syllable

When Nicole says *Honestly! You're impossible sometimes!* she uses two PHRASES in one UTTERANCE (*Honestly* and *You're impossible sometimes*). Each phrase has one stressed syllable: *'Honestly! You're im'possible sometimes!* Notice that the PITCH of the voice changes on the stressed syllable in a phrase →27. We usually stress CONTENT WORDS, which carry meaning; if students know this, it will help them to LISTEN FOR SPECIFIC INFORMATION →60.

When students learn new phrases, they need to learn where the main stress is →29.

We can change where and how we place stress in a phrase

With most English phrases, the stressed syllable is at the end of the phrase, because that is where we usually put the most important new information. For example, *Robert gave me a lovely 'present*.

Katazyna doesn't hear correctly. She thinks that Roger (not Robert) gave the present. When Nicole replies, she puts the main stress in a different place and says *'Robert gave me a present* because now it is Robert that is the important new information – or at least this is the information that Nicole wants Katazyna to be clear about. When we move the main stress to give special emphasis like this, we call it CONTRASTIVE STRESS.

However, if Katazyna had instead suggested that Robert's present was not nice, Nicole might have replied *No, Robert gave me a 'lovely present*, because it was the loveliness of the present that was the new and/or important information that she wanted to give.

When Nicole says *If you say so*, she is not taking her friend's comment (*I am dependable*, etc.) very seriously. But Katazyna wants Nicole to agree 100% that she is dependable, and so she replies *I 'do say so* – stressing *do* because she wishes to be emphatic about it.

Giving presentations

Many teachers gain a lot from presenting their ideas to their colleagues - and later at teachers' conferences. It is one of the best ways for us to reflect on what we do and contributes towards TEACHER DEVELOPMENT →78. Using PRESENTATION SOFTWARE such as *PowerPoint*, *Keynote* or *Prezi* can help to get our ideas across.

27

Intonation

The end?

T6 Steve has gone to see Ana at the café where she works.

Ana: Hello, Steve. What are you doing here?
Steve: I called in to see you.
Ana: That's really nice of you. Any special reason?
Steve: No.
Ana: No?
Steve: Well ...
Ana: Come on, then! Out with it!
Steve: I've got a job.
Ana: At last! That's fantastic! Well done! What is it?
Steve: I've got a teaching job.
Ana: You've got a teaching job?
Steve: Yes. Don't sound so surprised.
Ana: Where is it, this job?
Steve: Well, that's just it.
Ana: You don't want to tell me, do you?
Steve: No, it's not that. It's just ...
Ana: You're going abroad, aren't you?
Steve: Yes. To Dubai.
Ana: You're going to Dubai?
Steve: Yes.
Ana: So that's the end for us, is it?
Steve: No. Not necessarily.
Ana: Why? What are you suggesting?

What is intonation?

When Ana asks Steve if he has any reason for seeing her, he says *no* but he doesn't *sound* completely sure. She repeats the word (*no*) but when she says it, it *sounds* different: like a question. And when Steve says *well*, we know from the *sound* of his voice that he wants to tell Ana something. Those sounds – the different music tunes that Steve and Ana use – are examples of INTONATION.

- When Ana says *That's really nice of you*, the main STRESS is on the syllable *nice*. But something else happens when Ana says *nice*. The PITCH of her voice (that is whether it is high or low) falls from the higher level it had for *That's really* ... as if it was falling off the edge of a cliff. Intonation is all about pitch change like this.
- Syllables which are stressed and have a pitch change (like *nice*) are called TONIC SYLLABLES. There is one tonic syllable in every spoken phrase.
- When Ana says *You don't want to tell me, do you?* there are two tonic syllables, *tell* in the first spoken phrase (*you don't want to* ***tell*** *me*) and *do* in the second (***do*** *you?*).

The three most common intonation tunes (pitch changes) are the RISING TONE ↗ in sentences like *So that's the end for us,* ↗ ***is*** *it?*, the FALLING TONE ↘ in questions like *What are you doing* ↘ ***here****?* and the FALL-RISE TONE ↗↘ in phrases like *not neces*↗↘***sarily***.

What do pitch and intonation mean?

- When Ana says *That's fantastic! Well done!* she sounds really enthusiastic. We know this because the pitch of her voice is higher than normal. Higher pitch often conveys emotions such as fear, excitement and enthusiasm.
- When Ana says *You don't want to tell me, do you?* the overall pitch of her voice is lower than usual and this make her sound fed up or resigned. Lower pitch often indicates displeasure, resignation or boredom.
- Even though Ana's pitch is lower than usual at the start of *You don't want to tell me, do you?* she uses a falling tone on ↘ ***do** you*? This suggests that she is expecting Steve to agree with her. She uses a falling tone on *You're going abroad,* ↘ ***aren't** you?* for the same reason. We discuss TAG QUESTIONS in →3.
- We generally use falling tones for statements like *I've got a **teach**ing job* and we often use them for questions which start with QUESTION WORDS such as *what*, *when*, *how*, etc. in questions like *What are you doing here? What is it? Where is it, this job? What are you suggesting?* We use falling tones for QUESTION TAGS like ***do** you?* and ***are** you?* when we think we know the answer, or when we expect the other person to agree with us.
- In conversation, we use a falling tone when we have finished speaking and we are giving another person a chance (TURN) to speak.
- We can use rising tones to show that we haven't finished – that there is more information to come – or when we want the other person to speak. This often happens when we ask questions which expect the answer *yes* or *no*, as in *Any special* ↗ ***rea**son*? We often use a rising tone with question tags when we are not sure of the answer, e.g. *So that's the end for us,* ↗ ***is** it?*
- We use a fall-rise tone when we are unsure of what we are saying or asking: when we are surprised or doubtful. This often happens when we are repeating what someone else has just said, as in questions like *No*? *You've got a* ↗↘ ***teach**ing job?* ↗↘ *Why*? and *You're going to Du*↗↘***bai***?

Showing intonation

- We can show intonation with arm gestures - a falling arm for a falling tone, a rising arm for a rising tone and a u-shaped gesture for a fall-rise one.
- We can draw intonation tunes on the board in a number of different ways. For example:

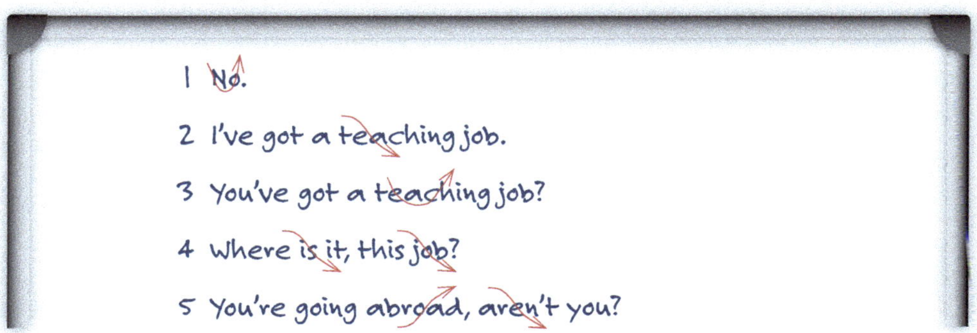

Note that in examples 4 and 5 there are two tonic syllables.

- Some people even whistle intonation tunes! See also →29.

28

Teaching sounds

Distinguishing between sounds

Before we can expect students to say sounds correctly, they need to be able to hear them. The students' HOME LANGUAGE can sometimes make this difficult →37. Many speakers of Chinese and Japanese often say /laɪs/ when they mean /raɪs/ because they find it difficult to distinguish between the sounds /l/ and /r/. Spanish speakers may say /beri/ instead of /veri/. In the following examples, the students listen first and then say the sounds.

1 Same letter, different sound

T7 The students hear a list of words which all contain the same letter (in this case *o*). They have to write them in the correct column, depending on their sound.

/ɔː/	/ɒ/	/ɔɪ/	/ə/	/əʊ/	/aʊ/	/uː/
worn	song	boy	lesson	go	cow	pool

compare conquest contrast (noun) contrast (verb) divorce do enjoy fool frown go horse long no poison prison saw soldier source sew torn town toy

2 Same sound, different letters

T8 The students hear a number of words which all have the same sound (in this case /ɒ/). They have to say what the sound is, underline it in each word and then list the different spellings which the sound has.

because bottle clock dog fog quality knowledge sausage topple watch what

3 Minimal pairs

T9 The students see pairs of words (MINIMAL PAIRS), which differ in only one sound.

a) could good
b) cave gave
c) clue glue
d) lock log
e) ankle angle

Listening to the words on their own helps students to focus on the sounds. However, hearing the words in sentences such as *I could help you* or *It's very good* may be more helpful since they will be hearing the sounds in a natural context.

We show an example of a minimal pairs exercise in DVD6.

4 Same sound rhymes

The students have to draw lines to connect words which have the same vowel sound.

anything hat dress fleece work first welcome many shirt belt jeans several gloves some much please every heap sweater cap

Another way to get students to see/hear rhyme like this is to have them reorder jumbled lines of POETRY →63 and DVD7 or SONG LYRICS →64.

5 Odd one out

The students hear a list of words and they have to say which is the odd one out on the basis of sounds. For example, in the list *sun moon love must one*, *moon* is the odd one out because it doesn't have the sound /ʌ/.

6 Weak or strong?

T10 The students listen to a number of sentences with the word *to*. They have to say whether it sounds like a) /uː/ in *food* or b) /ə/ in *photograph*.

1. I want to ask you a question.
2. I didn't want to see this film anyway!
3. How is this film going to end?
4. I'll do everything I can to help you.
5. You have to open the package first.
6. Do I want to learn to play the tuba? Yes, of course I want to.

Note that *to* is usually pronounced /tə/ if it is followed by a consonant, but is pronounced /tuː/ if it is followed by a vowel or if it is on its own.

7 Sounds and grammar

T11 When we are teaching grammar, such as PAST TENSE *-ed* endings (→4), the PLURAL 's' or the third person singular of the PRESENT SIMPLE, we can draw the students' attention to the different sounds of the MORPHEMES. The students have to listen and put the verbs in the correct columns. For example:

/s/ walks	/z/ plays	/ɪz/ watches

get go live march practise seem sing take wash write

Every time they learn a new verb, they have to say which column it goes in.

8 Tongue twisters

Some teachers like to give their students tongue twisters: sentences which are difficult to say quickly.

Even if students and teachers are not very keen on tongue twisters, it is often a good idea to invent sentences for our students to say which have a lot of the sounds we want them to practise.

a) A proper copper coffee pot
b) Pink lorry, yellow lorry
c) Red leather, yellow leather
d) Nine nice night nurses nursing nightly

9 *Your* pronunciation

When the students have a list of words (at the end of a unit, for example), they have to underline the sounds that *they* personally find difficult. They then have to find these words in a dictionary and practise saying them correctly.

Not all students have the same sound 'problems'. We need to encourage each individual to recognise their own strengths and weaknesses.

29

Teaching stress and intonation

Hearing stress and intonation patterns

The main objective when teaching stress and intonation is to develop the students' ability to hear where the stress falls in words and phrases so that their listening and speaking skills improve. We want them to understand why speakers use certain STRESS and INTONATION patterns – and what they mean. We want them to be able to vary their own stress and intonation so that they can express a variety of meanings and emotions when they want to.

1 Word stress: syllables and stressed syllables

T12 Students at the INTERMEDIATE level hear a list of words. They have to write each one in the following table in the column which has the correct stress pattern.

▪■▪	■▪▪	▪▪■▪	■▪▪▪
announcement			

announcement application calculator camcorder computer electric electronic internet microphone microwave organiser personal television video

The students then say the words and think of/find other words with the same stress pattern.

2 Sentence stress: stress and meaning

T13 Students at the intermediate or UPPER-INTERMEDIATE level hear a sentence said in four different ways. They have to match the sentences with four possible responses that a listener might have.

1 JOHN wrote the music while he was at university.
2 John wrote the MUSIC while he was at university.
3 John WROTE the music while he was at university.
4 John wrote the music while he was at UNIVERSITY.

a) He wrote the music? That does surprise me. I thought he wrote the words.
b) How surprising. I thought he did it at school.
c) I am amazed. I thought he just took someone else's melody.
d) I don't believe you; I thought Paul wrote the music!

The students can then say similar sentences. Other students have to show their surprise, changing the stress appropriately, e.g. A: *John wrote the music while he was at university.* B: *JOHN wrote it? I don't believe it! I thought Paul did.*

3 Intonation 1: question, exclamation or answer?

T14 The students hear the following phrases and they have to put a FULL STOP, an EXCLAMATION MARK or a QUESTION MARK, depending on what they hear.

a) She won some money
b) She's going to give it to a cats' home
c) She's going to give all of it to a cats' home
d) She loves cats
e) She won fifty thousand pounds

4 Intonation 2: bored, interested or surprised?

T15 The students listen to two speakers. They have to say if the second speaker is bored, interested or surprised.

a) I passed my driving test.	Did you?
b) I'm feeling really happy.	Are you?
c) I've bought myself some new shoes.	Have you?
d) I'll drive to Boston this evening.	Will you?
e) I love driving.	Do you?

5 Stress and intonation 1: nonsense words

T16 The students read the following comments. They are in answer to the question *What did you think of the film?*

a) I absolutely loved it.
b) I really enjoyed it.
c) Fabulous.
d) Absolutely terrible!
e) It was one of the worst films I've ever seen.
f) It was really wonderful.
g) I have never been so bored in all my life.

The students then hear the comments said with nonsense syllables (e.g. *do-de-do*). They have to identify which phrase is being said. They can then try the activity for themselves.

6 Stress and intonation 2: tonic syllables and intonation tunes

T17 The students listen to the following extract from a dialogue. They have to mark the TONIC SYLLABLES and say whether the speaker uses a FALLING TONE, a RISING TONE or a FALL-RISE TONE.

A: Have you got anything you want to say?
B: Have you?
A: Listen, John, I ask the questions.
B: Says who?
A: Says me. Now tell me, where were you last night?
B: At home.
A: I'd like the truth.
B: That is the truth.

We look at more ways of using drama in →64.

7 Stress and intonation 3: reading aloud

READING ALOUD (when students read sentences from a TEXT) has been very popular for many years, but it is often not very useful since it does not help them to understand a text, and many of them do it very badly.

If we want our students to read aloud, they should have a chance to prepare what they are going to read first so that they can decide where the tonic syllables are and where to pause, etc. We can help them to do this by looking through texts with them and discussing how sentences should be read.

A good (and realistic way) of getting students to read aloud is to ask them to underline their favourite sentence in a text. They can then think about how to read it in the best way. Then they can say *It says here* ... before reading out their favourite sentence **DVD8**.

(Reading aloud is, of course, a very good way of TESTING a student's pronunciation.)

30

Language functions

The after-school club

Hiro and Mari are getting a room ready for a test.

Hiro: It's really cold in here.
Mari: Do you think so? I don't. I like a bit of fresh air.
Hiro: No, it is. I'm freezing.
Mari: Poor Hiro! Would you like to borrow my sweater?
Hiro: No, it's OK. Couldn't you close the window instead? Just a little bit?
Mari: Oh all right, anything to make you happy! Hey, you don't have to worry about finishing here. I'll do it.
Hiro: No, it's OK. I have a meeting with Mr Sakamura, but it's not for another twenty minutes. Hey, Mari?
Mari: Yeah?
Hiro: I was wondering if you wouldn't mind helping me out this evening.
Mari: Might do. It depends.
Hiro: On what?
Mari: Well, what exactly does 'helping out' mean?
Hiro: It's just that I have an after-school club and ...
Mari: Sure I'll help you.
Hiro: You will?
Mari: Yes. As far as I'm concerned, after-school clubs are really good for the kids' morale.
Hiro: Yeah, that's true. So see you at about five?
Mari: Yeah.
Hiro: Promise?
Mari: I promise.

What we say and what we mean

When Mari says *I promise*, the word and the act are the same. In other words, when we say we promise something, we are actually performing the act that the word says. If all language was like that, it would be very easy to understand! But when Hiro says *It's really cold in here*, things are not so clear. In one sense he is just commenting on the temperature. But what he is really doing is suggesting that Mari should close the window or do something else to make the situation better. The words and the intention do not match in the same way. We call *promising* and *suggesting* LANGUAGE FUNCTIONS.

Language and language functions

In Hiro and Mari's conversation both speakers perform a number of different language functions, although it is quite difficult to describe them exactly.

- *I'll do it* and *I'll help you* are examples of offering help, whereas *Would you like to borrow my sweater?* is an example of offering something to somebody.
- *It's really cold in here* is an example of suggesting a course of action, but so is *Couldn't you close the window instead?* (although we might also describe this as requesting somebody to do something). However, the main difference is that *Couldn't you close the window instead?* is more DIRECT than *It's really cold in here*.

- When Hiro says *I was wondering if you wouldn't mind helping me out this evening*, he is requesting someone to do something (we could also describe this as asking for help). However, his request is quite TENTATIVE, rather than direct (in other words, he sounds unsure). Perhaps this is because he is worried that Mari might say no.
- Mari is asking for clarification when she says *What exactly does 'helping out' mean?* and she gives an opinion when she says *As far as I'm concerned, after-school clubs are really good for the kids' morale*. Hiro is agreeing with an opinion when he says *Yeah, that's true*, but Mari disagrees with Hiro when she says *Do you think so? I don't*.

Teaching language functions

Students of a foreign language need to be able to do things like offer help, give their opinions, suggest courses of action or disagree.

- Many functional language exponents are examples of either fixed or semi-fixed LEXICAL PHRASES. Students can learn and practise them so that they can produce the phrases without hesitation (and without pauses in between the words). This will make them (sound) much more fluent.
- The same function, such as requesting, can be expressed by a wide range of different LANGUAGE EXPONENTS (the actual phrases that are used). Hiro can say *Could you close the window? Close the window, please. Would you mind closing the window? I would be grateful if you would close the window* – or just *The window!* In order to make ourselves clear, we use a variety of INTONATION 'tunes' – and perhaps GESTURES.
- The difference between language exponents is often a difference between directness (*Close the window!*) and tentativeness (*Could you possibly, perhaps close the window?*). It can also be between FORMALITY (*Could you possibly close the window, please?*), INFORMALITY (*Close the window, yeah?*) or the use of a more neutral exponent (*Could you close the window?*). When we teach functions we need to be sure that our students understand differences of REGISTER →33.
- We need to be careful when we choose which language exponents to teach. We will base our choice partly on the students' level, and partly on what functions the students want or need to be able to use.

Teaching ideas: functional dialogues

We often use functional dialogues to teach typical language exchanges, as in the following example for elementary students DVD9:

Would you like *a drink*?
Yes, please.
Coffee or *tea*?
Coffee, please.
Would you like *milk*?
Yes, please?
Sugar?
Yes, please.
Here you are.
Thanks.
You're welcome.

The students can then substitute different items and language for the phrases in italics. SUBSTITUTION DIALOGUES like this have been used in language teaching for a long time. Notice that some phrases like *Thanks* and *You're welcome* are the kind of LEXICAL CHUNKS that all students need to learn.

31

Written and spoken English

Looking forward to the conference

Shengmei is chatting on *Skype* with her friend Nicole Harrison in Canada.

Wang Shengmei
Hi, Nicole.

Nicole Harrison
Heeeeeeeeeey! Shengmei, how ARE you?

Wang Shengmei
I'm great.

Nicole Harrison
Cool.

Wang Shengmei
I'm really happy.

Nicole Harrison
Why?

Wang Shengmei
My paper got accepted for the teachers' conference in the UK.

Nicole Harrison
Wow! Wow! Fantastic!!! That means we're both doing talks! Hey!!!
We'll finally get to meet f2f.

Wang Shengmei
Yes. And I'm looking 4ward to meeting 2 teachers called Manuela and Ratih, and being in the UK for the first time. Manuela's from Argentina & Ratih's from Indonesia.

Nicole Harrison
Cool.

Wang Shengmei
Yeah, met them on Twitter.

Nicole Harrison
Sounds great. When ru arriving?

Wang Shengmei
24th eve u?

Nicole Harrison
I'm arriving on the 24th, too. Can't wait. Big hug

Wang Shengmei

Speaking or writing?

- The communication between Shengmei and Nicole is, in many ways, a written text because both of them are using their computer keyboards to write messages. But it is also like a spoken conversation, in some ways, because they use conventions such as one-word sentences or short exclamations like *Can't wait* and COLLOQUIAL expressions like *Big hug*.
- Sometimes it is easy to identify text as *spoken* (e.g. in a face-to-face conversation) or *written* (in a novel or a newspaper), but at other times it may be easier to talk about text as being either SPEAKING-LIKE or WRITING-LIKE. When Nicole writes *Heeeeeeeeeey! Shengmei, how ARE you?* it 'sounds' very like speech. When Shengmei types *My paper got accepted for the teachers' conference in the UK*, it looks very much like written prose.
- The conversation between Shengmei and Nicole also includes a number of ABBREVIATIONS such as *when ru arriving* (= are you), *f2f* (= face to face), and *looking 4ward to* (forward). Shengmei and Nicole also use EMOTICONS (smiling faces, etc.) to express their feelings quickly and efficiently. These are all typical of INFORMAL digital writing.

Differences between speaking and writing

- When we write, we normally use complete sentences such as *The weather forecast is very bad*. We use appropriate **PUNCTUATION** and we expect grammar, spelling and vocabulary to be more correct than in speaking.
- In speech, we can say things like *Forecast's bad* – using **CONTRACTIONS** (*forecast is* → *forecast's*) and missing out words that we don't need (**ELLIPSIS**).
- When we speak informally, we don't have to be so careful with grammar. For example, many speakers say things like *There's two people at the door* in speech even though they should/would write *There are two people at the door*.
- When we write, we need to be coherent and we use a number of linguistic devices to make sure that our writing hangs together in a logical and easily understandable way. We discuss **COHERENCE** and **COHESION** in **→34**.
- When we speak, we use spoken 'tricks' to keep the conversation going and to organise what we are saying. For example, we **STRESS** **→26** the syllables which contain the most important information, repeat what other people say to us and use a variety of **INTONATION** **→27** patterns so that people can understand the logic of what we are saying. We use words and phrases like *erm*, *you know* and *well* as spoken punctuation.
- When we write, we can use punctuation such as question marks (?) and exclamation marks (!) to show emotion and grammatical function in sentences like *Why?* and *That means we're both doing talks!* In informal writing, some people use a lot of exclamation marks (*Fantastic!!!*) something which we don't do in more **FORMAL** writing (see **REGISTER** **→33**). We can also use devices such as capital letters (*How ARE you?*) or repeated words – such as *Wow! Wow!* – to show emotion in informal writing.

Punctuation

- We use a **FULL STOP** (.) when we finish an idea, as in sentences like *We'll finally get to meet f2f.*
- We use a **QUESTION MARK** (?) to show that we are asking a question, such as *Why?*
- We use an **EXCLAMATION MARK** (!) to show surprise, humour and other emotions, e.g. *Wow!*
- We use **COMMAS** (,) to separate clauses and as breathing spaces between ideas in sentences like *And I'm looking 4ward to meeting a couple of teachers called Manuela and Ratih, and being in the UK for the first time.*
- We use **COLONS** (:) when we list things in sentences like *There are many punctuation symbols: full stops, commas, exclamation marks, etc.*
- **SEMICOLONS** show pauses that are bigger than those shown by commas, smaller than those shown by full stops. We use them to join clauses in sentences like *I like being a teacher; life is never boring.*
- We use **CAPITAL LETTERS** for the beginnings of sentences (*That means we're both doing talks*), for the pronoun *I*, for proper names (*Nicole*) and for certain important roles/jobs (*the President of the USA*).
- We use **HYPHENS** in multi-word adjectives and phrases such as *good-looking* and *out-of-work actor*. But it is sometimes difficult to find rules for when to use them. It is often best to consult a **DICTIONARY**.
- We use **APOSTROPHES** to show contractions in sentences like *I'm really happy* and to show possession, as in *teachers' conference*.
- We use **BRACKETS** (or **DASHES**) when we want to insert an extra idea (or comment) into a sentence.
- We use **INVERTED COMMAS** to show direct speech in sentences like *'I'm coming to the UK teachers' conference,' she said*. Notice that the comma (or question mark, exclamation mark, etc.) comes before we close the inverted commas.

32

Genre

1

NEW MESSAGE

To: shengmei.wang@springmail.com

From: conference.registration@btinternet.com

Dear Shengmei Wang,

Thank you for registering for our annual conference. Your registration form will be processed as soon as possible. If you haven't included payment details, we advise you to pay before arriving at the conference to avoid delays. Your registration number is:

KLG217

(Please quote the above registration number on all communications.)

Your conference registration will not be completed until full payment is received.

2

Manuela

Got my talk accepted 4 conference, cu all there Yaay!

12 hours ago ☆ Favorite Undo Retweet Reply

3

4

The leaves are falling
Like winter love at its end
Two bare twigs remain

5

The day started in the normal way, but it did not go on like that.

Grace got up, made herself a cup of coffee, and went to the door to collect her mail. And that's when she saw him, blurred through the frosted glass of her front door. He was not moving. He just stood there. There was something familiar about him, she thought.

What is genre?

The five written texts above are examples of five different types (GENRES) of writing.

- The writer of extract 1 has used well-formed grammatical sentences such as *Thank you for registering for …* and PASSIVE constructions such as *Your registration form will be processed …* and *Your conference registration will not be completed until full payment is received.* The text gives Shengmei a registration number and then offers the instruction *Please quote the above registration number on all communications.* Lastly, there is no personal signature. All this clearly tells us that this is an official communication, perhaps produced automatically.

- Extract 2 is the TWEET that Manuela published on TWITTER, a social-networking program. We recognise that this is a kind of digital informal writing because she uses SPEAKING-LIKE →31 features such as ELLIPSIS and ABBREVIATIONS such as *cu* and *4*.
- Extract 3 is a billboard advertisement that Brittany saw on her way to work the other day. She knew it was an advertisement because a) it was on a billboard and b) it is written in a typical advertising style.
- Extract 4 is a poem that Hiro wrote (he has recently started writing poetry in English). We know it is a poem because the lines are uneven and because it uses imagery in a poetic way. Many people will also recognise that it is an English-language version of a HAIKU (a Japanese poetry form which has three lines of five, seven and five syllables, and which usually refers to seasons and emotions).
- Extract 5 is the start of a novel called *Glass Doors*. We know that it is a literary story because of the first sentence, which is clearly a dramatic introduction and because of the way sentences start with CONJUNCTIONS (*and*) or are very short, to create effect (*He was not moving*). Novelists often write like this.

How do we know about genre?

- Imagine that you had never seen a billboard before. How would you know that the London advertisement (extract 3) was actually an advertisement? But you *have* seen a billboard before and so you do know what it is. We recognise different writing genres because we have seen them before and because we are accustomed to seeing them. However, if you have never seen *Twitter* before, Manuela's message (extract 2) may be difficult to identify.
- When we write, we obey the rules or conventions of the genre we are writing in so that everyone else in our DISCOURSE COMMUNITY (people who share the language customs of a social group) will recognise what we are doing. This will help our writing to be more successful.
- Sometimes we have opportunities for creativity (there are many different kinds – or SUB-GENRES – of advertisements, for example, and so we have quite a lot of freedom to write what we like). But sometimes the rules of a particular genre are much stricter, as with haiku, a sub-genre of poetry. If we don't write three lines with the correct number of syllables in each, our poem will not be a real haiku.
- Sometimes writers – especially poets and novelists – disobey genre conventions on purpose in order to create an exciting effect.

Teaching ideas: genre

Students can't be expected to write or speak successfully in a genre unless they have seen examples of it beforehand. If we want them to write a speech, a business letter or a report, they need to have seen a speech, a letter or a report already so that they know what the conventions are. If we want them to write newspaper headlines, they should see examples such as *First snowfall blocks roads* or *Hamilton takes poll position in Monaco race.*

When students see examples of a genre, we should ask them to analyse how they are constructed: how many syllables per line for the haiku, what verb tense is very common in news headlines (the present simple), where the address goes in a letter, etc.

We want our students to read and analyse examples of a certain genre, but that doesn't mean that they have to copy them exactly. If we only show them one example of a genre (e.g. an advertisement), they will write one that is more or less the same. If we show them more examples of genres and sub-genres (different types of advertisement), they can select the kind of language and layout that they like best.

33

Register

A new life

① Part of the flight announcement on Steve's plane

Ladies and gentlemen, I would ask that you please direct your attention to the flight attendants as we review the emergency procedures for this flight. There are six emergency exits on this aircraft. Take a minute to locate the exit closest to you. Note that the nearest exit may be behind you. Should the cabin experience a sudden loss in pressure, oxygen masks will drop down from the panel above your seat …

② Part of the novel that Steve was reading on the plane

Emilio had made what for him was the long journey to Tesquiliapan, leaving his nets bunched on the shore and his wooden-hulled boat to scorch in the glaring sun, to tell the old revolutionary's wife, and all her people, of the death of a mutual relative, a woman who had lived an astounding number of years, being famous all along the coast, and beyond, for her magical medicinal remedies which cured every manner of ill from heartache to problematic pregnancy, from disappointment to indigestion.

③ Steve walks out of the customs hall

A: Steve? Steve Olsen?
B: Hi.
A: I'm Caroline Green. Welcome to Dubai.
B: Nice to meet you.
A: Good flight?
B: Yeah. They had some great movies.
A: That's good. Anyway, let's get going. The car's over there.
B: Yeah. Er, I was wondering if I could just use the bathroom.
A: Sure. I'll wait for you here.

④ Steve's quick email to his friend Ana

NEW MESSAGE

To: ana@coolmail.com
From: steve@coolmail.com

Hey Ana
It was a rubbish flight. Miss you already.
Come and visit. Soon.
Steve x
Sent from my iPhone

⑤ Steve's first tweet from Dubai

Steve
Dubai. New life. Gr8 2b here. I think!
09 Apr 19:20

What is register?

When Steve writes *Gr8 2b here* (*It's great to be here*) he uses ABBREVIATIONS because he doesn't want to use too many characters (letters) and because that is the style that some people use on TWITTER (a social networking site) →32. However, when Steve says *I was wondering if I could just use the bathroom* he uses a PAST TENSE with present meaning and the modal *could* because he is feeling TENTATIVE and thinks he needs to sound more FORMAL. In both cases he has chosen the type of language to use. We call this kind of language choice REGISTER.

- When Steve arrives at the airport, he is met by Caroline, his new boss. They use a mixture of fairly NEUTRAL language (*Welcome to Dubai/Nice to meet you*), INFORMAL language (*Good flight?/Yeah. They had some great movies*), and formal language (*I was wondering if I could just use the bathroom*), but they are always POLITE to each other. Politeness is different from formality; in other words, we can be polite whether or not our language is formal.
- When Steve says *I was wondering if I could just use the bathroom*, he is tentative because his new boss has just said *The car's over there* and he doesn't want to upset her by making her wait. We choose our words based on the PARTICIPANTS in a conversation and the relationship we have with them.
- Steve writes *It was a rubbish flight. Miss you already* in a very informal and friendly TONE. He uses an informal adjective (*rubbish*) and ELLIPSIS (*Miss you already*). He can write like this because he and Ana are close friends and because of the MODE (type of communication) he is using (an email).
- The chief flight attendant uses more formal language when he says *I would ask that you please direct your attention to the flight attendants as we review the emergency procedures for this flight*. This is because of a) the TOPIC he is talking about, and b) the mode (an official announcement – a MONOLOGUE).
- The sentence from the novel that Steve reads on the plane is extremely long, uses a number of subordinate clauses, very LOW-FREQUENCY vocabulary (*nets bunched … scorch in the glaring sun … medicinal remedies*). It is typical of a kind of LITERARY prose.

Register, therefore, is a combination of the kind of activity and topic we are writing and talking about (sometimes called FIELD), the *tone* we wish to use (based on the participants and their relationship to each other) and the *mode* of the communication (for example email, formal oral announcement, literary novel or tweet).

What do u think? R txt msgs gr8 or not?

When young people started sending TEXT MESSAGES in the 1990s, many people were very worried. They said that the language would be damaged and that nobody would write well anymore. In fact, this has not happened. Text messaging was (and is) just a different language register.

However, there *would* be something to worry about if students started to use abbreviations like *r* (for *are*) and *gr8* (for *great*) in more formal writing because it would not be appropriate. We need to be sure that they recognise this, and one way of doing it is to draw their attention to the register of the texts they read and hear.

When students write themselves, they should consider field, tone and mode so that they can use APPROPRIATE LANGUAGE: language that is right for the situation. If they are writing a formal essay, they need to use formal language rather than the kind of colloquial language and abbreviations that are found on social networking sites. But if they are communicating informally, they will want to be able to use some of these written devices in order to be appropriate.

34

Cohesion and coherence

Ratih's conference blog

About · Services · Get Ideas · Blog · Events

My first day!

by RATIH on NOVEMBER 1 · LEAVE A COMMENT

This is my first blog from the teachers' conference in the UK. The organisers gave me the 'first-time' speaker scholarship. They really liked the topic of my talk! It is all about what should be in a pre-service teacher-training course.

I arrived from Jakarta in the afternoon. Then I went to the opening ceremony and party. I met some really interesting people including Hassan (from Egypt), Arnulfo (from Mexico), Isil (Turkey) and Begoña (Spain). She used to live in Jakarta so we had a lot to talk about!

Today I went to four presentations. The first was by a Chinese woman called Shengmei. She organised a fantastic workshop about the problems that Chinese speakers have when they are learning English. After that, I went to a talk by a Canadian teacher called Nicole about teaching writing. She described her class and the kinds of lesson she teaches so that they learn about coherence and cohesion in writing.

In her session, Roberta, a secondary school teacher from Brazil, showed us how to teach using *Twitter*. Her students formed a 'Twibe' and wrote collaborative stories together. It was great fun. On the other hand, I couldn't imagine doing it with my young learners. They would be too scared!

The last one I went to was by someone called Manuela from Argentina. Her session was all about using *Skype* for private lessons. I have never had private students but it sounds very challenging.

So that's my first day! All in all it's been great! But tomorrow it's my turn! I'm really nervous.

What is cohesion?

COHESION is the use of certain stylistic devices to guide readers and show how the different parts of a TEXT relate to one another. These devices are the 'glue' that helps us to connect different sentences and phrases to each other.

- Ratih uses the words *teacher*, *teach* or *teaching* quite a few times in her blog. This repetition gives it LEXICAL COHESION.
- Ratih glues her blog together by using SEMANTIC FIELDS (groups of words that have related meanings – another form of lexical cohesion). She writes about *presentations*, *workshop*, *talk* and *session*. She also mentions *learning*, *teaching*, *class*, *lesson*, *students*, *learners*, *private lessons*, etc.
- Most of Ratih's blog is written in the PAST TENSE. Consistent tense usage helps to make a text cohesive.
- When Ratih says ***They** really liked the topic of my talk*, '*they*' refers back to the organisers. We call this PRONOUN reference 'ANAPHORIC' (see also ***She** organised a fantastic workshop* … which refers back to Shengmei and ***it** sounds really challenging*

where she is referring back to using *Skype* for private lessons). We also use CATAPHORIC REFERENCE to refer forward (for example *Here* ***she*** *comes, the next speaker*) and EXOPHORIC REFERENCE to refer to things outside the text (for example, ***This*** *is my first blog*, where *this* = this thing that you are reading).

- She uses a number of TIME ADVERBIALS →11 (*then, today, after that, tomorrow*) to structure her narrative.
- Ratih uses ELLIPSIS like *The first* (instead of *the first presentation*) to refer back to something she has already mentioned (*I went to four presentations*).
- She joins ideas together by using LINKERS such as *then* (***Then*** *I went to the opening ceremony*), *so* (*She used to live in Jakarta* ***so*** *we had a lot to talk about*), *after that* (***After that****, I went to a talk*), *on the other hand* (*it was great fun.* ***On the other hand****, I couldn't imagine doing it*) and *all in all* (***All in all****, it's been great*). Linkers show the sense relationships between different elements.
- When Ratih writes *The last one I went to* … she is substituting *one* for the word *presentations*. We use substitution with words like *one, kind*, etc.

What is coherence?

Even if we use COHESIVE DEVICES, it doesn't mean that people will automatically understand what we say or write. We need to be able to put our ideas together in such a way that people understand us – and understand our purpose for writing or speaking.

- If Ratih had written *She organised a fantastic workshop about the problems that Chinese speakers have when they are learning English. The first was by a Chinese woman called Shengmei. Today I went to four presentations*, we wouldn't understand what she meant because the ideas are in the wrong order. Sequencing our ideas appropriately – so that they have internal logic – makes our texts (written and spoken) COHERENT.
- For a text to be coherent, we need to be able to understand the writer or the speaker's purpose.
- Ratih assumes that her AUDIENCE will know more or less what she is talking about. But if she gave this text to a group of cement engineers, it might not be coherent because there would be too much there that they did not understand. We need to consider our audience if we want people to understand what we write and say.

Teaching ideas: cohesion and coherence

Students need to understand how cohesion works. They need to think about how to present their ideas coherently. Most of all they need to consider the audience they are writing for – since this will affect what they write and what REGISTER they use →33.

We will draw our students' attention to cohesive devices so that they can use them. We should also try to make sure that our students plan their writing so that they express themselves coherently.

Going to conferences

Teachers' conferences are good places to learn about other people's experiences and to get new and exciting ideas. They also offer great opportunities to meet people and discover that teachers share many of the same triumphs and preoccupations.

We discuss teacher development (including conferences) in →78.

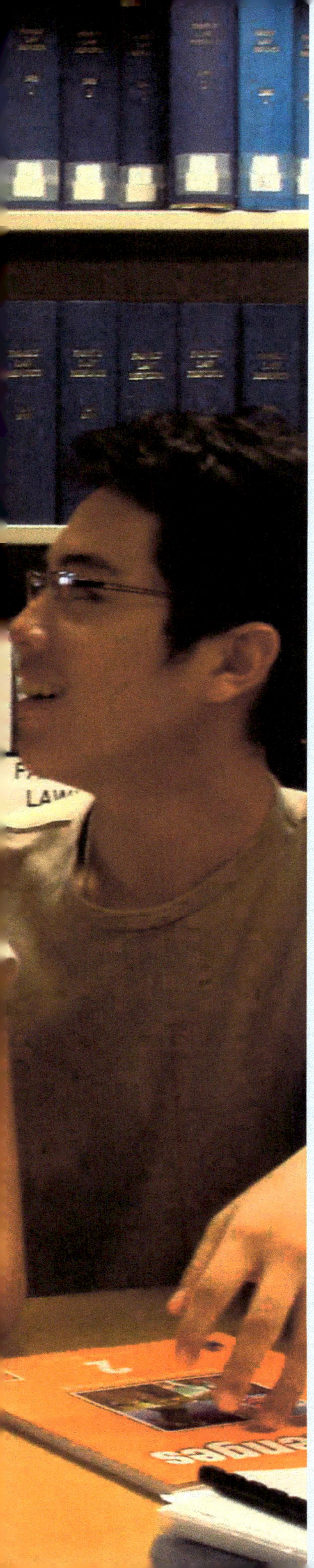

Section B: Background to language teaching methodology

In this section we look at some of the background issues which language teachers need to think about when they plan how they want to teach and what kind of lessons they want to offer their students. For example, we look at what people have said about how we learn languages and we list some of the most prominent learning and teaching methodologies that people have used.

We consider student mistakes and errors as part of the learning process, rather than something terrible that they do wrong!

We look at various differences in language learning. For example, learning takes place in many different situations. But whatever the situation, learners are not all the same: a lot depends on what level they are at, how old they are and what kind of learners they are (because different individuals are, well, different). We discuss how to deal with these differences.

We emphasise the importance of student engagement and consider how students can take responsibility for their learning – and we look at the crucial issue of student motivation.

35

How people learn languages 1

Acquisition and learning

Unless some physical or mental condition gets in the way, all of us speak and understand at least one language well. We got that language from our parents and from other people around us. As far as any of us can remember, we didn't have to think about the process of getting that language; it just happened. All we had was a lot of EXPOSURE to the language (we heard it all the time, especially when people talked to us) and opportunities to use it as much and as often as possible. In other words, this kind of LANGUAGE ACQUISITION is a subconscious process.

- Many children acquire more than one language in childhood. Indeed, in many countries and societies it is unusual for people to be MONOLINGUAL (able to speak only one language).
- Age seems to be an important factor in language acquisition →38. Children often acquire (and forget) languages easily, partly because they get such a lot of exposure to them, and partly because of their DEVELOPMENTAL STAGES →91 and the lives they are leading. TEENAGERS and ADULTS don't seem to acquire languages so automatically. However, they may, in fact, be more efficient *learners*, in part because their circumstances and developmental stages are different.
- If acquisition is a subconscious process, LEARNING, by contrast, is something we do consciously – for example, when we study how to use the PRESENT PERFECT →6, think carefully about what order ADJECTIVES go in →15, or concentrate on which part of a word we should STRESS →26.

Why does the difference between acquisition and learning matter?

In classrooms all over the world, students *learn* languages. They are taught GRAMMAR, FUNCTIONS and VOCABULARY. But perhaps that's the wrong way to do it. Perhaps we should only give students a lot of exposure to the language, together with opportunities to use it – just as we do with children.

- In a theory that he called the INPUT HYPOTHESIS, the linguist Stephen Krashen suggested that people *acquire* language if they get COMPREHENSIBLE INPUT. This means that they are exposed to language that is just above their own LEVEL→41 but which they more or less understand. He suggested that this is *all* they need.
- Krashen also suggested that the language that we *learn* consciously is different from the language we acquire through comprehensible input. We can use 'learnt' language to check (or MONITOR) our conversation (or writing), but these checks may stop us being fluent because we are worrying about whether we are speaking correctly. In the 1980s, Krashen said that *learnt* language could not become *acquired* language.
- Many researchers questioned Krashen's Input Hypothesis. They said it was difficult to test because people cannot usually say if their language was acquired or learnt, and if you can't say which it was, then the theory cannot be proved or disproved.
- Many people suggest that exposure to comprehensible input is not, in itself, enough for people to know and be able to speak a language. There has to be an element of conscious attention to the actual language that is being used in the input. This is especially important for learners who have reached (or gone through) puberty →38–39 – i.e. teenagers and adults.

Which way is best?

Perhaps the best way to get a new language would be to go and live in a country where the language is spoken. There would be both exposure to the language and opportunities to use it. But would that be enough for children or adults?

- Most people learn languages in classrooms. They don't have the opportunity to live in a foreign country, and they don't get the same amount of exposure to the language that children do when they learn their first language.
- Most educationalists believe that children are not ready to *learn* language – to STUDY grammar, etc. – because of their age →38. For them, acquisition-like activities may be the best.
- Some students seem to acquire a new language without too much effort. Many others, however, like, need and want to examine and understand what they are being exposed to.
- Most language-learning lessons today include a mixture of activities, some more focused on acquisition and some more focused on learning.
- Many teaching methods have focused more on learning than acquisition. Teachers following these methods have offered their students individual grammar and vocabulary items one by one. We look at these methods in more detail in →44–48.
- Some teaching methods have concentrated more on acquisition than learning. Teachers have involved their students in communication and encouraged them to think more about the CONTENT of what they say or do than the FORM of the language they are using.

How Fernando learnt English

Fernando Torres, a footballer from Spain who has played in the UK, says that he learnt English there by listening to the radio a lot and (while he was doing it) trying to *concentrate* on what he was hearing. He also looked at big advertisements at the side of the road and tried to see – to NOTICE – what they said and what the meaning was. When he had noticed the words in the advertisements (= concentrated on the words so that he could recognise them again), *then* he could learn them. In other words, he had exposure to the language, but then he thought consciously about what he was seeing and hearing.

36

How people learn languages 2

Four methods

Although there have been many attempts to find the perfect language-learning method, no one has yet come up with the 'best' one. This is partly because different students learn differently (we discuss DIFFERENTIATION in →42), and partly because teaching methods often change as society itself changes. However, some methods are worth discussing because they are either a) widely used, b) talked about a lot or c) still have influence in modern teaching practice. Methods 1 and 2 below are more LEARNING-based, whereas methods 3 and 4 are significantly more ACQUISITION-like →35.

1 Grammar-translation

GRAMMAR-TRANSLATION was the most common way of learning languages for hundreds of years. Students studied the grammar of sentences in the TARGET LANGUAGE (the language they wanted to learn). They translated them into their own language – or the other way round.

Adrian's story

At his English secondary school Adrian learnt French up to lower-intermediate level with grammar translation. He had to translate sentences such as *My uncle's garden is bigger than my aunt's pen* into French and he had to learn the rules of French grammar. When he went to France at the age of 17, he could say very little for a few days, but then suddenly he started to be able to communicate and he became more and more fluent over the next three weeks.

Many people learnt (and continue to learn) languages in ways that are similar to this.

Grammar-translation became unpopular because students translated written sentences rather than spoken conversation, and because they didn't do enough speaking. However, it is clear that asking students to translate into and out of their language and English can teach them a lot about the similarities and differences between the two languages.

2 Audio-lingual methodology

AUDIO-LINGUAL METHODOLOGY (A-L) gave students a lot of speaking practice by using habit-formation DRILLS. Students repeated sentences again and again until they were memorised. A-L methodology is connected to the theory of BEHAVIOURISM.

Pavlov's dogs

Perhaps the most famous example of early Behaviourist theory is the story of Pavlov's experiments with dogs. The dogs responded to a stimulus (a ringing bell) by salivating. This is because they had been conditioned to expect a reward (food) when they heard the sound of the bell. Every time they heard the bell, they salivated and this response was reinforced, in their minds, when food arrived.

- A-L methodology uses a STIMULUS-RESPONSE-REINFORCEMENT approach to language learning. A stimulus (a teacher's prompt) provokes a student response (a sentence), and this response is reinforced by the reward of, for example, teacher PRAISE and student satisfaction. If you repeat this procedure often enough, some people suggested, the language will be learnt.

- Behavourist theories of language learning were heavily criticised. It was argued that if all language was the result of stimulus-response-reinforcement, how come we can all say new things that we have never said before? These new things can't be the result of Behavourist conditioning, surely! One of the results of this was that teachers stopped using *only* A-L methodology.
- However, one the main ingredients of audio-lingualism (language drilling →47) is still used in many lessons because we believe that frequent repetition is a key to successful learning. One of the most popular ways of teaching new language, PPP (PRESENTATION, PRACTICE AND PRODUCTION →44), mixes drilling with contextualised explanation and opportunities for language use.

In →73 we discuss a method called the SILENT WAY.

3 The communicative approach/communicative language teaching

- THE COMMUNICATIVE APPROACH/COMMUNICATIVE LANGUAGE TEACHING (CLT) focuses on the idea that people get language if they have opportunities to use it, and that if students have a desire to communicate and a purpose for communicating (rather than just practising a grammar item), then language learning will 'take care of itself'.
- In CLT, students do many speaking and writing tasks, trying to use any and all of the language that they can. CLT focuses more on CONTENT than on FORM; it concentrates on how successfully students can *communicate*, rather than on whether they are speaking or writing correctly. CORRECTION often takes place *after* the students have tried to speak or write communicatively →74.

We look at examples of communicative speaking activities in →52–53 and communicative writing activities in →58–59.

4 Task-based learning (TBL)

- TASK-BASED LEARNING (TBL) is an approach where teachers set their students larger tasks, such as writing a newspaper article, giving an oral presentation, creating an online film reviews page or arranging a meeting, rather than concentrating only on the language. The students may STUDY language, too, of course, but only if this will help them do the task; it is the planning and the completion of the task that is most important. A TBL approach would base its SYLLABUS →80 on tasks rather than lists of grammar items. In some versions of TBL, language study comes after the task – to deal with any mistakes that occurred during the task.
- In a task-based sequence we might get INTERMEDIATE or UPPER-INTERMEDIATE students to plan a trip to a city in a foreign country by looking for information on the INTERNET and then writing an itinerary; we might ask the students to design a questionnaire which they can then use for video or audio interviews in the street.

How people learn; how people teach

Most teachers don't follow any one method, but use elements of many different approaches. This ECLECTICISM seems to be the best response to different claims about how different students learn. Everything will depend on the balance of exercises and activities – how we get students ENGAGED, how we get them to study and the opportunities we provide for them to ACTIVATE their knowledge →80.

A lot depends, too, on the role of the teacher. Should we *transmit* knowledge as lecturers do, SCAFFOLD learning (provide guidance and support) by helping students to do what they want to achieve or *facilitate* learning by providing the right kind of activities? We look at the ROLES OF THE TEACHER in →65.

37

Students make mistakes

We all make mistakes

When people are learning a language, they never get it right first time: they make MISTAKES. This is a normal part of learning a first, or any other, language. Native speakers of a language make mistakes, too, especially in informal conversation.

Why do learners make mistakes?

- When people are learning a second language, they make DEVELOPMENTAL ERRORS. These happen as a natural part of language learning because (either consciously or subconsciously) the learners are trying to work out how the language system works.
- When children are learning English as their first language, they often learn early on how to say past tense forms such as *went*, *came*, *ran*, etc. However, later, when they become aware of regular PAST TENSE endings, they start saying ~~*goed*~~, ~~*comed*~~, ~~*runned*~~, etc. We call this OVER-GENERALISATION because the child is using the new 'rule' too widely. In the same way, learners of English as a second language often say things like ~~*He must to go*~~, because they appear to be over-generalising *to* + INFINITIVE, which they have become aware of in sentences like *He has to go*.
- When students are learning a second language, they often make INTERFERENCE errors. These happen because they are (consciously or unconsciously) trying to use their first-language knowledge to speak the new language. For example, Japanese speakers may make sentences such as *Skiing is very interesting* (because the Japanese word which they would use in this sentence, *omoshiroi*, means both great fun and interesting), Spanish speakers may get their word order wrong and say ~~*She is a woman beautiful*~~ (because in Spanish the sentence would be *Es una mujer bonita*), Arabic speakers may say ~~*When I can see you?*~~ (because in Arabic there is no subject-verb inversion for questions) and Turkish students might say ~~*I happy*~~ (because in Turkish *Ben mutluyum* doesn't contain an overt verb).
- Researchers talk about a language learner's INTERLANGUAGE – that is their own version of the language they are learning at a certain stage in their language development.
- There is a danger that if mistakes are left uncorrected for too long – or if the learner is unaware of them – they may become FOSSILISED. They are then more difficult to put right.

What kind of mistakes do students make?

Students make several different kinds of mistakes.

- Sometimes they make SLIPS. We can think of these as the result of tiredness or because the students are speaking quickly and are careless. In other words, they know how to use the language correctly, but it just comes out wrong.

- Sometimes students make ERRORS. These suggest that they either don't know something, that they have learnt something incorrectly, or that their knowledge of the language has been affected by developmental or interference factors.
- Sometimes students make ATTEMPTS to say things which are beyond their language knowledge and so they have a go and make a bit of a mess of it!
- We need to be aware of what kind of mistake is being made so that we can CORRECT it appropriately →73. Students can often self-correct slips, but may need more help and explanation if they have made an error. Attempt mistakes are perfect opportunities for teaching new language because it is language that the students clearly want.

What do mistakes look like?

- Language learners may make pronunciation mistakes, many of which are caused by L1 interference. For example, Chinese speakers might say *I* /fi:wɪw/ instead of *I feel ill*.
- Learners may make grammatical mistakes, such as word order problems (~~*I like very much it*~~), the omission of ARTICLES (~~*She is teacher*~~) or the addition of words that are not necessary (~~*They must to help us*~~).
- They may make mistakes in word formation, such as *cooker* instead of *cook*, or misuse grammatical categories, such as *I am interesting* (PRESENT PARTICIPLE) instead of *I am interested* (PAST PARTICIPLE).
- Students may use wrong or inappropriate vocabulary; they may select the wrong word in COLLOCATIONS, saying *childish crime* instead of *juvenile crime*, for example.

Do mistakes matter?

We all know people who speak fairly 'broken' English (or another language), and yet they can make themselves understood perfectly well and no one worries too much about the errors they make. However, in certain circumstances, both inside and outside the classroom, mistakes do matter.

- When students speak, they may have an accent which is influenced by their first or second language. There is nothing wrong with this unless what they are saying is UNINTELLIGIBLE. PRONUNCIATION teaching →28–29 is all about making sure that the students are as intelligible as possible to as many people as possible. We will need to concentrate on STRESS →26 and INTONATION →27, especially, since when mistakes are made with these, they can affect meaning.
- Mistakes matter in writing. This is partly because writing doesn't flash past like conversation, but stays there for us to look at again and again. People can think that someone's English (or other language) is worse than it is if they see spelling mistakes, bad handwriting and poor vocabulary use – whereas if they heard the same person speak, they might have a better impression.
- In lessons we often make a difference between language activities which concentrate on ACCURACY (the students' accurate and correct use of language) and activities which concentrate on FLUENCY (the students' ability to communicate effectively and spontaneously) →73.
- When we are working on the students' accuracy, we are helping them to study language (that is, to understand the construction of GRAMMAR, a LEXICAL PHRASE, a LANGUAGE FUNCTION, etc.). Because of this, we will probably correct mistakes when they occur and try to help the students to say or write things correctly.
- When we are trying to encourage fluency, we probably won't correct quite so immediately since the students are learning how to communicate.

38

Learning at different ages

Young learners

Many people think that children are better language learners than other age groups →35. As a result, English is taught to young and very young children in many countries around the world.

- Children need a lot of good exposure if they are to acquire a language. One or two hours a week is usually not enough for successful ACQUISITION, though it may a) give students a taste of the new language, b) make them feel very positive about languages other than their own and c) be a lot of fun.
- Children take in information from everything around them, not just what is being taught. They learn from things they see, hear, touch and interact with. This is often just as important as more formal explanations.
- Children are usually curious about the world and like learning.
- Children often find abstract concepts (such as grammar rules) difficult to understand. However, this depends on what DEVELOPMENTAL STAGE they have reached. We look at developmental stages in more detail in →91.
- Many children are happy to talk about themselves, and like learning experiences which involve and relate to their own lives.
- Children are pleased to have the teacher's approval.
- Children often find it difficult to concentrate on the same thing for a long time.
- The Russian educational psychologist Vygotsky (1896–1934) said that children learn best when they are in the ZONE OF PROXIMAL DEVELOPMENT (ZPD): when they are *ready* for the next bit of learning. Later experts have suggested that teachers should SCAFFOLD →91 students' learning (provide guidance and support) until the students can do it for themselves.
- We need to remember, however, that children develop at different rates and that there is a clear difference between a child of five, for example, and a child of ten.

Tips for teaching young learners

- Change activities frequently.
- Combine learning and play.
- Use appropriate activities (including songs, puzzles, games, art, physical movement, etc.) for different kinds of student.
- Make the classroom an attractive, light and convenient learning environment.
- Pay special attention to your own English pronunciation – children are good imitators!

We discuss YOUNG LEARNERS in more detail in →91–101.

Adult and older learners

How are adult learners different from children?

- Adults can think in abstract ways and so there is, perhaps, less need for them to engage in activities such as games and songs in order to understand things.
- We can introduce a wide range of topics into adult classrooms and expect that the students will have some knowledge of what we are talking about.
- Many adult learners have strong opinions about how learning should take place, often based on their own schooldays. They sometimes dislike teaching methods that are either different from those they are used to or which remind them of earlier learning.

- Although some adults have good memories of learning success, others have experience of learning failure and are worried that they will fail again.
- Adults usually (but not always) behave well in class – at least better than some other age groups.
- Many adults (but not all) understand what they want and why they are learning. This means that even when they are a little bored, they can still keep working.

Tips for teaching adults

- Find out what interests different student *individuals* in order to plan the most appropriate lessons.
- Be prepared to explain things (such as grammar rules). But remember that many adults learn by doing things, too.
- Discuss the best ways of learning with your students so that everyone is happy with your lessons.
- Provide clear short-term goals so that the students can achieve success at each stage.

We discuss teaching adults in more detail in →39.

Adolescents

For many teachers, ADOLESCENT students are the most exciting – but also the most challenging – people to have in classrooms.

- Depending on their stage of development, teenagers can start to think in abstract terms. In other words, they can talk about ideas and concepts in a way that younger children probably cannot.
- Many adolescent students become passionate about the things that interest them.
- Many adolescent students have a large amount of energy. This is sometimes a good and creative thing, but sometimes, if we don't channel it correctly, it can lead to more or less serious DISCIPLINE problems →71.
- Many adolescents are extremely conscious of their age and find it irritating when adults continue to teach them as children – even though, in many ways, they still *are* children.
- Adolescents usually have not chosen to come to our English lessons. They are there because they have to be there. They may not see any good reason for learning English.
- Many adolescents want and need PEER APPROVAL (the good opinion of their classmates) far more than they want and need the approval of the teacher.

Tips for teaching teenagers

- Encourage teenagers to have opinions and to think critically and questioningly about what they are learning.
- Use the students' own knowledge and experience as much as possible.
- Treat the students like adults but remember they are still children.
- Encourage the students to have AGENCY →39 (take responsibility for their own learning).
- Be super-organised! Teenagers like to know what they are doing and why.
- Be consistent when there are discipline problems. Criticise the behaviour, not the student.

We discuss teaching adolescents in more detail in →39.

39

Student-centred teaching

The right priorities

The most important thing in a classroom is not how the teacher teaches, but whether (and how) the students learn.

Personalisation, agency and learner training

There are things we can do to help our students have some control over their own learning.

- PERSONALISATION is one of the most important stages of any learning cycle. When students use new language to talk about themselves, or to say things that matter to them (for example in the PRODUCTION phase of the PPP procedure →44), they have to think about the right language to use to express their own ideas and to talk about their own lives and what interests them.
- When learners have some responsibility for their own learning, they are more likely to be engaged than if they are just doing what the teacher tells them to. In other words, if students are sometimes 'in the driving seat', they have some AGENCY – some control over what is happening in their learning. They might decide such things as which words from a list they want to focus on, what topic they want to discuss, what activity they want to do next, or what HOMEWORK →76 *they* think would be most useful to them. We might discuss with them how and why they want to be CORRECTED →73–75.
- Many students find it extremely useful to think about *how* they learn and we can help them by providing LEARNER TRAINING. This means getting them to think of the best ways of doing things, such as writing words down to remember them, what to do in conversation when you don't know a word, or how to take notes.

Talking about adults

Adult students bring a lot of previous learning experience to the classroom and they bring their own ideas about what good learning looks and feels like.

- Some adults are not keen on COMMUNICATIVE LANGUAGE TEACHING →36, for example, because it is not like the way *they* were taught at school. As a result, we need to explain why we use PAIRWORK and GROUPWORK →67: to help the students to ACTIVATE their language knowledge because we think activation helps them to process the language they have ACQUIRED and LEARNT →35.
- We need to listen (where possible) to our students' own learning preferences. For example, they may want to TRANSLATE every word of a reading text into their own language (or have every word explained), but we want them to read for GIST →54. We can make a bargain, where they agree to try to do what *we* want (read for gist) and we agree, when they have done this, to work with individual word meaning.
- Some older learners have (or appear to have) more problems with memory than younger students. We need to RECYCLE and REVISE what we have done constantly, and we should back up what they STUDY with visual and other resources.
- When we teach middle-aged and older adults, we should find out how they like to be addressed (not everyone likes to be called by their first name) and take care that what we show and tell them is both clearly visible and audible.

Talking about teenagers

Although teenagers often learn faster than children or adults, there are other issues we need to take account of.

- Teenagers don't always see (or want to see) why we are asking them to do the things we are suggesting. It is important, therefore, to explain what benefit they will get from an activity or a lesson. They need to understand the LESSON OUTCOMES →79 we expect for them.
- Because some teenagers have unresolved problems with SELF-ESTEEM, we need to be sure that we don't do anything that will make them feel vulnerable or embarrassed in front of their PEERS. For example, instead of making them READ ALOUD from a text they have never seen before (and therefore risk them not reading very well), we may let them choose what they want to read and give them a chance to practise reading it so that when they do, they can have some confidence that they will be successful →29.
- Teenage students can be incredibly creative – offering ideas, energy and enthusiasm. We need to direct that creativity, pointing them in the right direction and helping them to focus on how to make TASKS manageable.
- Students at this age are far more likely to enjoy (and be engaged with) lessons if they can see the relevance of what they are doing to their own lives and interests. For example, instead of making our students work with music that *we* like (although there is nothing wrong with that), we may try to get them to talk about music that *they* like. Instead of using the STORIES of famous historical people, for example, we may have the students work with stories of their contemporaries, people in the school or characters from TV shows that they watch or online games that they play. However, it is worth remembering that teenage students do not necessarily want to share their world with adult teachers, so we have to be careful about how much we become involved with their interests.
- Teenage students want to know and see that their teacher is interested in their progress and their wellbeing and that, above all, the teacher is fair and treats all students the same. This is especially important so that DISCIPLINE does not become a problem →71.

40

Learner characteristics

Getting to know our students

If we want to know how to teach our students, we need to know what the students are like. How are they different? How are they the same?

The good learner

Many studies have tried to identify the characteristics of GOOD LEARNERS. There are variations in the conclusions that are reached, but most people say that good learners:

- try to guess when they don't know something – and often succeed;
- try to get their message across even if their knowledge of the language isn't very good;
- are prepared to make mistakes;
- try to figure out how language works;
- practise whenever they can;
- analyse the way they and others talk;
- have a good self-image and confidence.

We need to remember that many good LEARNER CHARACTERISTICS tend to represent a 'western' view of learning. Nevertheless, we should encourage our own view of good learner behaviour, in particular by rewarding appropriate efforts and by talking about how to learn.

Talking about differences

- Many people suggest that some students have more APTITUDE for language learning than others – in other words, some students will automatically be better at it than others. However, it is difficult to know how to measure this, and a lot will depend on how, when and where people are learning and what their MOTIVATION is →43.
- Some people suggest that intelligence plays a part in language learning. However, it is clear that most people are capable of learning a language whatever their intellectual level.
- The psychologist Howard Gardner proposed a theory of MULTIPLE INTELLIGENCES (MI THEORY) to show how we can think about people's knowledge and abilities. 'It is not,' he wrote, 'how intelligent we are that matters, it is how we are intelligent.' He suggested that everyone has the same intelligences: *spatial* (the ability to visualise things), *linguistic* (the ability to use, understand and memorise language), *logical-mathematical* (the ability to reason with and understand numbers and other abstractions), *musical* (the ability to respond, reproduce and interpret music), *bodily-kinaesthetic* (the ability to understand, use and control one's bodily actions skilfully), *interpersonal* (the ability to empathise and interact with others), *intrapersonal* (the ability to think and reflect internally), *naturalistic* (the ability to understand and enjoy the natural world) and *existential* (the ability to see and empathise with spiritual, religious and psychic belief). However, according to Gardner we are all different: for some of us, perhaps, our musical intelligence is more developed than our interpersonal intelligence. Others may have a strong bodily-kinaesthetic intelligence, and this may be more developed than their logical-mathematical intelligence.
- *Emotional intelligence* – which is similar to Gardner's interpersonal intelligence – has been described by a number of different psychologists as the ability to understand and deal with our own emotions and the emotions of others.
- Many people have tried to categorise students according to their LEARNING STYLES – the way they behave when they are learning in classrooms. According to these categories, *enthusiasts*, for example, try to take part and listen to the teacher, whereas *rebels* want to do it 'their way'; *communicative* learners try to do everything by letting the language flow, whereas *analytic* learners spend their time trying to understand everything.

- The only problem with these descriptions is that very few students *remain* one 'type' or the other, even if we could clearly establish what the different types were. Perhaps it is more helpful to think of different lesson stages where different styles are more or less appropriate.
- NEURO-LINGUISTIC PROGRAMMING (NLP) – which is a model for psychotherapeutic counselling – has been used to explain learner differences. The founders of NLP, Richard Bandler and John Grinder, wanted to help people to re-frame their experiences (visualise things in a different way) to help them perform better. They also suggested that all people respond to the same stimuli – *visual* (what we see), *auditory* (what we hear), *kinaesthetic* (associated with physical movement, touching, etc.), *olfactory* (what we smell) and *gustatory* (what we taste) – but that for each of us one of these VAKOG elements has more 'power' because it stimulates us more than the others do, and this is different for different people.

People have raised doubts about the scientific status of both NLP and MI theory (and about many attempts at learner categorisation). However, they all remind of us of an essential truth: different students are good (and not so good) at different things. They respond better to some things than to others.

What to do about student differences

- We need to make sure that we use different lessons to cater for different kinds of student preferences. We might use visual stimuli in one lesson, but rely on music for the next. We will give the students exercises for analytic learners at one stage of the lesson, but balance them with more holistic communicative activities at other times.
- We should keep a record of what kinds of activities are successful with which kinds of student so that we can make effective future decisions.
- We need to try to encourage LEARNER AUTONOMY (the students learning on their own and relying on their own abilities) by offering LEARNER TRAINING, where we get the students to think about how they learn best. Learner training involves tasks such as showing the students different ways of note-taking and asking them to think about which ones they prefer, or talking about different types of listening text and the SKILLS and the SUB-SKILLS that are appropriate for them. It involves thinking about the best ways of remembering words →22 and what the students can do to help this happen, etc.

We discuss DIFFERENTIATION in →42.

41

Different contexts, different levels

Different kinds of English learning

English language learning takes place in many different situations and for many different reasons.

- The vast majority of students are learning GENERAL ENGLISH: they are learning the language for no special reason. This is the case in many school situations and in many (private) language institutes, where groups are made up of students from a range of ages and backgrounds.
- In some schools around the world, teachers use CONTENT AND LANGUAGE INTEGRATED LEARNING (CLIL), especially at primary and secondary level. CLIL marries the learning of new language to the learning of school-curriculum SUBJECTS. We discuss CLIL in →102–110.
- Many students study ENGLISH FOR SPECIFIC PURPOSES (ESP). If they are aircraft engineers, they may study the special English of engineering. If they are air traffic controllers, they will learn language specific to that occupation.
- Many people study BUSINESS ENGLISH. Classes can a) take place in schools where students are learning business and English at the same time (pre-service) or b) can be given to people who are already working in the business world (in-service). The teacher may travel to a company to give lessons.
- ENGLISH FOR ACADEMIC PURPOSES (EAP) is studied by many people who need to use English at college and university.
- We need to think about why our students are learning English and what kind of English they want and need. We can do a NEEDS ANALYSIS to find out what future contexts they will need to use English in. Business English teachers, for example, will find out what situations their students need English for (perhaps business meetings) and what they will need to do in such situations (make presentations, give opinions, ask for clarification, etc.).
- Students around the world study in anything from classes of one to groups of 30, 60 and even more than 100. We discuss LARGE CLASSES in →42.
- In ONE-TO-ONE CLASSES (one student, one teacher), we can find out exactly what our student needs and wants. We must be well prepared for lessons, but at the same time we will need to be flexible as the lesson progresses.
- In one-to-one classes we can adapt to our student's feelings and wishes about language learning. We can negotiate the content of the course.
- In countries such as the USA, Canada, Australia, Ireland, New Zealand and Britain, students in a group may have a range of first or HOME LANGUAGES (L1). As a result, English is both the language of instruction and the language of communication. In other places, the students all share the same first language and, as a result, teachers can teach and students can learn in different ways. We discuss the uses of the L1 in →77.

Language levels

For many years, people have suggested that there are six different language learning levels (see diagram 1): BEGINNERS (with little or no language), ELEMENTARY, LOWER-/PRE-INTERMEDIATE, INTERMEDIATE, UPPER-INTERMEDIATE and ADVANCED. Although these terms can mean different things to different people, it is often said that students can complete a level in between 90 and 120 hours.

- Some people make a difference between REAL BEGINNERS (who know nothing at all) and FALSE BEGINNERS (those who have already picked up a few words and bits and pieces of English).

- Many teachers enjoy working with beginners because their delight in learning is obvious – and because there often seems to be a clear connection between what is taught and what is learnt.
- Teachers sometimes talk about the PLATEAU EFFECT, which often happens when students have reached the intermediate level. The students feel that they can speak English and find it difficult to see when they are making more progress. It is vital that we should provide clear goals for them to aim at, and explain what they are learning and what progress they are making.
- There are other ways of describing levels, too. The Council of Europe and the Association of Language Testers of Europe (ALTE) produced the COMMON EUROPEAN FRAMEWORK OF REFERENCE FOR LANGUAGES (CEFR), which is now used in countries around the world. As you can see in diagram 2, the CEFR has six levels from A1 (beginner) to C2 (very advanced).
- What makes the CEFR special is that it can be used for any language because levels are described in terms of CAN-DO STATEMENTS, such as (for writing) 'can complete basic forms and write notes including times, dates and places' (B1) or (for speaking and listening) 'can contribute effectively in meetings and seminars within their own area of work or keep up a casual conversation with a good degree of fluency, coping with abstract expressions' (C2).
- Students can use the CEFR to judge their own language level. In recent years, many COURSEBOOK writers and CURRICULUM designers have encouraged students to evaluate their own progress by checking whether their learning has been successful. For example if, at the end of a unit, they tick the statement *I can invite people out and accept and refuse invitations*, it means that they have learnt one of the language functions that were being taught.
- We need to give students more support when they are beginners, and teaching procedures such as PPP →44 may be more appropriate than for students at higher levels. It may be easier to encourage LEARNER AUTONOMY →43 at higher levels than at beginner level. At lower levels we will use a lot more demonstration when we give instructions →69 than we do at higher levels.
- We need to choose appropriate tasks, topics and language for students at different levels. We will not expect beginners to discuss complex issues and we will not ask advanced students to do simple language drills.

Different student levels

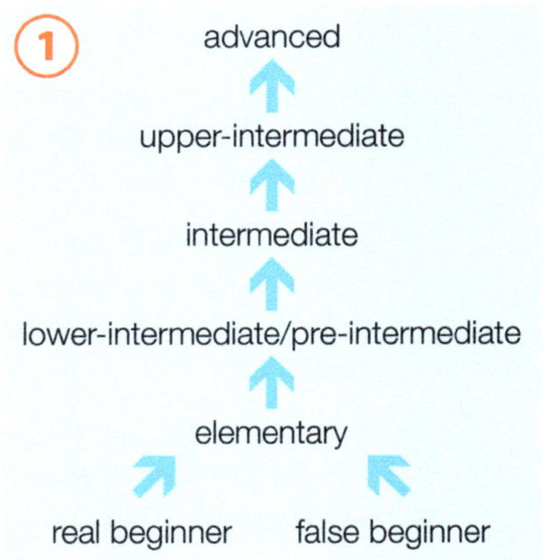

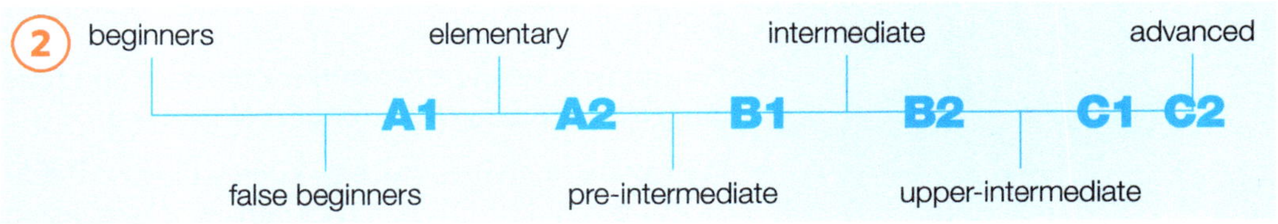

Levels and CEFR levels

42

Large and mixed-ability classes

Teaching large classes

Some teachers dislike the idea of teaching large classes (30 to 100+ students), and it is true that it is more difficult to give individual attention to students when there are so many of them. However, teaching in such circumstances can be rewarding and productive. Big classes can develop a strong group identity, and the atmosphere can be exhilarating.

- It is important to be very organised when teaching large classes. We must be sure that we have all the material that we and the students need. We need to have a clear idea of what we are going to do.
- The bigger the class, the more important it is to give very clear INSTRUCTIONS (and check them) →69 so that everyone understands exactly what they need to do. We should plan exactly how we are going to explain things and think about how to demonstrate what we want the students to do.
- We need to make it clear when we are moving from one STAGE OF A LESSON to the next. All the students, even the ones at the back, should know exactly what is going on. We need to vary our voice and the pace of the lesson when we move from one stage to the other.
- It helps to establish clear routines. Students need to know when they should quieten down at the end of an activity →70 and what signs and signals we use to indicate this. We also need to have a clear system of collecting in and giving back HOMEWORK →76, etc.
- We will maximise the use of PAIRWORK and GROUPWORK →67. For example, students can do INFORMATION-GAP activities →50 or rehearse scenes from plays →64. We can ask them to reconstruct stories DVD10 or do STORY CIRCLE-type activities →58.
- Students can complete WORKSHEETS and do reading and listening tasks in pairs and groups.
- We can use CHORAL REPETITION for reaction and practice →47. We can divide the class into two or three groups for choral practice DVD11.
- We can use activities (such as poetry fill-ins →63, 'It says here' reading aloud →29, 69 and DVD8 or 'stand up, sit down' listening DVD12) where we give all the students the same input, but they have to think and respond individually.

Teaching mixed-ability classes

In a sense, all classes are mixed ability because students are all individuals and have different LEARNER CHARACTERISTICS →40. And even in a class where everyone is supposed to be at the same level (UPPER-INTERMEDIATE →41, for example), it is unlikely that the students will all be able to speak, listen, write or read as well as each other. In primary and secondary education, children learn at different speeds and there is often a much greater range of ability, even where classes are STREAMED from, say, group 1 (high achievers) to group 3 (low achievers).

- DIFFERENTIATION (teaching different individuals in a different way) means trying to provide different learning experiences for different individuals – for example, offering different learning material or activities to suit different abilities and needs.
- We need to try to ensure that every student has a chance of success so that they can enjoy praise which they believe they deserve →72.
- We can give different students different material. For example, we can give out TEXTS at different levels. We can refer students to different online websites or give them different exercises and activities to do. However, this creates a lot of extra work for teachers.
- We can put the students in ability groups so that groups of stronger students work on different content or tasks from the weaker groups. In effect this is like in-class streaming.
- We can put students in groups where weaker and more able students are working together. We can give the group a task and say that it will not be complete until all the students (stronger and weaker) have completed it. As a result, the stronger students have to help out the weaker students.
- We can give students different roles when we give them tasks so that the stronger ones act as 'chairpersons' and take on the more difficult parts of the activity.
- We will take great care to respond to each individual student in a way that is appropriate for that student. This will affect such things as our choice of CORRECTION techniques →73, 75, how we reward and PRAISE students →72 and how we respond to DISCIPLINE problems →71.
- We can give all the students the same task, but expect different responses. For example, we can get some students to answer all 20 questions about a reading text, but only expect others to deal with the first ten. We can give a series of tasks which start by being general but then go into more detail. Some students do the first set of tasks, the others do the second.
- We will remember that weaker students need more help, not less. For example, when the students are working with a reading text, the stronger ones may go straight into the reading tasks and then move quickly to the FOLLOW-UP TASKS →56, whereas the weaker students may spend longer in a pre-reading prediction phase, and we may give them more help with the language that they are likely to encounter in the reading text.
- We need to have material ready so that we can give those students who finish early something interesting to do whilst the rest of the class catch up.

One of most important ways of dealing with both large classes and mixed-ability classes is to include LEARNER TRAINING →40 so that individual students can take responsibility for their own learning and progress.

43

Motivation

The importance of motivation

It almost goes without saying that students who are not motivated find learning difficult, whereas students who are motivated usually have more chance of success. But what is MOTIVATION and how can teachers have an effect on it?

Where motivation comes from

When we want something badly enough, when we want to feel better about ourselves or when we want to know that other people like what we are doing, we get into a state of mind that provokes us into doing something. In other words, if we want something badly enough, we act on that desire. That state of mind is what we call motivation.

- Experts talk about EXTRINSIC MOTIVATION, which comes from outside the learner and may, for example, be related to a need to pass an exam, or the desire to elicit praise from the teacher, or because the learner has a forthcoming trip where the foreign language would be an advantage. INTRINSIC MOTIVATION, on the other hand, comes from the task itself – and exists because the learner has a drive to learn.
- Differences have also been drawn between INTEGRATIVE MOTIVATION (where a language learner wishes somehow to integrate into the target language culture) and INSTRUMENTAL MOTIVATION (where a language learner is studying because with English they will get a better job – or for some other more materialistic reason). It has been suggested that integrative motivation has a more positive effect on student success than instrumental motivation, but perhaps it is more sensible to say that the strength of a student's motivation is what matters, wherever it comes from and whatever kind it is.
- The students' motivation may be affected (negatively or positively) by a number of factors such as a) the society they live in and that society's attitude to language learning, b) the people around them and how important those people think that learning a foreign language is, c) whether or not they have a definite goal for language learning (students who are preparing for exams are often highly motivated →89) and d) by the natural curiosity that most students possess.
- The students' motivation will also be affected by their learning experiences. Although motivation is personal to each learner, what teachers do can have a profound effect upon it.

Sustaining motivation

Most teachers can motivate their students. It is, after all, one of the things we are supposed to be able to do, and when, for example, we are asked to substitute for a colleague, it is not difficult to produce our 'best' lesson for the students to enjoy. Being a SUBSTITUTE TEACHER can be great fun. In the same way, the students' natural curiosity often makes the first lesson of a semester with a new class an enjoyable event. Helping our students to sustain their motivation throughout a semester or a year requires more effort, however.

- Students are far more likely to stay motivated if they think that their teacher cares about them – if their AFFECT (feeling) is positive. We need to listen, watch and respond to our students in a genuine and interested way. We discuss the importance of RAPPORT (the relationship between teacher and students) in →66.
- Nothing succeeds like success, and students who succeed in language learning are far more likely to remain motivated than students who constantly fail. However, it is important that students' ACHIEVEMENT should be the result of some effort. If everything is either too easy or too difficult, achievement will be either meaningless or impossible. Good teachers set an appropriate LEVEL OF CHALLENGE so that individual students can experience appropriate success (we discuss DIFFERENTIATION in →42). They set achievable GOALS at every stage of the language learning process.
- Students are far more likely to remain motivated if they think their teacher has a professional ATTITUDE. The way that we present ourselves to the class is important. Students need to know that we have thought about what we are going to teach (PLANNING →79–80) and that we know what we are doing. Part of a teacher's job is to convince the students, whatever the reality, that they have this kind of professional competence.
- Students will always stay more motivated if we involve them in enjoyable and challenging ACTIVITIES. However, not all students enjoy or respond to the same things in the same way. It is important for teachers to keep a record of what works and what doesn't (for the class and for individual students). REFLECTIVE TEACHERS do this anyway, and it helps them to decide what to do next.
- Students are far more likely to remain motivated if they have AGENCY (that is, if they have some control over what is happening). When students can make some decisions themselves – when they are the agents of their own actions – then they stay engaged in the process of learning because they have a stake in it.
- Because we believe that students should have agency, we encourage LEARNER AUTONOMY, where students do some or a lot of the work on their own. We want them to take charge of their learning by doing such things as DISCOVERING things for themselves →46, doing a lot of EXTENSIVE READING →54 and listening to PODCASTS, completing HOMEWORK tasks →76 and doing their own language investigation. We will provide LEARNER TRAINING, encouraging our students to think about the best techniques for their own individual learning. For example, how can they remember vocabulary best? What is the best way of studying at home?

None of these things will sustain motivation on their own, but taken together they offer us a clear guide about how to keep students motivated over a period of time.

ədˈventʃə]
[ænsKeip]

Section C: Teaching language and language skills

In this section we look at ways of teaching the language *system* (grammar, vocabulary, etc.), and we also look at ways of teaching language *skills* (reading, writing, listening and speaking).

We start by looking at ways of introducing, researching and practising language – and give examples of a large number of different types of exercises and activities.

In the language skills units we discuss different issues to do with speaking, reading, writing and listening – and then we go on to look at a range of different activities for each skill.

There are activities which involve poetry, too, as well as ideas for using music and drama.

44

Introducing new language 1

A popular way of introducing new language

Many teachers use a procedure called PPP (PRESENTATION, PRACTICE AND PRODUCTION) to introduce simple language at ELEMENTARY and INTERMEDIATE levels. We present the FORM (the construction), the meaning and use of the new language, and then the students practise it (often using DRILLING and CONTROLLED PRACTICE →47). Finally, when they have become familiar with the new language, we ask them to produce their own sentences or phrases using what they have just learnt.

An example of PPP in action

In this example DVD13, the teacher is introducing the third person singular (*he*, *she*, *it*) of the PRESENT SIMPLE tense to describe habitual actions. He wants to make sure that his students understand the way we use the present simple to talk about what people do on a regular basis. He wants to ensure that they understand that we need to add the *-s* MORPHEME to the verb with the third person singular. He also wants the students to hear the different pronunciations of *s* (/z/ in *goes*, /s/ in *works*, etc.).

Stage 1

Conor (the teacher) shows his elementary students a picture of a young woman. He tells them that her name is Meera. He asks them to guess what Meera does, before confirming them that she is a doctor. Guessing helps to engage the students' attention and we often ELICIT language or information from the class in this way.

Stage 2

Conor puts the picture of Meera next to a clock face, which shows six o'clock. He now introduces the idea of habitual actions by saying (with the students): *Monday*, *Tuesday*, *Wednesday*, *Thursday*, *Friday … every day*. He then MIMES the action of getting up and elicits the sentence he wants.

Stage 3

Conor MODELS the sentence by saying: *She gets up at six o'clock … get … sss … gets … she gets up at six o'clock.*

Notice how he says the sentence normally but then he ISOLATES the main grammar point (*gets*). He distorts it (*get … s … get … s*) before modelling the sentence again in a clear voice.

Conor could also have written the sentence on the board like this:

But in this case he didn't think it was necessary.

Stage 4

Conor now gets the students to repeat the new sentence using CHORAL REPETITION →47 (they all say the sentence at the same time) and then INDIVIDUAL REPETITION.

Stage 5

The students now see different pictures to teach sentences such as *She works in a hospital*, *She goes to work by car*, etc.

Stage 6

Conor now organises a CUE-RESPONSE DRILL →47. He points at different pictures and the students have to say the sentence for the picture.

Final stage

When the students have practised all the sentences about Meera's daily routine, Conor encourages PERSONALISATION →39 by asking them to make their own sentences about what they themselves do every day (*I get up at seven o'clock*, *I take the train to work*, *etc*.). This is the point at which the students take the language for themselves and make it their own.

Teaching ideas: showing language construction

We can use fingers and arms to show language construction (word order, contractions, etc.) DVD5.

We can use diagrams to show grammatical relationships. For example, we can use a squiggly line to show the meaning of the present perfect continuous in the sentence *They've been playing together in the orchestra since 2009.*

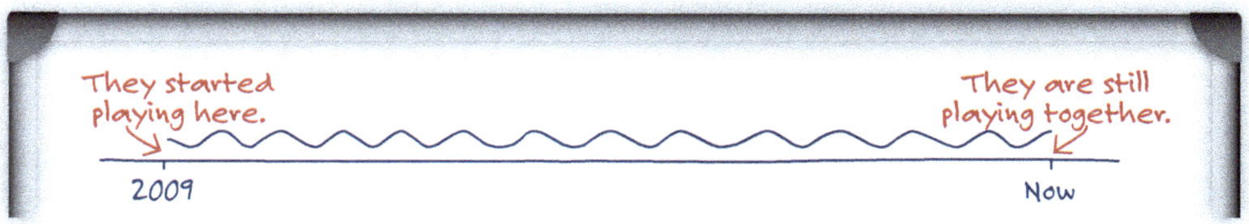

We can also use lines, boxes and arrows to show such things as the relationship between statements and questions. We can use different coloured pens to highlight such things as verb tense construction or show agreement between subject and verb.

At various stages during a PPP procedure we can CHECK MEANING (make sure the students have understood the new structure) by asking concept questions, such as *Does she get up at six o'clock on Thursdays?* (Yes, she does because she gets up at six o'clock every day), *Does she go to work by bus?* (No, she doesn't. She goes to work by car). We discuss checking meaning in →69.

Apart from PPP there are other ways of introducing new language →45.

45

Introducing new language 2

Ways of introducing new language

There are a number of ways in which we can introduce new language.

Situations

We used a SITUATION (Dr Meera's daily life) to introduce the PRESENT SIMPLE using PPP →44. Situations like this are extremely useful for introducing language at lower levels, as the following few examples will show:

- We can teach the WILL FUTURE with an imaginary visit to a fortune teller (the fortune teller can say *You will meet a handsome stranger*, etc.).
- We can teach *can* and *can't* by talking about someone in prison (*He can't go to the cinema, he can exercise for one hour every day*, etc.).
- We can teach PREPOSITIONS OF MOVEMENT by describing an adventure trail (*Run to the tree. Climb up the rope ladder. Walk along the wire*, etc.).
- We can teach POSSESSIVE PRONOUNS (*mine*, *his*, *yours*, etc.) by describing a lost property office. The students are told what colours certain people like so that when they hear that there is a blue purse in the office, they can say *It's hers*.

Stories

Stories can be used to contextualise new language. For example, we can tell the students the following STORY (and use pictures to illustrate it, if we want):

> *One day seven years ago, TV presenter Mary woke up late because her alarm didn't go off. She ran out of her door and fell down the steps. A neighbour called an ambulance and Mary went to hospital. In the hospital she met a handsome doctor. She offered him a job on her TV programme. They started to work together. They fell in love and got married. Now they have three children.*

Now we ask the students to imagine if things had been different, using the THIRD CONDITIONAL →2. For example, *If Mary's alarm had gone off, she wouldn't have got up late. If she hadn't got up late, she wouldn't have run out of her door*, etc.

We can tell stories about our own lives and experiences to contextualise new language. We can get our students to tell stories about their lives (where appropriate) and use these stories to introduce and explain the language that they need. Students can also read stories →54–56 or listen to them →60–62 on an audio track.

Dialogues

Dialogues can be used to introduce language. At pre-intermediate level, for example, we can draw two faces on the board (or show two people on the screen). We can then pretend to be each of the characters, one by one. We can stand in front of each picture in turn and elicit a dialogue as in the following example:

A: Would you like a drink?
B: Yes, please.
A: Coffee or tea?
B: Coffee, please.
A: Would you like milk?
B: Yes, please.
A: Would you like sugar?
B: Yes, please.
A: Here you are.
B: Thanks.
A: You're welcome.

We will need to use MIME, GESTURES and exaggerated INTONATION so that students can understand what is happening DVD9.

Texts

Many teachers get their students to meet new language in TEXTS; they read (or listen to) a text and then study some of the language they find there.

Pictures, objects and mime

Even in a technological age, teachers still need to be able to draw quick pictures and diagrams when they are needed. For example, we can show pictures of people *getting off*, *onto*, *out of*, *into* cars, buses, etc. We can draw happy and sad faces, or rain or snow. But we can mime these things, too, just as we can mime people sleeping, having a shower, making a cup of coffee or frying an egg.

Learning by doing

Learning by doing is especially useful for students at low levels. Using GESTURES and movement, we can get our students to follow instructions such as *Stand up! Sit down! Go to the window! Open the window!* etc. They can then start giving instructions themselves. This way of doing things, first suggested in the 1970s, is called TOTAL PHYSICAL RESPONSE (TPR) →4.

We look at more ways of introducing (and practising) language in →7, 17, 22.

Alternatives to *introducing* new language

In DISCOVERY LEARNING we ask students to RESEARCH language. We look at this in more detail in →46.

We can change the sequence of PPP and put the production stage at the beginning (rather than at the end) of the sequence. This was once amusingly called the DEEP-END STRATEGY – like throwing people in at the deep end of a swimming pool to teach them to swim! In other words, we can put the students in situations where they have to use language – and then, later, teach them the language they couldn't manage, or which they used incorrectly. Some people call this procedure TEST-TEACH-TEST. It has the advantage of making the students *need* to use the new language, and so it helps them to see what they need to learn.

In TASK-BASED LEARNING (TBL) →36 we ask students to perform TASKS rather than just learn new grammar and vocabulary, and perhaps we only deal with language they had difficulty with after the task is over. In many ways this is like test-teach-test – a kind of bigger *deep end strategy*. What is special about TBL is that language learning only happens because of the task; the task comes first and the students learn language in order to do it.

All the ways of introducing language in this unit are appropriate for grammar teaching or for a more LEXICAL APPROACH, where we introduce vocabulary, lexical phrases, etc., for example in the teaching of language functions →30.

46 Researching new language

Making discoveries

Many students often learn and remember new language well if they have to do some work to get it – for example, if they themselves have to go and look for it in DISCOVERY ACTIVITIES, and use their intelligence to understand (with the teacher's help, of course) →22.

Puzzling it out

We can give our students puzzle-like activities to get them thinking. They can work out the 'rules' for themselves (see below).

Looking for information (research)

- We can get the students to find out information by themselves by searching DICTIONARIES and GRAMMAR books. They can also search language CORPORA →87 or use INTERNET search engines such as *Google*.
- We have to suggest search tasks carefully. Students have to be able to understand the information they find. Some search tasks may not be appropriate if the students are not at intermediate level or above.
- It often helps if the students have to explain what they have discovered to their colleagues. Explaining makes us concentrate on what we know.
- It is often a good idea to give research tasks as follow-ups to CORRECTION →73–75.

Mining texts

All TEXTS, whether written or spoken, are goldmines full of language. We can train our students to be language 'miners', digging for the treasure of interesting language examples. For instance, we can ask them to identify the different PAST TENSES in a story; we can ask them to find any two or more ADJECTIVE combinations in a text and say what order they are in; we can ask them to listen to a conversation and say how the people feel, also get them to identify how they know this (INTONATION), etc.

Accidental meetings

- We should encourage our students to bring to class any English they have come across accidentally. They can do this regularly – perhaps at the start of the week, for example. Is there a song lyric they want to understand? Have they heard something in the street that they don't understand? Students often learn best when they really *want* to know something.

Teaching ideas: discovery puzzle

We can ask intermediate students what the rule is for QUESTION TAGS →3 in these sentences. They can discuss this in PAIRS or GROUPS.

It is worth noticing that many question tags can be replaced by *right*, e.g. *You're Brazilian, right?* but this is often only done in more INFORMAL situations.

You're Brazilian, aren't you?
You are not a teacher, are you?
You didn't arrive yesterday, did you?
You flew from São Paulo, didn't you?
You can't stay for the whole week, can you?
You can stay for a few days, can't you? etc.

Teaching ideas: research

1 We can ask INTERMEDIATE or UPPER-INTERMEDIATE students to research the uses of *make* and *do* and find out what nouns COLLOCATE with them. For example, we can give them a list of NOUN PHRASES, such as:

> a diagram a difference a drink a fool of yourself
> a good job a headstand a list a lot of work a noise
> a promise a survey the bed the dishes the ironing
> the shopping your homework

and they have to find the nouns in a dictionary or on the internet to see whether they are used with *make* or *do*.

2 We can ask BEGINNER and ELEMENTARY students to find out how to use FREQUENCY ADVERBS by looking at a grammar book. The kind of information they might find is shown here.

3 We can ask INTERMEDIATE students to find out how we use *sprained*, *broken* and *swollen* when we talk about parts of the body. They can use a search engine like *Google*. If they type in *sprained*, *Google* will immediately suggest a number of possible search terms involving the word *sprained*; this amounts to a list of common collocations. From this, they will discover that *sprain* collocates commonly with *wrist* and *ankle*.

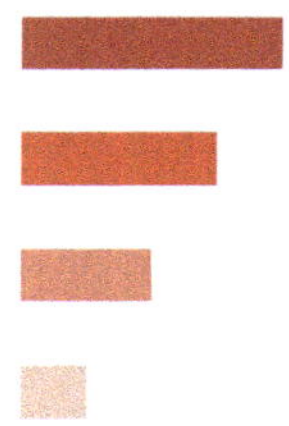

The bus is **always** crowded.
She **always** walks to work.

The bus is **usually** crowded.
She **usually** walks to work.

The bus is **often** crowded.
She **often** walks to work.

The bus is **sometimes** crowded.
She **sometimes** walks to work.

The bus is **never** crowded.
She **never** walks to work.

- We use adverbs of frequency to describe how often somebody does something, or how often something happens.
- Adverbs of frequency come after the verb *be*: *The bus **is always** crowded.*
- And they come before other verbs: *She **sometimes walks** to work.*
- In negative sentences, they come between *don't/doesn't* and the verb: *I **don't usually buy** magazines.*
- In questions, they come before the verb: Do you ***always have*** breakfast?

⚠ We can use *every* + noun, too (e.g. *every day, every week, every year*). *Every day/week*, etc. come at the beginning or end of the sentence:
*I phone Emma **every day**.*
***Every month** we visit my grandparents.*

From Grammar Practice for Elementary Students *by Viney Walker and Elsworth (Pearson 2007)*

Teaching ideas: mining a text

In this example, at the intermediate level, we can ask the students to underline any sentences with the word *if*. The purpose is to differentiate between different CONDITIONAL SENTENCES and to introduce the concept of the THIRD CONDITIONAL.

- Students will find out that apart from the ZERO CONDITIONAL (*I always help if I can*), the FIRST CONDITIONAL (*I will if you want me to be*) and the third conditional (*If I had seen him, I wouldn't be asking for help*), there are also different combinations (*I am going into town if ..., I thought I would ... if you don't mind*).
- They will learn that the *if* CLAUSE can come first (*If I had seen him ...*) or second (*... if you want me to be*).
- We can also mine the text for other interesting language, such as *leave something with you, lend, asking for a favour, call in*, etc.

A: Will you be in tomorrow?
B: I will if you want me to be.
A: That's great because I am going into town if I can finish answering all this morning's emails.
B: And?
A: So I thought I would call in and leave something with you if you don't mind.
B: Of course I don't. What do you want to leave?
A: A guitar. I'm lending Steve my guitar.
B: Didn't you see him last night?
A: If I had seen him, I wouldn't be asking you for this favour, would I?
B: Don't get upset! I always help if I can. You know that.
A: Yes I do. And if I can think of a good way to thank you properly ...

47

Repetition and drilling

Repetition: choral and individual

We frequently ask students to repeat things that we have said or that they have heard. We do this because it is useful for them to try to make the new sentences or try out new words – to see what it feels like. REPETITION is usually part of an introduction sequence →44, but we can also use it at any stage if we want to re-present things (for example, if we just want to have the students say a word correctly in the middle of some other teaching).

- We can use CHORAL REPETITION to get the students to repeat a sound, a word, a PHRASE or a SENTENCE all together. This helps them learn how to say the new language using correct sounds, stress and intonation. It gives individual students confidence and it can be enjoyable for them.
- When we want our students to repeat in chorus, we have to give a clear MODEL →44. We must make sure that all the students start at the same time so we will use GESTURES, like a conductor, to get them going. We can beat time with our hands, arms (and even stamping feet!) to establish a clear rhythm and to try to keep the whole class together.

An example of choral repetition DVD14

Teacher:	She gets up at six o'clock ... listen ... gets ... gets ... get ... s ... get ... s ... gets ... gets ... she gets up at six o'clock. Everybody.
Students:	She gets up at six o'clock.
Teacher:	Again.
Students:	She gets up at six o'clock.

- Choral repetition is highly motivational when we get the students to CHANT phrases, sentences, rhymes, poems and songs, etc.
- Choral repetition works well with words, phrases and short sentence. It is more difficult to organise for longer sentences.
- We can use BACK CHAINING to build up sentences and phrases from the end. For example, if the sentence is *You should've told her*, the teacher can have students repeat: *her ... told her ... should've told her ... you should've told her*. (The teacher, Conor, does this in DVD5.)
- We can use HALF CHORUS work by dividing the class in two. For example, we can have half the class say a line from a dialogue, and then get the other half of the class to say the next line of the dialogue DVD11.
- We often use INDIVIDUAL REPETITION to give the students a chance to say a sound, word, phrase or sentence on their own, and to check that choral repetition has been a success. First of all, we NOMINATE a student and then, when they have repeated the phrase or sentence, we give feedback. We can nominate by using a student's name, by looking at individual students or by gesturing towards them. However pointing can seem rude. It is better to use the hand with the palm upwards as Conor does in DVD15.
- It is important not to nominate students in order (by going along a row from left to right, for example); it is much more dynamic to nominate individual students in random order. The students will then pay more attention because they don't know when they will have to speak.

Drills and drilling

When we start nominating individual students one after the other and we ask them to repeat, we call this a **DRILL**. When we have more than one target sound, word, phrase or sentence and we get the students to *choose* which one to say, we call this a **CUE-RESPONSE DRILL**.

- In a cue-response drill we give a **CUE** (we indicate what we want the students to say), then we nominate the students we want to speak and they respond.
- Cue-response drills are especially useful when we want the students to practise *questions* and *answers*. We can, for example, give a question word as the cue and the student has to make a question with that word.

An example of a cue-response drill

Teacher:	*(gives a cue by holding up a picture of a clock saying 6 o'clock)*
Teacher:	*(nominating a student)* Alice.
Alice:	She gets up at six o'clock.
Teacher:	*(gives a new cue by holding up a picture of Meera the doctor at work)*
Teacher:	*(nominating a different student)* Mohamed.
Mohamed:	She works in a hospital.

In the example of a cue-response drill on the DVD, the teacher (Conor) uses gesture rather than calling the students by name DVD15.

An example of a question and answer cue-response drill

Teacher:	Question ... what ... Mohamed.
Mohamed:	What does Meera do?
Teacher:	Answer ... Alice.
Alice:	She's a doctor.
Teacher:	Question ... what time ... Piotr.
Piotr:	What time does she get up?
Teacher:	Answer ... Yumiko.
Yumiko:	At six o'clock ... she gets up at 6 o'clock.

Have a good mumble!

Sometimes, when we ask students to say something in a drill, or in other practice or speaking activities, it is a good idea to allow them think about what they are going to say before we ask them to speak. In fact, we can suggest that they **MUMBLE** the words to themselves for a bit before they have to say the word, phrase or sentence out loud.

When all the students are mumbling to themselves in a classroom, it does sound a bit strange, but it gives them a chance to try something out and, as a result, gives them confidence when they have to speak in front of the teacher or their classmates.

How much repetition and drilling is the right amount?

We have said that drills help students to get used to the new language. But if we continue with drills for too long, they quickly lose their appeal. We have to judge when they stop being useful and challenging. That's the moment to move on to something else.

48

Practising new language 1

Controlled practice

In CONTROLLED PRACTICE activities we want the students to use and think about specific language item(s) as often as possible. In this unit we will look at SENTENCE activities, DICTATION, DICTOGLOSS and MATCHING activities. We generally use very controlled practice activities at lower levels. When students are more advanced, the practice is often freer and less teacher-controlled.

There are more controlled practice activities in →49.

Sentence activities

Sentence completion

We can have our students make and complete sentences in a number of different ways.

Example 1

Complete the sentence/text with the correct form of the verb in brackets.

When I (*see*) ____ Mike yesterday he (*sit*) ____ in a café. He (*read*) ____ a newspaper.

Example 2

Complete the following sentences with one word for each gap. The first letter is given to you.

In the evening Shelly likes w____ television before she g____ to bed.

Example 3

Complete the following sentences with *some* or *any*.

I went shopping but I didn't see ____ shoes that I liked.

Example 4

Rewrite the following sentences using the word in brackets.

If you don't arrive on time, you will miss the bus. **(Unless)**

Example 5

Complete the sentences with words from the box.

adventure	animated	comedy	
documentary	horror	romcom	western

In ____ films people draw the characters with pens or on computers.

Sentence pictures

We can show the students a picture and have them make as many sentences as they can, using certain target structures or vocabulary.

Example 1

The students are shown a picture of a kitchen with many ingredients on the table and the worktops. They have to write/say as many sentences as possible using *There is/there are* + *some/any* (e.g. *There is some sugar on the table*).

Example 2

The students see a picture for 45 seconds. In the picture people are sitting in a café doing different things (drinking coffee, talking on a mobile phone, playing the guitar, etc.). The picture is then taken away and the students are asked what they can remember. Who can remember what everyone was doing? Who can remember the most sentences using the past continuous (*A girl was talking on her mobile phone*, etc.)?

Many INFORMATION-GAP ACTIVITIES →50 encourage students to make sentences in similar ways.

Dictation

- We can DICTATE short texts to the students using specific language items.
- The students can dictate sentences and texts to each other.

- We can use a RUNNING DICTATION. The students are in groups. They each send representatives to the front of the class to read a text, line by line, and take the lines back to the group and dictate them. Who can finish first? This is especially effective with short poems →63.
- We can do a SHOUTED DICTATION. The students shout a sentence or paragraph to a partner (the other students are all doing the same). It is noisy, but fun (and good for listening practice) DVD16.

Dictogloss

- Dictogloss is not quite a dictation as the students don't write down every word.
- The students hear a short text. The text is written to illustrate a particular language item(s). In this example, for elementary students, Emily wants her students to notice the use of *would* to talk about habitual actions in the PAST. She uses this text:

> When I was a child, we used to go to Spain every year by car. We'd take the ferry to France and we'd drive from France to Spain. In Spain we'd spend most of our time on the beach.

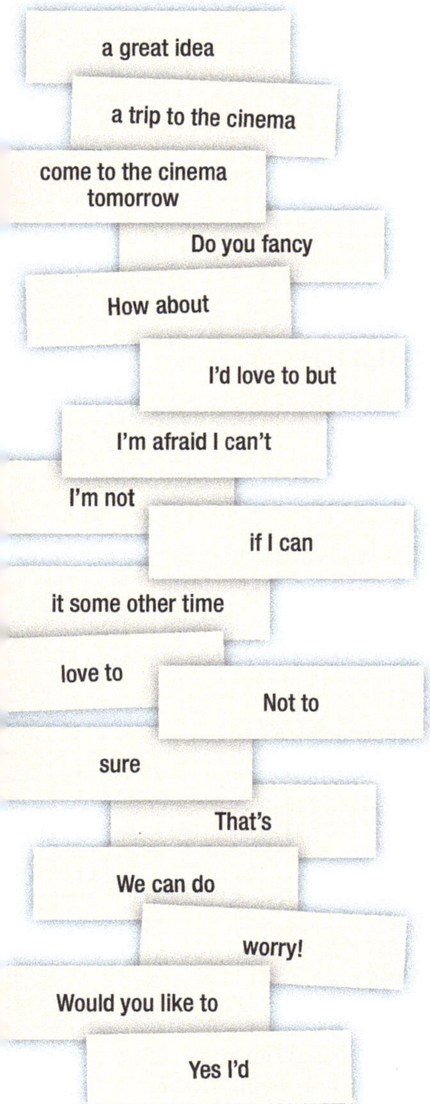

- The students try to understand what they hear (they can make notes, but they don't write down everything). They then try to reproduce it as accurately as possible.
- The students compare their text with the original. They see the difference between what they have written and what was in the original. This helps them to focus on the language in the original (***we'd** take the ferry*, ***we'd** drive*, ***we'd** spend most of our time on the beach*).

You can see this sequence on DVD17.

Matching activities

We can get students to match lists and cards to practice questions and answers, phrases and sentences.

Example 1

In the following activity to practise questions with *how*, the students have to match the questions in column A with the answers in column B.

A	B
1 How many brothers has Mary got?	**a)** He's one metre 82.
2 How often does John go to the gym?	**b)** He's twenty three.
3 How old is John's brother?	**c)** She's completely fluent.
4 How old is Mary?	**d)** He's nineteen.
5 How tall is John?	**e)** Three times a week.
6 How well does Mary speak Chinese?	**f)** Three.

When they have done this, they can practise asking and answering the questions. They can then ask each other the same questions.

Example 2

Each student is given a card like the ones in the margin with half a phrase on it. They walk round the class and find another student who has the other half of their phrase.

You can find more practice activities for PRONUNCIATION in →29, VERBS →7 and the NOUN PHRASE in →17.

49

Practising new language 2

Practice of specific language items

CONTROLLED PRACTICE ACTIVITIES (like the ones in this unit and in →48) are different from more COMMUNICATIVE SPEAKING ACTIVITIES because we want the students to use specific language ACCURATELY, rather than trying to use any or all of the language that they can. We look at more communicative speaking activities in →52–53.

Most of the activities in this unit can be adapted for a number of different specific language items.

Story chains

Example 1: things I have never done (present perfect)

The students sit in a circle. The first student says, for example, *My name is Roberta and I have never eaten raw fish.* The next student has to say *Roberta has never eaten raw fish. My name is Thais and I have never climbed a mountain.* The third student has to say *Roberta has never eaten raw fish, Thais has never climbed a mountain. My name is Marcus and I have never …*, etc.

Example 2: the never-ending story (first conditional)

The students are told to imagine a woman having breakfast. They are then asked to imagine the consequences if she has another coffee. Student 1: *If she has another coffee, she might miss her bus.* Student 2 has to continue the story: *If she misses her bus, she will be late for work.* Student 3 continues: *If she is late for work, her boss will be angry.* Student 4 goes on: *If her boss is angry, …* We can keep the story going until the students cannot think of anything more to say.

Interviewing each other

Students can INTERVIEW each other in order to practise specific language items.

Example 1: what can you do? (questions for beginners with *can* and *can't*)

The students have a CHART like the one in the margin. They have to walk around the room interviewing their colleagues, using *can* + one of these verbs:

bake   paint   play   speak   use   write

They ask *Can you play the guitar? Can you bake a cake?* etc. If a student replies *Yes, I can*, they write that student's name in their chart.

We can extend this kind of chart activity by designing a FIND SOMEONE WHO … chart. The students have to find someone who *likes watching movies*, *has at least one brother and sister*, *got up early this morning*, etc.

Example 2: present perfect with *since* and *for* (lower-intermediate)

This example is slightly more complex. The students have to complete some or all of the following SENTENCE STEMS about themselves – some suggestions are given in brackets:

I live in …
I study English at …
I have (pierced ears/a tattoo) …
I play (football/tennis/the violin, etc.) …
I work in a …

They then give their sentences to a partner. The partner has to ask about their sentences. For example: *How long have you lived in England? How long have you played the violin?*

And they have to answer: *I have lived in England since 2008. I have played the violin for ten years.*

Quizzes

QUIZZES can be good fun and provide a lot of practice of specific language items at the same time.

Example 1: superlative adjectives (elementary to lower-intermediate)

The students have to write general knowledge questions about world geography (or any other world facts). They may have to do some research for this. For example:

> What is the tallest mountain/building in the world?
> What is the highest capital city in the world?
> What is the biggest ocean/desert/country/lake in the world?

The students now divide into two teams and ask each other their questions.

We can get the students to write general knowledge questions about discoveries, works of art, buildings, etc. They can practise SUBJECT QUESTIONS →3 (*Who discovered penicillin? Who wrote Romeo and Juliet*) or questions using the PASSIVE →1 (*Who was penicillin discovered by? Who was Romeo and Juliet written by*? etc.).

(We need to remember that 'general' knowledge isn't necessarily shared by everyone. Different people know different things, especially when they come from different cultural backgrounds.)

Example 2: our students' lives

We can make a class quiz with questions about the students themselves. They can ask questions such as *Who lives furthest from the school? Who is the oldest student in the class? Who has the most cousins?* etc.

Games

Many games (some of which were designed for radio or for general use) can also be used for language practice.

Example 1: 20 questions

The students have to find out what a mystery object is by asking 20 (or fewer) YES/NO QUESTIONS →3. The person who uses the fewest questions wins the round.

Example 2: mystery description

Students at the intermediate level have to make sentences about a 'mystery' object using passive sentences (*It's made of/used for* ...). For example:

> It is often made of plastic.
> It is sometimes made of metal.
> It is used in the kitchen.
> It is used for stirring soup and things like that.

How many sentences can they make before their classmates guess what the object is?

Example 3: backs to the board

One student from each team (Student A) sits with their back to the board. The teacher writes a word or phrase on the board. The other students in the team have to give Student A information so that they can guess the word or phrase on the board.

Example 4: charades

The students take turns to act out the names of books, play and films. Their team has to guess what it is by asking questions. The acting students can only answer *yes* or *no*.

We will look at more GAMES (for younger learners) in →93. See also NOUGHTS AND CROSSES →23.

50

Practising new language 3

Information-gap activities

Many practice activities (and COMMUNICATIVE ACTIVITIES, too) have an INFORMATION GAP to make the activity/practice more meaningful.

- An information gap is created when two (or more) students have different bits of information. They have to share these pieces of information if they want to understand the whole thing – a bit like the way in which different jigsaw pieces make a whole picture.
- The students don't show each other their information. They have to talk to each other to close the information gap.
- We can make information-gap activities CLOSED (the students can use only specific language items) or more OPEN (they can use a range of language items). When they can complete the task using any of the language that they know, we say that the activity is a communicative activity.

Describe and draw

- In DESCRIBE AND DRAW activities, Student A describes a PICTURE to a partner, Student B. Student B cannot see the picture, but has to try to draw it as exactly as possible from Student A's description. The following picture could be used for this:

- Student B can ask Student A for more information or for clarification.
- We can use these activities to practise various prepositional phrases, such as *at the bottom of the picture*, *in the top right-hand corner*, *in the background*, *behind*, *in front of*, etc.

Finding similarities, finding differences

- Student A and Student B have different pictures. They have to ask each other questions like *What colour is the woman's hat in your picture?* or *What is the woman wearing on her feet in your picture?* in order to find either what is similar about them or what is different.
- We can use almost any pair of pictures for this activity. For example, they can show street scenes, groups of people, different buildings or different scenes from films. Teenage and younger learners can compare two pictures of a teenager's bedroom before and after it was tidied! (*In my picture the jeans are on the floor. In my picture the jeans are on the chair – very tidy!*)
- We can use this activity with poems, too, as we shall see in →63.

Information-sharing

- Students can use CHARTS to ask and answer questions, using specific language. In the example below, both students in a pair have information about different countries. For example, Student A has the following information:

A's information:
Name: Wales
Where: Western Britain
Capital city: Cardiff
Languages: English, Welsh
Most popular sport(s): rugby, football, cricket
Interesting information: Wales has its own parliament.

- A and B also each have the following chart. They have to complete their chart by asking their partner questions, such as *Where is your country? What's the capital? What languages do people speak there?* They can answer each other's questions but must not say the name of their country. When they have completed the chart, they try to guess their partner's country.

Where?	
Capital?	
Language(s)	
Most popular sport(s)	
Interesting information	

Using texts for information-gap language practice

We can use TEXTS for information-gap activities.

- We can give Students A and B texts with different words blocked out. In the following extract, the students have to ask each other questions (A: *What did Mandela do at school? What happened to Mandela in 1962?* etc.).

Student A
After school (where he was a keen (1) ____ and runner), Nelson Mandela became an important member of the African National Congress, which fought against the anti-democratic racist government of South Africa.
Mandela was (2) ____ in 1962 and stayed in prison for 27 years. Many of those years were spent on (3) ____, a notorious prison outside Capetown.
Mandela was relased from prison on (4) ____.
He was elected president of South Africa in 1994 and served until (5) ____.

Student B
After school (where he was a keen boxer and (1) ____), Nelson Mandela became an important member of the (2) ____, which fought against the anti-democratic racist government of South Africa.
Mandela was arrested in 1962 and stayed in prison for (3) ____ years. Many of those years were spent on Robyn Island, a notorious prison outside (4) ____.
Mandela was relased from prison on February 11, 1990.
He was elected president of South Africa in (5) ____ and served until 1999.

- In JIGSAW READING, students can be given three different texts which each tell only part of the same story. They have to ask each other questions about their texts to complete the whole story. We will look at reading in more detail in →54–56.

51

Teaching speaking 1

The reasons for speaking activities

There are a number of reasons why we ask students to do speaking activities in class.

- We want to get our students to speak so that they have to retrieve and use the language that they know. RETRIEVAL AND USE is one of the ways in which students are helped to remember language →22.
- In genuinely COMMUNICATIVE SPEAKING ACTIVITIES we want to give the students a real desire to speak and a communicative purpose for doing so. The content of the communication – and the achievement of the speaking task – are as important, in a way, as the language they use.
- We will not tell the students exactly what language to use because we don't want them to focus on specific language items in the same way as we do for PRACTICE ACTIVITIES →48.
- Speaking activities give the teacher and the students a good idea of how well everyone is doing.

We should take care to match the speaking task with the LEVEL →41 of the students. BEGINNER students will not find it easy to have a discussion unless it is very structured. ADVANCED students will not be motivated by simple speaking tasks.

Building the speaking habit

The following activities (mostly game-like) aim to make students relaxed and enthusiastic about speaking.

- We can DICTATE sentences to the class, such as '*One of the most beautiful things I have ever seen is …*'. The students have to complete the sentence with a word or phrase. They then read their sentences out. Any SENTENCE STEMS can be used in this way.
- We can write topics on pieces of paper and put them in a hat or bowl. The students take turns to pick out a piece of paper and have to say at least one sentence (instantly) about the topic they have chosen.
- The students have a dice. They choose one topic for each of the numbers 1–6. One student throws the dice and has to speak immediately (one or more sentences) about the topic for the number that occurs. If we use two dice, then we can list 12 topics.

- The students have to talk about a topic, such as *What I did yesterday*. Every time they say a sentence, they can pick up a counter. Who has the most counters at the end of the discussion? We can also turn the activity around so that the students each start with five counters. Every time they say a sentence, they can put a counter into a bowl. Who finishes their counters first?
- We can choose two or three students. They have to construct an instant 'letter' to a writer, thinker, artist, musician or celebrity of their choice. But they have to speak their letter one-student-one-word at a time. For example, Student A: *Dear*, Student B: *President*, Student C: *I*, Student A: *am*, Student B: *writing* … When they have finished their letter, three other students have to reply in the same way. This game is funny, makes the students think about words and syntax (what can follow what), and takes away speaking performance nerves.

Interviews

We can use INTERVIEWS to practise specific language items, but we can also use them for more communicative speaking activities.

Example 1: the hot seat

- The students have to prepare short statements about what they did last weekend or their favourite sport or hobby, etc.
- One student now sits in the HOT SEAT and delivers a statement. The other students ask as many questions as they can about it.
- When the student runs out of things to say, someone else goes to the hot seat.

Example 2: interview the picture

- The students look at a PICTURE which shows several people – perhaps a famous work of art or a photograph. They have to write questions for the people in it.
- Several students come to the front and pretend to be the people in the picture. The rest of the class ask their questions and the students at the front have to imagine how the characters might answer.

Turning on the inner voice

In a lesson there is usually not enough time for individual students to do as much speaking as they or we would like. We can compensate for this by getting the students to use their INNER VOICE – the voice we all use in real life when we imagine conversations we could have or could have had.

- We can encourage the students to use their inner voices for 'silent' speaking activities. For example, we can tell them to imagine that they are going to an English-speaking doctor and have to explain what is wrong with them. They can imagine that they meet their favourite film actor by accident. What will their conversation be?
- We can encourage the students to think about what they are going to say (using their inner voice) before we ask them to speak out loud in a DISCUSSION or a SIMULATION (or ROLEPLAY) →53. This will give them a better chance of speaking success.
- We can set inner-voice tasks for students to do on their own. For example, on the way home they could imagine that they have a blind person sitting next to them and they must describe everything that they see. When they notice (in the street) a person that they think is interesting, they could imagine how they would introduce themselves and the conversation that they could have with that person. After school they can imagine ringing up an English-speaking friend and telling them about their day.

52 Teaching speaking 2

Discussions

When **DISCUSSIONS** are organised well, they can be highly motivating and successful.

Example 1: buzz groups

At almost any stage we can put the students into **BUZZ GROUPS**, where they can quickly discuss anything from what they are going to read about to what they want to do next. Buzz groups are normal events in the life of a classroom.

Example 2: from sentence to discussion

We can give the students a topic, such as boxing or mass tourism or school uniforms (anything that people hold strong opinions about). They have to write three sentences in favour of the topic (e.g. *Boxing is exciting to watch* or *Mass tourism helps poor countries*) and three sentences against the topic (e.g. *Boxing encourages violence* or *Mass tourism destroys the environment*). Then one student reads out a sentence and another student has to either agree (*Yes, I agree and boxers are very brave*) or disagree (*I don't agree; boxing is a horrible sport*). We can also put the students into 'for and against' teams.

Example 3: prompt cards

We can give the students **PROMPT CARDS**, each with a point of view about a topic, as in the following examples:

School uniforms look smart and give the school a good image.

School uniforms are too expensive for some parents.

School uniforms make all the children look the same.

When students wear school uniforms, they don't have to worry about fashion and competition.

Children need an opportunity to express themselves through the clothes they wear. School uniforms don't allow this.

We then give the students time to think about what they can say to support the points of view on their cards before we start the discussion.

Example 4: formal debate

We can decide on a motion (an idea, a proposition) for a debate, such as *Women have better lives than men* (or the other way round). We divide the class into two groups, one for the motion, one against. Each group has to prepare arguments for their position and think of three questions for the other side. Each group then chooses someone to speak first and someone to speak second. The others (from both groups) are the audience. The debate sequence is Team A speaker 1 followed by Team B speaker 1. Then the audience can speak and ask questions. Then Team B speaker 2 makes concluding remarks and Team A speaker 2 makes concluding remarks. The audience votes. Who won the debate?

Example 5: panel discussions

We can set up a panel discussion on just about any topic – or indeed replicate the kinds of 'contemporary issue' panel debates that are common on television in most countries. Students may feel easier if we give them **ROLES** →53 to 'hide behind' so that they are not judged on their own opinions.

Although successful discussions are frequently prepared in the ways we have discussed, some happen quite by accident, in the middle of a lesson. When this happens, we have to take an instant decision about whether to let the discussion continue (often a very good idea) or whether to stop it because there are other things we have to do. We will discuss MAGIC MOMENTS like this in →79.

Reaching a consensus

Consensus-reaching activities work because the students have to speak in order to reach a decision.

- We can give the students a situation (such as *You see a parent treating their child badly in the supermarket*) and five options about what they could do:

  1 Do nothing.
  2 Look at the parent and show them that you disapprove.
  3 Go and speak to the parent and ask them to stop.
  4 Ask the people around to help you stop the parent.
  5 Call the police.

  The students reach a CONSENSUS on the best option.
- We can guide the conversation by giving each student a ROLE-CARD →53, telling them which option they should argue for.
- Any decision-making activity (e.g. which out of five video clips should win a prize) is good for this kind of discussion.
- In PYRAMID DISCUSSIONS, we start by putting students in pairs to decide, for example, on five things to put in a time capsule for future generations to find. When they have made their lists, two pairs join together to form new groups of four. They have to negotiate their five-item lists so the new list is agreed by the group. We then join two groups of four and the new groups of eight have to negotiate their lists.

The teacher's roles in speaking activities

When students are trying to express themselves in speech, we should do everything we can to make this work.

- We will often need to be a PROMPTER →65, pushing students forward, suggesting things they might say next, and helping them out of difficulties. We may also need to keep on encouraging them to speak in English rather than using their first language →77.
- Sometimes we may decide to take part in the activity as a PARTICIPANT. This will allow us to keep the conversation going from within. However, we need to be sure that we don't dominate the activity.
- At the end of a speaking activity we need to give FEEDBACK, showing not only what errors may or may not have occurred, but also (perhaps more importantly) telling the students what was successful, and commenting on the content of the speaking activity →72.

Turn-taking

We can help our students to be good at TURN-TAKING (knowing when we can speak in conversations). We can teach them expressions such as:

Could I just say something here? *You may have a point, but on the other hand ...*
I'd like to say something if you don't mind. *Before you go on, I'd just like to say ...* etc.

53

Teaching speaking 3

Telling stories

Storytelling is good for speaking, not only because it encourages the students to use a lot of language, but also because we tell stories all the time in real life.

Example 1: reconstructing a story

For a STORY RECONSTRUCTION activity, we can put the students into six GROUPS. Each group is given one or two of a series of PICTURES that tell a story DVD10.

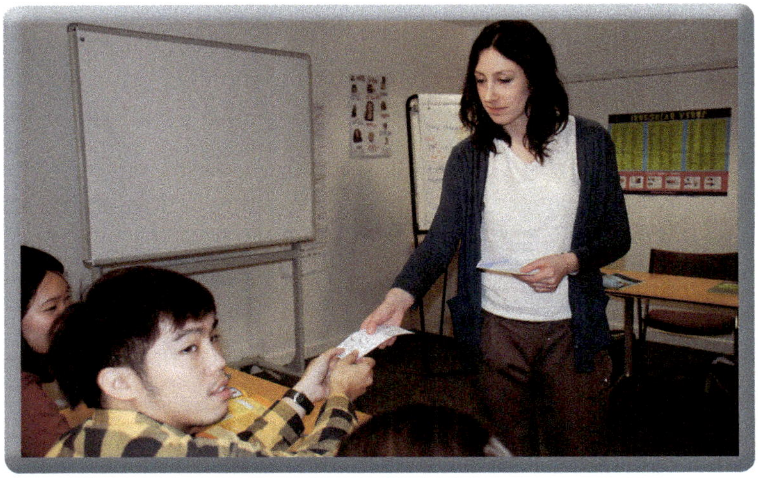

After each group has had a chance to study the pictures, we take the pictures away. Now we form new groups of six; each of the new groups has one student from each of the original groups. They have to tell each other what was in their pictures and try to work out a story that connects them all. When they have finished, the different groups compare stories.

Example 2: string things together

We can give the students pictures of any four items and ask them to work out a story which connects them.

Example 3: what happens next?

We can show the class a FILM CLIP from *YouTube* or *Vimeo* and stop it half way through. The students have to imagine what happens next. When they have made their suggestions to the class, we show them the whole video to see if they were right.

Example 4: taking time away

A student tells a story, based on a text they have read or something that has been discussed in class. They have a time limit to tell the whole story. The next student has to tell the same story, but the time limit is shorter. Each time a new student tells the story again we take some time off so that they have to tell it more and more quickly. This activity is good fun. It also ensures that the storytelling will get more and more efficient.

Example 5: truth and lies

In groups of three, the students prepare three stories. One of them is true, the other two are false. They tell their stories to the class. Can the class guess which is the true story?

Making oral presentations

When students make an ORAL PRESENTATION, we should give them time to prepare what they are going to say. If we want oral presentations to be successful, we need to find tasks, too, for the students who are listening to the presentation.

- We can give the students topics to choose from and questions to guide their presentations. For example, we could prepare the following questions for students who choose to give a presentation about sound effects in radio, TV and film: *Who was the first sound effects expert? Where are sound effects used? Can you describe some typical sound effects and how they are made?* etc.
- We can help the students to research their topic by finding WEBSITES and other sources for them to look at.
- We can encourage the students to use PRESENTATION SOFTWARE and the INTERNET to back up their presentations.
- In a multilingual/multicultural group, the students can prepare talks about their countries or their region.
- We can show the students model presentations and discuss how to introduce and develop a topic. We can give them language for the different stages, such as *I'd like to start by … Another thing I would like to say is … In conclusion, I would just like to say that …*
- We can set up POSTER PRESENTATION sessions. The students prepare a talk and create a poster to back it up. Half of the class stand in front of their posters. The other half visit them one by one and listen to the presentations. They have to report back on the two or three presentations they enjoyed the most and why. Then the two halves of the class swap round. We can also get the students to stand in front of pictures and describe them as if they were art gallery guides.
- We can ask the students to write at least two follow-up questions as they listen to each poster presentation. We can choose students to summarise the presentations they have heard.

Simulation and roleplay

- In SIMULATIONS, we give the students a chance to rehearse real-life encounters. For example, we can move the classroom furniture so that we represent a station office with a ticket window. The students simulate an exchange between a passenger and a travel clerk.
- In ROLEPLAY simulations, the students are given a role. For example, Student A (the passenger) can be given the following ROLE-CARD:

> You want to buy a ticket to Boston. You are very nervous and you are in a great hurry because the police are chasing you.

Student B (the travel clerk) can have a card saying:

> You don't like your job and you hate it when passengers start trying to make you do everything in a hurry.

- Because they are playing roles rather than being themselves, students often find roleplays very liberating.
- Some simulations and roleplays can involve considerable preparation and time. For example, we can set up a job INTERVIEW situation. The interviewing panel can prepare the questions they want to ask, and we can give the candidates role-cards. At the end of the process, the panel have to choose the successful candidate.
- Students can roleplay TV programmes, parties, United Nations debates, etc.

See also using DRAMA →64.

54 Teaching reading 1

The need for reading

We all need to be able to read in our own language, whether from books, documents, computers, mobile devices, signs or billboards. Students of English need to be able to read these things in English, too. But reading also helps them to learn and acquire English.

We can divide reading into EXTENSIVE READING and INTENSIVE READING.

Extensive reading

Reading at the appropriate level is one of the best ways for students to get COMPREHENSIBLE INPUT →35 – that is, language that they can understand. The more comprehensible input they receive, the better their English gets.

- When students read extensively, they are not just looking for specific language or trying to do vocabulary and comprehension exercises. They are reading either for pleasure or for information that interests them.
- We need to encourage our students to read on their own so that they can keep learning and acquiring language even when there is no lesson and no teacher to help them.
- Students will get the most benefit from extensive reading if they read at an appropriate level. If the text is too difficult, it will be more like work than pleasure. If it is too easy, it may not be very engaging.
- Students will get most benefit from reading texts that they themselves want to read. Different students have different interests: this means that they should, if possible, read different books.
- Many publishers offer GRADED READERS (sometimes called *learner literature*). These range in level from beginner (CEFR A1) to advanced (CEFR C1) →41. Some of them re-tell stories from famous books or films. Some describe the lives of famous people. Some are original stories written especially for the appropriate level.
- Where possible, we should have a collection of books (or texts) that individual students can choose from. When they themselves choose what to read, they are more likely to be enthusiastic about reading.
- We can give students time to read in lessons – say ten or 15 minutes a week. Some teachers (and schools) have DEAR (drop everything and read) moments to encourage this.
- We can ask our students to tell other students about what they have been reading. They can do this orally, or they can fill in fairly simple report forms such as the following (for intermediate students):

TITLE: ______________________

AUTHOR: ______________________

Type of book (non-fiction, thriller, romance, etc.) ______________________

What you like/don't like about it

____

Would you recommend the book to your colleagues? Why? Why not?

- Students can also, of course, fill in WORKSHEETS with language exercises based on a book, but they should only do this after they have read the book, usually as HOMEWORK →76 or private study.
- Some students enjoy reading more than others. Some of them will read extensively (and enthusiastically). Some will not. Nevertheless, we should encourage extensive reading, explain why it is such a good idea, have DEAR moments and make our classes 'reading friendly'.

Intensive reading

We often get students to read intensively in class. This means that they will look at a short reading text and do various exercises based on it. Texts for more advanced students are usually longer than those for students at lower levels.

- Good reading exercises help students with TOP-DOWN PROCESSING (getting a general idea of meaning) and BOTTOM-UP PROCESSING (understanding individual words, phrases and text construction).
- Intensive reading is often used to train students in different reading skills, such as READING FOR GIST (getting the general meaning from a text) or READING FOR SPECIFIC INFORMATION (looking for particular things, such as the times of a film at a cinema, rather than trying to get the general picture).
- Reading for gist is sometimes called SKIMMING. We often ask students to read a text quickly (skimming over its surface) and get the main idea(s) first, before we ask them to read for more detailed information.
- Reading for specific information is sometimes called SCANNING – because the eye is searching around just for the special information that we want – a bit like a computer scanning for only the information it needs.
- Some people say that we don't need to teach reading skills like scanning and skimming because these are things that people do in their L1 anyway – and they can transfer them to learning English. Others say that many students (especially those from certain cultural and language backgrounds) don't read very much even in their L1, so it is a good idea to train them when they read in English. What is certain is that it is a good idea for students to read in different ways as often as possible since this helps them to practise reading. It also helps them to see new and previously learnt language in context.
- When we get students to read in class, we often give them a more general task first (such as skimming or scanning) before asking them to look for more detailed information (relating to both meaning and language).
- Although we use intensive reading for showing vocabulary and grammar in context, we should never forget that the best response to any text is to ask whether or not the students like the text and why. This makes them think about the content and the language and encourages them to re-use both.
- Any text can be MINED for language →46.

We look at ways of using intensive reading in →55.

55

Teaching reading 2

12 The Gliding Lesson

1 Read the text and choose the summary of it.

a The narrator was given a gliding lesson as a present and loved it. He wants to do it again.
b Christophe took the narrator's daughters for a flight in his glider.
c The narrator was given a gliding lesson as a present. It terrified him and he is unlikely to go again.
d Christophe bought his daughter a gliding lesson as a present. She really enjoyed it.

2 Look back at the text and answer these questions.

a How many people were in the car?
b Where were they going?
c Why were they going there?
d What happened when they got there?
e What did the narrator think of the experience?

3 Find words or phrases in the text that mean the following:

a a place where planes and gliders take off and land
b people who travel with you
c playing with, moving something
d the place where a pilot sits in a plane or glider
e beating strongly

Speaking

4 IN GROUPS, talk about:

- whether you have been – or would like to go – gliding
- the most exciting thing you have ever done
- what you would like to try that you have never tried before

It was a cold windy day as they approached the airfield. He was driving. He wondered if he should turn back and go home. But they were sitting there, one beside him and the other behind him. If he said he didn't want to do it, they would laugh at him. So he kept quiet.

They drove up to the clubhouse and got out. The man in charge of the airfield opened the door and let them in.

'Come for your flight?' he said.

'Yes,' he replied, more cheerfully than he felt.

'First time? Looking forward to it?'

He looked round at his two companions. They were smiling and happy with the present they had chosen for him. How could he tell them that he was absolutely terrified?

A new man came up to them. 'Hi,' he said, 'My name's Christophe. I'll be taking you up.'

He greeted Christophe and shook his hand.

And so, a few minutes later he found himself walking over the grass, the wind ruffling his hair. His two daughters walked alongside him, chatting away and giggling. Then Christophe helped him on with his harness and explained how to use the parachute. The parachute?!

He couldn't back out now. He got into the tiny cockpit and strapped himself in. Christophe got in behind him. And then suddenly, far far too quickly, they were bouncing over the grass behind the tow-plane and before he could say 'Stop, I want to get out' they were bouncing up into the air.

He tried to remain clam. Tried to tell himself that he was safe and that Christophe knew what he was doing. But it didn't work. His heart was thudding in his chest and his knees were literally knocking together. Every time they slipped in the wind, he thought he would be sick.

Christophe was chatting away happily. 'Look!' he said. 'Look down there. That's Royston.'

So he looked from their height of 2,000 feet. And felt sick again.

The flight only lasted about 25 minutes, though it seemed to go on for ever. But in the end they dipped to the right and came thudding down onto the grass, stopping a few feet from where his two daughters were standing, their hair flying in the wind.

He got out onto the grass and suddenly as he walked up to the two girls he felt a sense of huge excitement, a great feeling of triumph, a feeling of something big and important.

But he hasn't been gliding again.

What texts should we give students for intensive reading?

We should give our students TEXTS that are appropriate for their level. We need to give them material on a variety of topics and let them read in a variety of GENRES →32 (stories, advertisements, reports, poems, newspaper articles, etc.).

What to do before students read a text

It helps if we give the students a chance to think about what they are going to read. That's why we give them PREDICTION activities so that they are thinking about the topic and getting their brains ready for reading with the knowledge they have about the genre or the topic of the text.

- We can tell the students what the topic of the text is and ask them to guess what they will find in it. Sometimes they can form BUZZ GROUPS →52 to do this.
- We can ask them to read some questions about a text before they read the text itself. They should try to guess the answers, and then read the text to see if their guesses are correct DVD18.
- We can tell the students what the text is going to be about and ask them to fill in a CHART like the one on the left about the topic.
- We can also get them to write their own questions about the text.
- We can show the students any PICTURES which accompany the text (or headlines, captions, etc.) and get them to guess what will be in the text.

Things I know
Things I think I know
Things I would like to know

- We can give the students words or phrases from the text and ask them to guess what the text is about. We can give different phrases to different students in a group (instead of the pictures we used for the STORY RECONSTRUCTION activity →53). They have to guess the story which links all the phrases.
- We can project the first line of a text on the screen. The students have to guess what the next word will be. We show the next line and again they have to guess what the next word will be, as in this example:

> It is difficult to remember what it was like before educational technology changed classrooms for ever. Once we were lucky if we had a board and some chalk, but now many classrooms have a variety of educational

Like poetry with blanks for the students to complete →63, this keeps the students' attention and makes them think about language.

- We can display part of a text and ask the students to predict what comes next. They then read the next section of the text to confirm their predictions before predicting what comes after that.

Reading activities

We can ask our students to do almost anything with a reading text. Here are some of the most common activities. They are designed so that the students get a general understanding of the text first.

- The students read the text and then tell each other if they liked it and why (or what they agreed with or didn't agree with). This kind of GIST reading exercise →54 makes them think about meaning in general, and invites them to ENGAGE →80 emotionally with the text.
- The text is presented as a reading puzzle. We cut it up and give the students the different paragraphs in random order. They have to work out how to put the text back into the correct order.
- For JIGSAW READING we can divide the students into groups of three (or more) and create an INFORMATION GAP →50. Each student has a text which tells part of a story (or contains part of the information they need). They cannot show each other their texts. They have to ask each other what is in their texts in order to tell the whole story. Jigsaw reading gives the students a reason to read and understand what they are reading.
- We can ask students to TRANSFER INFORMATION from texts to graphs, charts or other graphics. We look at this in more detail in →105.
- We can ask students to answer gist questions about the text, such as the following:

1. Which of the following topics are mentioned in the text? Tick the boxes.
2. Choose a title for the text.
3. Read the text. What three things does the writer suggest?
4. Read the text and match the statements to the different paragraphs.
5. Read the advertisements. Which one is about a…., b…., c….? etc.
6. Say whether the following statements about the text are true or false.
7. Say which of the statements about the text are true.
8. Read these short summaries. Which (a, b or c) is the best summary of the text?

- We can set a time limit for reading tasks and stress that the students should use the appropriate SUB-SKILL to get what they need from the text in the time they have.
- At higher levels, many teachers help their students to get used to reading TEST exercises, such as MULTIPLE-CHOICE questions →89 and other question types.

56

Teaching reading 3

Responding to a text

When the students have read a TEXT in class, we can ask them to respond to it in various ways. They may answer questions which they chose or which they were given. They may discuss whether they liked the text or not. Or they may go back to the text and read it for different reasons.

Before we ask individuals in the class to give us their responses to questions, it is a good idea to let them compare answers in PAIRS or small GROUPS →67. This is good for co-operation and helps to reduce any tension that the students may be feeling.

More comprehension

When the students have read a text for the first time (for general comprehension), we often ask them to read it again and look for more (detailed) information. This allows them to absorb more information and language and helps to ensure that they have really understood what they have read.

- We can get the students to look for details using WH-QUESTIONS →3. For example, if they have read a text about the Wright brothers, the inventors of the first aeroplane, we can ask them questions such as *Who first had the idea? What did Wilbur Wright do next? When did the Wright Flyer 1 first leave the ground?*
- We can give the students a series of numbers such as *2*, *7*, *12* and *1903*. They have to search the text and say what the numbers refer to (*2* = the wings on their flyer, *7* = the number of Wright brothers, but only Wilbur and Orville were involved, *12* = the seconds in the air of the first flight, *1903* = the date of the first flight, etc.).
- We can ask the students to give more detailed answers to questions such as *In your own words how would you describe …?* about characters, places, ideas or things.
- Different students can be asked to find out detailed information about different people or things in the text.
- We can ask the students to find sentences in the text which either confirm or contradict different statements that we give them.

Language questions

We often ask students to look at a text to find out things about words and phrases, as in the following examples:

Vocabulary

1 Find a word or phrase in the text that means …
2 Match the words in blue (in the text) with the following meanings …
3 Replace the underlined word in these sentences with a word which means the same thing.
4 Explain the meaning of the phrases in blue.

Grammar

1 Find all the uses of *had* in the text. Which are examples of the past perfect? Which are examples of something else?
2 Look at the text. Find comparative forms of the following adjectives … How do we make comparative adjectives?
3 Read the text again. How many different ways of referring to the future can you find? What is the difference between them?
4 Find six verbs in the text. Do they refer to the past, the present or the future?

Follow-up tasks

When the students have read a text and done the exercises that go with it, we will often want them to do some kind of FOLLOW-UP TASK, using the topic of the text or exploiting some of the language in it.

- At the INTERMEDIATE level (or above) students can discuss any issues that were in the text. They can get into groups to decide whether they agree or disagree with what the text said. We can use the text as preparation for a FORMAL DEBATE →52.
- The students can read a text and then tell the same story from different points of view. For example, if they have read a story about an argument between two neighbours (about how each neighbour's children are behaving), they can tell the story as if they were one or other of the neighbours, or one of the children concerned.
- Students can ROLEPLAY →53 a situation leading from the text. For example, if the text is about a neighbours' argument (see above), they can roleplay a police INTERVIEW or a TV or radio interview about what happened.
- The students can do more research (in the library or on the INTERNET) about the topic of the text.
- The students can rewrite the content of a text as a dialogue, a newspaper report, etc. They can write a real or imaginary letter to the characters in the text or to a newspaper about the content of the text.
- We can introduce or practise some of the language that was in the text. For example, if the text contains some MODAL AUXILIARY VERBS →8, we can ask the students to look at how they are used and practise saying or writing sentences using them.
- We can use the content of the text as the springboard for some new language presentation. For example, if the text tells a story, we can retell the story imagining what *would have happened if* … to introduce the THIRD CONDITIONAL →2. We can use a text about an animal or animals as the start of a longer lesson in which we teach vocabulary about animals.
- We can MINE →46 a text for any language that is interesting, such as how ADVERBS →11 or PREPOSITIONAL PHRASES →16 are used in it.

57

Teaching writing 1

The importance of accuracy

When we make mistakes in spoken English, we can correct ourselves quickly – or say the same thing in a different way. But when we write, we need to be more ACCURATE. People don't tolerate mistakes in writing as generously as they do spoken errors.

Teaching the 'nuts and bolts' of writing

Students need to learn a range of technical skills if they are to write successfully.

- Although many people use COMPUTERS or MOBILE DEVICES →86 for written communication, there are still many occasions when we use handwriting in English.
- Some students find English script difficult to master, especially if the way people write in their language (the symbols that they use) is very different from English. We will need to give them training in letter formation by using specially lined paper to help them imitate typical handwriting.

  We can also give them gradually disappearing letters to teach them the pen strokes for each letter.

  This kind of training is vital because readers sometimes judge people on the basis of what their writing looks like.

- Students need to learn when to use PUNCTUATION features in writing →31. We can explain the rules and we can give them unpunctuated paragraphs like this and ask them to put in capital letters, FULL STOPS (PERIODS), COMMAS and INVERTED COMMAS (QUOTATION MARKS):

> he remembered the day they had met in a café in new york after five minutes he said you're the one for me and she laughed that was twenty-five years ago

The process of writing

When we write in our first language, we usually think about what we are going to say before we do it, and we often check what we have written to see if it looks OK before we put the paper or card in the envelope or we click on *Send* on the computer. This is part of the WRITING PROCESS.

- In the PLANNING STAGE we think about what we want to write and, where appropriate, make notes. We also think about the AUDIENCE we are writing for →34.
- We can then start the first DRAFT (the first attempt) of what we want to write.

- We REVIEW what we have drafted and EDIT it before writing the final version.
- The writing process does not go in only one direction, however. For example, sometimes we plan what we are going to write, but after we have drafted it we go back and plan all over again. Sometimes at the last moment (the final version) we rethink what we have written and go back to the planning or the editing stage. The writing process is a bit like a wheel, in other words, and we tend to go round it and across it in many directions.

The writing process

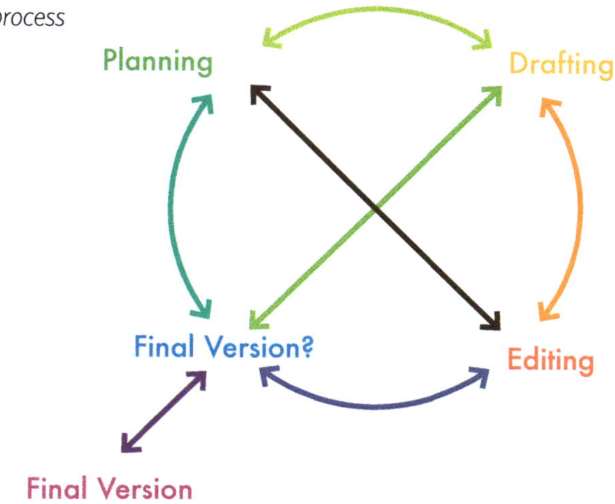

- Sometimes (but not often) we have a thought, and with almost no planning we write a TWEET →32 or an EMAIL (for example) and send it without reviewing or editing it. As a result, our writing may have spelling and/or typing mistakes and if we had thought longer, we probably wouldn't have sent it! Reviewing and editing are almost always a good idea.
- We can encourage our students to think carefully about writing by having them plan what they are going to say. They can discuss ideas in BUZZ GROUPS →52. They can research ideas on the INTERNET or in the school library and make notes either on paper or on the screen.
- We can encourage the students to review and edit what they have written before they produce a final version. This is important for exam training. Students need to check through their answers before they hand them in.
- We can give the students a checklist to use while they are reviewing their work. For example, if they are writing emails, we might give them the following questions:

Checklist

1 What have you put in the subject line? Does it give a clear idea about the content of your message?
2 How do you greet the person you are writing to? Is it appropriate (not too informal or formal, for example)?
3 Have you made your message clear? Have you separated parts of your message into paragraphs? Why? Why not?
4 Have you used correct punctuation? Do you think it is necessary for this email?
5 How do you sign off? Is it appropriate for the person you are writing to?

- When the students have written a first draft, we can look at their work and RESPOND →72 to what they have done, making suggestions about the CONTENT, their use of English and whether or not their writing is COHERENT →34. We can become a kind of EDITOR →65.
- We can ask the students to look at each other's work and to make suggestions. This kind of PEER REVIEW only works when the students trust each other. We will have to watch carefully to make sure that everyone is happy with the idea.

58

Teaching writing 2

Encouraging writing

Many students don't enjoy writing very much and so our task is to make them comfortable and enthusiastic about it.

Spontaneous writing

We can ask our students to write things instantly (without worrying too much).

- We can say *Write down three things you want to do before you are 35* or *Write down one thing you like about learning English and one thing you don't like about it.*
- We can ask the students to write an 'instant sentence' about someone in the class (or someone well known). The students pass their sentences round the class. Can they identify the people in the sentences?
- We can give them a simple sentence, such as *A man was playing the guitar*. They have to expand the sentence using as many adjectives, clauses, etc. as they can, but the sentence still has to make sense →17.
- We can give students in PAIRS →67 a time limit. Student A suggests ideas and Student B has to write as quickly as possible. Then it is Student B's turn to write. They correct each other's work.

Students writing together

There are a number of activities which provoke COLLABORATIVE WRITING.

- We can get the students to write a sentence and pass it on to another student, folding the paper first so that the next student cannot see what the person before them has written. In the example below, Student A completes the first blank (e.g. *Peter*) and hands the folded piece of paper to Student B who writes, for example, *Sally*. The paper now goes to Student C who has to write where they met, for example *at the swimming pool*. The paper then goes to the next student to continue the story. When the activity is finished, the paper is straightened out and the students can see the whole story.

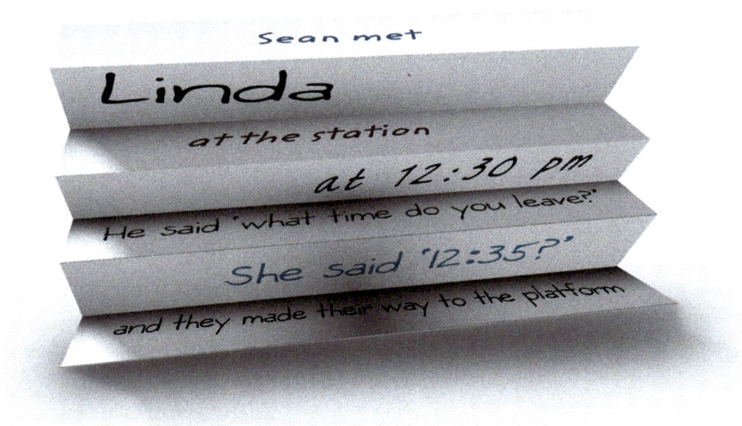

- The students sit in a STORY CIRCLE and each has a blank sheet of paper. We dictate a sentence, such as *When he opened his eyes that morning, he did not know where he was.* We then ask them to write the next sentence in the story. When they have written the sentence, they all pass their papers (in the same direction) to the person next to them. Each student now writes a sentence for the story they have in front of them (which is not the one they started out with). For each new sentence, they pass the papers to the person next to them again. When the papers get back to the original writers, they have to write a conclusion.

- The students work in groups. We give them a controversial sentence, such as *Everyone likes football*. The groups have to rewrite the sentence so that everyone in the group agrees with it.
- We can get the students to write EMAILS to each other. If they don't have access to a computer, we can give them sheets of paper which look like email windows.
- We can get the students to TEXT each other (using their mobile phones) to arrange a meeting.
- The students can complete a *wiki story* using an online WIKI →87. Each student adds a sentence to the original story (with, perhaps, a different colour for each). They can do this activity on the board, too (perhaps in teams): one by one the students have to write a story, sentence by sentence.
- The students have to compose a story using social media such as TWITTER, where they can only use a certain number of characters each time.
- We can give the students the first and last lines of a story. In groups, they have to write what comes between them.
- Students do a RUNNING DICTATION or a SHOUTED DICTATION →48.

Pictures and writing

- We can give the students a series of holiday postcard PICTURES. They have to write imaginary messages, such as *Today the snow was really beautiful. I went down three red slopes and one black one*. The other students have to guess which postcard they are writing about.
- We give the students famous portraits. They have to write a diary entry for each one. They can also write letters or emails from one portrait to another.
- We give the students pictures. In pairs or groups, they write a story to connect them.

Music and writing

There are various activities which use MUSIC (without words) to stimulate writing.

- We can play music and ask the students to write down what they think the composer is describing.
- We can play any music which has a strong feel (sad, happy, dance-like, etc.) and ask the students to write words that come into their minds while they hear it.
- We can tell the students that they have to write a description of a scene in a movie. They should listen to a piece of music and then write directions, such as *Night. A street. It is raining …*
- We can dictate a sentence to the students, such as *As he came round the corner he saw her*. We tell them that this is the first line of a story. They have to continue the story when we play them some music. Perhaps we play them some really sad music. We then dictate the same sentence again and they have to write a new story, but this time the music is cheerful. The students then swap papers and read out one of the stories in front of them. The rest of the class have to guess which piece of music it was.

We discuss music in more detail in →64.

Many teachers use POETRY ACTIVITIES to engage their students in creative writing. We look at poetry in →63.

59 Teaching writing 3

Producing a finished product

We will involve our students in an extended WRITING PROCESS →57 if they are going to produce something which they are going to display in public or put in their portfolios – or which is going to be graded.

Preparing for writing

Before we ask our students to do any substantial writing, we need to encourage them to start planning what they are going to write.

- Students can get into BUZZ GROUPS →52 to discuss the topics they have chosen and think of any words and ideas that might be involved.
- We can put a SPIDERGRAM or WORD MAP →22 on the board. The students can come up and extend the diagram with new ideas.
- We can ask the students to group their ideas in a logical sequence.
- We can give them a checklist to think about as they start (and continue) to write and review their work.

From analysis to production

- We can demonstrate COHERENCE and COHESION →34 by giving the students paragraphs and sentences in the wrong order. They have to reorder them and discuss why they made their choices.
- If we want our students to write within a certain GENRE →32 or type of writing, we will get them to start by doing GENRE ANALYSIS. This means looking at various examples of the kind of writing they are going to do to see how the genre is normally written. For example, if we want INTERMEDIATE or UPPER-INTERMEDIATE →41 students to write their own online newspaper article, we might ask them to look at a number of online texts in order to answer questions like the following:

1. What is the audience for the article? In other words, who do the writers expect will read it?
2. Who wrote the article?
3. How many headlines are there?
4. What language is used in the headlines? What tenses are used? What language (if any) is left out?
5. How many paragraphs are there in the text?
6. What content is in the first paragraph?
7. What is the content of the other paragraphs?
8. What verb tenses are used in the article?
9. How does the article end?

Portfolio writing

We can ask our students to keep a PORTFOLIO (a collection) of their writing. At the end of a semester or a year we (and they) can use this as part of their FINAL ASSESSMENT →88.

- We can give the students examples as models for their own writing. For example, we can show lower-level teenage students a text like the one on page 133. The students now have to write about their own friends, saying where they live, where their parents are from, what languages they speak, how long they have known their friends and what they do together.

- Portfolios can also contain the students' POETRY →63, emails, letters, cards and any other kind of writing they wish to do. They can keep their work in folders or online if they are using an ONLINE LEARNING PLATFORM.

Writing journals

We can encourage our students to write JOURNALS in which they talk about the things that interest them most.

- It is a good idea to encourage students to write journals because they can use them to reflect on what they are learning – and the more writing they do the better.
- Journals are a good place for teacher–student dialogue. We can find out what our students are thinking, and encourage them to use writing for real communication.
- When we respond to journals, we should always focus on the content of what the students write before correcting mistakes. We can ask the students if they want us to correct their mistakes or not.
- We can give class time for our students to write their journals. This will encourage them to continue writing.
- We cannot respond to all our students' journals all the time. There are not enough hours in the day (or week) for that! We can look at different students' work over a period of time, making sure that we read and respond to every student's work during that period.

Blogs, wikis and contacts

- We can get our students to write BLOGS →87. They can do this either on an INTRANET (which is only viewable by the class or the school) or online (where everyone can see it).
- We can tell them how often they should post a message on their blog (perhaps once a week). We can set a time limit of, say, a month or two months for them to keep blogging. If we don't do this, they may well lose interest.
- We will encourage our students to comment on each other's BLOG POSTS.
- We can get the students to build up a WIKI with their writings, pictures, audio or video clips. We discuss blogs, wikis and other ways of sharing information in →87.
- Students can exchange information with students in other countries. They can do this via EMAIL or on blog sites using WEB 2.0 tools such as *Eduglogster* and *Wallwisher* →87.

We discuss writing for HOMEWORK in →76.

60

Teaching listening 1

The importance of listening

For many people, speaking on the telephone is one of the scariest things to do in a foreign language because, when you can't see the speaker, you just have to rely on what you hear. In a face-to-face conversation we get clues from the speaker's facial expressions, gestures, etc., but when all we have is the sound of the voice, these clues aren't there to help us.

Many students feel the same about listening in classrooms! But listening is a vital skill in any language, and in language learning it also helps students ACQUIRE (and LEARN) →35 WORDS, LANGUAGE CHUNKS, GRAMMAR and PRONUNCIATION.

Types of listening

Most of the listening that students do happens when their teacher is talking. This kind of COMPREHENSIBLE INPUT →35 is very useful for language ACQUISITION. However, there are two other main sources of listening input.

- We use RECORDED LISTENING when we want our students to hear dialogues and monologues from COURSEBOOKS →81, news broadcasts, radio programmes, PODCASTS, phone messages, film announcements, etc.
- Recorded listening TRACKS are great for letting students hear different voices and different accents. They are extremely useful because students can listen to them again and again – and they will always hear the same thing.
- Recorded listening gives students potential access to the whole English-speaking world.
- Although we hear recorded listening in real life (in phone messages, automated information on company phones, on the radio, etc.), it sometimes seems unnatural to have a class of 30 people all listening to the same audio track at the same time, especially since speaker–listener interaction is not possible.
- We use LIVE LISTENING when a speaker (the teacher or some other visitor to the classroom) is in the same room as the students.
- Live listening includes GENRES →32 such as lectures, conversations between two teachers (which the students watch and listen to), face-to-face interviews, readings from books, poetry, drama, etc.
- Live listening works because the students can see who is talking, observe their body language and their facial expressions and, sometimes, interact with the speakers. When the speakers are in front of other people, they often speak differently from the way they speak in front of a microphone.
- Live listening is more likely to expose students to speech phenomena such as hesitations, repetitions, interruptions, etc. than some recorded listening does (especially in some COURSEBOOK DIALOGUES). It is important for students to experience speech phenomena.
- When students listen to audio tracks (or a live speaker) in the classroom – and do activities and exercises – we call this INTENSIVE LISTENING. When they listen outside the classroom, often by themselves and for pleasure, we call this EXTENSIVE LISTENING.

Audio devices and who uses them

A wide range of AUDIO DEVICES can be used for recorded listening.

- In some classrooms around the world teachers still use cassette recorders. These are extremely versatile, especially if they have counters, which can help you find where you are on the cassette. *Rewind*, *fast forward*, *play* and *stop* are easy to use. However, cassette machines are rapidly disappearing as newer devices take their place.
- Many teachers use CD and DVD players. These are easy to use when they have track numbers, but can sometimes be more difficult (than cassette recorders) for fast forwarding and rewinding within a track.
- Many teachers play audio (or VIDEO →62) from computers or the interactive whiteboard (IWB) →85. This is ideal since by using *sliders* with a mouse, a pen or your finger it is easy to find your place on the track or control the volume.
- Students can listen to recorded audio in LANGUAGE LABORATORIES. Sometimes the whole class listens to the same thing at the same time, but at other times we can have different students listen to different audio tracks. Language laboratories are now much less common than they once were.
- Many students have their own listening devices. These can be used for INDIVIDUAL WORK →67 in lessons. The students can all download the same track, or listen to different tracks for JIGSAW LISTENING (where each student listens to part of a text so that, by sharing what they have heard, they can reconstruct a story or a report).
- When we use audio devices it is vitally important to try them out before we go into class so that we know how to find the track we are looking for and so that we don't waste time and look unprofessional.
- Although teachers usually control the audio device, we can sometimes let our students be the controllers, too.
- We can let the students become 'remote controllers'. They can tell a live speaker to *stop*, *pause*, *rewind* or *fast forward*.

How often should students listen?

There is disagreement, sometimes, about how many times students should listen to the same thing, whether recorded audio or live listening.

- In real life, students often only listen to something once and they need to practise that skill. We can make sure that our students are given 'one-listening' tasks to help them get used to this. These are often GIST (LISTENING FOR GENERAL UNDERSTANDING) or SCANNING-type tasks (listening for specific information) →54.
- A language class is not, however, like the outside-the-class real world. In intensive listening, we want to give our students chances to listen more than once so that they get the maximum benefit from what they are hearing. When they listen for the second or third time, they can focus on different things, such as sounds, intonation or stress or the way speakers use certain words or grammar.

61

Teaching listening 2

Prediction

There is almost no limit to what can be done with RECORDED AUDIO or LIVE LISTENING →60. However, it is important to give the students a chance to PREDICT what they are going to hear. This will allow them to get ready and to remember what they already know about the topic and the listening genre that is coming. We call this knowledge SCHEMATA.

Before listening

There are many things that we can do before the students actually listen to the speaker or the audio track:

- The students can look at the questions which accompany an audio recording (or a live listening session). They have to predict what the answers will be.
- The students see a picture or pictures related to the SITUATION or topic of the listening and they have to predict what they will hear.
- We can give the students words or phrases from the audio – perhaps in the lesson before – and ask them to guess what it will be about.
- We can give the students a form, telephone message pad or chart which they are going to fill in when they listen to the audio. They use this to predict what kind of information they will hear on the audio before they listen to it.
- If we can bring a visitor to the lesson to speak to the students, we can tell the students the general TOPIC that the visitor is going to talk about. They then have to think of questions to ask the visitor.
- The students are told the topic they are going to hear about. They have to do some research (or form BUZZ GROUPS →52) about the topic. They can say what they know about the topic, what they think they know, and what they would like to know.
- We can play a short extract from the audio recording and ask the students to tell us anything they heard – and what they think about the speaker(s). They can predict what is coming next.

- We can play the whole recording but tell the students not to listen for meaning. Instead, we ask them to tell us about any other information they have understood: the location, relationships between the speakers, etc. Using this, they predict the content of what they will hear when they listen for a second time.
- Should we PRE-TEACH VOCABULARY before the students listen? If we don't, there is a chance that they will not understand enough. If we do, however, they may concentrate too much on the words we have taught and so not hear all the other words that are rushing past. A sensible compromise is to pre-teach only that vocabulary which is absolutely necessary for the topic – or vocabulary which is impossible to guess from the context.

Listening tasks

- If we are organising live listening, we can teach the students to be good listeners. They do this by showing their agreement or disagreement, and by asking questions when something is not clear.
- We can give the students a live listening lecture. Every minute or two we can stop and let pairs or groups of students reconstruct what we have said before moving on to the next stage of our talk.
- Each student can be given a bingo card with, say, 12 words from a listening text on it. Each card has different words. The students cross out their words when they hear them. Who crosses out all their words first?
- We can choose a text to read to the class. We take some (not all) the words from the text and arrange them in random order (or alphabetically) on the board. Each student then has to choose one of the words, whichever one they like. They can talk to their neighbour to make sure that they haven't both chosen the same one. We then divide the class into two teams and get all the students to stand up. We read the text aloud and each student can only sit down when they hear their word. Which team sits down first? DVD12
- We can ask different students to read different texts aloud (or tell different stories) all at the same time. It will be very noisy! Other students have to try to listen to just one of the speakers and write down what they say. How much can they hear and understand? This SHOUTED DICTATION →48 is a way of making students feel less anxious about listening in general DVD16.
- We can play an audio track (or tell a story), but keep stopping. Each time, the students have to say what they think is going to happen next. Then we continue and they see if their predictions are right.
- The students can listen to a series of vox pop (mini) interviews on a topic, such as favourite hobbies. They have to match the speakers to different hobbies (football, reading books, playing chess, going to the cinema, playing music, etc.).
- The students listen to a NEWS BROADCAST and have to list the five topics they hear.
- The students listen to a picture description and have to choose which one of four pictures is being talked about.
- The students listen and put a sequence of pictures in the right order.
- The students listen to an audio track and identify some differences between what they hear and a written version of the same content.
- The students listen to phone messages. They have to fill in phone message pads.
- The students listen to an interview or a conversation and have to fill in a form, chart or graph with the information they hear.

62

Teaching listening 3

Listening again

When the students have listened to a live speaker or an audio recording for the first time, we can ask them to listen again and do a variety of tasks.

- We can ask them to listen again to try to identify more detailed information, such as names, facts, numbers, times and dates.
- We can ask them to listen again and transfer the information in the audio recording (or what a live speaker has told them) to a different genre. For example, if they hear a story, they have to rewrite it as a newspaper article.
- When the students hear a NEWS BROADCAST or a story, we can ask them to retell it as if they were one of the people in it.
- Students can act out the roles of people from the original audio recording.
- Students have to retell what they have just heard, making one (or more) mistake(s). Can their colleagues find the mistake(s)?
- Like real filmmakers, the students have to draw/design STORYBOARDS showing the scene and the camera angle for the speakers they have just heard. They film the scene with video cameras or their mobile phones →87.

Listening again: language matters

We can also ask students to listen (again) in order to study language.

- Students are given a section of the written TRANSCRIPT with blanks in it. They have to complete the blanks and then listen again to check if they were correct.
- We give the students a WORKSHEET with excerpts from the listening. They do a language exercise. They then have to use the language in sentences of their own.
- The students look at a written transcript of what they have just heard. They rewrite a section so that any grammatical MISTAKES, hesitations and other speech phenomena are cleaned up. With the teacher, they discuss the differences between speaking and writing →31.
- The teacher and the students MINE →46 the listening for interesting language.
- When the students have listened to a dialogue, the teacher displays it on the BOARD. The students read it aloud. Then the teacher starts to remove words and phrases one by one. Each time, the students have to continue speaking the dialogue. By the end of this DISAPPEARING DIALOGUE activity, they can do the whole thing from memory.

Extensive listening

If students really want to improve their English (especially their PRONUNCIATION →23–29 and speaking →51–53), they should listen to as much spoken English as possible.

- EXTENSIVE LISTENING means listening for pleasure, usually outside the classroom. Most audio material can be heard on CDs, MP3 players or online via COMPUTERS and MOBILE DEVICES.
- Extensive listening is most successful if the students choose what TOPICS they want to listen to and the level they want to listen (or feel comfortable listening) at.
- We can encourage our students to listen extensively by talking about the advantages of listening in this way and showing them where they can find material.
- We can ask our students to keep a record of what they have listened to, including language that they have found interesting or puzzling. We can ask them to recommend good listening material to other members of the class.
- Students can download PODCASTS →87 from English-language-learning sites (we can help them find sites like these with a simple internet search), from news organisations, radio programmes and any other podcast outlet.
- Students can listen to English-speaking radio online.
- Students can access the wide range of freely available VIDEO CLIPS on sites such as *YouTube*, *Vimeo* and *Videojug*.
- Students can listen to audio recordings of books, including GRADED READERS →54, and COURSEBOOK audio material (although some teachers prefer them not to do this before the lesson because it spoils the 'surprise' of coursebook-based lessons).

Using video

VIDEO is an extremely useful resource for listening, especially now that we can share FILM CLIPS on sites such as *YouTube* and *Vimeo*. But students can also watch video clips from DVDS, COMPUTERS or MOBILE DEVICES and IWBS, for example →85.

- We can play the students a video clip and then stop it so that they have to guess what happens next. They can do this in PAIRS or GROUPS. When they have discussed their predictions, we show them the end of the video.
- If we are using a DVD, we can fast forward a video clip. Students then discuss what they have seen and try to work out what happened and what the people in the video said. Then we play the video clip at normal speed.
- We can play a video clip with the sound turned down. The students have to guess what the people are saying and/or what background sounds they will hear.
- We can play a video clip so that the students hear the sound but don't see the picture. They have to say where the speakers/participants are and what is going on.
- We can let the students watch a video clip without sound. They do this two or three times. Then they have to invent their own conversations and speak along with the people in the video clip. 'Doubling' like this can be very funny.
- Students are given a list of the VERBS →4 (or NOUNS →12, etc.) from a video clip. They have to watch the clip and put them in the right order.
- After the students have watched a video clip for the first or second time, we can give them the transcript (if it is short enough) with BLANKS. They have to try to FILL IN the blanks before they watch again.

63 Using poetry

Choosing the right poems

Because poems can express big ideas and stories in just a few lines, they can be used for comprehension, writing and language work. However, we have to choose the poems we use very carefully because some poetry is extremely complex and culture-bound. We need to find short, clear poetry at the right level for our students.

Predicting poetry

As with a lot of reading, we can get our students to make PREDICTIONS about poems they are going to read or hear.

- We can give the students the title of a poem (or poems) and ask them to guess some of the words that might be in it.
- We can give them some or all of the words from the poem – perhaps in a WORDLE like the one below. The students have to guess what the poem is about.

- We can give the students words from a (short) poem. They have to try to use them to write their own poem. They then compare their attempts with the original.

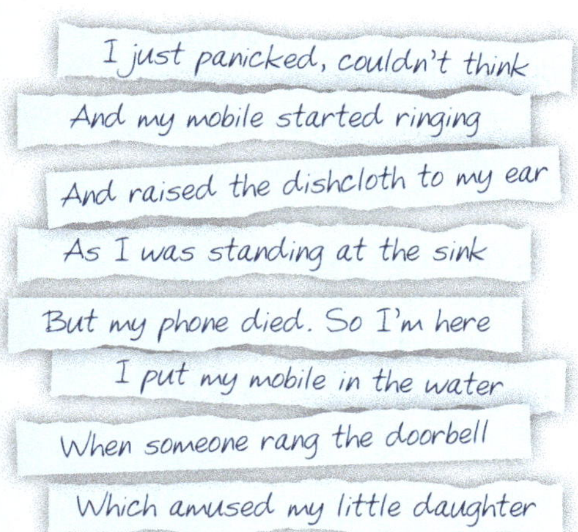

Poetry and language

- We can use POETRY REORDERING ACTIVITIES like the one shown below. For this, we put students in GROUPS of eight. Each student is given a line of poetry on a STRIP OF PAPER. They can speak their line, but they must not show it to anyone else. They have to put the lines in the right order to make a poem called *Buying a new phone* DVD7.

  We will need to go round the groups helping them, where necessary.
- Using a COMPUTER with a DATA PROJECTOR, or an OVERHEAD PROJECTOR (OHP), we can reveal (and speak at the same time) the lines of a poem with a large number of BLANKS (spaces where words should be). We use a nonsense word or sound for the blanks. The students have to try to guess the missing words. They will find this very difficult! Next we reveal and read the poem again, but this time the students can see the first letter of each blanked word. When we read the poem for the third time, they can see the first two letters of each blanked word, and so on. This is a very good activity for making students search their own mental lexicon (their store of words).
- The students study a poem and think about how they would speak it. We give them a chance to MUMBLE →47 the poem to themselves. We then read the poem or play a recording of it (which we can make before the lesson if we have to). The students read as they listen and try to work out where the pauses are, what words are stressed →26, etc. They mumble the poem again. We can then use SHADOW SPEAKING (they speak along with the recording). Finally, after more mumbling, the students will be able to speak the poem well.

Poetry and meaning

- We can give the students different poems. Without showing each other their poems, they have to discuss the similarities and difference between them. This is a kind of INFORMATION-GAP activity →50.
- We can ask the students to write a word, phrase or sentence saying what a poem means to them (they can write 'nothing' if that's how they feel). They do this in silence. They then go round the classroom (still in silence) reading each other's sentences.
- We can ask the students to discuss who they would like to read a poem to and why.

Writing poems

We don't expect our students to be great poets (though some of them may be!). But we can use POETRY FRAMES and shapes to help them produce something enjoyable.

For all poetry-writing activities it is important that the students have a chance to BRAINSTORM ideas and vocabulary first, perhaps in BUZZ GROUPS →52. We cannot expect them to be instantly creative.

- We can get our students to fill in frames which make simple poem-like verses. For example, we can choose any topic (such as food, music, clothes, sports). They have to fill in the following frames:

I like ...
I like ...
I like ...
But I don't like ... because ...
How could anyone like ...?

- We can ask the students to write acrostic poems. They write a vertical word on the left-hand side of the page. Each line of the poem then starts with a letter of the word. For example:

Liking English is not
Easy because grammar is
Always difficult but it's
Really good fun and I will
Never stop trying to speak it well

- We can ask more advanced students to write SPINE POEMS. They take titles from the spines of books (for example *The Old Man and the Sea*, *War and Peace*, *The Girl with the Dragon Tattoo*). They write the words vertically down the page and then write poems similar to acrostic poems, with each line beginning with one word from the title.
- We can have the students write HAIKU →32.
- We can take one copy of a poem to the lesson and use it for a RUNNING DICTATION. We put the poem on a desk at the front of the classroom. The students are in small groups. One representative from each group comes up to the desk and reads (and remembers) the first line. They go back to their group and dictate it. Then another student comes up to the desk and does the same for the second line. For each line, new students come up to the desk to take their lines back and dictate them. Which group finishes the poem first?

64

Using music and drama

Using songs and music

Many (but not all) students love working with English-language SONGS. They provide memorable and engaging ways of working with the language.

- We can give the students words from a song and ask them to predict what the song is going to be about.
- We give the students the jumbled lines of a song. They have to reassemble the lines in the correct order. They listen to the song to check that they have done this correctly. This is similar to poetry reordering →63.
- We give the students the lyrics of a song. The last word of each line is missing. We give them the words and they try to put them in the right place, using meaning and rhyme to help them.
- We give the students the jumbled verses of a song. They have to listen to the song and put them in the right order.
- If we type a grammar point such as *If I had* or *I should have* or *I wish I'd* and then *lyrics* into *Google* (or another search engine) we can find a wide range of songs with that specific piece of grammar or lexical chunk.
- Each student chooses a song that they like. They explain the meaning to the rest of the class and play the song.
- The students listen to a song (which we hope they have not heard before) by a singer-songwriter. They have to decide whether to tell the artist either a) Write more songs – you've got real talent, b) If you must sing, sing other people's songs, or c) If you must sing and play, do it in private – why should other people suffer?

We discuss using songs with YOUNG LEARNERS in →94.

Talking about music and songs

We can use songs and other types of MUSIC in many different ways.

- We can ask the students to tell the class about a song that is really important to them and why it is so special. This is a very good activity for getting classes of adults and young adults to introduce themselves to each other at the beginning of a course.
- Students discuss which five songs they would take to a desert island or a trip to the moon and why.

- We can ask adults and young adults to discuss their 'inheritance tracks': the music they have inherited from their parents/during their childhood. We can then ask what music they would like to pass on to their children.
- The students listen to a song and discuss what kind of a video they would make to accompany it and why. They can do this in pairs or groups.
- We can show the students a music video without the sound. They have to guess what the song will be.
- We can play excerpts of music. The students have to say what colour the music is, what mood it is describing, what temperature it is (boiling hot or freezing cold, for example), where they would like to hear it and who they would like to hear it with.
- We can show a FILM CLIP without any sound. The students have to guess what music goes with the film clip. They then watch the clip with sound to see if they were correct.
- We can play the students some music from a film. They have to guess what kind of SCENE it might be describing. They then watch the scene to check if they were right.

Being careful with music

We can use music to motivate and engage students, but not all students love music – or singing.

- We should keep a record of who is engaged (or not engaged) by the music we bring to class.
- We can discuss music with the students and find out who likes it and who doesn't.
- We can ask our students to bring their own music to class. The other students can say if they like it or not.
- We should ask our students if they would like us to play background music, while they are working in groups, for example, rather than just making the decision ourselves.

Using drama

We can use DRAMA for a number of different purposes.

- After the students have read and understood a drama extract or short PLAY, the teacher can discuss it with them. Which words and phrases should be STRESSED →26, for example? They practise and then act out the scene.
- The students read a scene (or extract) from a play. They have to write in their own stage directions, including ADVERBS OF MANNER →11 (such as *angrily*, *in a strange voice*, etc.). When they practise (and then perform) the scene, they have to speak and act in the way that the adverbs say.
- The students read a PLAY EXTRACT. They have to tell someone else what happened.
- They read a play extract and each student chooses to be a character from the play. The class INTERVIEWS that character and asks them how they are feeling, why they did what they did, what they are going to do next, etc.
- The students write the scene that occurs immediately before a play or after it ends.
- The class chooses a location (such as *a street*) and an event (such as *someone gets knocked off their bicycle*) and the participants (such as *the cyclist*, *a pedestrian*, *the people watching*, *a policeman*, *first aiders*, etc.). They discuss what each person would do and say. They then write the scene and act it out.
- In groups, the students act out a story in MIME (without using any words). The other students have to guess the story.
- In CHARADES, students have to act out the title of a book, play or film without using words. The others have to guess what it is.

Image courtesy of Asociación Peruano Británica Lima, Peru

Section D: Managing learning and teaching

Whatever we are teaching, the way that we manage the classroom is of vital importance. In a well-managed classroom, students can learn and they are likely to be engaged. In a badly-managed classroom, this is not nearly so easy for them.

In this section we consider pairwork and groupwork and how to use them, as well as looking at using the whole class or having the students work as individuals.

We discuss the issue of students and teachers talking in lessons. Who, for example, should do most of the talking, and if and when teachers talk, what kind of talking should they do? (Note: there is an appendix of teacher classroom language on pages 247–249.)

Teachers need to be sure that their students have understood instructions and meanings and so there is a unit on this. We also need to know what to do at the beginning of a lesson or if a student is late, for example.

We especially need to know how to prevent discipline problems, and what to do when they happen.

One of the most sensitive areas for learners and teachers is correction – how and when to do it. In this section there are four units on giving feedback and on offering appropriate and effective correction.

We also discuss the use (or non-use) of our students' home language (L1) – and we discuss ways of making homework 'work' for teachers and students.

65

Teacher roles

A variety of roles

When we think of people who have taught us, we can, perhaps, remember times when they stood at the front of the class and told us things; there may have been times when we were working in groups and they came to help us; or perhaps sometimes we were working on our own and the teacher didn't seem to be doing very much at all. In each case they were fulfilling one or more of the different ROLES OF THE TEACHER.

- Teachers are at all times FACILITATORS of learning. This means that we must always do everything we can to make learning happen smoothly and appropriately for the learners – making learning possible, but without making it too easy.
- TRANSMISSION TEACHING (when we are giving the students information or explaining things) is only one way for students to learn things. We must make sure that that we also play many other roles in the classroom.
- We need to be CONTROLLERS when we are explaining things, taking the CLASS REGISTER or telling the students what to do. This often involves standing at the front of the class and being very clear.
- When we are acting as ORGANISERS in order to set up and start an activity, we should 1) ENGAGE the students in the task, 2) give our INSTRUCTIONS clearly and where possible demonstrate the activity, 3) start the activity and 4) organise FEEDBACK →72. We look at instructions in detail in →69.
- We often act as EVIDENCE GATHERERS. When students are doing a groupwork activity, for example, we will want to MONITOR and make notes (gather evidence) of what they say or do so that we can provide feedback later. We will check that the students know what to do and are doing the right thing.
- We often act as PROMPTERS, pushing students to make new sentences and encouraging them to speak when they are reluctant. We can offer words and phrases to help them say what they want to say. However, we must be careful not to intervene too much if they are trying to learn how to communicate on their own.
- We need to act as a RESOURCE for our students. They can ask us questions about things they don't understand. When they are involved in individual or groupwork activities, we should be available to help them and answer their questions. However, we should remember that no teacher knows everything about the English language and so we also need to be able to tell them where they can find the answers to their questions (in a GRAMMAR BOOK, a COURSEBOOK, a DICTIONARY, etc.).
- We often act as FEEDBACK PROVIDERS when we CORRECT students' mistakes, make a comment on what they have said or praise their efforts. Feedback is discussed in →72.
- We often act as a kind of EDITOR, for example, when the students are writing in English or preparing an ORAL PRESENTATION. This means responding to what they have written (or what they plan to write or say) with comments, questions and suggestions. We should try not to insist on what they should do, but instead try to make them think more carefully about what they want to achieve.
- We can act as TUTORS to individual students. This means giving them personal advice and information about English and going through their work with them. We can correct or edit their work – or make suggestions about what they can do. It is helpful to organise tutorial sessions while the rest of the class is working on some other task. If we can tutor a few individual students in a lesson, we can, over a period of time, see all of them individually.
- We should remember, too, that one of the teacher's most important jobs is COMPREHENSIBLE INPUT PROVIDER to the students, speaking to them in ways that will help their language acquisition →35.

What *scaffolding* means

Many people use the term **SCAFFOLDING** to describe the role of the teacher. Scaffolding derives from the work of Jerome Bruner, amongst others. It means supporting the students, providing the framework to hang their knowledge on, just as we use scaffolding to support a structure that is being built.

People who talk about scaffolding say it is like a music teacher guiding a child's arm as they move the violin bow from side to side until the child can make the correct moment alone – or like parents helping their children to ride bicycles: they hold on until the child can keep upright on their own, but even then they stay close to provide emotional support until the child is truly independent.

Although both examples concentrate on teaching *children* to do things, scaffolding is, perhaps, a good **METAPHOR** for supporting students at any age.

We discuss scaffolding for **YOUNG LEARNERS** in →91.

The teacher's role, the teacher's place

Because we have many different roles in a classroom, we tend to move around quite a lot. For example, if we are transmitting information or taking the register, we will often be at the front of the class. But if we are gathering evidence, we may want to move round the class listening to (and observing) the different groups at work.

- Sometimes we will act as a prompter, resource and feedback provider while working with just one pair of students.
- Sometimes we will set up a desk at the side of the class so that we can tutor individual students.
- We need to think of the best place to be for the different roles we play.

66

Teachers and students

Establishing rapport

One of the most important elements of a successful lesson is the relationship between the teacher and the students. If this relationship goes wrong, learning is difficult because everyone is preoccupied with emotions like nervousness, mistrust, anger or boredom. When the relationship is satisfactory, everyone can concentrate on the lesson, rather than their negative feelings.

We call the relationship between teacher and students RAPPORT (which is very important for MOTIVATION →43). Although it is difficult to say exactly how to create good rapport (because so much depends on the individual personalities in a classroom), we do know how to *help* it flourish.

The teacher in the classroom

- Some teachers are loud and extrovert; some are quiet and shy. Some teachers like to command the class; some prefer to take a back seat. As teachers, in other words, we are just as varied as any other human beings.
- However, whatever our personality, we are always performing in class, playing different roles →65. So whatever our personality outside the classroom, it is how we behave in the class that matters.
- Students expect to see teachers behave like professionals. The way we walk into a lesson matters. The way we stand in class matters. The way we dress matters (though different schools – and different cultures – have different ideas of formality).
- We should think about where to stand or sit in the classroom. We should not always be at the front. We should be prepared to move around when the students are working in GROUPS, etc.
- Students like it when they can see clearly that we know what we are doing. Even if we have not prepared the lesson in detail →79, the students should have the sense that we have thought about an appropriate lesson just for them.
- We need to be able to react to what happens in the lesson. Students will respect teachers who can react quickly and appropriately →79.

Celebrating success

We should celebrate the good work that our students do.

- All students – not just the really good ones – react well to PRAISE (but they have to deserve it →72). We must find something to praise for every student. It might be a piece of HOMEWORK →76 they have done, the fact that they have tried to answer more questions than usual or even the fact that they have not interrupted as much as before.
- When we praise students for what they have done, we should then give them a GOAL (a mission) for the future. We might say: *That was a very good piece of homework. Well done* (praise). *For your next piece of homework I want you to concentrate more on punctuation – when to use commas, for example* (future goal).
- When students produce good pieces of work, we may put them up on the classroom walls or show them round to the rest of the class.
- We can collect work from all the students in the class and put it in a special 'achievement' folder.
- If students submit good work online on a learning platform such as MOODLE or BLACKBOARD, we can tell the other students about it or make it available for them to see as an example of good work (we will ask the students if they mind this – and if they would prefer it if we didn't say who did the work).
- We can encourage the students to write BLOGS and/or record short video and audio clips to upload onto public or internal WESBITES →87. However, we may want to make sure that the work is of a particularly high standard before the students put it online (where it may be seen by people outside the school/institution).

Respecting students

If we are to have good rapport with our students, the students need to feel that we respect them.

- Students need to feel that we know who they are. This is not easy when we teach six or seven groups in a week. But over time we need to try to show them that we know who they are. Students often say that a good teacher is 'someone who knows our names'.
- We can ask the students to put name cards in front of them so that we can see who they are.
- We can make notes in the CLASS REGISTER next to our students' names to help us to remember which student is which.
- We can ask the students to sit in a pre-arranged class plan. However, we have to be careful to make sure they do this, and we may want to change seating arrangements for GROUPWORK, etc. →67.
- We need to try to respond to different students differently, especially when CORRECTING them →73–75.
- We need to listen to what our students say and show them that we are interested in it. This means sometimes stopping what we are doing so that a student can complete a sentence or a thought.
- We need to show – by the way that we look at them – that we are interested in our students. We create rapport with our eyes, our expressions and our gestures just as much as with our mouths and ears!
- We should respect what our students say and do rather than being critical and sarcastic. This is especially important when we correct them →73. If we suggest that they are stupid (for example) because they are making mistakes, it will be difficult for them to feel comfortable in the classroom and rapport will suffer.
- It is especially important to treat all students the same, particularly when we have DISCIPLINE problems →71.

67 Where students sit

What classrooms look like

Traditional classrooms have straight lines of chairs or benches facing the front – where the board and the teacher are. This can be very useful for some forms of WHOLE-CLASS TEACHING, such as explaining things, demonstrating, showing pictures or films and making announcements. However, there are other possibilities, too:

- Students often have individual chairs with a fold-down surface at the side which they can write on. This is an ideal situation since they can move their chairs round if they want to work in pairs or groups. It is always a good idea to insist that they lift their chairs up when they move them, otherwise it can get very noisy.
- We can organise the class in a *horseshoe* shape, with the teacher (and the board, etc.) at the open end. This is an ideal arrangement since the students can all see each other and it is easy for the teacher to get round the horseshoe.
- Some teachers seat their students in a *circle*. This can help to create a feeling of equality and inclusiveness.
- Some teachers have their classrooms organised with groups of students seated round *individual tables*. This is appropriate for a large range of GROUPWORK tasks, but it can sometimes make teaching the whole class more difficult.
- If the chairs are not fixed, we can ask the students to move around, sometimes sitting in horseshoes, sometimes sitting alone and sometimes in groups around tables, depending on the activity we are organising. We can have them stand up and move around the room, forming pairs and groups in different corners. For many students, moving around helps them to learn and concentrate.

Working alone, working together

Students can work alone or in a number of different pairings and groupings.

- Whole-class teaching helps to build class spirit, the feeling that everyone is involved, together. It is highly suitable for lecturing, explaining things and controlling what is going on →69. However, it is less appropriate for COMMUNICATIVE SPEAKING ACTIVITIES, and many students don't like speaking or performing in front of the whole class.

- When we involve students in SOLOWORK (working on their own), we can go round the class helping them one by one. Students can work at their own pace, reading texts, doing exercises, writing compositions, planning talks, etc. Classes are often quiet when students are working on their own. However solowork does not always help to promote class harmony and it may be difficult for the teacher to get round the whole class.
- PAIRWORK greatly increases the amount of speaking time that each individual student has. It promotes LEARNER AUTONOMY (because the pair is doing the work, not the teacher). It is highly sociable and is very useful for comparing answers, creating and practising DIALOGUES, rehearsing dramatic scenes →64, etc. However, it can be very noisy and students can get distracted and go 'off-task' (they start talking about something else). Some students don't always enjoy pairwork; they prefer to work with a teacher or in groups.
- Groupwork increases individual STUDENT TALKING TIME (STT) →68. It encourages co-operation and allows the students to work on a range of tasks, such as BUZZ GROUPS, discussion →52, story-circle writing →58, story-reconstruction →53 and planning. However, some students do less work in groups than in a whole-class setting. We need to create tasks that involve MANDATORY PARTICIPATION (every single student has to take part). Some students are not very keen on groupwork and it can be very noisy.
- Good teachers use a variety of different student groupings and use them for different tasks.
- We can sometimes vary student groupings during a task as, for example, in story reconstruction.
- For pairwork and groupwork to be successful, teachers need to give good instructions and clear demonstrations →69.

Putting students into pairs and groups

We have to decide who should work with whom and there are various ways of doing this.

- We can put the students into pairs with the people sitting next to them, in front of them or behind them. This is ideal when chairs are fixed to the floor in straight lines.
- We can tell the students to get into pairs or groups and let them choose who they work with. This is very easy but it can be chaotic and it may be difficult for some students to find friends to work with.
- We can tell the students who to work with, making sure that they have to move so that they are not always working with the same people.
- We can have the students stand in inner and outer 'wheels'. They work in pairs with the person in front of them. When the outer or inner wheel moves, they work with the new person they are standing opposite.
- We may want to group students according to ability so that we can give them different tasks. We can also mix students of different abilities so that the stronger students can help the weaker ones (and learn more by doing it).
- We can group students by chance. For example, we can have them all stand in a line in order of, for example, their birthdays or the first letter of their name and then group the first five, then the next five, then the next five, etc. DVD19
- We can ask the students (privately, in confidence) who they do and don't want to work with. We can draw a SOCIOGRAM (a diagram with arrows between students who say they can work together) for this.
- When we want our students to move, it is often less confusing (and more efficient) if we make them stand first before we tell them where to move to.

68

Teacher language

Who does the talking in class?

If you walk into some classrooms, the only voice you hear is the teacher's. In a language learning lesson, however, this may not be in the best interests of the students.

- When there is too much TEACHER TALKING TIME (TTT) in class, there will not be enough STUDENT TALKING TIME (STT), even though it is the students who need speaking practice, not the teacher!
- One of the ways of maximising student talking time is to have the students working in PAIRS and GROUPS →67.
- There are, however, good reasons why some teacher talking time is a good thing. Teachers are the best source of COMPREHENSIBLE INPUT →35 (language that students more or less understand the meaning of, even though it is above their own speaking or writing level).
- If we want to be comprehensible, we need to 'rough-tune' the language we use. In other words, we will simplify what we say, use repetition, say the same thing in different ways and (sometimes) use exaggerated intonation. ROUGHLY-TUNED INPUT is not the same as baby talk (although that *is* a form of roughly-tuned input in a different context); it is, instead, a way of helping students to ACQUIRE language.
- Most of the everyday language that students hear (especially at LOWER LEVELS →41) comes from their teacher, and it is the teacher's voice that is the main model for the students' way of speaking the foreign language – at least at the beginning.

The teacher's voice

Our voices are perhaps the most important CLASSROOM RESOURCE that we have. We need to use them wisely and well.

- We need to be audible in class so that even the students at the back can hear us clearly. However, this does not mean shouting! Shouting usually sounds unattractive – and when teachers shout too often, students no longer listen (or just talk more loudly so that they can hear themselves). This is especially true when we are trying to quieten students down or regain control.

- When teachers shout, it often looks as if they are not calm, and calmness is important when there are DISCIPLINE problems →71 in a lesson.
- It is important to vary our voice in a lesson. If we always speak at the same volume, at the same speed or in the same tone of voice, then our students will get bored – and it is more difficult to play different ROLES →65 for different STAGES OF A LESSON →80.
- Teachers need to look after their voices. We should try to relax our shoulders, breathe properly (from the diaphragm, not just the upper chest), and make sure that there are moments in every lesson when we are not straining our voice.
- When teachers have throat problems, they should speak as little as possible and avoid caffeine, alcohol and very cold drinks.

Giving instructions

One of the most important things that teachers do is GIVING INSTRUCTIONS, for example when we want to put students into GROUPS →67, start an INFORMATION-GAP ACTIVITY →50 or set up a DEBATE →52 or a team GAME →49.

- When we give instructions, we should keep them as simple as possible and try to put them in a logical order.
- If we are going to give students a handout or ask them to open their books, it is a good idea to do this after we give our instructions. If we do it before, the students will look at the handout or book: they will not listen to us.
- When we have given instructions, it is often a good idea to check that the students have understood them. We can ask the students to repeat the instructions back to us. We can ask them questions, such as *What must you do first? Is it OK for you look at each other's pictures?* (for DESCRIBE AND DRAW →50), *How long have you got for this activity?*
- If the teacher and the students share a language, the teacher can ask the students to translate the instructions into their L1 →77. This will clearly indicate whether or not they have understood the instructions. However, this may break the 'English atmosphere' in the class.
- The best kind of instruction is DEMONSTRATION. If we really want our students to know how they should do an activity, we can get them to do it first with our help. One of the best ways of doing this is for the teacher to do the activity with one student (or a group of students) while the rest of the class watch. The teacher can guide the demonstration students through the activity and then everyone knows exactly what to do DVD20.

Teaching ideas: demonstrating a *Find someone who …* activity

When we use a FIND SOMEONE WHO … activity →49 for the first time, the students need to understand exactly how it works. They have to go round the class finding someone who does/has done/will do (etc.) the things on their chart – and writing down the names of people who say *yes*.

One of the best ways of doing this is to put the chart on the board (or have a student at the front of the class with their chart in their hand). The teacher can ELICIT the questions for the chart and show the students what to write – depending on the answers they get.

We look at giving instructions and checking meaning in more detail in →69.

69

Giving instructions, checking meaning

Giving instructions

There are a number of things we need to do when giving instructions.

- We should keep our instructions simple, using short simple sentences. For example, instead of saying (for a DESCRIBE AND DRAW activity →50):
  Today I would like you to get into pairs with the person next to you and when that's all sorted out, then I'll give you one of the pictures I've got here which I'll hand out pair by pair and then one of you takes the picture and he or she mustn't show the picture that I have given them to their neighbour …
  we can say:
  OK, I want you to work in pairs. You and you. You two. I'm going to give one student a picture. Do not show it to your partner … etc.
- We need to break down the instructions we want to give into manageable chunks so the students don't have to take in too much information at the same time. We discuss SCAFFOLDING in →65, 91.
- We must make our instructions logical and COHERENT →34. For example, instead of saying 1) *Don't show the picture to your partner.* 2) *I'm going to give you a picture*, we will give the instructions in the sequence 2, 1.
- Where possible, we will demonstrate the task. We can get a student or several students to help us.
- Where possible, we should let the students see us doing the activity. For example, if we want them to get involved in a DEAR reading activity →54, they should see us reading, too. If we want them to learn how to use dictionaries, they should see us using them appropriately.
- We don't have to give our instructions all at once. We can feed in new instructions as an activity progresses.

An example of instruction giving DVD21

The teacher (Conor) wants the students to do an activity called 'It says here …' →29. Notice the times that he 1) gives clear instructions, 2) marks stages of the activity and 3) DEMONSTRATES parts of the activity by reading himself so that the students can see him, and then modelling what he wants them to do.

Conor: (1) What you need to do is read the text and find your favourite sentence. OK? Cool.

(3) *Conor reads the text, too, as an example.*

Conor: (2) OK, one more minute.

Conor: (2) OK, so we've all read the text. What we're going to do now is look at the text and this time (1) I want you to choose your favourite sentence, OK, and then practise reading it. Choose your favourite sentence and then practise reading it.

(3) *Conor practises reading himself.*

Conor: (2) OK, good, so what you're going to do now is (1) read your sentence to the class and make it sound like the most exciting, crazy thing you have ever heard. For example (3) (*he exaggerates*) 'The largest number of extras in a film was for *Gandhi* 1998; 300,000 for the funeral scene' Wow! Yeah, I know, it says here. (*He reminds the students of the task*) OK?

Checking instructions

We need to be sure that the students have understood our instructions.

- We can ELICIT the first answer (or get the students to do the first part of a task) to see if they have understood what to do.
- We can demonstrate the activity and make deliberate mistakes to see if the students notice that we are getting it wrong.
- We can ask small detailed questions about the task, such as *OK, so how long have you got for this activity?* or *Can you look at your partner's picture?* DVD22.
- We can stop activities at any stage, and say things like *Can anyone tell me what Student A should be doing right now?*

Checking meaning

When teachers ask *Do you understand?* students often say *yes*, because, perhaps, they think that is the answer we want – even if the answer should be *no*! We have to find better ways of making sure they know what is going on.

- We need to include CONCEPT CHECKING when we introduce new language →44. For example, if we have presented the sentence *I managed to open the window*, we can ask the students to choose the best way of explaining it:

  a) It was easy but I did it.
  b) It was difficult but I did it.
  c) It was difficult so I couldn't do it.
  d) I tried and I did it, etc.

- We can use questions to check meaning. For example, if the students are studying the THIRD CONDITIONAL →2 with sentences like *If the alarm clock had gone off, he wouldn't have been late*, we can ask CONCEPT QUESTIONS such as *Did the alarm clock go off? What time does he usually get to work? What time did he get to work today? What was the reason?* etc.
- We can get our students to give us more examples of the concept we have introduced. For example, if we have introduced the word *vehicle*, we can ask members of the class to come up with more examples of *vehicles*. This will tell us if they understand the word.
- We can ask the students to draw PICTURES of the words we have introduced. We can also get them to act out the meanings of new words.

70

Classroom moments

How to start a lesson

- Some teachers put on music before the students start coming into class. This sets the mood for what is to follow. However, we need to remember that music may not be popular with everybody →64.
- We can make TAKING THE REGISTER/ROLL an enjoyable activity. Instead of just saying *yes* when we call their names, the students have to answer with a word in a category we give them (such as food, transport, feelings or PHRASAL VERBS →9) or with a sentence about what they did at the weekend, etc.
- Some teachers start their lessons with WARMERS to get the students in a good mood for a lesson. These are often connected with the topic of the lesson that is coming. Activities like this are also sometimes called ICEBREAKERS. They are often games or activities such as RUNNING DICTATION →48, POETRY REORDERING →63 or MATCHING activities →48, where the students have to move around or puzzle things out.
- We can go straight into the lesson by asking for a class story. We give the students the first line and they have to continue sentence-by-sentence; the storyteller changes every time we throw a ball, blow a whistle or use some other method.

When students are late

There are a number of things we can do when students arrive late.

- We can get class agreement on what to do about lateness. We can include this in an agreed CODE OF CONDUCT →71.
- We can make sure that we start lessons with an engaging activity so that the students don't want to be late. For example, we can say that at the beginning of the next lesson they can ask us about a forthcoming test and that we will answer honestly.
- We can get late students to explain why they were late and allow the class to give their excuses a 0–5 GRADE.
- We can get the rest of the class to summarise what has happened so far for the students who are late.
- We can tell late students that they will have to give their reasons for being late at the end of the lesson.
- We can say that students cannot come into the lesson if they are more than five minutes late.

We need to be sure that our actions are in line with the policy of the school and that they are not hurtful to the students involved.

We discuss DISCIPLINE in →71.

When the class needs to be quiet

We often need to be able to quieten the students down – especially after a noisy activity. When we want to end an activity, we need the students to stop what they are doing.

- When teachers shout too often, the students ignore them and the noise level increases. However, if the teacher speaks very loudly and this is unexpected, it may make the students stop what they are doing because they are curious.
- Some teachers start talking very quietly to the people at the front of the class and hope that the others will quieten down because they are all interested in what the teacher is saying.
- Some teachers raise their arms. When they do this, the students have to raise their arms, too, to show that they have seen and to indicate that they are quietening down and finishing the activity.
- Some teachers use little bells or miniature cymbals or a whistle (or some other musical noise) to indicate that an activity is over.
- Some teachers count backwards from five or ten. When they finish, the class has to be quiet and stop what they are doing.
- Some teachers stand (usually in the same place each time so the students know what is happening), watch and wait until the class has quietened down. It helps to maintain eye contact with the class when we do this.

We need to find the technique which suits us and our students best. It is important that we talk about it with the students so that they recognise the technique when we use it.

Finishing the lesson

One of the most difficult things for many teachers is to finish the lesson before the bell goes! Getting our timing right can be challenging, especially if MAGIC MOMENTS or UNFORESEEN PROBLEMS have happened →79. However, if we can, it is sensible to finish the lesson properly and end on a positive note.

- It is a good idea to summarise what has happened in the lesson and ask the students to tell you what they have learnt.
- Some teachers like to tell their students what they can look forward to in the next lesson. They want the students to be enthusiastic about coming back to class.
- Some teachers like to end their lessons by asking the students to write down (three) things that they have learnt, or (three) things that they think are the most useful for them now or will be in the future.
- Some teachers like to end lessons with an enjoyable activity such as a GAME →49, a SONG →64 or some other fun activity to send the students away in a good mood.
- Some teachers like to end with some quiet EXTENSIVE READING →54 or, especially with young learners, with a READING CIRCLE →96 where they read to their students.
- We can ask our students to write their own TEST question →89 which they can give to a colleague to take away (and bring back in the next lesson).

The most important thing, perhaps, is to vary the way we end our lessons so that our students look forward to the end of the lesson for the right reasons!

We discuss PLANNING in →79–80.

71

Discipline

Reasons for discipline problems

All teachers have had to deal with DISCIPLINE problems in their lessons at various stages in their careers. It is part of the life of being a teacher.

There are many different reasons for discipline problems.

- Some students have low SELF-ESTEEM (they doubt themselves and have no confidence). They seem to need the approval of the teacher or their peers (fellow students). They may try to get approval by asking for attention all the time or by behaving badly. We discuss self-esteem in YOUNG LEARNERS in →91.
- Some students become very DEMOTIVATED →43 when they fail.
- Some students are afraid of the strongest members of the class and so they do what those stronger members do, even when they know that it is wrong.
- Students feel very upset if they think that the teacher does not respect them or if they think the teacher treats individual students differently. 'It's not fair!' is often stage 1 of future discipline problems.
- Some younger learners come from families where education is not important. It is difficult for teachers to change that attitude.
- Some students are unhappy in their home life and they bring this unhappiness into class.

Preventing discipline problems

If we create successful well-behaved classes, discipline problems are unlikely.

- We can talk to the class about what good behaviour means. We can ask the students what they think is acceptable (e.g. *We will respect other people's opinions. We will wait till the lesson finishes before getting up and leaving the class. We should not interrupt people before they have finished speaking*, etc.).
- After a discussion about good behaviour we can negotiate a CODE OF CONDUCT, a kind of contract between us and our students. They can help us by agreeing 'rules', such as (for YOUNG LEARNERS →92) *No laughing at each other*, *Everyone has a turn*, *No speaking when someone else is speaking*, *We put our hands up if we want to say something*, etc.

- It is a good idea to remind the students about the code of conduct from time to time – and sometimes we may need to discuss it again so that everyone understands clearly what is acceptable and what is not acceptable.
- Discipline problems are much less likely if the teacher focuses on success rather than failure.
- Discipline problems are always less likely if teachers know what they are going to do. If the teacher is in control, the students are less likely to get out of control!
- Discipline problems are less likely if the students are engaged with the lesson. We should always think about how to make this happen before we go into the classroom.
- Discipline problems are much less likely if we treat all our students equally. If we have obvious favourites, for example, the students may resent this.
- Discipline problems are less likely to continue if we always act in the same way – and with determination – when things go wrong.

But when there *are* discipline problems, what then?

The most important thing to do when things go wrong is to stay calm – or at least to look calm, even if we don't feel it! Students of whatever age find it difficult to respect teachers who panic.

- When something goes wrong, we should act immediately. If we wait and hope that things will get better, they probably won't.
- Most discipline problems (but not all) disappear when the teacher shows that the behaviour is wrong.
- We can make students go and sit somewhere else so that they are not next to the person who is helping them to cause trouble.
- We should always try to respond to the behaviour rather than the character of the student. If we use sarcasm or personal insult, it is more difficult to regain control. But if we focus on what happened instead of who was responsible, it will be easier to stop the problem.
- We can use the code of conduct to stop discipline problems. We ask the class what everyone agreed to do and what not to do and then show that someone is behaving in a way that breaks the code.
- When we praise students, we try to give them a GOAL for the future →66. In the same way, we should always look towards the future when a discipline problem happens. Once we have stopped what is happening, we should talk about what will happen next or how things could be better in the future.
- Sometimes it is better to walk up to a student who is behaving badly. However, we don't want this to look like a physical challenge. We should keep our distance, keep eye contact and remain calm at all times.
- We should never threaten to do things that we are not going to do because students will soon stop listening to our threats.
- When it is possible, we should talk to students in private. We can ask what they think is the problem. We can discuss what happened. We will only tell them off (lecture them about their behaviour) if the discussion does not go well.
- If we are having difficult and worrying discipline problems, we should *always* talk to colleagues and to the co-ordinator, head teacher, etc. There is no shame in this. All teachers have discipline problems sometimes.
- We should find out exactly what the discipline policy of the school is and always act according to that policy. The students should know what the policy is, too, so that they are clear what will happen next if a discipline problem goes on being serious.

72

Giving feedback

Teacher feedback

When students say or write things, they usually expect feedback from the teacher. This often comes in the form of some kind of **EVALUATION**. Here is a typical example (the teacher is organising a question and answer drill →47):

Teacher:	Question … what … Guido.
Student (Guido):	What's the boy doing?
Teacher:	Good.

When the teacher says *Good*, she is giving feedback. She is telling Guido that he said the question correctly. This kind of evaluation feedback is extremely common and useful, but there are many other ways of responding to students' work too, as we shall see in this unit.

Acknowledgement and evaluation

- It is important that our students know that we have heard what they have said or read what they have written. We need to **ACKNOWLEDGE** their contribution and comment on both the language they have used and on how well we think they have performed a task.
- Students like to know if their writing or speaking is correct. When we say *Good* (like the teacher above) or just repeat what the student says without comment, this indicates that we are happy with what they said, e.g.

Student:	Last night I went to the cinema.
Teacher:	You went to the cinema.

However, we need to be careful to use approving and enthusiastic intonation →27 so that the students understand that we are happy with what they have said.

- We should be careful not to praise students too enthusiastically too often. If we say *Fantastic!* or *Well done!* to everything that they say, the words lose their meaning. Students don't enjoy being praised if they cannot see a good reason for it.
- We often need to show the students that what they have said is incorrect. They can often correct themselves when we do this. We look at how to correct students in →73–75.

Going further

Instead of only giving evaluation feedback, we can follow up what students say or write with repetitions and comments which will make them say or write more.

- We can **REFORMULATE** or **RE-CAST** what the student has said, e.g.

Student:	I have been to the cinema yesterday.
Teacher:	Oh, you went to the cinema yesterday.

This is a popular correction technique →73, but it is also a useful (and communicative) way of encouraging the students to hear and think about other ways of saying things.

- We can repeat what the student has just said with a rising **INTONATION**, e.g.

Student:	I went to the cinema yesterday.
Teacher:	You went to the cinema yesterday?

Depending on our facial expression and the intonation we use, this shows *either* that we want them to tell us a bit more (about what they have just said) *or* to think a bit more about what they have said to see if they think it was correct.

- We can ask our students to clarify what they have just said, e.g.

Student: I went to the Arts Picture House last night.
Teacher: Oh, you mean you went to see a film?

This is a useful way of making them try to explain themselves more fully or in a different way.

- We can comment on the CONTENT of what the students have just said, e.g.

Student: I saw 'The King's Speech' at the cinema last night.
Teacher: Oh you saw that film, did you? I hope you enjoyed it. I did when I saw it.

Students appreciate this kind of (genuine) acknowledgement and it may encourage them to say more.

- We can use FOLLOW-UP QUESTIONS to encourage students to say more, e.g.

Student: I saw 'The King's Speech' at the cinema last night.
Teacher: Oh really. Did you like it? What was your favourite bit?

Which kind of feedback?

We have to decide on which kind of feedback (or follow up) we want to use.

- If the students are involved in DRILLS or CONTROLLED PRACTICE, we often use evaluation feedback →73.
- When they are involved in more genuine communication, we often ask for clarification, comment or use intonation to show that we want to hear more.
- There are many occasions, however, when any of the types of feedback and follow up might be useful for students. We have to decide instantly which is more useful for a) their accuracy, b) their creative use of the language or c) getting them to remember language they know but aren't using much.

Giving feedback on written work

As we shall see when we discuss CORRECTING WRITTEN WORK →75, we give feedback on written work in a variety of ways.

- Evaluation means telling the students when they have done well or made mistakes. We often use CORRECTION SYMBOLS for this →75.
- COMMENTING means reacting to the content of what the students have written. We might write something like:

I really like your description of the town that you visited. Do you think you will go there again?

This shows the students that we are interested in what they have written, not just how well or badly they have done it.

- RESPONDING means commenting on students' written work and suggesting ways that they might want to change it. This is especially useful when they are involved in PROCESS WRITING →57. We might write something like:

Your story is very exciting, but you only use the past simple tense. Can you think of times when you could use the past continuous or the past perfect? It might make your story more interesting.

73

Correcting speaking 1

Different kinds of correction

The way we CORRECT mistakes will depend on the kind of mistake the student makes →37 and what kind of activity the students are involved in DVD23.

- We can make a difference between activities which focus on ACCURACY and those which focus on FLUENCY →37. When students are trying to say (new) language correctly – during PPP sequences, for example – we call this *accuracy* work. But when they are engaged in COMMUNICATIVE SPEAKING ACTIVITIES →51, we say that they are focusing on *fluency* – trying to speak spontaneously using any and all of the language they know.
- We tend to correct more during accuracy work. We help the students to say new language correctly, partly by showing them what mistakes they are making so that they can fully understand what they are learning.
- When students are involved in fluency work, we are, perhaps, more careful about when and how to correct. If we correct too much, we will stop the students expressing themselves; we will stop the RETRIEVAL AND USE →22 which are important elements for remembering language. However, correction can still be appropriate during fluency work. It depends how we do it.

Students correct themselves

If we think that students can correct themselves, there are a number of things we can do to make this happen.

- We can show that something is wrong by using FACIAL EXPRESSION (for example a raised eyebrow or some other surprised or quizzical expression), or by using GESTURE and/or body language to show surprise. This can be amusing, but it can also offend certain students, so we must be very careful and try not to do this inappropriately.
- We can echo what the student has said using rising INTONATION. This indicates that we expect something more. The students may realise this and then be able to correct themselves:

Student:	If I won a million dollars, I buy an aeroplane.
Teacher:	If I won a million dollars, I buy an aeroplane?
Student:	Oh, yes. If I won a million dollars I would buy an aeroplane.

- We can draw the student's attention to the actual mistake by stressing the part of the sentence where the mistake was made:

Student:	If I won a million pounds, I am travel round the world.
Teacher:	If I won a million pounds, I AM TRAVEL round the world?
Student:	Oh, yes. I would travel round the world.

- Or we can just repeat one word or phrase so that students know what part of the sentence to try to correct:

Student:	I have winning a million pounds, I would buy a house for my mother.
Teacher:	Have winning?
Student:	Oh, yes. If I won a million pounds, I would buy a house for my mother.

- We can also use explicit statements and questions to show incorrectness in the hope that the students can correct themselves:

Student:	If I won million pounds, I would help the poor.
Teacher:	Do we say 'million pounds'?

The teacher could also say *Do we use an article with million, hundred, etc.?*

Students correct each other

If the students cannot correct themselves, what do we do then?

- We can ask other students in the class to help the student who is having problems.

Student (Yutaro):	If I am winning a million pounds I am stopping work.
Teacher:	If I AM winning?
Student:	… (*the student is uncertain and cannot correct himself*)
Teacher:	Jun, can you help??
Student (Jun):	If I won a million pounds I would stop work.
Teacher:	Yutaro?
Student (Yutaro):	If I won a million pounds I would stop work.
Teacher:	Very good.

- We should be careful when using students to help each other. Some people don't like being made to look 'weaker' in this way.

The Silent Way

Caleb Gattegno (1911–1988) promoted a teaching method called **THE SILENT WAY**, so called because teachers do as little talking as possible.

After modelling new language, the teacher nominates the students in turn (usually with a silent gesture). The students each have to say the new language. If they cannot do this, the teacher silently nominates other students and keeps doing this until one of them says the new language correctly. The teacher then uses that student as a model until everyone else can say the new language as well as the successful student.

The students' reliance on each other is very powerful and forces them to pay attention really carefully. However, it can also be quite stressful.

Reformulation

We can **REFORMULATE** (or re-cast) what students say →72, using the correct language form.

Student:	If is raining, I am getting wet.
Teacher:	Yes you're right. If it rains, you will get wet.

For some students (but not all) this may be enough to make them (and the rest of the class) think carefully about what they have just said. They may correct themselves – or at least notice the difference between what they said and what the teacher says.

From correction to (re)teaching

Sometimes we have to break off from what we are doing and (re)teach something that our students are having difficult with.

- As an example, imagine that a teacher is not getting any response when she tries to correct students who are using *furniture* as a **COUNTABLE NOUN** →12.
- The teacher stops the sequence and puts two headings (*Countable nouns*, *Uncountable nouns*) on the board. She elicits nouns that the students know (including *furniture*) and writes them (or gets the students to write them) in the correct columns.
- The teacher then reviews the rules for countable and uncountable nouns before returning to the previous activity.

74

Correcting speaking 2

When should we correct?

As we saw in →73, we use correction differently if the students are involved in a COMMUNICATIVE SPEAKING ACTIVITY.

- If we correct our students all the time when they are trying to say something interesting, we may make them feel nervous. We may stop them trying to find the best way to say things in English – one of the main reasons for doing activities like this.
- Many students say that they want to be corrected at the exact moment when they make a mistake. However, if we do correct all their mistakes in this way, they generally become frustrated and the speaking activity is less successful.
- However, it may sometimes be appropriate to correct students when they are trying to say something that is important to them. They may have a strong MOTIVATION to speak correctly.
- We have to decide how much to correct while a communicative speaking activity is taking place. If correction will stop the activity, then it is probably better to wait until afterwards. But if it is fairly easy to help the students out through correction – and this does not stop the conversation – then we may decide to go ahead.
- It is a good idea to ask the students when and how they want to be corrected and to come to an agreement with them about how it will happen.

Correcting while the activity is taking place

- If we correct while a speaking activity is happening, we will try to do so without disrupting the activity too much. Our correction will often be more like SCAFFOLDING →65 than direct teaching.
- We can use REFORMULATION →72 as a gentle reminder to the student who is speaking, as in the following example:

Student:	So I like listen to music when I driving and also in the house.
Teacher:	You like listening to music when you are driving.
Student:	Yes, when I am driving and I like listening to music in the house, and …

  Notice that once the teacher has reformulated the student's sentence, she does not insist on the sentence being said again. She hopes that her gentle reformulation will be enough.

- We can, of course, say things like *Remember 'furniture' is an uncountable noun* in the middle of a communicative activity, but as with reformulation we don't usually insist on the students stopping to correct themselves.
- However, if the mistakes that are being made are having a bad effect on the activity, the teacher may feel that they should stop the activity and do a bit of (re)teaching →73.

Making a record of what is being said

When our students are involved in a speaking activity, we will make a record of what they say so that we can give FEEDBACK and correct them when the activity is finished.

- We can 'eavesdrop' on what is happening. In other words, we listen without interrupting – and without dominating the event. We can sit just outside a group or stand to one side of the class, listening to what is being said.

- While we are eavesdropping on groups or on the class, we can make a note of anything that we want to talk about later – both mistakes that we hear, and also things that students do or say well. However, we should not be too obvious about this since this will be almost the same as instant correction.
- We can use a chart to help us record both the successful and the less successful aspects of what we hear, such as the following:

Content	Grammar	Words and phrases	Pronunciation

- We can use a microphone or video camera to record a speaking activity, though this will only work if the microphone quality is good enough.

Correcting after the event

We can use the information we recorded to make corrections after the students have finished a speaking activity.

- We will respond to the CONTENT of what the students said, not just the language they used.
- We will tell the students what we liked (content and language). Positive feedback has a strong motivational effect.
- We can write a few mistakes that we recorded on the board. We can ask the students to say how they could correct these. However, we will not say who made the mistakes on the board because we don't want to make any particular student feel bad DVD24.
- We can watch or listen to our audio or video recordings with the class and point out where things were successful or not successful.
- We can play the audio/video recording and ask the students to comment on successful and less successful uses of language.
- We can ask the students to transcribe a short section of a video or audio recording. We can then analyse the transcriptions and a) say what we like and b) make any necessary corrections.

Correcting for the future

The point of correction is to help our students achieve more success in the future.

- When the students are preparing to make an ORAL PRESENTATION →53, we can let them practise their presentation and give them feedback (making suggestions and corrections) so that when they do their (final) presentation again, it will be even better.
- When students are creating DIALOGUES for acting out, we can go round the class helping them to say things in a more correct and appropriate way.
- If we have the students tell stories more than once →53, we can comment on what we hear the first time round so that the next (and subsequent) tellings of the story will be better.

75 Correcting writing

How much to correct

It is often difficult to decide how many mistakes to CORRECT in a student's written work and how to do it. We do not want to cover their paper in a discouraging mass of red ink (or its equivalent).

- We have seen that it is important to comment on the CONTENT of our students' work rather than just focusing on the language that they use →72.
- We have said that when we are helping students in PROCESS WRITING →57, we respond to their work and suggest ways that they can improve it. This is rather different from giving correction.
- However, when we return corrected students' HOMEWORK →76 or other written work, we want them to look at the corrections and suggestions and, where possible, to rewrite their work correctly.

What to correct

If we correct everything, then students may be DEMOTIVATED →43 by the number of corrections we make. There are ways of correcting only some things:

- We can select what we are going to correct and tell the students before they do the work. For example, we can say that we will only be correcting SPELLING. As a result, the students are likely to think more carefully about how to spell than they would otherwise have done.
- We can ask the students to choose what we should correct when we check their work. We can give UPPER-INTERMEDIATE students a list which includes grammar, vocabulary, spelling, PARAGRAPH CONSTRUCTION, good text organisation (introduction, argument, conclusion, etc.) and ask them to put them in order of importance. Students will pay more attention to correctness in the areas they have put at number 1!
- We can give our students a writing checklist to use when they have finished their writing. We can ask questions such as *Does the first paragraph of your text introduce the topic? Do your verbs agree with their subjects (singular – plural)? Have you put your adjectives in the right order?* etc.

Using correction symbols

Many teachers use CORRECTION SYMBOLS to try to avoid too much 'red-ink' marking. Although there is no agreed list, the following symbols are common.

Correction symbols

Symbol	Meaning	Example error
S	A spelling error.	*The asnwer is obvious.*
WO	A mistake in word order.	*I like very much it.*
G	A grammar mistake.	*I am going to buy some furnitures.*
T	Wrong verb tense.	*I have seen him yesterday.*
C	Concord mistake (e.g. the subject and verb agreement).	*People is angry.*
⋏	Something has been left out.	*He told ⋏ that he was sorry.*
WW	Wrong word.	*I am interested on jazz music.*
{ }	Something is not necessary.	*He was not {too} strong enough.*
?M	The meaning is unclear.	*That is a very excited photograph.*
P	A punctuation mistake.	*Do you like London.*
F/I	Too formal or informal.	*Hi Mr Franklin, Thank you for your letter …*

- We need to train our students to understand our correction symbols. We can do this by a) getting them to find mistakes in sentences, b) asking them to say what kind of mistake it is and c) choosing a symbol for each type of mistake.
- When the students submit work on paper, we can underline a mistake in a written sentence and put the correction symbol in the margin.
- When our students submit work electronically, we can underline words and phrases and put correction symbols in brackets.
- We can get the students to try correcting each other's work using correction symbols.
- We should remember to include ticks (✓) or **EMOTICONS** and other symbols to show when we approve of what the students have written.

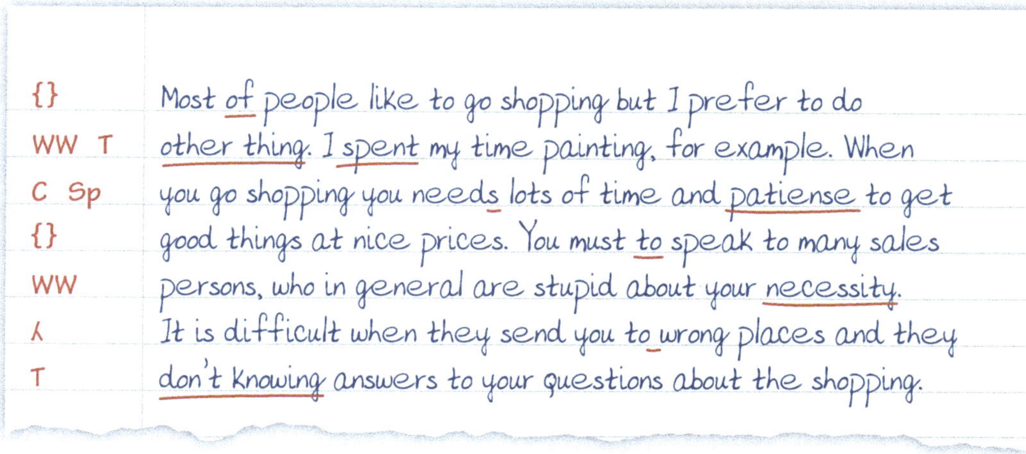

Other kinds of correction

- When we correct written work that has been submitted electronically, we can write our own comments (in different colours) or use reviewing tools (such as *Track Changes*) to add comments.

- However, it is just as demotivating to over-correct electronically as it is to do it with a pen.
- We can send our students **AUDIO** or **VIDEO FEEDBACK**, with a mixture of comments, corrections and suggestions. Students can listen/watch as they read through their own writing. Some teachers record themselves making corrections on screen, using software like *Jing* or *Camtasia*. The students can hear what the teacher says and, at the same time, see on the screen what corrections the teacher is making to their work.

76

Homework

The magic of homework

HOMEWORK is like magic! The more that students do it, the better their English becomes. This is especially important when lessons provide the students' only other exposure to English.

Homework is like music practice or physical training. It encourages LEARNER AUTONOMY →43 because we will be asking the students to work on their own.

What kind of homework?

It is important to set varied homework tasks so that the students don't get bored with the whole process, and also because different students respond to different things and often have different LEARNING STYLES →40.

- We can ask our students to complete exercises in their WORKBOOKS or on WORKSHEETS that we give them.
- The students can submit audio and video material via email or by using an ONLINE LEARNING PLATFORM such as MOODLE, BLACKBOARD, etc.
- We can ask them to do exercises on a learning platform and submit their work ONLINE →87.
- We can ask the students to submit homework with photographs and drawings attached. In other words, homework does not always have to be words only.
- We can ask the students to research a topic for homework. For example, we can ask them to find facts about a topic (such as tourism) in preparation for a FORMAL DEBATE →52. We can ask them to collect six different newspaper headlines from online sites, bring them to a lesson and explain them to the class. We can ask them to look at dictionaries, newspapers, magazines or WEBSITES and find, for example, six new PHRASAL VERBS →9.
- We can ask our students to learn a POEM or a SPEECH by heart →63.
- We can ask them to write a text to be included in their writing PORTFOLIO (a collection of their work that they add to over a semester or a year) →59.
- We can ask the students to write a new BLOG POST →87 or to comment on at least two other students' blogs.

Using mobile devices for homework

Many students have a range of MOBILE DEVICES →86: MOBILE PHONES (cellphones), digital cameras or TABLET COMPUTERS. These can be used for doing a variety of homework tasks.

- We can ask them to make short VIDEO or AUDIO RECORDINGS. For example, they can describe their day or show their house or their street (with commentaries).

- We can ask the students to use their mobile devices to record interviews with family, friends or strangers (provided that we are sure of their safety).
- We can ask the students to record ORAL PRESENTATIONS →53.
- We can ask them to take 'mystery photographs' (pictures from strange angles) on their mobile devices. They then bring them into the lesson and the other students have to say what they are. We discuss more uses of mobile devices in class in →86.

Making homework 'work' for students

There are a number of ways in which we can make homework a positive experience for students.

- We can include doing homework in the CODE OF CONDUCT we agree with our students →71.
- We should find out what homework our students have to do for other lessons. We don't want to overwork them.
- When students submit homework, we should do our best to mark it and give it back as promptly as possible. This is not always easy, but if we give homework back late, students may start to submit it late, too.
- One of the best ways of making sure that students do their homework is to give GRADES for each piece of work that is completed. This grade can be instead of (or as well as) any other mark that we give. The 'completion' marks all go towards a final grade.
- We can ask the students to decide what homework they want to do. They could discuss this in groups. They can choose anything, such as working with a song or watching/listening to a football commentary, provided that it either uses English or helps them to learn English. We can use their (sensible) choices as homework tasks.
- Students can decide (with our guidance) how their homework should be graded.
- Teachers should keep a HOMEWORK RECORD so that they know who has done homework and when.
- Where it is appropriate, with younger learners, teachers should give each student a homework notebook. In this book the teacher writes each homework task. The student's parent or guardian signs the record to show that they know the homework has been assigned. The teacher signs the book when the homework is done.

Making homework 'work' for teachers

Teachers are happy when students do homework well, but marking and record-keeping can take up a lot of our time!

- We shouldn't ask different classes to submit homework all at the same time.
- We should set clear homework limits (number of words, etc.) and ask the students to respect them.
- We should encourage the students to suggest ideas for homework. This will be interesting to mark.
- We can try selective marking. In other words, we don't need to comment or correct everything in a piece of homework. For example, we might concentrate on verb tenses but not comment on minor SPELLING mistakes.
- We can mark only a selection of papers each time (and make sure that every student's work is marked over a period of weeks).
- We can get the students to mark (and/or comment on) each other's homework (and check that they are doing it well).

77

Using the L1

L1 in the classroom

For many decades, teachers have discussed the following question: Should we allow students to use their HOME LANGUAGE(s) in the *English*-language classroom?

Some background facts

There are a number of reasons why people have different attitudes to the use of the L1 in the English-language classroom.

- When people reacted against the GRAMMAR-TRANSLATION methods →36 of the past, they wanted to replace them with the DIRECT METHOD. The direct method encouraged speaking the TARGET LANGUAGE in class instead of speaking *about* it.
- Many English teachers (NATIVE SPEAKER TEACHERS →13 and others) travel to different countries around the world to teach. If they can't speak their students' language, their lessons have to be in English all the time.
- Many classes (especially, but not only, in countries such as Australia, Britain, Canada, Ireland and the USA) are MULTILINGUAL: the students come from a variety of different language backgrounds.
- Many people around the world grow up speaking two, three or more languages. When we discuss this topic, however, we tend to talk about a student's L1 to refer to their first/home language.
- When people are learning languages, especially at the beginning, they translate from one language to another in their heads whether we like it or not!

Arguments against using the students' L1 in the classroom

Even in MONOLINGUAL classes using the L1 may not be a good idea.

- The more the students speak in their L1, the less English they speak.
- Students get fantastically good COMPREHENSIBLE INPUT from the teacher in English. If the teacher uses the students' L1, they won't get as much English exposure.
- We want our students to think in English, not in their L1. We want to create an English environment in the classroom.
- Students learn best by trying to express themselves in English. The more they communicate in English, the better. There is no point in COMMUNICATIVE ACTIVITIES if the students are using their L1.

Arguments in favour of using the students' L1 in the classroom

There are also a number of reasons why using the L1 may have advantages.

- Part of a student's identity comes from the language(s) they speak. We should encourage our students to celebrate their multilingual identities.
- Using the students' L1, especially at lower levels, allows us to talk to them about many different matters to do with class management, etc.
- We can help our students with any problems if we can communicate with them in their L1.
- The use of the L1 can make a good contribution to the atmosphere in the class and the RAPPORT →66 between teacher and students.
- Students learn a lot by comparing English with their L1. They will do it anyway, so it is better if we help them.

An L1 'policy'

Since using the students' L1 has both advantages and disadvantages, we need to make up our minds about what to do.

- We should always acknowledge the students' L1 (and other languages which they speak), for example by asking them to contrast that language with English, or talking about pronunciation differences.
- Teachers should not overuse the students' L1. Remember, it is an English lesson!
- The more advanced the students are, the less need there is to use their L1 in class. However, we may want to make use of a range of TRANSLATION ACTIVITIES at any level (see below).
- We should make sure that the students know when it is OK to use their L1 (when they are discussing answers in pairs, for example) and when it is not (when they are trying to communicate in English, for example). It is a good idea to get them to agree a policy about this, perhaps as part of a CODE OF CONDUCT →71.
- We should use the L1 (if we are able to) to help our students understand differences between English and their L1.
- If our students start using their L1 at inappropriate times (e.g. during a speaking activity), we should use encouragement, persuasion and prompting to get them to go back to speaking in English.

Translation activities

Translation can aid motivation and help the students to think more carefully about language.

- We can evaluate our students' progress at the end of a course of study by asking them if they can translate the phrases and structures they have been studying back into their L1.
- The students can translate different sections of a text and then share their translations to build up the complete story in an activity similar to JIGSAW READING →55.
- Students can translate short texts and then compare their translations with those of their classmates.
- Student A translates an English sentence into their L1. They give the translated sentence to Student B (who shares the same L1). Student B translates it back into English. Is Student B's English sentence the same as Student A's?
- The students discuss different idioms in different languages and cultures.
- We can get our students to use online web translators and ask them to say what, if anything, is wrong with the translations.

Teaching ideas: translating a poem

Amanda Wilson asked a multilingual group of students in the UK to translate an anti-drug-use poem into their different languages. The activity was a big success and very motivating because the students:

- wanted to 'parade' their L1s when they read their translations aloud.
- enjoyed hearing each other's languages and comparing them with their own.
- had to think really hard about grammar, lexis, syntax, etc. when translating.
- could recite the original poem in English from memory by the end of the lesson.
- felt empowered because they had been able to translate a whole poem from English into their own language.

Amanda's students' poems on display

78

Teacher development

Continuous professional development

The best (and happiest) teachers continue to learn and discover new things all through their teaching careers. Development activity is just as important for teachers as it is for students. It can make us more enthusiastic about teaching (and about our lives) and it can also help us through episodes of **BURNOUT**.

Burnout just around the corner?

Many teachers and trainers worry about the possibility of teacher burnout.

- Burnout happens when teachers lose interest in (and enthusiasm for) teaching. It can cause (or be caused by) stress.
- Burnout does not mean the end of a career (though it can do). It is often a temporary state of affairs. Most teachers get through it and come out the other side.
- Burnout is caused by such things as teaching too many **CONTACT HOURS** (hours in the classroom), having too much **HOMEWORK** →76 to mark or by other conditions at work. But it can also be the result of factors such as time spent travelling to and from work, pressures at home or things going on in teachers' private lives.
- The best route out of teacher burnout is to re-engage with teacher development activities.

Doing it ourselves

There are many things that teachers can do to help themselves continue learning, thinking and enjoying teaching.

- The best teachers are **REFLECTIVE**. This means that they reflect on (think about) what happens in their lessons. Some teachers keep journals to help them do this.
- Teachers can do their own **ACTION RESEARCH**. This means a) asking themselves a question about teaching (for example, *Why are some students quiet during groupwork?*), b) trying to answer the question by doing something different in class (for example giving each student in a group a specific task), c) reflecting on what happened when they did this (for example, did those different tasks mean that all the students took part?) and d) deciding what action to take next.
- An effective type of personal reflection takes place when teachers watch themselves teaching on film. Even if this only means putting a small video camera at the back of the classroom and leaving it there while we teach, we can learn a lot by watching it afterwards.

- One of the best ways of thinking about our own teaching is to write an article for a teachers' magazine, present a seminar or talk at a teachers' meeting or conference. This makes us think about what we do and why we do it. It may make us feel nervous, but other teachers are usually very supportive.
- One of the best things we can do for our teaching is to become learners ourselves. Perhaps we can study for a further teaching qualification or take a postgraduate course, for example. But it is also extremely invigorating to learn something (anything) completely new, whether it is a new language (it helps to put ourselves in our learners' shoes), a new sport, a new musical instrument or any other fresh and exciting challenge.

Doing it with others

Some of the most effective teacher development takes place when we work and share with colleagues and other professionals.

- We learn a lot (and develop) when we co-operate with others. For example, if we have just tried a new activity in class but we don't know what to think about it, talking about it with a supportive colleague will often help us to clarify our ideas.
- The worst thing we can do if we are having problems or suffering from burnout is to keep it to ourselves. We need to talk to other people about it.
- It is a very good idea to set up regular sessions where two teachers take turns to be the *listener/understander* and the *speaker*. The listener/understander listens non-judgementally – in other words, they don't say 'that is good' or 'that is bad' – before asking questions to try to get the speaker to clarify their thinking. Having a non-judgemental listener gives the speaker confidence. After a set time, the two teachers change roles.
- Teachers can organise their own teacher development groups which meet at pre-arranged times. All the teachers in the group can vote on what they want to talk about, and every week a different teacher can lead the session.
- Teachers can write or comment on BLOGS →87. This can be like a very good conversation with colleagues.
- Teachers can have discussions (and form groups) using social networks such as TWITTER. They can take part in WEBINARS or other ONLINE meetings.
- We can keep our eyes open for seminars which are organised in our locality. If possible, we can attend some of the many teachers' conferences, either in our region, our country or abroad.
- Fellow teachers can plan, discuss and observe each other's lessons. However, such PEER OBSERVATION will not work if the teacher being observed feels that they are being judged. The main reasons for peer observation should be a) for the observer to learn new things and reflect on their own teaching, and b) for the observed teacher to have a chance to talk about their lesson with an observer they can trust.
- When schools organise peer observation, it is a good idea to have a meeting afterwards where people talk about the good things they have observed. This means that everyone gets to hear new ideas.
- Many teachers feel nervous when a director of studies (for example) comes to watch. If the OBSERVATION is going to be really helpful for the teacher (rather than just an evaluation), the teacher should be able to negotiate the time and content of the lesson, the follow up should be a conversation (rather than a report) and the emphasis should be on future success, not past failure. It is worth remembering that anyone in a senior academic position has almost certainly been observed many times themselves.
- Teachers can watch VIDEO RECORDINGS of each other teaching and discuss what they see.

LONGMAN
Diccionario Pocket Plus
energy
LONGMAN
English Language and Culture

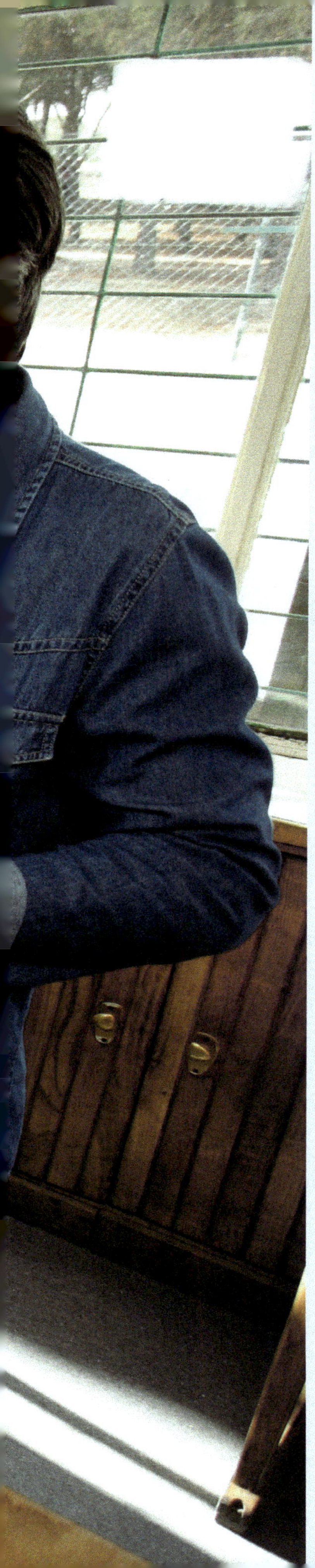

Section E: Planning, resources and assessment

In this section, we discuss a range of issues to do with planning lessons, what resources we can use and how to test students along the way.

We look at the essential elements of lesson planning and of how to plan a sequence of lessons. (Note: there is separate lesson planning appendix on pages 250–256.)

We look at a range of materials, both in book form (coursebooks, supplementary materials, dictionaries, etc.), and also using other forms of technology (whether this is a class board or a tablet computer or other hand-held mobile device, for example). In addition, we discuss teaching without any materials at all.

Finally, we look at the basics of assessment and testing. (Note: we also discuss testing for young learners in Unit 101 and for CLIL in Unit 110.)

79

Planning lessons

Different attitudes to planning

Some teachers spend hours PLANNING what to do in their LESSONS the next day. Others don't seem to need the same amount of time to think about what they are going to do. Some schools and institutions expect teachers to provide detailed plans. Some teacher qualification exams expect teachers to present plans for the lessons they are going to teach.

To plan or not to plan?

- When teachers don't plan – and leave everything to chance – they sometimes have wonderful lessons, full of creativity and fun. But it's a big risk. Sometimes the lesson is just chaotic and no one learns very much. If this happens too often, the students may start to think that the teacher is unprofessional and this is bad for teacher–student RAPPORT →66.
- When teachers plan too much and then follow the plan exactly, without changing a single thing whatever happens in the lesson, the lesson may be uncreative and boring.
- We need to be ready for MAGIC MOMENTS (when students do or say something really interesting) and be prepared to change our plan to take advantage of them. We also need to be ready for UNFORESEEN PROBLEMS (when something happens which we had not anticipated) and be prepared to change our plan to deal with them.

What are lessons like?

- We need to have an idea of what we hope the students will achieve in a lesson. We need to think of the best ways to help them do this. When we start to think what the AIMS of a lesson are and how we will help the students to achieve those aims, we are already planning, whether we write the plan down or not.
- Lesson plans are like maps. They tell us where we are going and help us to take the best route to get there. But we still have to make decisions as we travel. Should we take a detour? Do we prefer the motorway or a country road, for example?

- When we think of a lesson as a journey, it is just one METAPHOR →21 we can use. We might also think of a lesson as a film or a novel or a meal – and use those metaphors to help us put the pieces together to make, for example, a narrative or a fantastic dining experience.
- Lesson ideas can come from many different places. They can be inspired by films we see or something we read. They can come from the ideas of our colleagues or from something we have read about in a teachers' magazine or heard from an online community. They can come from the SYLLABUS we are following or the COURSEBOOK we are using – or they can simply arise because we think our students need some extra work on something. They may be part of a SEQUENCE OF LESSONS →80, perhaps planned around a central TOPIC or THEME →100.

What goes into a plan?

Different schools and institutions (and exam boards) have different plan forms and formats. But they all have several things in common:

- The most important part of the planning process is to decide what our precise learning aims are. In other words, we need to consider the learning OUTCOMES. We can think of a learning outcome as the answer to the question *What will my students know or be able to do at the end of a lesson (or lesson stage) that they could not do or didn't know at the beginning?*
- We need to consider TIMETABLE FIT. In other words, we will say what the students have been learning recently and what they will be doing in the next lesson(s) after this one.
- We need to have (or write) a good CLASS DESCRIPTION. This needs to say who the students are in as much detail as we can give. We can say what they find easy and difficult, how well they participate in lessons, etc. When we know who our students are, we can plan especially for them – and plan activities that DIFFERENTIATE between different students →42.
- We need to list the LANGUAGE EXPONENTS (GRAMMAR, VOCABULARY or PRONUNCIATION items) that we are going to teach or the LANGUAGE SKILLS (reading, writing, speaking and listening) we will focus on.
- We will say what ACTIVITIES we are going to include in our lesson and what TEACHING AIDS we need to achieve them.
- We will describe the PROCEDURES that will happen in our lesson and what INTERACTIONS will be taking place – in other words, who is working with whom. For example, perhaps the teacher is talking to the whole class. Or perhaps the students are working in PAIRS or GROUPS →67.
- It helps to estimate the TIMING of each lesson stage. If we include this in our plan, when we are teaching we will know if we can slow down or if we need to speed up.
- We often include PERSONAL AIMS. In other words, we say what we (the teacher) hope to achieve. This is different from our aims for the students. We might say something like *In this lesson I am going to evaluate what it feels like to teach without using any technology at all.* All lessons are opportunities for TEACHER DEVELOPMENT and ACTION RESEARCH →78 like this.
- It helps to ANTICIPATE PROBLEMS that our students might have with the lesson we are preparing. If we do this, we can then imagine POSSIBLE SOLUTIONS to these problems.
- We will list ADDITIONAL POSSIBILITIES so that if the class goes more quickly than we anticipated (or in a different direction), we have something ready.

We discuss planning for CLIL lessons in →109.

For examples of LESSON PLANS, see Appendix C on pages 250–256.

80

Planning sequences

Lesson shapes, stages and sequences

- When we plan lessons, we may use **METAPHORS** like maps, films, books or meals to come up with a **LESSON SHAPE** →**79**.
- We think about establishing different episodes or **LESSON STAGES** within a lesson period (the total time of the lesson). This is because we believe that **VARIETY** within a lesson is important.
- When we teach a lesson, we need to make it clear when one stage is over and the next one begins.
- We need to plan a *coherent* sequence of stages (and the activities and sequences within them). Variety is important, in other words, but chaos probably isn't.
- We discuss activities and how to evaluate them in →**83**.

ESA

Any teaching sequence needs three essential elements:

- We need to **ENGAGE** the students so that their hearts as well as their minds are involved – so that they are emotionally connected because they are curious, happy or provoked.
- Students need to **STUDY** something at some stage during every teaching sequence, whether this is grammar, vocabulary, pronunciation or paragraph/text construction.
- We need to give the students a chance to **ACTIVATE** any and all the language they know. They do this when they speak freely, but they also do it when they read a text for meaning and use the language they know to understand it.

Some lesson sequences (such as **PPP** →**44**) follow the pattern E-S-A. We *engage* students with en enjoyable situation or picture. Then we present the new language and practise it (*study*) before we let the students try to *activate* (use) it.

Some lesson sequences follow an E-A-S sequence. For example, we might get the students *engaged* in a situation before getting them to *activate* their language in a **ROLEPLAY** →**53**. Afterwards we might do some language repair by *studying* grammar or vocabulary that they had problems with in the roleplay.

Many sequences are much more like a patchwork, where the **ESA** elements are jumbled up.

Planning a sequence of lessons

When we plan a sequence of lessons (say for two, three or four weeks or longer), there are a number of things we will want to consider.

- We may decide to base our sequence on TOPICS AND THEMES →100. For example, we could take *photography* as a topic and then plan lessons which look at a) the development of photography, b) photographs that have changed the world, c) snapshots that we take, d) the impact of digital photography on film, e) the way we use photographs for social networking and f) the photographs we wish we had been able to take (such as photographs of an event from history).
- We can base our sequence on the language which we want our students to learn, including GRAMMAR, VOCABULARY, LANGUAGE FUNCTIONS and TEXT AND DISCOURSE features. Over a two-week period, for example, we might concentrate on narrative, with an emphasis on tenses (PAST SIMPLE, PAST CONTINUOUS, PAST PERFECT), time LINKERS (*first, and then, later on, after that*), LEXICAL PHRASE starters (*I hadn't intended to, I realised that I had, When I found that* ...) and vocabulary that we have decided is important for our students to know.
- When we plan a sequence of lessons, we try to ensure a balance between the different LANGUAGE SKILLS that the students need to work with and the different ACTIVITIES we are going to ask them to do.
- When we plan a sequence of lessons, we think about short-term and long-term goals. SHORT-TERM GOALS are the OUTCOMES which we hope the students will achieve by the end of a lesson or a sequence within a lesson. LONG-TERM GOALS are the ones which we hope they will have realised at the end of, say, a month or even a semester.
- Students need short-term goals so that they have something to aim for, something which is not so far away that it is invisible. Short-term goals keep students MOTIVATED →43, especially when the long-term goals seem too remote and far away.
- Although we may plan a sequence of lessons in advance, we must be ready to change and amend our plans as the sequence continues and the lessons in it take place. If things are going faster than we expected, we may need to add extra activities or material. If things are taking a longer time, we may need to speed up or cut some activities or material we had planned to use. If the students are not responding to a topic or theme, we will have to decide on how to make changes so that they respond better.
- It is probably not a good idea to plan a sequence of lessons just on language, just around a topic or only based on the range of activities we want the students to take part in. Instead, we will create a MULTI-SYLLABUS which includes all of these elements threaded together.

Syllabus, curriculum, course

Some people use the terms *syllabus* and *curriculum* to mean the same thing, but this is inaccurate.

- A CURRICULUM is the overall plan for a school or a SUBJECT. It expresses the content, the overall goals, the philosophy (ideology) behind the programme, and the way(s) in which evaluations will take place.
- We call a particular number of weeks of teaching at the LOWER-INTERMEDIATE level (for example) a COURSE. We can say what course are you studying?
- Most courses have a SYLLABUS: a list of the language or other content that will be taught and the order that it will be taught in. For example, we can talk about a GRAMMAR SYLLABUS (a list of grammar items), a TASK SYLLABUS (a list of tasks), a FUNCTIONAL SYLLABUS (a list of language functions), etc.

81 Using coursebooks

The coursebook issue

All over the world people use COURSEBOOKS to help them teach or learn foreign languages.

- Coursebooks are often well planned. Language progression has been carefully considered and there is adequate RECYCLING (REPETITION OF ENCOUNTER →22) of vocabulary and grammar.
- Good coursebooks have a wealth of attractive-looking material, TOPICS and activities to engage students and teachers and to support them as they get to grips with the new language.
- Modern coursebooks are often accompanied by a range of SUPPLEMENTARY MATERIAL (such as WORKBOOKS, ACTIVITY BOOKS and DVDs) and online provision (such as CYBER HOMEWORK, which stores and grades homework online).
- Some people don't like coursebooks. They say that no single coursebook is exactly right for any particular class of students. They argue that most are based on (and have too much) GRAMMAR, and that the language used in COURSEBOOK DIALOGUES is not natural. Above all, they claim that over-reliance on a coursebook stops teachers and learners being creative. We look at MATERIALS-FREE TEACHING in →84.
- As more education providers offer online and mobile resources, there is a move away from coursebooks in some educational institutions and regions. However, for now, paper-based educational materials are still widely used.

Thinking about the next coursebook

When teachers, directors of study and co-ordinators are thinking about choosing a new coursebook, there are a number of things they need to consider.

- It is important to make sure that the course materials are affordable for the institution and the students – and that all the components that are needed (such as audio, TEACHER'S GUIDE, etc.) are available.
- We need to think carefully about the layout and design of the materials we are going to be using. Are the pages attractive? Is the style of illustration pleasing to the eye? Are the pages too cluttered? Can the students clearly see what is going on and in what order? Are the RUBRICS (instructions) written clearly and in a way that the students can understand?
- We need to decide whether the CONTENT of the book is appropriate for our students. Are the topics interesting, stimulating and culturally appropriate for the age, gender and social background of the students?

- We need to evaluate the methodology of the course. Does it use a largely PPP methodology →44 (many coursebooks do) or is there a variety of activities and procedures within it? Does the coursebook reflect the way(s) that we like to teach?
- We need to be sure that the coursebook has the right balance of LANGUAGE SKILLS (reading, writing, listening and speaking) for the goals we want our students to achieve.
- We will want to check the syllabus in the coursebook to see if we are happy with the selection of grammar and VOCABULARY and the way that it is graded (the sequence of language areas).
- We will look at the coursebook to see what LEARNER STYLES it is designed for and whether it offers any activities for DIFFERENTIATION →42.
- We will want to look at the supplementary materials that come with the coursebook (workbook, AUDIO RECORDINGS, DVDs, etc.). Are they appropriate for what we want our students to achieve?
- A good coursebook has a helpful TEACHER'S GUIDE – either in paper form or as online notes.
- Does the coursebook have a COMPANION WEBSITE →87 or is there some other ONLINE material that can be used with it? We discuss BLENDED LEARNING (using coursebooks together with INFORMATION TECHNOLOGY) in →87.

How to choose a coursebook

- It may help if we talk to colleagues (before we look at any books) and discuss what to look for in a coursebook. We can come up with our own list of desirable characteristics, based on the situation we are working in. Many of these may be the same as those listed above, but we may also have our own special concerns. We can then use our list to compare the different books we are considering.
- Where possible, we should PILOT coursebooks before we make a definite decision about whether to use them. Piloting means using the coursebook with a trial class and comparing the results and the experiences with older books and/or books we are thinking of using.
- It is a good idea to show the students the coursebooks that we are thinking of adopting. They may have strong opinions about many of the issues discussed above, especially topics and layout.

Using coursebooks

Using a coursebook is a teacher skill. But if teachers follow the book word for word, never varying the way they do it, students may not be ENGAGED →80 and as a result they may lose their MOTIVATION →43.

- We need to engage our students with a coursebook. We can ask them what they think about the exercises or TEXTS. We can encourage them to give their own opinions on the topics in the book. We can use the coursebook as a springboard for discussion about the topics in it.
- We can OMIT COURSEBOOK MATERIAL completely →84 or REPLACE it with material that we prefer or which is more appropriate for our class. However, if we do this too much, the students may resent having to buy the books and bring them to lessons.
- We can add to what is in the coursebook – by bringing in our own material, or by finding information online, for example.
- We can REWRITE parts of the book. For example, we may want to use our own (or the students') questions with reading and listening material. We discuss simplifying material for CLIL lessons in →106.
- We can REPLACE or REORDER activities and lessons to suit our own needs.

82 Using dictionaries

Different kinds of dictionary

Dictionaries are one of the most useful resources for language students, whether in book form, ONLINE or, as is becoming more and more common, on handheld and MOBILE DEVICES, such as SMARTPHONES and TABLET COMPUTERS.

- BILINGUAL DICTIONARIES have words in two languages. In the first section, language 1 is translated into language 2. In the second section, language 2 is translated into language 1. BILINGUAL LEARNERS' DICTIONARIES (BLDs) are designed especially for language learners.
- MONOLINGUAL DICTIONARIES (written in one language) are used by NATIVE SPEAKERS and other competent speakers of the language.
- MONOLINGUAL LEARNERS' DICTIONARIES (MLDs) are written in the TARGET LANGUAGE. They use a simplified language for their DEFINITIONS and have information which is especially useful for language learners.
- PRODUCTION DICTIONARIES, such as a THESAURUS, group words in topic areas so that we can look for new words to use.

What students can find in good learners' dictionaries

Monolingual and bilingual learners' dictionaries give a wealth of information which can help learners understand and use words effectively. The numbers in the paragraphs below refer to the numbers in the illustrations on page 183.

- MLDs list a series of HEADWORDS – and the different meanings for them. (1) For example, the VERB *teach* has more than eight different meanings.
- Good MLDs give information about the FREQUENCY of a word. The top 3,000 words are often in red in paper dictionaries, and sometimes information is given, such as S1 (the word is one of the top 1,000 words of spoken English) or W3 (the word is one of the top 3,000 in written English). (2) More than 84% of all language use employs the most frequent 3,000 words in the language.
- MLDs say what PART OF SPEECH →1 a word is (NOUN, PHRASAL VERB, TRANSITIVE VERB, etc.). (3) Sometimes, especially in paper dictionaries, this is abbreviated, e.g. *n* = noun, *adj* = adverb, *phr v* = phrasal verb.
- MLDs give the PRONUNCIATION of words. In books this is usually done in PHONEMIC SCRIPT →23. Online and mobile dictionaries have audio recordings of the words being said. (4)
- In good MLDs word definitions are written in simple language that students can understand.
- MLDs give examples of the word in the context of sentences and expressions. (5)
- Good MLDs give the COLLOCATIONS →20 that the headword is part of and they list typical phrases and IDIOMS →21 that the word occurs in. (6)
- Good MLDs list words with similar meanings and explain the differences between them. (7) They provide thesaurus entries – groups of words and expressions with similar meanings.
- MLDs give different spellings and pronunciations for varieties such as British English and American English (8), and give extra information such as if a word is FORMAL or INFORMAL →33 or if it is TABOO (it is a word that should not be used in 'polite society').
- Good MLDs give SYNONYMS and ANTONYMS for words. (9)
- Good BLDs offer the same features as MLDs. The word from Language 1 is grouped under different meanings in the L2 and clear examples are given in the L1.

Using dictionaries with students

Students are unlikely to use MLDs or even good BLDs unless we tell them, time and time again, how incredibly useful they are. But this will not be enough.

- We need to train our students to understand dictionaries and what they contain, whether they are in paper, online or mobile form. When students first get their new dictionaries, we will ask them to identify things such as what part of speech a word is, when a word can be used (so they look for descriptions such as *formal*), how frequent a word is, what words it collocates with, etc.
- It is a good idea to give the students repeated short training experiences in the middle of lessons, but not try to include everything all at once. If we include little two- or three-minute training sessions over a number of lessons, our students will become familiar with the dictionary they are using.
- When the students read a text, we can get them to decide which new words they want to know (after reaching a CONSENSUS first in pairs, then in groups, then in bigger groups). We then tell them to look the words up in the dictionary.
- We can start a lesson or week by giving the students a word WORKSHEET or quiz which asks them to find words they are going to use during the lesson (or week) in their dictionaries.
- Students can find words and test each other by giving the definitions. The others have to guess the words.
- We look at researching collocations, etc. in →46.

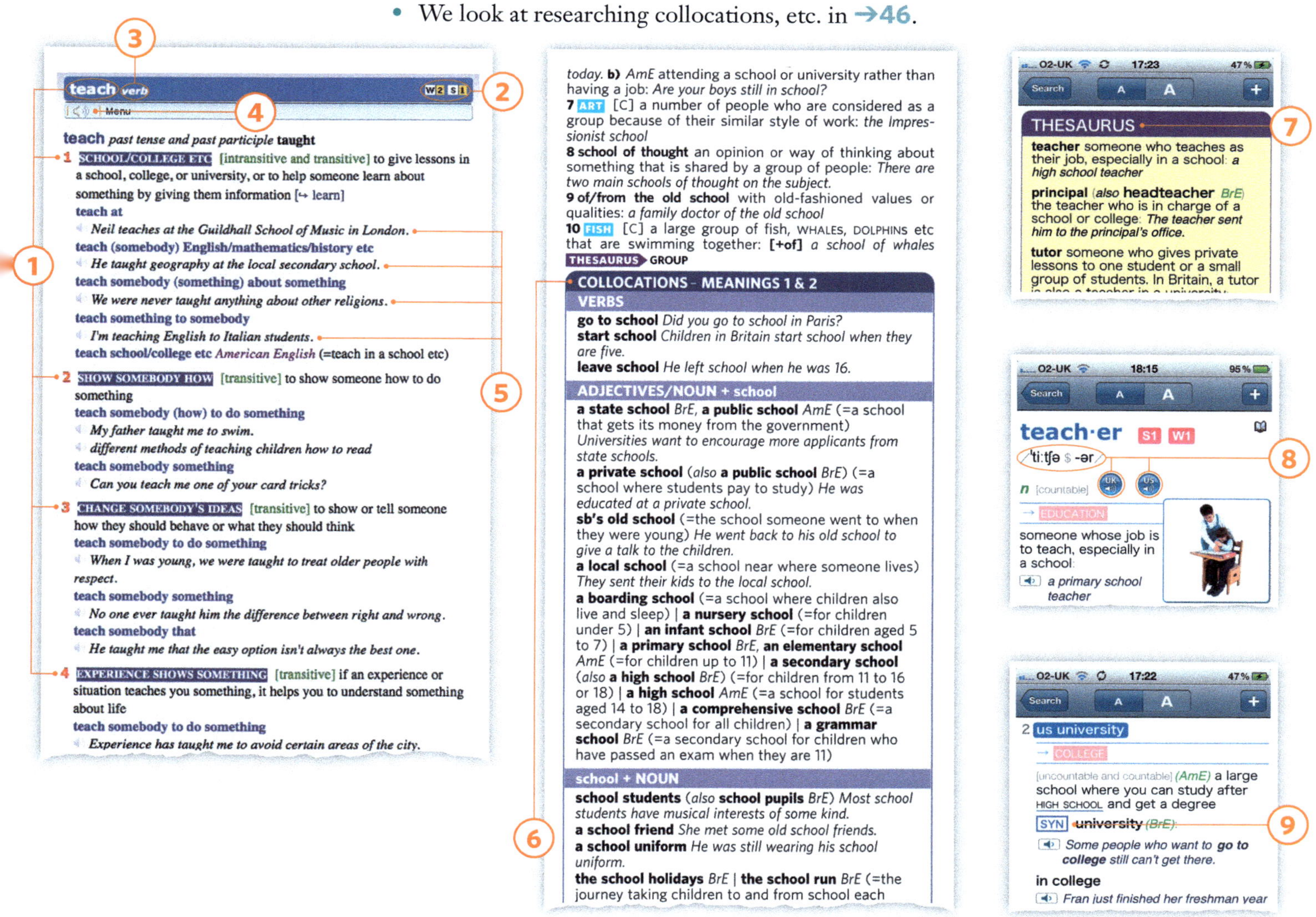

83 Supplementary materials and activities

Why use supplementary materials and activities?

Many teachers like to bring SUPPLEMENTARY MATERIALS and ACTIVITIES into the classroom.

- When we use COURSEBOOKS, we often find that we want to introduce some variety because the coursebook may sometimes feel all a bit 'the same'.
- Many of us have our own favourite activities and lessons that we like using.
- We often think that our students need extra PRACTICE with a particular language item or LANGUAGE SKILL or SUB-SKILL.
- We often take particularly ENGAGING activities (or supplementary material) into a lesson because we think the students need a bit of extra stimulation or a reward, or to add some variety to the course.
- When we are working in a MIXED-ABILITY CLASS, we may want to give different materials (or activities) to different groups of students. We discuss DIFFERENTIATION in →42.

What supplementary materials can teachers use?

There is a wide range of materials that teachers can use in the classroom.

- Many teachers encourage their students to read GRADED READERS because they believe that EXTENSIVE READING is good for language learning. We discuss extensive reading in →54.
- Many teachers take in supplementary material to practise language skills. This provides extra practice for reading, writing, speaking or listening.
- There is a wide selection of TEACHERS' RESOURCE BOOKS on the market. They contain many different ideas for activities and lessons.
- There are many WEBSITES that offer activities, language practice and LESSON PLANS.
- Students often do activities from LANGUAGE PRACTICE BOOKS or EXAM PRACTICE BOOKS.
- Many teachers like to design their own materials and activities for their students. Sometimes these might be STORIES they tell in materials-free lessons →84 or DIALOGUES they invent. Sometimes they might be WORKSHEETS with EXERCISES or CARDS or STRIPS OF PAPER →86.
- Some teachers like to copy/photocopy material from books and other sources. There is nothing wrong with this provided that a) the material is not covered by copyright and b) the students don't end up with a large collection of random pieces of paper.

Deciding what materials and activities to take into class

Before we decide to use activities and supplementary materials, there are a number of questions we will want to ask.

- *Is it easy to prepare, explain and manage?* The best activities and materials, from the teacher's point of view, are those which don't take a lot of time to prepare and don't cause problems in terms of classroom management.
- *Is the time balance attractive?* If an activity takes a long time to set up in the classroom but finishes very quickly once it starts, then the time balance is wrong. It should be the other way round. If an activity lasts for a long time but the students don't achieve or experience very much, then, again, the time balance is wrong.
- *Will the students understand what to do and how to do it?* If the material or the activity confuses the students because they don't understand how it works, then we may decide not to use it again.
- *What will the students achieve or experience?* We need to know what the OUTCOME →79 will be for the students. Will they learn something new? Will they consolidate their knowledge of some piece of language? Will they gain an understanding of how some language works? Will they increase their CONVERSATIONAL SKILLS or learn more about READING SKILLS? In other words, we need to decide what the students will get out of the activity or the materials they use.
- *Is the activity appropriate for the students?* We need to make sure that what we bring into the classroom is appropriate for the age, level, interests and cultural background of the students. This is not always easy, especially since our students have different LEARNER CHARACTERISTICS →40 and may not all feel the same about content and activities. However, we will do out best to make sure that what we bring into class is not too childish, too adult, too serious or too silly for our students – and that it is not offensive to any of them.

Deciding on games

One way of deciding whether or not to use an activity is to make a list of what a good activity *should* be like – and then see if the activity really *is* like that. We can do this if and when we are thinking of using a GAME in the classroom.

- We might, for example, decide that a good game should have the following characteristics: it should a) be engaging, b) be fun, c) involve all the students, d) have clearly understandable procedures and rules, e) be easy to organise, f) be competitive (although some people think that games should be non-competitive), g) not go on for too long and h) have a pedagogic (learning) purpose.
- When we have decided on these characteristics, we can use them to evaluate any game we want to use.
- When we have used a game in class, we can use our characteristics as a checklist to see how well it went.
- It is worth remembering that some students like games more than others. Some students are good at puzzles and competitions, but others think more slowly and don't enjoy these activities as much as their colleagues do. We should keep a record of who does and doesn't enjoy games and decide how often/whether to use them with this information in mind.

84 Teaching without materials

Teaching unplugged

Some people think that learning is more successful when the teacher doesn't use any – or at least not very many – materials. This is sometimes called **TEACHING UNPLUGGED**. There are arguments both in favour of this and against it.

Why teaching without materials is a good idea

- A lot of learning happens when people talk to (and participate with) each other, rather than when they are studying with books. That's why we include **PERSONALISATION** in much of our teaching →39.
- The students' own lives and interests may be just as interesting as the **TOPICS** and **CONTENT** that can be found in books.
- All teachers have experienced **MAGIC MOMENTS** in lessons →79 when students suddenly become **ENGAGED** in a topic (which is often about themselves and their lives) and start to talk about it enthusiastically. When students are engaged like this, they often learn better than when they are not.
- Students learn new language best when they need it and are ready for it. It may be better to let language **EMERGE** from the students' brains because they want or need it rather than trying to teach something just because it is in the syllabus.

Why teaching without materials may not be a good idea

- Some students are very good at **CONVERSATION**. Others are not so comfortable with this style of learning.
- Some learning is individual. We think things through in our own heads. When we read a book, listen to a lecture or study we often do this by ourselves.
- Some students' lives are interesting but not all! There may be, and often is, material (from a **COURSEBOOK** or some other source) that is just as fascinating.
- Although it is true that language emerges when it is needed, some language may not emerge by accident like this. In such cases, it is sensible to teach language that we know that the students need.

What the teacher needs to do when teaching without materials

If teachers decide to teach without materials, and/or when magic moments happen (when conversation suddenly takes off in a classroom), they need to be able to take advantage of the language that the students are using, or trying to use, so that they learn more.

- We should always be ready for magic moments and be prepared to exploit what the students want to talk about. This may mean departing from our plan →79 but it will often be worth it.
- We should encourage our students' ATTEMPTS →37 to use language by praising them and giving them a chance to expand on what they are saying.
- We should REFORMULATE or RE-CAST →72 what students say to make it correct.
- We should get the students to try to REPEAT what they have said – but correctly this time. We can get other students to use the same language effectively.
- We should encourage our students to keep a record of the new language that has emerged in the lesson.
- We should RECYCLE the language that has emerged in subsequent lessons so that the students get a chance for RETRIEVAL AND USE →22 to help them remember it.
- We should REVISE the language that has emerged.

Examples of materials-light teaching

- We can start the lesson by telling the students about things we like and don't like and why, e.g. *I like Sundays because I can rest. I don't like Mondays because I have to get up especially early*, etc. The students then have to talk about what they like or don't like in the same way.
- We can tell the students five things about ourselves. They have to guess which of them is false. For example, we can use five different PHRASAL VERBS →9 in sentences such as *I grew up in West London, I don't get on well with my sister, I've recently taken up playing cricket*, etc. They then have to make their own 'Which sentence is false?' sentences using the same phrasal verbs DVD2.
- We might ask a class of business students to do a WEBQUEST →87. For example, they have to investigate the cost of living in different cities around the world (we can pretend that they are thinking of opening a new international office). When they report their information back to the class, we can reformulate the language they use and get all the students to practise it.
- We can ask our students to tell STORIES about (or describe) a wide range of subjects, such as *the last concert I went to*, *my journey to school*, *my favourite place*, *a book I have read*, *an injury I had*, *a robbery I witnessed (or suffered)*, etc. As the students tell their stories, we help them to use the language they need. We get them to retell the story. As other students tell their similar stories, they use some of the same language.
- We can tell our own stories. For example, we might talk about a time that we had a discussion with a traffic warden who wanted to give us a parking ticket. The students have to retell the story from the point of view of the traffic warden or a passerby. They can also create and act out the discussion itself.
- Students can bring in their own photographs, pictures or objects and tell the class about them. This 'show and tell' procedure is popular with and for YOUNG LEARNERS, but can be used with any age group. We can also ask the students to talk about what they would rescue from their house if it caught fire and why, or the one book they would want to have with them if they went to the moon.

85

Classroom technology 1

Teaching with technology

From that first time when a teacher gave the students a slate to write on, teaching has involved the use of technology. In the modern world the variety of technological possibilities – and the speed of technological change – is extraordinary.

Deciding what technology to use

People are always encouraging teachers to use new things – for example, computers, online sites and MOBILE DEVICES. How should we respond to such offers?

- Before we spend time and money, we need to ask ourselves if there are better (sometimes older, more effective and cheaper) ways of achieving the same result.
- We should never reject something just because it is new, however. Teaching, as much as any other area of life, depends on innovation. We should always be prepared to try new things out for ourselves.
- Before we decide to say 'yes' to the new thing, we want to be sure that there will be training for using it, and that everyone who needs it has access to it. We also need to be sure that there is technical support for when things go wrong.

Using boards and other 'showing' technology

Teachers need to show students words, PICTURES and texts. They need to play AUDIO RECORDINGS and show VIDEOS.

- The most useful and versatile piece of classroom technology is the BOARD –whether this is a BLACKBOARD (used with chalk), a WHITEBOARD (used with marker pens) or an INTERACTIVE WHITEBOARD (IWB) – also called a SMARTBOARD.
- Current versions of the interactive whiteboard (IWB) allow teachers and students to do everything that is possible with a computer and a projector, but also much more. This is because all the material (whether writing, audio or video) can be controlled by tapping the board with the fingers, or with specially configured pens.
- Teachers and students can use IWBs to drag things around the screen. They can highlight phrases using a control which turns the pen or finger into a coloured marker. They can use a 'curtain' effect to hide some of what is on the board (much as we do with OHTs). Teachers can tap part of an AUDIOSCRIPT so that the students hear just that audio extract and they can use similar controls to show video extracts.
- Many teachers who use IWBs like to have an ordinary whiteboard in the classroom as well since there is less likelihood of any technical malfunction, and they are quick and easy to use.
- Boards can be used for an enormous range of activities. We can write up new GRAMMAR and VOCABULARY. We can show grammatical construction or DEMONSTRATE an activity by having everyone look to the front.
- We can write up students' errors and draw attention to them so that the students can think about how to CORRECT them DVD24. We can stick things like pictures and posters on the board.
- On the board we can draw faces, stick men, vehicles like cars and buses, trees, houses – anything that will help us contextualise the learning that is taking place. It is not necessary to be a good artist.
- It is a good idea to organise the board so that the students can clearly understand what they are being shown, rather than trying to make sense of a jumble of messy writing and pictures.

- Students can use the board, too. They can write sentences or fill in blanks. They can complete WORD MAPS DVD3. They can play games, such as noughts and crosses.
- FLIPCHARTS are very useful for students when they want to make notes for the rest of the class to see. If different groups are discussing something, they can summarise their points on flipcharts (one for each group). The whole class can then move round the room reading what each group has written.
- We can tear off the pages of a flipchart and stick them up in different parts of the classroom or keep them for future reference. Flipcharts are useful for activities like DICTOGLOSS →48, where a class try to recreate a story they have heard and one student writes the story up on the flipchart.
- The OVERHEAD PROJECTOR (OHP) is still used in some classrooms. It is useful for showing writing and because we can write on OVERHEAD TRANSPARENCIES (OHTs) while the students are watching. For example, if we ask a student to write something on an OHT, we can show it to the whole class and then write on it (or have the students write on it) to make changes. We can cover OHTs and then gradually reveal the contents. This is good for PREDICTION →55.
- We can use a computer (or TABLET COMPUTER →86) with a DATA PROJECTOR to show anything that is on the computer, such as presentations using software like *PowerPoint*, *Keynote* (for Apple computers) or *Prezi*. We can show video clips and films from CDs or DVDs, or, if we are connected to the internet, we can access anything there and project it onto the screen.
- Students can use presentation software, too, when they do ORAL PRESENTATIONS.

86

Classroom technology 2

Using pictures, cards and strips of paper

PICTURES, CARDS and STRIPS OF PAPER have a variety of uses:

- We can hold up (or project) large pictures for presenting and checking meaning, and to demonstrate and show information (for example a street scene showing what people are doing, how many cars are in the street, where the bank is, etc.).
- We can show pictures for a short time and then cover them up and ask the students if they can remember what they saw.
- We can use pictures to help the students predict the content of an audio extract or a reading TEXT →55.
- Many teachers use FLASHCARDS to show things – and as the cues in a CUE-RESPONSE DRILL →47. Flashcards (like the ones in the photograph on this page) are pictures which are big enough so that all the students can see them, but small enough for teachers to hold up in different sequences, changing them from hand to hand.
- We can give the students a selection of pictures of objects, places, people, etc. They have to choose one from each category and invent a story that connects them.
- We can give individual students different pictures. Each student has to write a story about (or a 'biography' of) their object, without saying what it is. The rest of the class then have to guess the object.
- We can get the students to draw pictures in activities like DESCRIBE AND DRAW →50 or in team games where they have to try to draw vocabulary items (or film titles, etc.). The other students have to guess what they are drawing.
- We can use strips of paper to give students roles in ROLEPLAYS →53. We can cut up material such as DIALOGUES, TEXTS or POEMS →63 and ask the students to put them in the correct order DVD1 and DVD7.

- Cards (and/or strips of paper) are especially useful when the students have to find other students whose cards MATCH theirs, perhaps because they have the other half of a sentence or the answer to a question →48.
- We can give our students cards where one side has a picture and the other has the word (for the picture) written on it. They can use the cards for team guessing games, etc.
- We can use a range of pictures, cards and strips of paper for INFORMATION-GAP ACTIVITIES →50.

Using realia and other devices

We can use real objects (REALIA) to contextualise and explain language and meaning.

- We can bring in a range of real objects (such as food items) to DEMONSTRATE meaning. Students can do a range of EXPERIMENTS (such as the famous 'Will it float?' activity for YOUNG LEARNERS).
- We can bring in clock faces, plastic fruit and telephones and any other objects and use them like theatrical props for classroom activities.
- We can put objects in a bag. Students feel (but can't see) the object. Can they guess what it is?
- We can give different students different objects. They have to find similarities and differences between them. They can write an autobiography for their object and the other students have to guess what the object is.
- Some teachers use a learning ball. When one student throws it to a classmate, the one who catches it has to answer a question or ask the next one, etc.
- We can use dice for a range of classroom games. For example, each number (1–6) represents a different topic. The students throw the dice and have to speak about the topic for the number which appears →51.
- We can use CUISENAIRE RODS (sticks of different colours and lengths) to demonstrate word order, stress and intonation – and for a range of other demonstrations of meaning.

Mobile learning

MOBILE DEVICES, such as SMARTPHONES and TABLET COMPUTERS, are becoming extremely useful in education – as in life.

- Some teachers get their students to use their mobile phone cameras to take pictures which are difficult to interpret. The other students have to try to guess what they are.
- We can have our students arrange to meet each other using TEXT MESSAGING only. Can they all manage to agree on a time and place?
- Some teachers have their students go to different rooms and phone each other to complete tasks. However, we need to be sure that the students have enough credit on their phones (and are prepared to use them).
- Some teachers encourage students to use tablet computers because a) they are easier/lighter to carry than laptops, b) they switch on and off more quickly than computers, c) students can carry them around in lessons and share them easily in PAIRWORK tasks, for example, and d) they can easily be passed from hand to hand.
- Students can use mobile devices to learn with APPS (applications). These are easier to use than many INTERNET WEBSITES. Because the students only use one app at a time, they are less likely to go to other internet sites such as *Facebook*, *Orkut*, etc. instead of working!
- Many apps have interactivity. Students can communicate with each other. They can make audio or video recordings and send them straight to internet sites.

87

Classroom technology 3

Software in the classroom

Modern software technology is extremely useful for certain learning and teaching activities.

Researching online (and on mobile devices)

- We can ask our students to research language in DICTIONARIES →82 and on WEBSITES such as *Wikipedia*, online newspapers, SONG LYRIC sites, etc.
- We can design WEBQUESTS in which we select a TOPIC for the students to research. We can supply them with tasks, websites to look at and evaluation activities to assess how well they have done.
- Students can use CONCORDANCERS on LANGUAGE CORPUS sites. These give evidence of how words are used and the COLLOCATIONS →20 that they appear in.

Making recordings

It is now easier than ever before for students and teachers to make recordings of all kinds, using smartphones or other RECORDING DEVICES. It is then relatively easy to learn how to use film and audio editing software such as *Audacity* (audio) or *iMovie* and *Windows moviemaker* (video) to cut and paste extracts.

- Using their recording devices, the students can INTERVIEW members of the public, act out their own plays, create mini films or make ORAL PRESENTATIONS. They can film their neighbourhood and give a commentary. They can post the results on sites such as *YouTube* or *Vimeo*, offer them as PODCASTS, or mail the results to friends, colleagues or teachers (for HOMEWORK →76) or post them on a website.
- Many programs (such as *Zimmertwins* and *Voki* – for children) allow students to make animated cartoon videos using AVATARS or user-created cartoon characters.

Presenting online

- Using programs like *Jing* and *Camtasia*, we can record our voices while the program records (films) what is happening on our computer screen. In other words, we can speak while we show a presentation using *PowerPoint*, *Keynote*, *Prezi*, etc.

- WEBINARS and LIVE STREAMING have become popular ways of letting people attend talks and presentations even though they cannot physically travel to conferences and seminars. Watchers of live streaming see the filmed talk as it happens. In webinars, people can see the speaker talking to a webcam while he or she also shows *PowerPoint* or *Keynote* slides. Participants can interact with each other by writing in CHATBOXES or with microphones. They can use icons for things like applause and laughter.

Using internet programs for learning and social interaction

The ONLINE world is now a great environment for people to share with each other across geographical boundaries and time zones.

- Some teachers use SOCIAL NETWORKING programs such as TWITTER, *Google+* and *Facebook* to get their students talking to each other, sending messages, writing group stories or sharing photographs and descriptions, for example.
- Teachers and students can share information, PICTURES and VIDEOS on sites such as *Wallwisher* and *Eduglogster*. These sites are really useful because all the information from the different students (wherever they are) is in one place.
- We can encourage our students to write BLOGS where they talk about their lives. We can get them to co-create WIKIS (like small versions of *Wikipedia*) where they share information or create stories together. Blogs and wikis work best when we ensure that the students interact with each other (though commenting and co-constructing); most students lose interest if we leave them alone to do it themselves.

Using virtual learning environments and learning platforms

A lot of teaching and learning now takes place using a variety of VIRTUAL LEARNING ENVIRONMENTS (VLEs) and ONLINE LEARNING PLATFORMS.

- Course designers use software such as BLACKBOARD, MOODLE or *Fronter* to run lessons and courses. Users often need a password to enter. Students and teachers can post material in the form of texts, exercises and video and audio clips. Everyone in the group (but only in the group) can access it. Discussions happen on DISCUSSION BOARDS, and assignments can be submitted, commented on and graded online.
- Some educators invite students to SECOND LIFE where users create their own AVATAR (a 3D computer identity) and can then move around in a computer-generated 3D environment. In the same ways that computer gaming provokes participation, so *Second Life* participants can speak, type, move and interact. Because there are no physical limitations (and 'environments' can be designed), the learning experience can be extremely varied and interesting. Learners can take part in tasks and challenges rather like gamers – a kind of virtual TASK-BASED LEARNING →36.

Blended learning

- Many teachers organise BLENDED LEARNING in which the students get some of the input from material such as a COURSEBOOK →81, and then expand on it with material and websites on the internet. For example, if the students read a text about water shortages around the world, they can go to the internet and see what they can find in the way of extra information or video clips.
- If their coursebook has a COMPANION WEBSITE, the students can go there and find a range of extra texts, exercises, references and activities. As with VLEs, they can do CYBER HOMEWORK, submitting HOMEWORK tasks →76 which the teacher can grade online. The software will then allow the teachers to keep automatically generated GRADE sheets and records of participation.

88 Assessment and testing

Assessing students

Students are often assessed and tested to see how well they have done, how well they are doing or how well they perform in standard (often national) exams.

Types of assessment

- Assessment can be either FORMATIVE or SUMMATIVE. Formative assessment happens when we test students so that we can help them to do better next time. We might say that a lot of CORRECTION →73–75 is a kind of mini formative assessment. Summative assessment happens when we want to see how well students have done – testing their knowledge at the end of something (a semester or a year) or in some PUBLIC EXAM.
- Teachers conduct INFORMAL ASSESSMENT all the time. We are constantly evaluating our students' progress and abilities so that we can decide what to do next in a lesson – or when we are PLANNING future lessons →79.
- We give students more formal DIAGNOSTIC TESTS when we want to know how much they know so that we can decide what to do next – like a doctor diagnosing a patient's symptoms. We can give diagnostic tests at any stage during a course to help us plan future lessons.
- A particular kind of diagnostic test is a PLACEMENT TEST. We give students placement tests when they first arrive at a language-teaching institution so that we know what level they should study at and which class they should be in.
- We give PROGRESS TESTS to see how students are getting on. Progress tests often happen at the end of a week, a month or when a unit of work (perhaps in a coursebook) is finished.
- We give students ACHIEVEMENT TESTS at the end of something, such as a semester or a year. We want to know what they have learnt in the past few months – what they have achieved.

- PROFICIENCY TESTS measure a student's language ability at a particular point in time. Most public exams are like this. We spend a lot of teaching time preparing students for these tests.
- PORTFOLIO ASSESSMENT is based on work that the students have done during a course. They keep examples of their work and this forms the basis of our assessment.
- Portfolio assessment is one example of CONTINUOUS ASSESSMENT – where we keep a record of students' work, giving marks for each piece of homework or mini-test, and we use this to decide a final grade. This is the exact opposite of a proficiency test. Some teachers prefer continuous assessment because students can feel very uncomfortable in proficiency tests and may not do as well as they should. For this reason, a combination of both can be much fairer.

Designing and making tests

Although as teachers we sometimes feel that we don't have a lot of influence on the design of public exams, we often find ourselves writing progress and achievement tests.

- When we design tests ourselves, we have to decide on our ASSESSMENT CRITERIA. We need to know what it is we are testing. For example, a question such as *Describe the hydrologic cycle in no more than 250 words* might be an appropriate task for CLIL ASSESSMENT →110, but if we only want to test the students' use of language, then it is unfair to test SUBJECT-SPECIFIC KNOWLEDGE →103 because some students may not know (or may have forgotten) about water evaporation and rainfall.
- Tests need to have VALIDITY. This means that if we tell the students that we are going to assess their writing, we shouldn't make it dependent on a lot of reading because they were not expecting a reading test. When we make achievement tests, we need to test things that the students have been learning (grammar, vocabulary, etc.), and we have to be sure that we use the same kinds of test items and tasks as the ones they have been using in their lessons.
- Before we start writing a test, we need to list exactly *what* it is we want to measure and *how* to do it. For example, we can use SENTENCE REORDERING items if we want to test SYNTAX (the order that words go in) →1 or we can get the students to put pictures in order to test comprehension of a story. However, putting pictures in order doesn't test syntax, and sentence reordering doesn't test comprehension!
- We have to decide on the balance of items in a test. Do we want all the questions to be 'discrete point' items (that is only testing one thing – such as a verb tense – at a time) or should we include more INTEGRATIVE items, where students have to read and write, for example, or use a variety of language items? What balance do we want to have between grammar and vocabulary or between the four skills?
- We have to be extremely careful to write RUBRICS (instructions) that are easy for the students/candidates to understand. If possible, every question should have an example so that the students have no doubt about what they are expected to do. For example:

> Rewrite each sentence using the word given so that it has exactly the same meaning.
>
> **Example:**
>
> Mary went to bed late and as a result she overslept. **(because)**
>
> Mary overslept because she went to bed late.

- When we write tests, it is a very good idea to give them to colleagues (or students who are not going to do the tests later) to try out (PILOT) first. This will help us to identify questions that don't work so that we can make changes before we use the test for real.

89

Test items and how to teach them

Types of test item

Test items and questions can be either direct or indirect. A DIRECT TEST ITEM asks the candidate to perform the skill that is being tested (for example, make an ORAL PRESENTATION). An INDIRECT TEST ITEM, on the other hand, examines the candidate's knowledge of individual items of language.

Direct test items

Direct test items come in many forms as the following examples show:

- In tests of *speaking*, students can be asked to do such things as give an oral presentation →53, do an INFORMATION-GAP ACTIVITY →50 with one or more colleagues or take part in an INTERVIEW.
- In tests of *writing*, students can be asked to do such things as write a letter or a report, or compose a newspaper report or a BLOG entry.
- In tests of *reading*, students can be asked to transfer information from a written TEXT to some kind of VISUAL ORGANISER →105 (a pie chart, a graph, etc.) or match texts with pictures and headlines.
- In tests of *listening*, students can be asked to transfer the information they hear to some visual organiser (a pie chart, graph, etc.) or they can put pictures (or events) in the right sequence, or choose between different written summaries of what they hear.

We discuss GRADING tests like this in →90.

Indirect test items

There are many different kinds of indirect test items.

- For GAP FILLS, students have to write a word or words in BLANKS. For example:

> **Complete the following sentences with one word for each blank.**
> She had a quick shower, but she didn't ____ any time to put on her makeup.

- In CLOZE texts, every sixth (or seventh, eight, etc.) word is a blank. The students have to understand the whole text in order to fill in the blanks. For example:

> At school none of her (1) ____ seemed to have remembered that (2) ____ was her birthday either and (3) ____ made her miserable, but at (4) ____ the children in her second (5) ____ class were in a happy (6) ____. It cheered her up and (7) ____ time one of them …

- In MULTIPLE-CHOICE items, the students have to choose the correct (or perhaps the best) from three or four alternatives. For example:

> **Choose the correct answer.**
> There were ____ people outside.
> **a** any **b** a lot of **c** much **d** none

- In TRUE/FALSE items, the students have to say whether a statement about a reading text is *true* or *false*. For example:

> **Circle the correct answer.**
> Brittany went to bed at nine o'clock in the evening. **true / false**

We can also add a third option, such as 'no information given in the text'.

- For JUMBLED SENTENCES tasks →1, the students have to put sentences in the correct order to make a coherent text, and in SENTENCE-REORDERING tasks they have to put words in order to make correct sentences. For example:

> **Put the words in order to make correct sentences.**
> call / finished / for / left / no / she / sleeping / the / there / time / was / When

- SENTENCE TRANSFORMATION exercises ask students to rewrite sentences in a slightly different form. For example:

> **Rewrite the sentence using the word given.**
> When she got home, Brittany was still tired so she lay down to have a bit of rest. **(because)**

- PROOFREADING exercises ask students to identify the mistakes in certain sentences. For example:

> **Underline the mistake in the following sentence.**
> Luckily, she doesn't wearing much makeup.

- Candidates can also be asked to do MATCHING tasks →48 and we can give them DICTATIONS →48 which test a range of competencies, such as listening, spelling, grammar, collocations, etc.

How to prepare students for tests

Students are often highly MOTIVATED →43 in exam classes because they have a clear goal to aim for. We can use their enthusiasm to help them prepare for ACHIEVEMENT and PROFICIENCY TESTS →88.

- We will give the students experience with the indirect test items that they are likely to meet. We will also give them strategies for dealing with MULTIPLE-CHOICE QUESTIONS. For example, they should find the most obvious DISTRACTORS (the choices that are wrong), eliminate them and then focus on the possibilities that remain and try to work out what is being tested.
- We will discuss with our students general exam skills, such as how to prepare, how to use PROCESS WRITING →57 techniques when writing and how to get exam timing right.
- We will let the students do MOCK EXAMS in real time. In other words, we will let them take a complete exam (not the real one, of course) so that they get used to timing, etc.
- We have to be careful of exam WASHBACK (where teachers only teach the kind of things that are in the test). Preparing students for an exam does *not* mean that we have to teach for the exam all the time. If we do this, we may damage the motivation that our students bring to their lessons.
- Students can do direct tasks which are similar to ones they will meet in the test, but we can also get them involved in any other activities and materials that will help them to improve their English.
- We can get the students to ROLEPLAY →53 oral interviews (one student plays the examiner).
- Students can try to write their own exam items and give them to their classmates. This will give them a good idea of what is involved.
- Students can give each other sections of tests to do or they can work in PAIRS and GROUPS →67 to discuss how to do them.

90 Marking and grading tests

After the test

Writing and giving tests is the first part of a complex process. When we receive students' papers, we have to mark and grade them.

The trouble with marking and how to deal with it

A good test has scorer RELIABILITY – in other words, whoever grades the test, the student should get the same result. But this is not easy to achieve.

- It is easy to be SUBJECTIVE when we grade tests and exams, because that's what we do in real life. Two people can go to a film and have totally different reactions to it. Two people grading the same student's composition can also react differently.
- It will be much better if the marking is OBJECTIVE – that is, if a candidate gets the same grade whoever is marking the test. When this happens, we call the test RELIABLE, and we can be confident that (provided we have designed it well) the test gives a clear picture of a candidate's real ability and achievement.
- Many INDIRECT TEST ITEMS →89 can be objectively graded. For example, when candidates answer well-designed MULTIPLE-CHOICE QUESTIONS →89 only one answer is correct. If the test is graded on a computer or by someone using an OVERLAY (which can be put over a student's answer sheet and which only shows correct answers), then we can have confidence that the grading will be accurate.
- If we want to include DIRECT TEST ITEMS →89, such as speaking tests and longer pieces of writing, we will have to find other non-mechanical ways of trying to achieve the same kinds of scorer reliability. ASSESSMENT SCALES like the examples below and on page 199 can help to achieve this.
- Whatever kind of marking we are using, the grading will always be more reliable if more than one person is involved. For example, two scorers can check each other's grades, or two scorers can mark the same paper to see if the same work gets the same grade.
- Where marking is subjective, we can still make grading more reliable if we organise scorer training so that everyone is clear about what an 'A' grade is, or what a 'fail' looks like, for example.

Using assessment scales

When we have thought about our ASSESSMENT CRITERIA (exactly what skills and sub-skills we want to assess), we can design an assessment scale (or scales).

Example 1: a basic five-level assessment scale for writing

1 Very difficult to understand, with poor spelling and many vocabulary and grammar mistakes.
2 Quite a lot of grammar and vocabulary mistakes, but the meaning is mostly clear.
3 The meaning is clear although there are some grammar and vocabulary mistakes.
4 The meaning is clear and there are few mistakes of grammar and vocabulary.
5 The meaning is clear and the writing is almost mistake-free.

We can make more complex assessment scales which allow us to assess a wider range of abilities in direct test items.

Example 2: an assessment scale for giving oral presentations (with a total of 25 possible marks)

	5	4	3	2	1
Content	Interesting, informative, clear	Enough interesting information to engage listeners	Quite interesting at times	Occasionally interesting, but unlikely to engage listeners	Listeners will find it difficult to find anything interesting here
Organisation	Excellent structure with good introduction and conclusion	Mostly clear and easy to follow	Easy to follow, though a little chaotic	Rather poorly organised and incoherent	Extremely difficult to follow because of extremely poor organisation
Pronunciation	Almost faultless with no problems for the listener	Very good pronunciation with only occasional difficulties for the listener	Clearly intelligible but some problems make listening a little difficult	Quite a few pronunciation problems make this speaker difficult to understand	Very poor pronunciation and very difficult to understand
Grammar	Use of varied grammar with no mistakes	Use of varied grammar with a few errors	Good grammar use with some mistakes	Often good grammar use but quite a few mistakes	Many and varied grammar mistakes
Vocabulary	A wide use of appropriate vocabulary with no problems	A wide use of vocabulary with occasional problems	Good vocabulary use with some problems	A lot of vocabulary problems make it difficult to understand	So many vocabulary mistakes that it is very difficult to understand

Involving the students

Students can be involved in marking and grading in a number of ways.

- We often use a grading system that has been decided at some stage in the past – whether by the school, the subject co-ordinator or by ourselves. However, we can also ask the students what grading system they would like us to use. Would they like A, B, C, D grades or would they prefer a simple pass, fail, distinction marking system? When we encourage our students to write JOURNALS →59, we ask them how much comment they would like from us. We can do the same with tests.
- Students can mark their own tests if we give them clear criteria for doing so.
- Students can use CAN-DO STATEMENTS →41, such as *I can write a simple email to arrange a meeting* or *I can make a two-minute oral presentation about a scientific topic* to assess their own abilities. Can-do statements can be included at the end of a week or month's work, for example, or at the end of a COURSEBOOK →81 unit so that the students can evaluate their own progress and ability levels.
- We can ask our students to take part in PEER EVALUATION (peer assessment) so that they grade each other's tests.

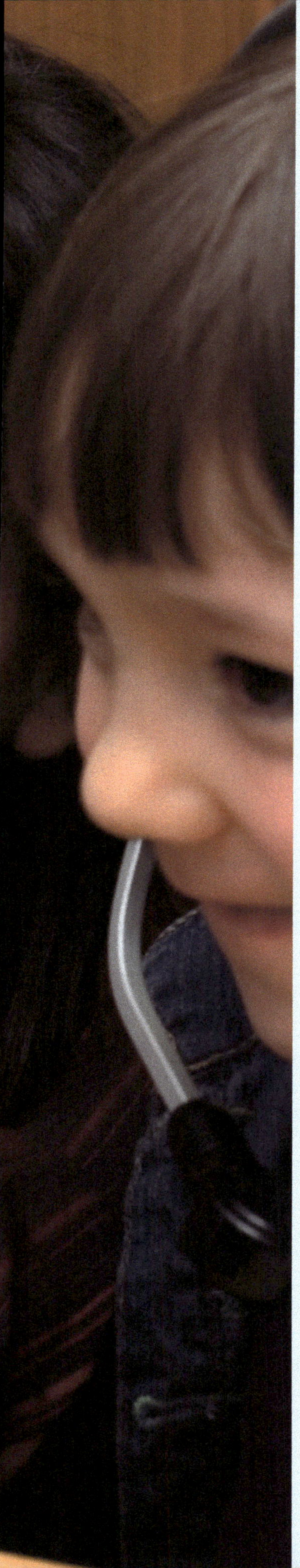

Section F: Teaching young learners

The units in this section discuss some of the characteristics of young learners, before going on to look at ways of teaching them and the activities we can use for this.

We use the term *young learners* to describe children up to about ten or eleven years old and in this section we look at how children develop, and what this means for us as (language) teachers.

We look at many activities for children – including songs, chants, games and stories – and we discuss how these activities can be used to improve young learner listening, speaking, reading and writing.

Finally we talk about a 'topics and themes' approach to lesson planning, before looking at how we can assess young learners.

91

Describing young learners

Theories of learning and child development

Many theorists have influenced the way we think about CHILD DEVELOPMENT.

- Jean Piaget (1896–1980) said that children move from *egocentrism* (thinking only of themselves) to *sociocentrism* (themselves and others) and that this maturation process involves four basic stages from the *sensorimotor* stage (when children experience everything through touch, sound, smell, etc.) through to the FORMAL OPERATIONAL stage when they can think in an abstract way and consider the practical and hypothetical consequences of their actions. His strong belief was that children construct personal meaning through action: playing, moving, making things, etc.
- Lev Vygotsky (1896–1934) suggested that children gradually develop understanding of abstract meaning through play – that action is eventually replaced, through play, by imagination. Through play, children learn social rules. Language becomes a tool for organising their thoughts (through inner speech) and for interacting with the world (external speech). Children learn best in the ZONE OF PROXIMAL DEVELOPMENT (ZPD) →38 when, with the help of someone more knowing than they are, they can understand and do new things.
- Abraham Maslow (1908–1970) suggested that there is a hierarchy of needs that learners have. Feelings of safety, being loved, belonging and SELF-ESTEEM are essential for learning to take place.
- Jerome Bruner (1915–) has said that we should realise that any learner (even at a young age) is capable of learning almost anything, provided that the instruction is organised properly. He developed the idea of *instructional scaffolding* as the way in which we can best help children to learn. In some ways this is similar to Vygotsky's idea of help and support to learners in the *ZPD*.

Instructional scaffolding

When parents (or teachers) use instructional scaffolding →65, they:

- make the children interested in the task;
- break a big task down into smaller steps;
- keep the children focused and on task by reminding them what the goal of the task is;
- point out what the important parts of the task or steps are;
- show the children other ways of doing the task.

- Based on these theories, we can say that children need safety and support if learning is to take place. They will (at first) learn best from doing things through play and action in a warm and ENGAGING environment where they feel safe. The job of teachers is to identify what developmental stage individual children have reached so that they can guide and help them to achieve appropriate learning objectives.

How young are young learners?

We generally call students between the ages of two and eleven young learners. Some people talk about children aged 0 to four as VERY YOUNG LEARNERS. But young learners are not all the same.

- There are many differences between a five-year-old child and an eleven-year-old child, and between six year olds and nine year olds, for example. We need to understand these differences if we want to know how to teach children at different ages.
- Although it is possible to suggest that in general eight-year-old children have certain characteristics which are different from those of ten year olds, this will always depend

on the individual maturity of the child and what stage they, personally, have reached. In other words, although we can make generalisations about children at certain ages, it is important to remember that these will never be exact and may not be true for individual children who are developing at different speeds and in different ways.

Children aged five to seven

If we consider children between the ages of five and seven we can say that in general, they:

- are enthusiastic about learning (if it happens in the right way);
- learn best through play and other enjoyable activities;
- use everything in the physical world (what they see, do, hear and touch, etc.) for learning and understanding things;
- use language skills without analysing (or being able to analyse) why or how they use them;
- like to do well and enjoy being PRAISED →66;
- have exciting imaginations;
- can't, sometimes, tell the difference between fact and fiction;
- have a short attention span and can't concentrate on the same thing for a long time;
- will talk (and participate) a lot if they are engaged: they can tell you what they are doing and what they have done;
- often don't understand the adult world – but they don't say 'I don't understand', they just go along with it;
- are very good at imitating people, so they pick up the teacher's INTONATION →27, etc.
- can't decide what to learn by themselves (or how to do it);
- are self-centred and like playing by themselves;
- are comfortable with the idea that there are rules and routines for things.

Children aged ten and above

By the time children reach the age of about ten, they are quite mature and they:

- understand basic concepts of the world around them; they are making sense of the adult world around them;
- can tell the difference between fact and fiction;
- have (sometimes strong) views about what they like and don't like;
- ask (a lot of) questions;
- can work with the spoken word only (they don't always need the physical world to help);
- can make some decisions about their own learning;
- can understand abstract concepts and symbols and can generalise;
- have a strong sense of what is right and fair.

92

In the language classroom

Creating the right conditions for language learning

We can help our students to feel safe, happy and eager in a young learner language classroom. This will make their learning more successful.

- We will organise activities so that each child has a chance of doing well. This will involve DIFFERENTIATION (doing our best to teach individual students in ways that match their LEARNING STYLES →40) so that every individual does work that can be praised.
- We will emphasise meaning rather than focusing on the ACCURACY of the language that the students are producing – although we will, of course, try to make sure that they do things properly.
- We will use routines (activities and procedures that happen often) in lessons so that the children feel secure and know what to expect when they happen again.
- Where possible, we will speak in the TARGET LANGUAGE to give instructions, explain things or organise PAIRWORK and GROUPWORK →67, for example. We need to take special care to use ROUGHLY-TUNED language →68 so that our students can understand what we are saying. We will accompany our words with gestures, facial expressions and visual demonstrations to help them understand. We discuss GIVING INSTRUCTIONS in →69.
- We can teach young learners some classroom phrases in English. This will help them to become comfortable when using the language, and it will help to create an English environment in the classroom.

Some examples of useful classroom English

I'm sorry.
I don't understand.
What do you want us to do, miss?
Good morning/afternoon.
Can I read a book/use the computer/go to the toilet, please?
What's this in English, please?
Is it my turn? / Now it's your turn.
Pass the ... / Can I have the ..., please?
Can you help me with this, please?
What is your painting/story about?
I like your painting/story.

- In young learner classrooms it is also very helpful if the children and their teacher can talk to each other using the children's HOME LANGUAGE (L1). However, some people believe that teachers should only use the target language in a foreign language classroom. We discuss this view in →77.
- We will use stories that the children enjoy (and which are useful for them) more than once so that they get to know them and feel comfortable and ENGAGED with them each time they appear. Many children enjoy hearing the same stories many times. We discuss reading in →54–56.
- If we spend too much time CORRECTING mistakes →73–74, rather than listening to what the students want to say and encouraging them through praise and showing interest, we may damage their emerging confidence and self-esteem.

The classroom as a learning environment

It is important to arrange young learner classrooms (if we can) in a way that contributes to the learning experience.

- A young learner classroom should, where possible, be light and spacious. It should be colourful and comfortable. The furniture should be child-sized and child-appropriate (so that the children can reach shelves or are comfortable sitting, for example).
- We can divide the classroom into designated areas so that there is, for example, a reading corner, a computer corner, a play area, a 'wet area' (where there is a sink and bowls for activities with water and other liquids), and clearly marked containers for things like pens, paints, glue, plasticine, etc. This makes it much easier for the students to move from one activity and area to another.
- We can put pictures, charts and objects around the classroom. It is especially important to display the children's own work on wall charts and posters, etc. We can encourage the children to bring things to the class so that they can 'show and tell'.
- We must decide how we want our students to sit →67. If they are all in straight lines, they will all be facing forward when we want to explain something or act as a CONTROLLER →65, and the students can still do pairwork →67 if the row in the front turns back to the row behind it. But at other times, the view of everyone who is not in the front row will be the back of another student's head!
- One of the best arrangements is to have the students seated in groups of, say, four at small tables. This helps them get used to working with others and makes groupwork and pairwork much easier to organise. It also helps if we want to use differentiation by giving different tasks to different groups.
- If we want to have our students work in different pairs or groups, we can hand out cards with pictures of animal families (ducks, cows, cats, etc.). The students then have to find the other members of their group by making the noise of their animal.
- We can vary the arrangement of tables (or where the students sit) depending on what the students are doing. For example, if we are reading a story to younger learners (5–7 year olds), we can have them sitting on the floor in a semi-circle around the teacher's chair. If they are playing a team game, they may sit in lines on the floor and send RUNNERS (individual group representatives) up to the front.
- It is important to let the students move around during lessons. Physical movement helps learning, especially for KINAESTHETIC learners →40. If the children have spent a lot of time sitting down, then we should let them get up and move, at least for a short period, to allow them to release some energy and get them in the mood for the next activity.

We discuss issues of classroom management and DISCIPLINE in →70 and →71.

93 Movement, games and special friends

Movement

Young learners should not be made to sit still all day. They need to move and to move around.

- We can ask our students to do movements with CHANTS, RHYMES and SONGS →94.
- When students are learning to tell the time, we can get them to be 'living clocks'. They have to use their arms as the hands of a clock (this is not as easy as it sounds!).
- We can ask pairs of students to mirror each other's movements and then say what they are doing.
- From time to time, we should let the children stand up and jump or wave their arms or run around (if there is a place where they can do this).
- If we want our students to work in pairs or groups, we can tell them to stand up and make a line along one wall of the classroom in order of birthdays, heights, etc. so that we can group them two by two or four by four, for example. We discuss PAIRWORK and GROUPWORK in general in →67.

1

2

3

Special friends

We can bring other 'characters' into the lesson. Children will enjoy engaging with them and imitating them.

- Many teachers like to use PUPPETS (1) when teaching young learners. We can use commercially-produced glove puppets or we can draw and cut out cardboard characters. We can use sock puppets or even just use paper bags which we draw faces on.
- The children can talk to the puppets and the puppets (the teacher) can answer. The children can take turns to talk to the puppet, be the puppet and talk like the puppet. (2)

- We can describe the puppet's life or tell stories about what it has done.
- We can give the students a number of characters who have special personalities, for example *nice Nick*, *horrible Harvey*, *clever Carol*, *happy Harriet*, *sad Sadie* and *silly Sylvester* (3). Every time the children meet these people, they are always horrible, sad or clever, etc. so they know what to expect and they enjoy their different characters. Children can also pretend to be the characters – and this gives them a chance to play at being horrible, sad, happy, etc. It makes speaking in the foreign language enjoyable and not frightening.
- It is important to consider the age of young learners when we use special friends. Ten year olds may not want to engage with puppets. They will usually respond better to more realistic characters or to the kind of AVATARS they can use with computer programs such as *Voki*, for example →87.

Games

When students play GAMES, they don't realise they are learning language. And if the game has built-in repetition, they will be practising words and phrases without even realising it!

- In the game *Please, Mr Crocodile*, one student is the crocodile and the other students are trying to cross the river. They say *Please, Mr/Mrs Crocodile may we cross the river?* The crocodile replies *You may cross the river if you have a blue T-shirt/glasses, white trainers*, etc. Children with the right clothes can walk across safely. The rest then try to cross and the crocodile tries to catch them. The crocodile can, of course, choose any category, for example *You can cross the river if you have a brother*, etc.
- We can give our students CARDS with PICTURES of objects. The teacher says a word. Which child can pick up the right picture card first? This can be very noisy!
- The learners use the word *teapot* instead of VERBS in sentences. For example, they say *Yesterday I teapot to the skating rink with my family* and the other students have to guess that *teapot = went*.
- We can write the names of famous characters (real or fictional) that the students know. They have to stick the names on their foreheads without looking at them (or someone sticks them on their backs). They have to ask *yes/no* questions →3 (*Am I a boy? Am I in a fairy story?*) until they find out who they are.
- The children can play *Snap* with two identical sets of picture cards. The first child to say the right word when they both put down the same card from their different packs keeps the two cards. Who wins?
- We can play chain memory games with students in a circle. The first student (Jack) says *I went to the market and I bought an apple*. The next child (Annie) says *Jack went to the market and he bought an apple. I went to the market and I bought an orange*. The third child has to remember what Jack and Annie bought and then add his or her own purchase, and so on.
- We can use dice. For example, each number represents a different animal. If the dice lands on a six (= tiger, for example) the child has to say a correct sentence, such as *I have four legs* or *I have a tail*.
- We can use board games. The children throw a dice. When they land on a square they have to say the word (if it has a picture) or answer the question there.
- We divide the BOARD into two columns, one for each team. The children line up in teams and take turns to write a word for each letter of the alphabet. Which team can write 26 words first?

Many speaking →51–53, listening →60–62, writing→57–59 and reading →54–56 activities for young learners have game-like characteristics.

94 Chants, rhymes and songs

Chants and rhymes

CHANTS and RHYMES with a clear rhythm help the students to get used to the stress and sounds of the language. They are easy to learn and they are fun. Because we can use them more than once, they help the students to memorise words and phrases.

- Children can do ACTIONS while they chant rhymes such as:

> Put your hands in the air.
> Now scratch your nose.
> Put your hands on your hips.
> Now touch your toes.

- Or they can do movements to accompany their rhymes:

> I'm a cunning little fox (*hands on head for ears, looking around*)
> And I live in the wood. (*hands waving for trees*)
> My favourite food is chicken. (*flapping wings*)
> Wow! It tastes so good. (*rubbing their stomachs*)

- We can put rhythm behind almost any questions and answers such as:

> What's your **name**? My name is **Sam**.
> Where do you **live**? I live in a **house**.
> Do you have a **bro**ther? Yes I have **three**.

- We can use counting rhymes such as:

> Five little elephants sitting in a boat.
> But elephants are heavy and the boat won't float.
> *So one jumps out and swims to shore.*
> Now there aren't five elephants, there are only *four*.
>
> (*So one jumps out and swims to a tree: three*)
> (*So one jumps out and runs to the zoo: two*)
> (*So one jumps out to have some fun*
> Now there aren't five elephants, there's only one.)

They can count on their fingers, or they can have picture cards of a boat and five elephants. They take one away each time and put it in the right place (in a zoo, on the shore, etc.).

Songs and singing

Many young learners (like people of all ages) like SONGS. They appeal directly to our emotions and, as a result, make the words (lyrics) more memorable. When young learners sing together, it can reinforce a sense of belonging, and when they perform their songs, they can feel a sense of pride and achievement.

- Students can sing songs →64 and do the actions to go with them. In the following two songs (used by teachers all over the world) they have to do a range of movements.

> **A** If you're happy and you know it, *clap your hands*. T18
> If you're happy and you know it, *clap your hands*.
> If you're happy and you know it, your face will surely show it.
> If you're happy and you know it, *clap your hands*.

For the second, third and fourth verses, we can replace *clap your hands* with *stamp your feet*, *shout hurray*, *turn around* – or any other action the teacher or the children want to use.

B This is the way we *wash our face, wash our face, wash our face,* T19
This is the way *we wash our face* so early in the morning.

For the verses that follow, the teacher can substitute actions such as *brush our teeth, put on our clothes, brush our hair*, etc.

- Students can sing a round: a song where the same lines are started at different times by different singers. Two popular ones are:

C London's burning, London's burning T20
Fetch the engines, fetch the engines
Fire, fire! Fire, fire!
Pour on water! Pour on water!

D Life is butter, life is butter T21
Melancholy flower, melancholy flower
Life is but a melon, life is but a melon
Cauliflower, cauliflower

- We can teach each child a word or phrase from a song (perhaps a pop song that they like) or give it to them on a STRIP OF PAPER. Every time they hear that word or phrase, they have to stand up or hold the word up.
- If the song has a STORY, we can give the students pictures of the main characters (or display them on the board/screen). The learners have to put the pictures in order and/or point to them when they come up in the song.
- We can give the students the words of a song. The students sing along with an audio recording. We fade out the audio and the children keep singing. When we increase the volume of the audio again, are the children in the right place (or have they sung too fast or too slowly)?
- We can conduct students while they are singing. We can make them sing softly or loudly, faster or slower. A student can then be a conductor.
- We can build up a song using different groups of students to sing different lines. For example, they can sing 'The lion sleeps tonight' in three parts. The first part has the words:

  In the jungle, the mighty jungle, the lion sleeps tonight

  The bass line is:

  A-wimoweh, A-wimoweh, A-wimoweh, A-wimoweh

  and the middle line can be sung as *We-ee-ee*, etc.

We discuss music in detail in →64.

95

Language teaching with young learners

Teaching language to children

As children approach puberty (from about ten onwards), they start being able to analyse abstract language concepts such as SYNTAX and GRAMMAR. They are reaching the FORMAL OPERATIONAL stage of their development →91. Before that, however, we need to think about teaching language to children differently from the way we teach it to TEENAGERS and ADULTS.

- Young learners absorb language through ACTION, GAMES, SONGS and RHYMES →94, STORIES and the senses. This is far more effective than trying to explain its rules or construction.
- We can, however, make young learners aware of *some* language features and differences. For example, we can show them the word *horses* (with the *s* in a different colour from the rest of the word) and say *Is that one horse or more than one horse?* We can say things like *Is that a yesterday question or a today question?* to make them aware of past and present tenses.
- We will give explanations when the *children* ask for them (rather than when *we* want to give them). We will try to find explanations which are appropriate for the stage the child is at.

Some examples of language teaching sequences

It is impossible to list all the many ways of teaching language to young learners, but the following examples give an idea of how children can learn and practise language.

- We can build up a conversation with two PUPPETS (or with their SPECIAL FRIENDS →93), such as:

Croc:	What shall we do *this evening*, Mr Ted?
Mr Ted:	Let's *watch television*.
Croc:	But I don't like *television*!
Mr Ted:	All right then, let's *play a game*.
Croc:	Yes, let's.

  The children practise the dialogue in CHORUS →47. We can then give the puppets to a pair of students and they have to try to perform the conversation. They can change the words and phrases in *italics* in the dialogue.

- We can MIME actions (representing language that we want our students to learn and/or practise) and the students have to guess what we are doing. We can mime a story and the students have to tell us what is happening. Students can then mime their own stories.
- If we want our students to hear (and produce) two of the different sounds of the 's' plural, we can ask them whether the words are *snake* words (*cats*, *cups*, *socks*) or *bee* words (*apples*, *bananas*, *dogs*).
- We can tell our students about the class puppet or another character and they have to say whether their lives are *the same* or *different*. For example, we can say *Mr Ted has a brother*. A student has to say *Same! I have a brother, too* or *Different! I don't have a brother. I have two sisters.*
- We get the students to think of all the things that you can find in people's bedrooms. We can draw or write up words (or show PICTURES). We then ask them to think of six things they have in their bedroom. They write them down or draw pictures of them without the other students seeing. The class now asks each student *Do you have a television in your room? Do you have a picture in your room?*
- We can get the students to be telepathic with words! One student thinks of a day of the week (or a word from another category such as an animal, a sport or a hobby). Can another student (or other students) receive that telepathic message and guess the day of the week?

- We can ask our students to write words showing where the **STRESS** is – the stressed syllable must be larger than the unstressed syllables (1).
- When we teach children who have started to read, we can use disappearing words or **DISAPPEARING DIALOGUES** as a way to help them remember words and phrases. We show a dialogue on the board (or the screen). The students practise saying it. Then we take words or phrases away, one at a time. Each time we do this, the students have to try to say the original dialogue until, finally, they can say the whole dialogue from memory.
- We can show the students 'spaghetti' or 'ball of string' pictures (2). They have to follow the lines from a person to a place so that they can say things like *John lives in a house*, *Justin lives in a flat*, *Peter lives in a caravan*, etc. We can use pictures like this for almost any language we want to practise.
- Students can look for the words in a wordsnake showing, for example, the months of the year (3), or do a wordsearch (4) puzzle. Who can find the most words?
- We can play a version of the **GAME** →93 *Battleships*. Each student has two charts, one for themselves and one for their partner. They don't look at their partner's chart. In the charts, the horizontal top line shows pictures representing *under the chair*, *on the table*, *in the basket*, *on the chair*, *behind the sofa*. Pairs of students put different animals in different places in their own charts (but they don't tell their partner) (5). For example in A's chart, Danny the dog is behind the sofa and Carrie the cat is under the chair, etc. Student A asks 'Is Danny under the chair?' and if the answer is *yes* (because Danny is under the chair in B's chart), Student A can put a cross on that square in their second chart (the one about their partner). The first student to put crosses on all the squares of their partner's chart is the winner.

(1) fifTEEN FIFty

(2)

(3)

(4)

O	R	A	H	O	U	S	E	B	S
R	O	Z	E	C	G	G	A	R	O
O	C	L	A	S	S	I	C	A	L
A	K	C	V	U	O	J	A	Z	U
R	C	E	Y	E	U	O	R	J	P
P	O	U	M	B	L	U	E	S	O
U	B	L	E	L	C	L	G	I	P
N	A	P	T	O	R	E	G	E	A
K	O	R	A	P	O	J	A	Z	Z
E	F	O	L	K	G	L	E	M	T

(5)

Danny the dog				X
Carrie the cat	X			
Mickey the mouse		X		
Simon the snake			X	

96

Young learner listening

The importance of listening

If we want young learners to use the foreign language they are learning, they have to listen to it first. There are a number of activities we can use for this.

Listen and do

- We can use RHYMES and CHANTS →94. The children have to do the actions in the rhyme, as in the following example:

> Sway from side to side like a tree in the breeze.
> Smell the beautiful flowers – but be careful, don't sneeze.
> Turn your face to the sun – but don't stay too long.
> Now here comes the rain with its pitter patter song.

- We can ask our students to do things with a range of instructions, such as *Bring me something green*. Each group of students sends a RUNNER (a representative from the group) to the front of the class with the appropriate object.
- We can tell the children things like *Put the lion in the cage* or *Clare is in the sitting room*. The children have to move pictures or drag them on the INTERACTIVE WHITEBOARD so that the animal goes in the right place in a picture of a zoo or the girl is put in the right room in a picture of a house.
- We can tell students to do things like *Stand on one leg and count to ten* or *Go to the window and open it*. With TOTAL PHYSICAL RESPONSE activities like this →4, 45 the students themselves can then give instructions to each other.
- Students choose words that we give them (one word for each student). They stand up. We read a TEXT with their words in it. When they hear their word they have to sit down (we can do this with adults, too DVD12).
- We can describe a picture. The students have to draw the picture. This is similar to DESCRIBE AND DRAW →50.
- When we are teaching colours, we can tell the students to do things such as *Colour the clown's nose red*, *Make the clown's right leg purple*, etc.

Listen for information

- We can give the students a picture of a town. We tell them they have to discover where we (or a PUPPET or a SPECIAL FRIEND) went yesterday. They hear things like:

> I walked out of my house and turned right. I walked past the cinema. I crossed the street and walked past the swimming pool. I turned left and walked past the baker's. Then I walked across the zebra crossing and it was right in front of me next to the …, etc.

- The students see PICTURES of four different children. We describe one. They have to say which one we are describing. For example, we say:

> I am quite tall. I have red hair and freckles. I have glasses and a stripy shirt. I am wearing blue trousers. Who am I?

  Or, for animals, we can say something like:

> It has four legs, two ears, two eyes, sharp teeth and a long tail. It has spots and it can run very fast. What is it?

  and the students have to find the picture of a leopard.

- We can describe a picture or tell a story (see below) and make a mistake such as *Cinderella's sisters were very beautiful*. The children have to find the mistake. We can give them information and they have to say whether it is *true* or *false*.

Stories

Children love stories. Stories teach them about the world. They can be funny, serious, happy, sad and uplifting. Children like it when stories are told and retold.

- When we read to children (as all parents know), we need to be animated and dramatic. We need to make the story come alive. When the wolf says *All the better to eat you with!* he should *sound* like a horrible wolf.
- When we want to tell stories (rather than read them) we need to think about what order the events should be in and then practise the different stages of a story. As with reading, we need to tell stories dramatically and interestingly.
- We can have a special story time, especially for younger learners (5–7). For example, it is often a good idea to end the day with a READING CIRCLE to settle the children (quieten them down and relax them). They can sit on the floor so that they listen and relax. We can show them all the illustrations in the book or on the screen (if we are using a data projector or an interactive whiteboard).
- We can show the learners the cover of a book (and the pictures in it). The children have to guess (or tell us) what the story is before we read it.
- With older children, we can read longer stories or books one chapter each time so that the children will look forward to the next week's instalment.
- When we read to younger children, we can invite them to join in with the story. We can say things like *So what did the princess do then?* or get them to speak the repeated lines with us.
- We can tell a story and the students have to MIME the actions.
- We can tell the students to close their eyes and try to imagine that they are in the story we are telling them. When we finish, we can ask them what they saw, how they felt, what smells they smelt, etc.

We discuss listening in general in →60–62.

97

Young learner speaking

Creating confident speakers

We want our students to become confident speakers in the foreign language. For some young learners this can be hard, but there a number of ways we can help them to overcome their difficulties.

Speaking activities

When we want our students to practise speaking, we can use a number of activities and techniques.

- The students sit in a circle. They pass or throw a soft ball around the circle. When a child receives the ball, they have to say something in English.
- The students can interview PUPPETS or their SPECIAL FRIENDS →93 and ask them questions about what they like, what time they get up in the morning, where they are going on holiday, etc. We can answer for the puppet at first, but later we can give the puppet to one of the children and they can make up the answer.
- When we ask our students to practise any language (for example *I like/don't like bananas* or *On Sunday I watched television*) they can speak in the voice of one of the special friends (such as sad Sadie or happy Harriet →93). The other students have to guess who they are.
- We can get our students to complete questionnaires. They write the names of other students along the top of a chart and then the names of some foods on the left. They have to ask the other students *Do you like chocolate? Do you like snails?* etc. If young learners are not writing yet, they can draw (or put) smiling/frowning faces to show the correct answers.
- We can have a collection of CARDS (or PICTURES on the board) of places such as a library, a swimming pool, a sweet shop and a skating rink, and some objects such as a book, a swimsuit, some money, some gloves, etc. One child chooses one of the places and the others have to ask *What do you have in your bag?* When the child answers, for example, *I have some money*, the others ask *Are you going to the sweet shop?* The child who asks the correct question chooses the next card.

Storytelling

We need to help younger learners become good storytellers in English.

- We can SCAFFOLD →65, 91 STORIES with our students, gradually helping them to include the elements that they need. For example, we can ask them things such as *Who is in the story? Where did they go? What happened next?* etc.
- We can get the students to tell stories to their puppet or mascot, saying things like *Tell Teddy what you did yesterday* or *Teddy wants to know what you saw when you went to the zoo.*
- We can get younger students to retell the stories that they have been enjoying in a READING CIRCLE (where the teacher reads a story to the students) →96. We will point out how the story begins and ends with typical phrases such as *once upon a time* and *they all lived happily ever after.*
- As young learners get older, we can get them to retell stories they have heard in class. We can have different GROUPS →67 hear or read different stories. They then have to tell the stories to the other groups so that everyone has heard all the stories.
- Older children can read or hear a story with several different characters. They then have to retell the story from the point of view of one of the characters in the story.
- Sometimes the simplest things can provoke good stories. For example, we can ask the students to tell the story of a day in the life of pebble on the beach, a five-pound note or a set of keys.
- We can tell older students two stories about our lives (or the lives of a person/ celebrity the students know) and they have to decide which story is true and which is false.

Using drama and playacting

Young learners are usually happy to become involved in PLAYACTING and DRAMA.

- We can get our students to act out situations using language they have been learning. For example, if they have been learning words to describe foods, we can set up a food store, and they can go to the store to buy different items, saying things like *Have you got any apples?*
- Students can ROLEPLAY →53 a visit to a restaurant and order meals.
- We can reconstruct a familiar story as a drama, and the children can help to create the scenes. They can decide who says what. For example, if they have been reading (or listening to) the story of Cinderella, they can decide what Cinderella's sisters say to her when they are getting ready for the ball, e.g. Cinderella: *I want to go to the ball, too.* Sisters: *Well, you can't! You haven't got anything to wear!* We can give different scenes to different groups so that the final version of the whole 'play' has been written by everybody in the class. We can help them with words and phrases from the original stories. We will rehearse our play for a few minutes every day in the weeks before the final performance.
- If the students have been reading comic-strip stories (for example in their COURSEBOOKS →81), they can rehearse the scenes and act them out. We will spend time helping the students to say their lines with correct pronunciation, using appropriate stress and intonation so that their scenes are dramatic and enjoyable.
- We can turn stories into the news. For example, the children can retell the episodes in a story as if they were doing a news broadcast. We can set up a table as if it was in a TV studio and have presenters 'read the news'.

We discuss more speaking activities in →51–53.

98

Young learner reading

1

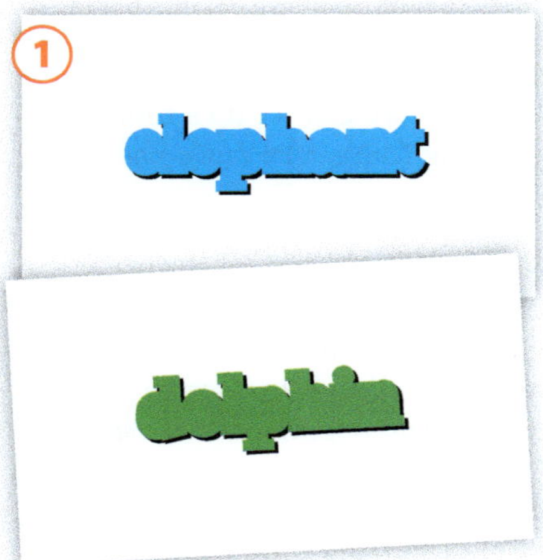

Encouraging reading

When young learners first start reading, they need to be able to recognise word shapes and sentences. But we also have to encourage them to love reading, and we can do this by demonstrating our own enthusiasm for reading, especially during READING CIRCLE sessions, for example, where the teacher reads to the students.

Learning sounds, learning words

In the first stages of reading, we want our students to recognise letters, whole words and sentences.

- When we read to our students using big books in a typical reading circle (where the students sit in a circle and the teacher reads to them), they can point to the words as we read them. If they have their own books (or if they are reading on screens), they can follow the words with their finger or a cursor.
- We can show the students word shapes (1). They have to match them with the words. The examples shown in the margin have to be matched with the words *elephant* and *dolphin* from a list of animal names given to the students. This helps them to get used to what words look like.
- We can give the students word CARDS. They have to MATCH them with PICTURES.
- We can give the students word and MORPHEME cards (for example, *S* cards for plurals). The words can be in different colours for verbs, articles, etc. The students have to say what the words are. For example, *It's a 'doing' word*, *It's a 'person' word*, etc. They can choose words to make their own sentences. They can put cards in order to make sentences →1.
- We can get our students to give us sentences about themselves such as *I live with my mum and dad* or *I have a cat called Timmy*. We write the sentence(s) on a piece of paper or card and give it to the students so that they can read it to themselves. Then they have to read their card back to us. Later they have to select one of their many cards and read it out.
- When we build up a DIALOGUE with the class →45, we can write it on the board. We can then give the students phrases from the dialogue cut up and written on cards. The students have to match the cards to put the phrases back together again. They can look at the dialogue on the board to help them do this.

A few things that young learners can do with reading

- We can give the students a STORY, together with pictures which come from it. The students have to put the pictures in order.
- Students read a story. They then retell it.
- We can give the students a story with pictures of the characters (but without names). The students have to identify them.
- We can give the students pictures from a book or story they are going to read. The students have to guess (and get prepared for) the story.
- We can give young learners a story to read and ask them to draw pictures about it.

Reading aloud

In many classrooms, teachers ask students to read from books in front of the whole class, student by student, line by line. This isn't usually very successful. Students often find it difficult to read well, and the other students get bored. However, reading aloud can be fun, and it helps us to know how well our students are getting on with their reading.

- If we want our students to read aloud, we must give them time to think about how to read the text. They can hear us reading the text first (or listen to an audio recording). They can then practise reading it aloud in pairs or groups (or just mumbling to themselves) before we ask them to read to us.
- Students can read (on a one-to-one basis) to the teacher (or parent or classroom assistant). This allows them to show us how well they are doing, and we can help them with any words they are finding difficult. We will only ask students to read aloud in front of the whole class if we are confident that they will not stumble over the words and feel foolish.
- Students can read sentences in CHORUS →47. This is good fun and focuses their attention on the sentence in the book or on the board. We can point to words as they read them.
- We can ask our students to choose their favourite sentence in a story. They can practise reading it by mumbling to themselves. When we ask them to read it aloud, they have to say *It says here* … and then read their sentence aloud as dramatically as possible →29, 69.

Let students read!

- We should encourage our students to read for pleasure (we discuss EXTENSIVE READING in general in →54). They can go to the reading corner in their classrooms →92 and sit there reading while other student groups do different things.
- We can make mini-books (short stories on cards with accompanying pictures) so that the students can read complete stories quickly.
- It is important that students should be allowed to choose the books that *they* want to read, even if this means that they are reading the same books again and again.
- We can include DEAR (drop everything and read) moments in lessons →54. This encourages the students to become comfortable with reading books, tablet computers, online sites, etc.
- We can get our students to comment on what they have read. At the beginning, they can put smiley or frowny faces on a feedback sheet (2), but later they can complete sentences such as *My favourite person in the story is* … and *The part I like best is when* … (3).

We discuss reading in general in →54–56.

(2)

Title:	The Snow Prince
Ivana	🙂 🙂 🙂 🙂
Sergei	🙂 🙂 🙂
Natalia	☹ ☹
Sasha	🙂 🙂 🙂 🙂 🙂
Veronika	🙂

(3)

Title:	The Mysterious Castle
Name:	Mehnan My favourite person in the story is Tiny the Giant The part I like best is when Tiny kills the nasty king

99 Young learner writing

The value of writing

When students start to write, they find another way to express themselves. Because the WRITING PROCESS →57 is generally less spontaneous than, for example, speaking, students have a chance to *think about* language, and this helps their linguistic development.

- Some students find it far easier to express themselves in writing than in speaking.
- When students write things down, it helps to consolidate their knowledge of the language they have been learning.
- When students write in their books, on posters or on the computer, they get to see what they have done, and we can celebrate their work →66 by displaying it around the classroom or online.

Copying activities

Students need to copy words so that they get used to writing. They should have a COPYBOOK in which they can record new words and sentences that they have met.

- Children need help in forming letters and putting letters into words. We can give them special lined paper to help them to do this, and show them what strokes are necessary to make different letters →57.
- Students can practise writing letters in the air. They can write letters with a finger on another child's back and the child has to guess which letter it is. They can make letters from plasticine or draw them on large pieces of paper.
- Students can have fun with words. For example, if they write *big*, they have to write a really big word. The word *small* has to be smaller and the word *tiny* has to be smaller still. Students can do this with words which describe size (*tall*, *short*) and shapes (*triangular*, *circular*, *square*, etc.).

- We can get our students to tell us any food words that they know. We then write them on the BOARD →85 and draw a chart with columns for *meat*, *fish*, *vegetable*, *fruit* and *cereal*. The students copy the chart and then they write the words in the correct columns, making sure they spell them correctly.
- We can get the students to copy down the words for parts of the body on sticky labels. They then have to stick the labels on one of their friends or on a picture.
- We can show the students words, sentences or very short paragraphs. They have to look at them for a short period. We then take the sentences away or cover them up and the students have to try to write them from memory.
- We can get the class to help us write a text. We write up the sentences they suggest to us. When we have finished, they have to copy the text into their copybook and we can check it. We discuss writing together in more detail in →58.

Dictation

We can DICTATE short sentences, especially if they are connected to topics or language which the students are working on.

- To begin with, the students put their pencils down. We then say a sentence and the students have to listen. When we finish, they try to write the sentence from memory. With very short paragraphs we can use the DICTOGLOSS technique →48.
- We hold up picture cards (with the word for the picture on the back). The students write down the words for the pictures. We turn the cards over and they check whether they have written the right word correctly.
- We can hold up CARDS with words (accompanied by pictures), such as *empty*, *big*, *hot*, etc. and the students have to write their opposites (*full*, *small*, *cold*, etc.).
- We can dictate half a sentence, such as *The best book I have ever read is* ... and the students have to complete it.
- Students can do a RUNNING DICTATION →48 with a poem or other short text.

Portfolio writing (and other writing tasks)

When teachers get young learners write POEMS, STORIES or descriptions (often with pictures and drawings attached), they can keep them in a folder (or PORTFOLIO →59). Later they can look at this collection in order to EVALUATE the learner's progress over time →88. The portfolios can be given to the parents at the end of the term or year.

- We can give our learners clear models to follow. For example, we can show them a text (with an attached photograph or drawing) such as the following *Gloria is my best friend. She's clever and funny. She likes chocolate and hamburgers, and she likes ballet and TV. She lives in Cambridge, in England. She speaks English and Spanish*. Now they have to write about their best friend (including a photograph or a drawing), saying what their friend is like, what they like, where they live and what languages they speak.
- We can ask our students to write POETRY →63 using models we give them.
- We can give the students cartoon strips with the words in the speech bubbles missing. They have to write words for the speech bubbles. They then compare their versions with the original.
- The students can watch a cartoon sequence without sound. They have to write the dialogue and then check with the original.
- Students bring in their favourite photographs (or post them on an ONLINE LEARNING PLATFORM). They write a paragraph explaining who or what is in the photograph. We can display these photographs and paragraphs on the classroom walls.
- We can ask our learners to keep a JOURNAL →59 in which they write about such things as what they have been doing and what they would like to do, or write an imaginary entry from a space diary.

We discuss writing in general in →57–59.

100

Topics and themes

Planning around a subject

Many teachers organise their teaching by grouping language lessons around topics and themes. In other words, instead of PLANNING one lesson after another based on language or activities alone, they base a series of lessons around a SUBJECT. We discuss lesson planning in general in →79.

Topic-based teaching is a form of 'soft' CLIL (CONTENT AND LANGUAGE INTEGRATED LEARNING) →102 where language and topic are taught alongside each other.

Thinking about topics and themes

One of the best ways of planning a sequence of lessons for young learners is to organise our classes around a TOPIC or a THEME.

- When we use a topic or a theme to build our lessons, we can decide how long (five lessons, ten lessons, 15 lessons) we want our topic or theme to carry on for.
- We don't do the same thing lesson after lesson just because we have organised everything around a theme.
- When we organise lessons around a topic or theme, we still need to think about what activities, language skills and language learning we want the students to practise. We need to see how we can fit all these different elements into and around the topic or theme we have chosen.
- When we choose a topic, we need to think about how to make it personal for our young learners. We will choose topic-related activities which are interesting and relevant to their lives. However, we will also use our topic to introduce the children to the wider world, including giving them some INTERCULTURAL UNDERSTANDING where this is appropriate.

Themes, topics and activities

Almost any topic can be used for a large variety of activities and lesson types. A lot will depend on the age of the children, and what DEVELOPMENTAL STAGE they are at →91. For our example in this unit, we will take the theme of bananas as our organising topic and show a range of CROSS-CURRICULAR activities based on this topic that could help our students learn English.

- We can get the students to research/look at different types of banana and categorise them.
- The students can learn about the life cycle of a banana. They can research the growing and harvesting of bananas.
- They can learn about where bananas are grown and make VISUAL ORGANISERS (such as graphs or maps) →105 showing which countries are the biggest producers.
- They can complete a class survey, asking each other about which fruits they like most, or how many bananas they eat in a week, a month, etc. They can transfer this information to a visual organiser of some kind.
- Students can hear or read about the daily life of a banana grower.
- The students can enjoy learning and singing *Day-o (The Banana Boat Song)*, a traditional SONG about dockworkers loading the banana boats in Jamaica and waiting for their work to be counted when daylight comes so that they can go home.
- Students can think about other work songs which have call-and-response verses to help people enjoy their work. We can introduce simple sea shanties, for example.
- The students can learn about how bananas are weighed and sold. They can act out a visit to the greengrocer's where they go to buy bananas and other fruits and vegetables.
- Students can make banana puppets and use them to create conversations.
- They can discuss different banana recipes. They can make a banana smoothie or other simple banana-based dish.
- They can read information about why bananas are good for you. They can discuss healthy eating in general and make lists about healthy and unhealthy eating options. They can design a healthy eating programme or leaflet.
- Students can write an *I like/I don't like* poem about bananas →63.

We can summarise (some of) the different activities in a TOPIC WEB. We can use the topic web as the basis for planning a SEQUENCE OF LESSONS →80.

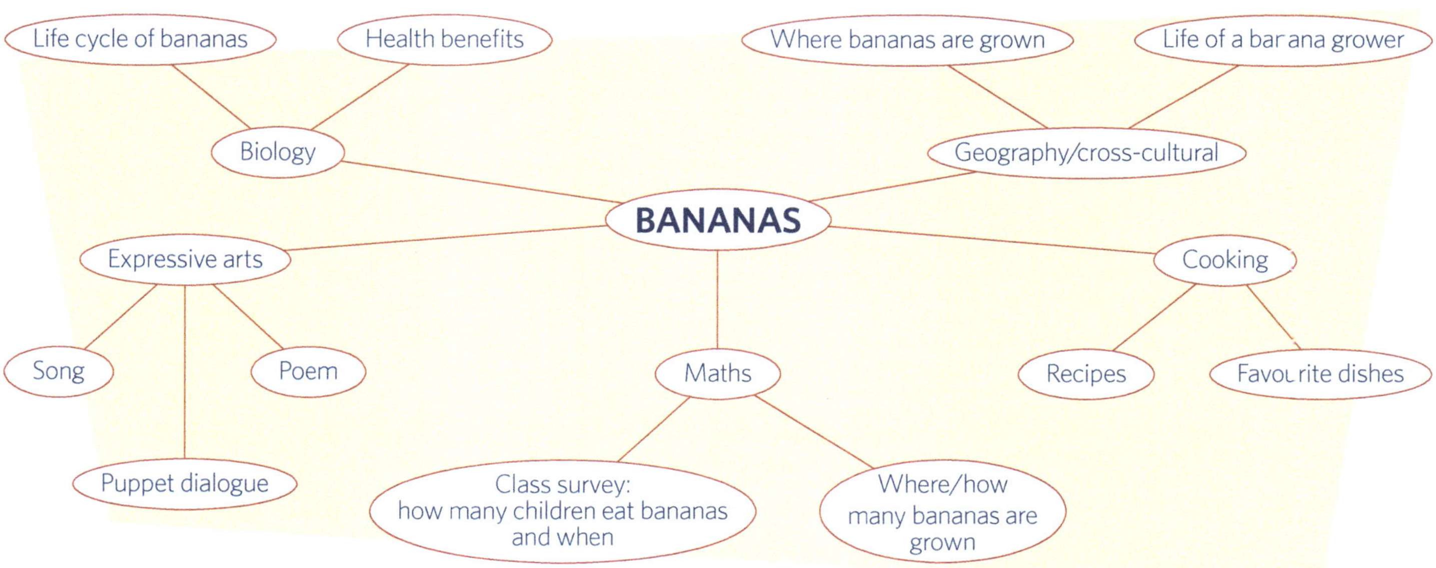

101 Assessing young learners

Why we test young learners

When we think about assessing (or testing) young learners, we have to decide what we are testing for and how we want to do it. There are a number of reasons for testing young learners.

- Sometimes we test students because we want to see what they *have achieved* or how proficient they are (e.g. what they know). We call this kind of assessment SUMMATIVE ASSESSMENT.
- Sometimes, however, we assess students because we want to see how well they *are doing*, in order to help them do better. We call this kind of assessment FORMATIVE ASSESSMENT; we use the results of the assessment to show our students how to improve.
- Some learners have to sit 'sudden death' tests at the end of a semester or year. Some students do very well in tests like this – it suits their learning style – but others don't because this type of testing isn't right for them.
- A lot of young learner assessment is based on CONTINUOUS ASSESSMENT, (including PORTFOLIO ASSESSMENT →88) where we are continually evaluating the students' work and helping them to improve over the semester or year.

We discuss assessment and testing in more detail in →88–90. We talk about testing for CLIL in →110.

Continuous assessment

Because children develop at different speeds and are constantly changing, we need to gather information about them as often as possible.

- We can look at our students' work as evidence (imagining that we are detectives). We can then see what the evidence tells us so that we can take action to help our students improve.

- When we look at a student's work, we can make a list of the strengths it has and then say what the student can do to improve and build on those strengths. For example, we might say *She knows when to use the* PRESENT SIMPLE →6 *tense* (strength) and *She needs help to understand that we add an 's' to the third person singular*, or *He knows how to tell a story* (strength) but *He needs help to organise the events of a story into a coherent order* →34.
- We can make a LEARNER LANGUAGE PROFILE (LLP) for each student. The profile might consist of a number of CAN-DO STATEMENTS →41 such as, for example, (in reading) *He/she can read and understand all of the words in word list A* or (for listening) *He/she can understand simple instructions.*
- Most teachers don't have time to fill in learner language profiles all the time, so it is helpful to divide the class up into GROUPS →67 and plan activities so that while Group A is doing some colouring, Group B is in the reading corner and Group C is watching a video, we can listen to Group D and fill in the LLP for the students in it. In the next lesson we can switch the groups around.

Students assess themselves

We can encourage older children to assess themselves.

- At the end of a SEQUENCE OF LESSONS (for example two weeks' work or a unit in a coursebook), we can ask them to say *yes* or *no* to statements such as *I can give my opinion about things with the expression 'I think that ...'* or *I can use more than two adjectives (in the right order) to describe objects and people.* If they say *no*, they can go back to the lessons they have studied and look again at that particular language point.
- At the end of a sequence of lessons, students can do tasks similar to the ones they have been doing. When they have done these tasks, they themselves say if they have been successful or not. For example, they have to listen to three descriptions of objects and write down what the objects are. If they can do this, they can tick (✓) a statement which says *I can understand descriptions of objects.* The statement is written in English and/or in their home language (L1). We might ask them do an exercise using the GOING TO FUTURE →5. If they are successful, they themselves can tick a statement (in English or in their L1) which says *I can say what people are/are not planning to do.*

Types of test items

When we design tests for young learners – or when young learners do PROFICIENCY TESTS →88 – we will write test items which are similar to things which the students have been doing in their lessons.

- In listening tests for young learners who don't yet write well, we can ask the students to point to the objects which we name or describe. We can also use pictures and picture cards so that we can ask them to do things, such as *Put the dog behind the sofa.*
- In speaking tests for older children (perhaps eight years old or more), we can ask them to FIND THE DIFFERENCES →50 between two similar pictures when talking to an examiner – or two children can do the activity and an examiner can listen and grade their speaking to each other. They can do a range of INFORMATION-GAP ACTIVITIES →50 or tell a story based on pictures that we give them.
- In reading and writing tests for younger children who have just started to read, we can ask them to put ticks and crosses (or *yes* or *no*) to say if statements are true (for example *This is a crocodile*) or unscramble letters (*c-c-d-e-i-l-o-o-r*) to make a word (*crocodile*).
- In reading and writing tests for older children (perhaps eight years or more), we can ask them to do FILL-IN tasks by choosing words from a box which have accompanying illustrations. We can ask them if statements about a picture (for example, *There are three monkeys on top of the car*) are true or false. We can ask them to complete a dialogue using lines we give them.

Irish Sea
Sea
English Channel
BIRMINGHAM
LEEDS
SHEFFIELD
Liverpool
Blackpool
LONDON
LEEDS
Oxford
Cambridge
1 : 1 000 000

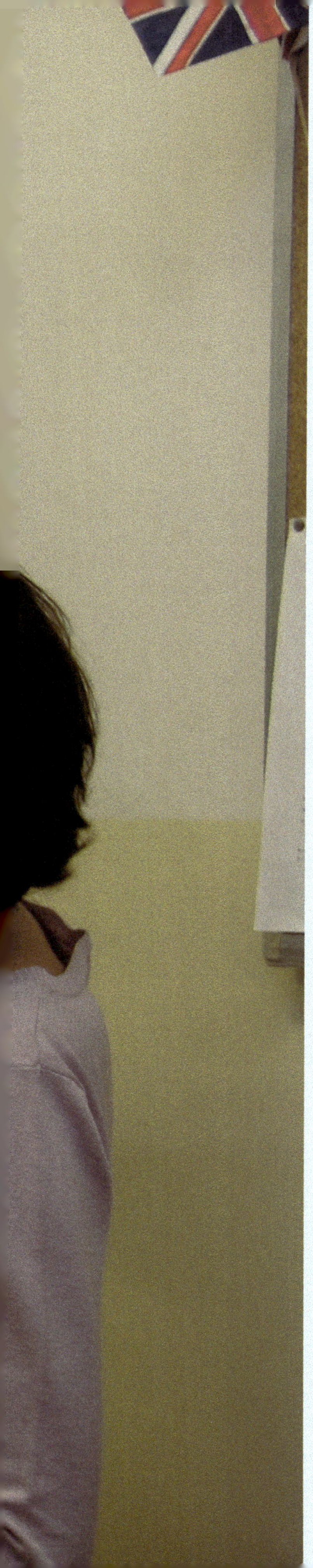

Section G: Content and Language Integrated Learning

Content and Language Integrated Learning (CLIL) is the name given to a kind of teaching (and learning) where the students study a subject such as biology, maths or citizenship and, at the same time, learn the language they need to understand and talk about the subject in a second language.

In this section we look at many aspects of teaching CLIL. After an introductory unit which explains what it is, we discuss the kind of language that CLIL lessons delivered in English focus on, and we show how genre is extremely important for CLIL lessons.

We look at the many visual organisers (diagrammatic ways of showing information) that CLIL learners need to be able to use, and we discuss the different kinds of material and activities that CLIL teachers can exploit. We also look at what the teacher's roles are for CLIL teaching.

Finally, we look at the issues that teachers need to consider when they plan CLIL lessons – and how they can assess their students' knowledge (and language).

102

Introducing CLIL

What is CLIL?

CLIL stands for CONTENT AND LANGUAGE INTEGRATED LEARNING. In other words, the students study content (geography, physics, music, maths, etc.) *through* and *with* a second language, and they study language through and with the content.

- People who like and use CLIL say that students (especially at primary and secondary levels) have more success as language learners when they are taught using CLIL. They also do well in their knowledge of the content.
- CLIL can be taught using a second language, an ADDITIONAL LANGUAGE (in other words a third, fourth, fifth language, etc.) or a mixture of languages – for example, the CLIL language together with the students' first language. This is sometimes called TRANSLANGUAGE CLIL.
- CLIL can, of course, be delivered in languages other than English (LOTE), but in this section we will concentrate on CLIL using English.
- Although both language and content are important in CLIL, we organise lessons on the basis of content. However, CLIL is successful when the content and the language are closely connected. For example, if the students are learning about the life-cycle of a butterfly, they will focus on the language we use to describe a process, such as the PRESENT SIMPLE →6; TIME ADVERBIALS →11 (*first*, *after that*, etc.) and the specific vocabulary they need (*leaf*, *egg*, *larvae*, *caterpillar*, *pupa*, *chrysalis*, etc.).

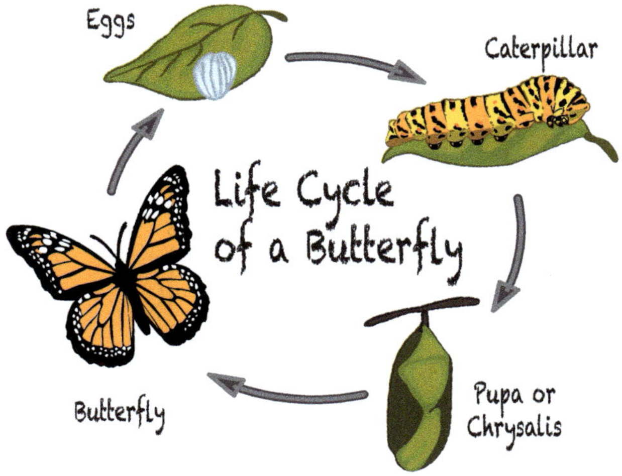

- The language in CLIL may not be the usual list of grammar items that we expect to see in language learning COURSEBOOKS and materials. Instead, we only teach what the students need for the content of the lesson – and this may be PHRASES and words rather than complete grammar patterns.
- CLIL is different from general English teaching because students use language to learn rather than learning language to use later.
- CLIL focuses on four special areas: CONTENT (the subject itself), COMMUNICATION (using language effectively), COGNITION (thinking skills – how we learn), and CULTURE (understanding our own culture and its relationship to other cultures). We discuss these 4Cs for planning in →109.

CLIL methodology

There isn't a lot of difference between good general language teaching and the teaching techniques which are necessary for successful CLIL lessons.

- CLIL experts say that teachers should stress social interaction in the classroom: between teacher and students, and between students and students.

- In CLIL lessons, the students should COLLABORATE with each other, often working in PAIRS and GROUPS →67 to solve problems, do research or report back on what they have found out.
- CLIL teachers try to support their students by SCAFFOLDING their learning – in other words, getting the students to experience things in stages to help them understand. We discuss scaffolding in →65 and →91.
- In CLIL lessons, the students are asked to use METACOGNITIVE SKILLS – in other words, to think about how they learn.
- In CLIL lessons, the students are asked to think creatively.

We look at some CLIL activities in →108.

How is CLIL offered around the world (and who teaches it)?

Many schools and education organisations say that they use CLIL. However, because CLIL is used in many different contexts, they may be talking about very different situations.

- Many people talk about SOFT CLIL and HARD CLIL. Soft CLIL happens when some language learning (but not all) is organised with strong SUBJECT content (such as geography, environmental science, etc.). However, when teachers deliver whole areas of the curriculum (science, history, etc.) in a second or additional language (and when language and content are both taught at the same time), this is hard CLIL.
- Some schools and teachers offer short (say, 15-hour) CLIL courses. Others have CLIL courses running through a whole semester or year.
- Some CLIL courses are taught by a subject teacher (a geography or physics teacher, for example) who speaks English well enough to do this, or by an English teacher who can manage the CLIL content.
- In some situations, the students study the content first in their L1 and then again with a language teacher who can focus on the CLIL language.
- In many situations, subject teachers and English teachers work together so that language lessons back up the subject lesson language.

How to make CLIL successful

CLIL is not a worldwide phenomenon yet. It is becoming more popular, but it is difficult to say if it will be the way that everyone teaches English and content in a few years. Perhaps some countries and teachers will say no to CLIL because (they believe) students learn better in their own language, and there are not enough language and subject teachers to make it work – or enough money!

- Teachers who are using the CLIL language need to have a good enough level of that language so that they can model the sentences and phrases that the students need.
- When language and subject teachers work together, they need time to prepare and liaise with each other. We look at PLANNING CLIL in →109.
- When teachers are using CLIL for the first time, they need proper training and support. This is especially true if they have been non-CLIL language teachers before.
- ASSESSMENT and TESTING of CLIL have to support CLIL teaching. We look at general assessment in →88–90 and at CLIL assessment in →110.

103

The language of CLIL

Types of language

Students need various different kinds of language to study a CLIL subject. Teachers need to be able to identify what these language types (and items) are when they are PLANNING CLIL activities and lessons →109.

- The language that students need for CLIL is sometimes more varied than the language they would need for general English.
- Many CLIL theorists make a difference between BICS (BASIC INTERPERSONAL COMMUNICATION SKILLS) and CALP (COGNITIVE ACADEMIC LANGUAGE PROFICIENCY). Whereas BICS are the kind of language and skills that are frequently taught in standard language learning classes, CALP relates to the kind of language that students need to study a curriculum subject, such as maths, science, geography, etc.
- When students are learning in the CLIL language, they will need CONTENT-OBLIGATORY LANGUAGE. This consists of words, structures and FUNCTIONS →30 which are essential for the particular topic they are studying. In general English language learning we often decide to teach more frequent vocabulary items first, but in a CLIL lesson the topic will help us to decide what words to teach (and what COLLOCATIONS →20 to include) even if they are not very frequent for other situations. For example, if students are learning about elephants, they will need specific vocabulary, such as *African elephant*, *Asian elephant*, *poacher*, *ivory*, *trunk*, *tusk*, etc.
- CLIL students will also need CONTENT-COMPATIBLE LANGUAGE – in other words, the everyday kind of language which is useful both for the study of a specific topic and also for general language use. When the students are learning about orchestral instruments and procedures, for example, they will use verbs such as *blow*, *hit*, *play*, *start*, *stop*, *sit*, etc., all of which are also used in everyday situations.
- In TRANSLANGUAGE CLASSROOMS →102 teachers and students will sometimes use the students L1 →77 for some explanation and discussion before reverting to the CLIL language for the main study.

Grammar and CLIL

Students need to be able to use appropriate grammar structures in the CLIL language – and these will depend on the topic being studied and what they are expected to do and say about it, as the following examples show:

- Students can use the PRESENT CONTINUOUS →6 to talk about something happening now (or a changing situation), e.g. *I am exposing the phosphorus to the air* (chemistry) or *The water is getting warmer* (physics).
- The PRESENT SIMPLE →6 can be used to talk about processes and general truths in sentences such as *A viola has four strings* (music) and *Orangutangs live in the tropical rainforests of Sumatra and Borneo* (geography).
- We use PASSIVE constructions →1 to talk about processes and events when we want to stress the action and the result rather than the person who does it, e.g. *Atahualpa was executed by the Spanish conquistadores in 1533* (history) or *The cocoa beans are dried in the sun* (science).
- PAST TENSES can be used to talk about historical events in sentences like *Benito Juarez lived from 1806 until 1872* (history) or to describe what happened in the classroom, e.g. *While Hiromi was preparing the experiment, Keiko was reporting on her actions* (science).
- MODAL AUXILIARY VERBS →8 are used to express concepts such as certainty, possibility, obligation, etc. in sentences like *Conditions below decks on the ship 'La Amistad' must have been terrible* (history) or *The potatoes can be boiled or roasted* (domestic science).
- CONDITIONAL SENTENCES →2 are used for expressing a general rule, prediction or hypotheticality in sentences like *If you multiply four by seven, you get twenty-eight* (mathematics) or *If Archduke Ferdinand had not been assassinated in Sarajevo in 1914, Europe might not have gone to war* (history).
- Students will often have to report →10 what people say in their CLIL language in sentences such as *The conductor told us to play more quietly* (music) or *He asked me to calculate the time it would take* (science).

Language for a purpose

In order to achieve the purpose for their communication in CLIL lessons students will need to be able to use various LANGUAGE FUNCTIONS →30, appropriate PUNCTUATION →31 and other conventions for writing, as the following examples show:

- Students may need to be able to give opinions if they are discussing a work of art or a piece of music, using language such as *I think* … and *In my opinion* … .
- They may need to describe processes, using language such as *First, the wood is chipped and then it is fed into steam-heated containers.*
- When primary students are discussing whether something will float in water, they may need to agree and disagree using language such as *I don't agree. I think it will sink* or *Yes, I agree. I think Paula is right because* … .
- Students will need to use language items and written conventions if they want to give examples, including *such as* and *for example*, and punctuation features such as BRACKETS ( ), SEMICOLONS (;), DASHES (–), etc. →31
- Students will need to be able to define things using language such as *kind/type of* (*a sturgeon is a kind of cold freshwater predator*) and RELATIVE CLAUSES →2 (*capillaries are small blood vessels which connect arterioles and venules*).
- Students may need to make generalisations (general statements) using language such as *tend* (*most people tend to eat their evening meal at around eight o'clock*), *in the majority of cases*, *in general*, etc.

104

Genre in CLIL

Language functions and tasks

Students will have to perform different LANGUAGE FUNCTIONS →30 and tasks in CLIL lessons. The specific tasks will depend on the particular curricular subject they are studying, as in the following examples.

- If students are studying music, we will expect them to do things in the CLIL language such as explain, demonstrate, identify and describe instruments, notes and styles.
- When students study science subjects, they will have to do things such as HYPOTHESISE about what will happen, describe EXPERIMENTS and processes and write up records of what they have found.
- When students study history, they will have to do such things as write biographical texts and draw TIMELINES.
- Geography students may have to interpret map features, write descriptions and use various graphics and VISUAL ORGANISERS →105 to explain facts, features and events.
- When students study mathematics, they will probably need to explain mathematical concepts, describe how they solved problems and draw and label geometric figures.

Genre and CLIL

A GENRE →32 is a particular type of art, music, text, etc., whether spoken or written. The specific examples in a genre share some features; for example, most letters start with a greeting. It is important for all students (whether in CLIL lessons or GENERAL ENGLISH →41 classes) to understand and to be able to use the features in various genres.

- CLIL genres are things like encyclopaedia entries, letters, poems, reports, scientific descriptions, oral presentations, newspaper articles, discursive essays, etc.
- A text within a genre is written in a particular REGISTER →33. The language may be FORMAL or it may be INFORMAL and it will have SUBJECT-SPECIFIC LANGUAGE. For example, a biology text will have biological words and terms.
- Texts in a genre (or oral presentations/discussions, etc.) have certain layouts. For example, in formal letters there is a special place for the address of the letter writer and the address of the person or organisation they are writing to. In oral presentations (with visual support) there is a special place for the title of the talk, etc.
- Texts or presentations within a genre need to be COHERENT →34. In other words, information must be presented in a logical sequence. For example, when describing a science experiment, we might organise our report by saying 1) what we wanted to find out, 2) how we decided to try to find it out, 3) what we did, 4) what happened, (5) what we found out and (6) what we are going to do next.
- Various sections in a genre tend to be constructed in similar ways. For example, newspaper headlines are often written in the PRESENT SIMPLE →6 and they omit small words such as ARTICLES →13, PREPOSITIONS →1 and MODAL AUXILIARIES →8, e.g. *Police arrest man after high-speed chase.*
- Texts in certain genres are often accompanied by a variety of visual organisers →105.

Helping students to understand and produce genre features

We must give our students guidance if we want them to write or speak in a specific genre. They should do GENRE ANALYSIS →59 by looking at a text, studying its construction and language features, and then using it as a model. For example, the students read the following text and answer questions, such as:

What is the purpose of the text?
Where does it come from?
How is the subject/name of the entry presented?
How are the subject's dates given (and where)?
What information is given in the first paragraph?
What order are the events in the entry presented in?
What time adverbials are used?
How and why are brackets used in the second paragraph?

Article | Discussion

Mustafa Kemal Atatürk

Mustafa Kemal Atatürk (1881–1938) was a Turkish army officer, revolutionary statesman and writer. He founded the Republic of Turkey and was the first Turkish president.

After the defeat of the Ottoman Empire in WWI, Atatürk led the Turkish national movement in the Turkish War of Independence. He set up a provisional government in Ankara, and then he defeated the allied forces (soldiers from the United Kingdom, France, Russia, Belgium, Serbia, Greece, Japan and Romania) who had invaded Turkey. His military campaigns gained Turkey independence. After Turkish independence, Atatürk started to introduce political, economic and cultural reforms. He wanted to make Turkey a modern and secular country. He was president of Turkey from 1923 until his death in 1938.

- The students now research another historical leader so that they will be able to write their own encyclopaedia entry.
- With the teacher's help, the students will use their genre analysis and their research to produce a text which follows the same model as the one they have been studying. We will guide them so that the subject's name is written **in bold** with the dates in brackets immediately after it. They will stick to the model closely: they will describe the subject briefly in the first paragraph before describing their life in chronological order. We will expect them to use time adverbials such as *after*, *then*, *from*, *until*, etc. and SUBJECT-SPECIFIC VOCABULARY such as *government*, *revolution*, *independence*, *president*, etc.
- At various stages during the procedure we will ask the students to look at more examples of the genre and compare them to the first one they have seen.

We discuss genre for general English writing in →59.

105 Using visual organisers

Presenting information in a visual way

When students read or hear information – and then have to present what they have learnt – they will use a number of presentation devices and visual organisers.

Why visual organisers matter

- The information that students see, read, watch or listen to is often presented as text, either in books or ONLINE, as material on BOARDS or INTERACTIVE WHITEBOARDS →85, with the use of video or AUDIO DEVICES, or via PRESENTATION SOFTWARE →87 such as *PowerPoint*, *Keynote* and *Prezi*.
- We often use VISUAL ORGANISERS (such as WORD MAPS →22, TABLES, VENN DIAGRAMS or PIE CHARTS) so that the information is clearer. This is especially useful for more VISUAL LEARNERS →40.
- When students present their own work, they must be able to use visual organisers, too.
- Visual organisers are useful devices for teaching. For example, we can ask our students to transfer information from a written text to a graph or table. They are also useful in assessment. For example, we can give the students information in the form of a visual organiser. They then have to transform it into written text.

Types of visual organiser

There are many types of visual organiser.

- A BAR CHART (1) uses rectangles of different heights to show frequency or quantity.
- A CYCLE (2) shows a typical sequence of events.
- A WORD MAP →22 shows how things and categories (types) of things relate to each other DVD3.
- A LINE GRAPH (3) shows how things are developing (or have developed).
- A PIE CHART (4) shows relative proportions by means of the size of different 'slices' of the same 'pie'.
- STORYBOARDS →62 are drawings or plans of a sequence of events. We sometimes include speech bubbles or thought bubbles.
- VENN DIAGRAMS (5) show similarities and differences between different groups.
- TREE DIAGRAMS show hierarchical relationships, such as (in a company) the relative importance of the chief executive, managing director, directors of departments, assistants to the director, etc. There is an example of a tree diagram showing SUPERORDINATES and HYPONYMS in →18.
- A QUADRANT (6) shows how things can be identified in two ways.
- A T-CHART (7) divides things into two categories.
- CARROLL DIAGRAMS (8) (named after Lewis Carroll the author of *Alice in Wonderland*) are used for grouping things in a kind of *yes/no* way.
- A TABLE can be used to put things in different categories and summarise information.
- CAUSE AND EFFECT diagrams (9) (PROCESS DIAGRAMS) show how certain effects happen – what leads up to them.
- FLOW DIAGRAMS (10) show processes and the order in which they happen.
- A BINARY KEY (11) divides information into a series of *yes/no* questions.

1

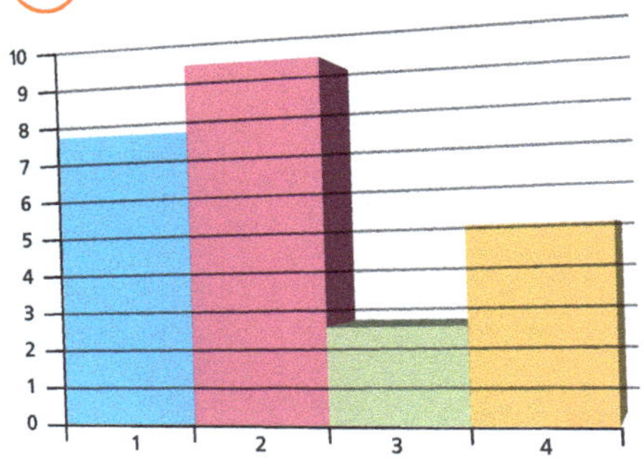

2

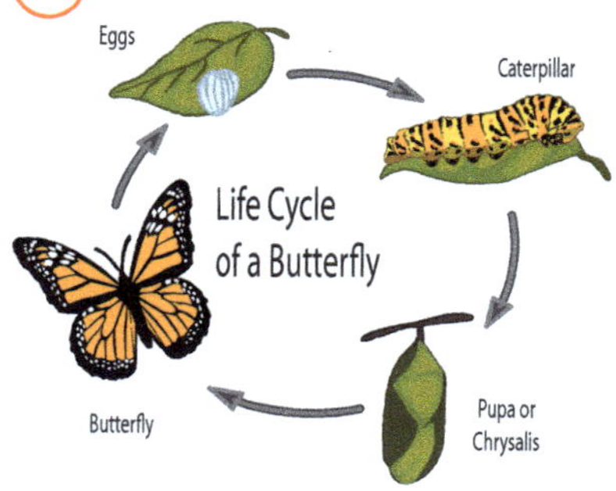

3

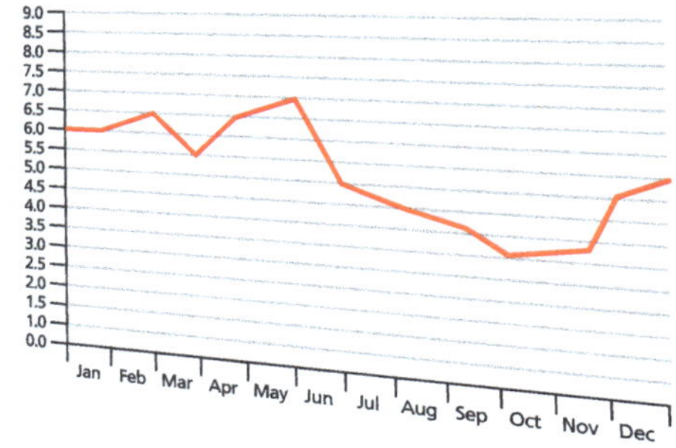

4

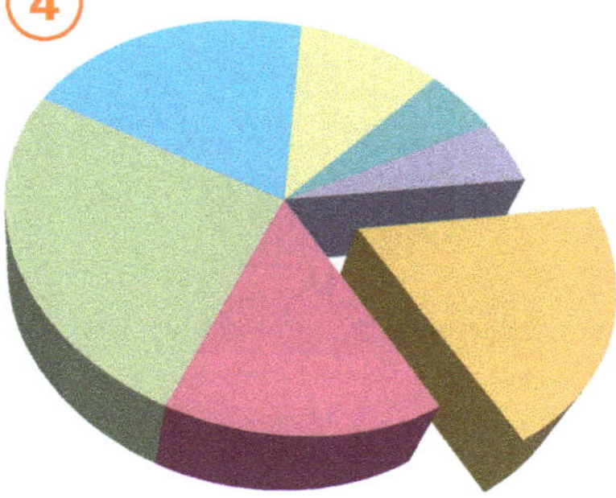

5

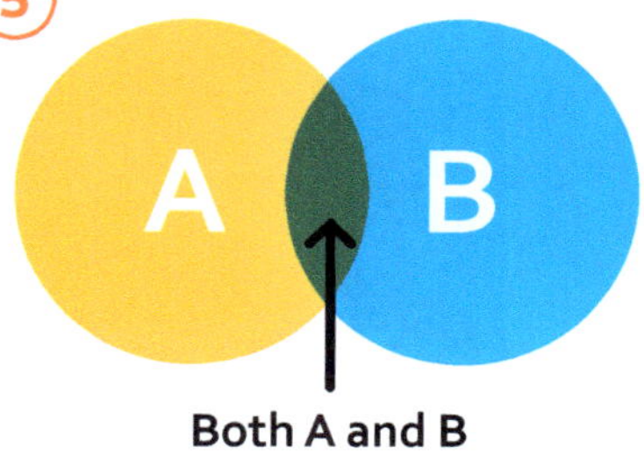

6

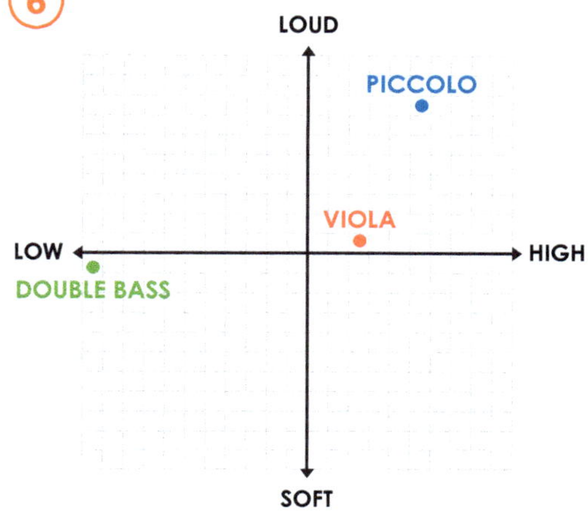

7

ADVANTAGES	DISADVANTAGES

8

PRIME NUMBERS	NON-PRIME NUMBERS
2, 3, 5, 7, 11, 13, 17, 19, 23, 29, 31	1, 4, 6, 8, 9, 10, 12, 14, 15, 16, 18, 20, 21, 22, 24

9

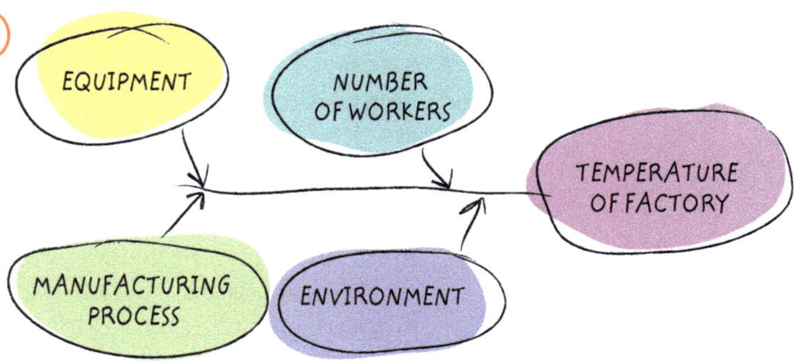

10

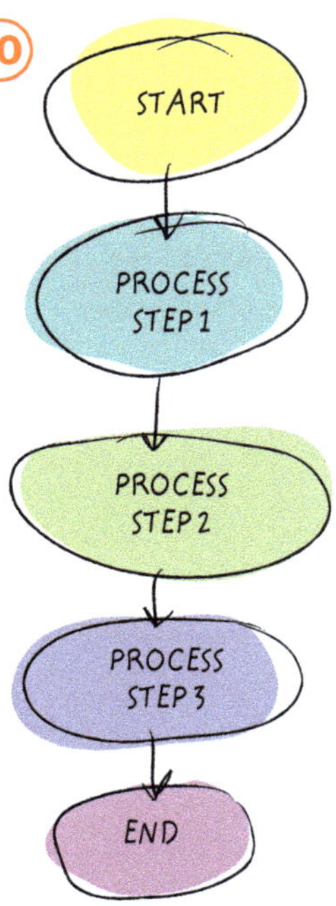

11

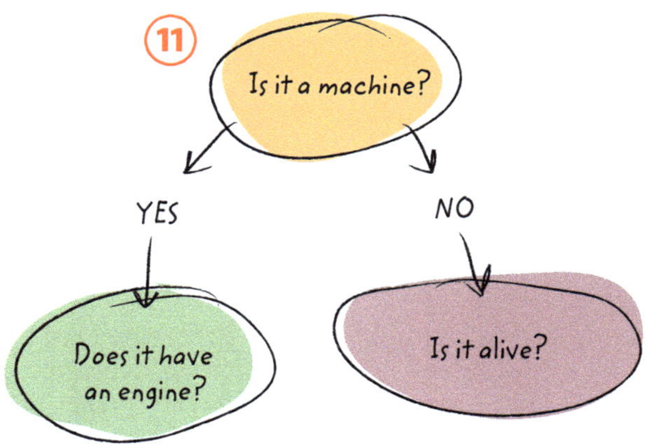

106 Materials and resources for CLIL

Differences between materials for CLIL and general English

There are many differences between materials written for GENERAL ENGLISH lessons, and those which are designed especially for subject-specific purposes such as CLIL or ENGLISH FOR SPECIFIC PURPOSES (ESP).

- General English materials are often organised on the basis of a grammatical syllabus: Unit 1 = the verb *to be*, Unit 2 = the present simple, Unit 3 = the present continuous, etc. CLIL materials are often organised by subject or content area, such as Environmental sciences 1: Water and where it comes from, Environmental sciences 2: Water and what it is used for, Environmental Sciences 3: How and why we use water in the home, etc.
- General English materials are often tightly graded so that the students only see the language which fits with the GRAMMAR and VOCABULARY SYLLABUSES. Material for CLIL and ESP lessons will often have a greater variety of language, however, because more complicated ideas and processes need to be explained.
- General English materials often deal with general themes, such as families, sport, great inventions of history or living in cities. CLIL and ESP materials usually focus on more specific topics, such as how city transport systems work, the life cycle of the emperor penguin, nutrition, etc.
- Whereas CLIL teaches content *and* language, ESP lessons frequently focus on the language *about* the content, which the students already know.

Adapting materials for CLIL

We can get material for CLIL courses from a variety of sources, such as the INTERNET, or from COURSEBOOKS written for general English.

- We can reorder or rewrite the RUBRICS (the instructions telling students what to do) so that they are easier to understand.
- We can add our own CLIL-based tasks. For example, in a general English text about different animals, we can ask questions such as *What do all the animals have in common?* or *Can you sort the animals into groups, according to what they eat and where they live?*

- We can rewrite the texts we are using and provide helpful illustrations or VISUAL ORGANISER backup →105. We can remove unnecessary detail or paraphrase the text (say the same thing in an easier way), using words that the students are likely to know. Compare the first text (the original) with the simplified version below it:

Violinists can alter the sounding pitch of their strings in two ways. They can use the tuning pegs on the pegbox to tighten or loosen the tension of the strings, or they can press down on a string anywhere on the fingerboard. When a violinist presses a string to the fingerboard, he or she is shortening its effective length, which causes the string to vibrate more rapidly. Violinists can also rapidly change the sounding pitch of a string by pressing a string against the fingerboard and subtly pushing and pulling the string, which makes the sounding pitch oscillate above and below the central pitch. This technique is called vibrato.

A violin player can make a string sound higher or lower in two ways. They can turn the tuning pegs (1) so that the string (2) is tenser (tighter) or less tense (looser). When the player puts their finger on a string (and presses it down onto the fingerboard (3)) they make the string shorter. This makes it vibrate (move) more quickly and so the note is higher. When they take their finger away, the string is longer and it vibrates more slowly and so the note is lower. If the player moves their finger backwards and forwards very quickly the note goes up and down. This gives a pleasant effect which is called vibrato.

Notice that CONTENT-OBLIGATORY LANGUAGE, such as *tuning peg*, *string*, *fingerboard*, *vibrato*, etc. are still there, but other terms (and some grammatical constructions) have been simplified to make it easier for students. Also, the simplified text will be accompanied by an illustration with numbers identifying the different parts of the violin.

CLIL resources

We will bring a wide range of resources to the classroom – and we will expect our students to use a wide range of resources themselves.

- We can use a variety of book-based material. This can be from encyclopaedias, DICTIONARIES, coursebooks (including general English coursebooks – though we will have to adapt these), stories and content-specific books which discuss such things as history, scientific processes or mathematical calculations.
- We will use a variety of materials, such as paper, cardboard, pens, glue and scissors (for example) when we want to make (or ask the students to make) models, large charts or displays of material. We will bring in REALIA (real objects) to help the students understand concepts and processes.
- We will present information using text, illustrations, visual organisers, AUDIO and video and any other appropriate resources.
- A CLIL classroom will often have a range of educational technology, such as BOARDS of various kinds (including the INTERACTIVE WHITEBOARD or smartboards, etc.). Many CLIL teachers use laptops and DATA PROJECTORS to show and explain a variety of concepts and processes or to show films and video clips →85–87.
- Successful CLIL teachers use a wide variety of media to explain concepts. For example, we can show paper charts to explain the life cycle of the emperor penguin, project photos of the penguins' habitat, give the students short texts to read, project video clips or use *PowerPoint* or other PRESENTATION SOFTWARE (such as *Keynote* and *Prezi*).
- Students can access materials from the INTERNET or via APPS (APPLICATIONS) or on CD/DVD, etc. They can do RESEARCH →46 using online or handheld dictionaries, encyclopaedias, etc. They can download a range of material onto their laptops or TABLET COMPUTERS (if they have them).

107

Teaching CLIL

The teacher's responsibilities

CLIL classes should foster co-operation rather than competition in an atmosphere of mutual respect. We can create a CODE OF CONDUCT →71 to ensure this.

- When students are working on difficult content areas, our job is to reduce their anxiety so that they have a good chance of success. We will encourage collaboration through PAIRWORK and GROUPWORK →67.
- We will SCAFFOLD student learning experiences by breaking learning tasks down into small, achievable, logical steps →65, 91.
- We will monitor learning and give positive and encouraging support and FEEDBACK →72 during and after tasks.
- We will activate the students' prior knowledge (SCHEMATA →61) and do our best to ENGAGE their interest when we start a new lesson sequence →80.
- We will summarise what the students have learnt, often in a PLENARY session at the end of the lesson.
- CLIL teachers use the students' L1 when it is necessary for the understanding of content or for classroom management →77.
- We will remember that students need thinking time (WAIT TIME) when they are working on a complex task, so we will not expect instant answers!

How teachers can help students with language

One of the main teacher roles in the CLIL classroom is to help the students learn the language that applies to the content they are learning.

- We need to highlight and model SUBJECT-SPECIFIC VOCABULARY. For example, if our physics lesson is about energy, we may want the students to know or be able to say words like *matter*, *mass*, *force* and *energy*, and COLLOCATIONS →20 such as *thermal energy*, *electromagnetic energy*, *transfer energy*, etc.
- We need to highlight (and MODEL) SUBJECT-SPECIFIC SENTENCES, such as (for a lesson on musical instruments) *The strings of a viola are tuned to A, D, G and C* or (for a brass instrument) *We change the notes by pressing different combinations of valves.*
- We can model the language that the students need to know by saying it clearly and isolating the elements that they need to concentrate on (e.g. *are tuned ... listen ... are tuned ... the strings of a viola are tuned ...* etc.).

- We can write sentences on the board which the students then have to complete. For example, we might write the following on the board: *The strings of the viola* ____ ____ *to A, D, G and C* and *We change the notes by* ____ *different combinations of* ____ . We give the students the words *are*, *pressing*, *tuned* and *valves*, and with our support they have to use them to do the task.

How teachers can help students with cognitive skills

We need to teach our students to use their THINKING SKILLS to help them understand the content and to help them understand the process of learning.

- We need to help the students to develop their CONCRETE THINKING SKILLS so that they can classify and organise information with the help of visual organisers such as TABLES, WORD MAPS and VENN DIAGRAMS. Such LOWER-ORDER THINKING SKILLS (LOTS) can be encouraged by asking YES/NO QUESTIONS →3, such as *Is a trumpet a brass instrument?* and *what* questions, such as *What do we call a cat's feet?*
- As children start to develop towards the OPERATIONAL STAGE →91, we will help them develop ABSTRACT THINKING SKILLS, such as reasoning and hypothesising. We can encourage such HIGHER-ORDER THINKING SKILLS (HOTS) by asking *why* and *how* questions, such as *How do you know that the people in the picture don't have much money? Why do rivers run in one direction?* and OPEN-ENDED QUESTIONS →3 with *what*, such as *What do you think will happen if we expose this phosphorus to the open air?*
- We can encourage our students to think carefully about their answers. We can prompt them to think in more detail/depth with more *how/why/what* questions, such as *What is it that makes you think that? Why have you coloured your elephant green?* etc.
- We should encourage the students to ask questions themselves. We can say things like *What questions would you like to ask the people in the picture?* Or *Think of the questions you would like to ask for your class survey*, etc.
- We will encourage our students to analyse GENRES →32 (whether they are reading a text, listening to a song, watching a video or accessing information on a computer). They can decide what kind of a text (or song, etc.) it is, and say who it has been designed for and what makes it successful.
- We can put individual students (or PAIRS) in the HOT SEAT →51. They have to answer all the questions that the other students ask them.

How CLIL teachers encourage good learning

We need to get our students to think about how to learn so that they will learn more effectively.

- We can get the students to compare the work they are doing with work they have done before. We will get them to see how and why they have made improvements.
- We can give the students different strategies for doing a task and ask them how effective they are. For example, we can show them four different ways of taking notes. They have to think about which one they prefer and why.
- We can discuss the best way of remembering words and encourage the students to keep VOCABULARY BOOKS in which they write down words and phrases that they need to remember.
- At the end of a lesson or unit of work, we can get the students to think about what was difficult and what was easy – and why. We can get them to think/take notes about how they will use what they have learnt and how they will follow it up.

108

CLIL activities

Balancing activities

CLIL teachers use many of the same activities that teachers of GENERAL ENGLISH use →41. However, in CLIL lessons, we balance the 4CS →109 in ways that give real CLIL activities a special 'feel'.

Cats and dogs

We can talk about cats and dogs with YOUNG LEARNERS aged between five and eight.

- The students can do a class SURVEY about who has cats or dogs as pets. They can then count the number of cats and the number of dogs and find out which are more popular.
- We can introduce the children to a cat and a dog (we can use photographs, drawings, computer animations or PUPPETS →93). They can decide on names for them and can imagine their lives, and tell or write a daily diary for them.
- We can find stories about dogs and cats to use in our READING CIRCLE →96.
- We can make a VENN DIAGRAM →105 about the similarities and differences between cats and dogs. This will mean that we have to teach some CONTENT-OBLIGATORY language →103, such as *bark*, *purr*, *claws*, *whiskers*, *tail*, *paw*, etc.
- The children can find out what cats and dogs like and need to eat and drink and the amounts that are necessary for them, and they can compare that with humans.
- They can talk about cat and dog 'families' and separate them into wolf and cat families.

Rivers

Slightly older children (7–12) can do work about how rivers are formed and how they function.

- We can ask them to tell us about any rivers or streams they know or have visited.
- Students can research the water cycle and label the stages of *evaporation*, *convection*, *condensation*, *wind shift* and *rainfall*. While they do this they will need to learn the specialist vocabulary for describing the process.
- Students can learn about the basic principles of how rivers work – flowing downhill – and how erosion (of river banks, etc.), transportation (how the rocks and materials that are picked up by a flowing river are carried along by its energy) and deposition (when the materials fall to the bottom because there is not enough energy to carry them along) change the shape of rivers over time.
- Students can do experiments to see what angle is needed for water to flow, what happens when the water stops falling downwards (it meanders) and why flowing happens.
- We can ask them to find out about the length, breadth and depth of some of the world's largest rivers. They can make visual organisers, such as bar charts, to compare them.
- Students can learn about some of the capital cities of the world that are built on and beside big rivers. They can discuss the languages, cultures, religions and activities of those cities.
- Students can learn about what humans use rivers for (transportation, irrigation, hydroelectric power, fishing, pleasure, etc.).

Music, anyone?

- We can introduce our students to four different instruments and teach the difference between blowing, bowing, plucking and hitting.

- We can play students recordings of different instruments. They have to say whether they are plucked, hit, bowed or hit. They can then do research in books or on the computer so that they can label a world chart showing where the different instruments are played.
- They can practise passive constructions, such as *Violins are made of wood. They are played with a bow. They are used in classical music and folk music*, etc.
- Students can make a WORD MAP →22 to describe different categories of instrument. For example, we can divide 'blown' instruments into woodwind and brass. We can divide woodwind instruments into single reed and double reed instruments, etc.
- We can play the students music from different countries. They have to say whether the music is sad, happy, good to dance to, etc.
- Students can learn to play percussion instruments. We can build up a class piece, where they learn about counting, rhythm, speed, etc.
- We can use music as a stimulus for writing words and POEMS →63.

Life on the edge

In the following example, for older children, we show how a photograph can be the source for COGNITION and COMMUNICATION SKILLS and how these can be SCAFFOLDED →65. Students can learn to empathise, and learn about different cultures before relating what they are learning to their own lives.

- We show the students the photograph and we ask them some lower-order thinking skills (LOTS) questions →107, such as *Where is the boy? What does he have in his hands? What is behind him?* before moving on to higher-order thinking skills (HOTS) questions →107, such as *Why is the boy there, do you think? What are your reasons for your answers?* We can ask them to speculate about how the boy feels and how they know this.
- We can teach language such as *I think the boy is … because he looks very …*
- We can ask the students if they would like to be in the picture and to give reasons for their answers.
- We can introduce the concept of recycling and show how the people in the photograph earn small amounts of money by rescuing rubbish that can be re-used.
- We can estimate how much household rubbish a family produces and discuss how much of it can be/should be recycled, etc.
- We can discuss how the life of the boy in the photograph could be/should be improved.

109

Planning CLIL

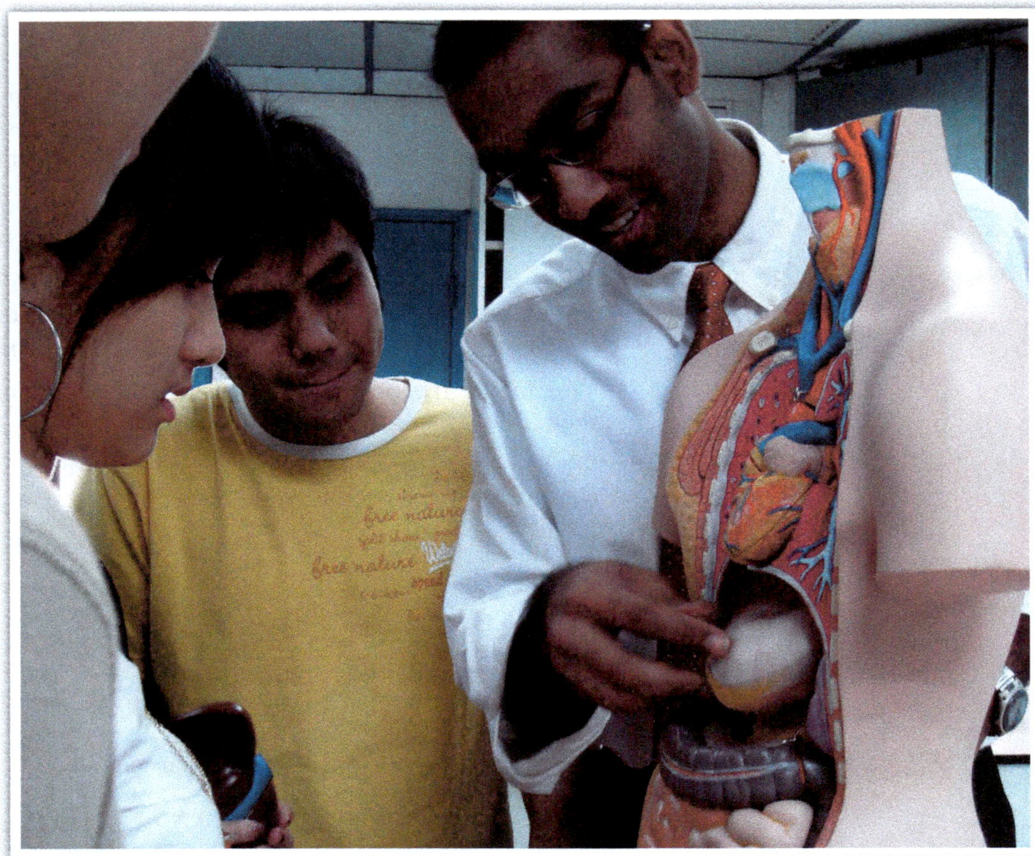

Planning CLIL lessons

We discuss planning in general in →79–80. However, there are some extra things that we need to think about when planning CLIL lessons.

Outcomes and demands

- As with all lesson planning, we need to consider the learning OUTCOMES →79 of any lesson we are going to teach. We want to know what our students will know or be able to do better at the end of the lesson than they knew or were able to do at the beginning.
- We should always be aware, however, that things don't always turn out as we plan them to. Good CLIL teachers respond to events in a lesson as they happen and, as a result, they may have to adapt their plan because of UNFORESEEN PROBLEMS or MAGIC MOMENTS (where we decide to follow our students' unplanned creativity) →79.
- When we plan CLIL lessons, we need to balance the demands of the 4Cs: CONTENT, COMMUNICATION, COGNITION and CULTURE. For example, if the level of cognition (the amount of thinking that the students have to do) is high, we may want to make sure that we don't ask too much of them in terms of their communication skills – because we do not want to make things too difficult for them. If our lesson has a lot of new content for the students to absorb, then we try not to make them work too hard on the other three Cs.

Lesson shapes

We discuss METAPHORS for lesson planning (such as 'a lesson is like a book, a play a film', etc.) in →79. Although there is no one perfect shape/metaphor to fit all circumstances, CLIL lessons probably have certain characteristics in common.

- In a successful CLIL lesson, the students should be encouraged to *think* about the content they are learning – and about learning in general.

- A CLIL lesson will ask the students to engage with things that they have learnt previously as well as with the new content and language for the class.
- CLIL lessons often start by activating the students' prior knowledge, often with a WARMER or ICEBREAKER →70.
- We often end CLIL lessons with some kind of PLENARY feedback (where the students are in a WHOLE-CLASS setting →67) in which we sum up what has been learnt and studied. We can ask the students to think about things such as what they have learnt, what was easy and difficult, and what they still need or want to do or find out.

What goes into a CLIL lesson plan

Different teachers write different kinds of plan, depending on factors such as their students, their own personal style, how long they have been teaching, whether they are being observed or whether their school expects detailed plans. However detailed (or not) the actual plan is:

- We need to decide what the CONTENT of our lesson is. Content means things such as geometric shapes (mathematics), different kinds of musical instruments (music), a historical event (history), the cultivation of maize (geography) or what objects are magnetic (science).
- We need to decide on our learning AIMS for the students – or the learning outcomes that the lesson will end with. What will the students have achieved when our lesson is over? We may want to divide our learning outcomes into three sections: what the students will *know* at the end of the lesson, what they will be *able to do* at the end of the lesson, and what they will *be aware of* at the end of the lesson.
- We need to be able to say how we will know if our aims have been met – in other words, how we will ASSESS their effectiveness.
- We will want to plan what VOCABULARY, GRAMMAR structures or LANGUAGE FUNCTIONS, etc. the students will need to use in the lesson. We will think of what they know, what we want them to recycle, and what language will be new. We will think of the LANGUAGE EXPONENTS that the students will want to use.
- We will want to be aware of the COGNITIVE SKILLS that the students are expected to display. What thinking processes are we expecting them to be able to cope with during the lesson?
- We have to decide what CULTURAL ELEMENTS we will include in the lesson. We might refer to other cultures and worlds, or to the students' own world. We might want to deal with issues of CITIZENSHIP or CULTURAL IDENTITY, for example.
- We need to think of what CLASSROOM RESOURCES our lesson needs. For example, we might need paints, large sheets of paper and tape if our lesson is art-based. On the other hand, we will need computers and internet access if the students are going to be using a LEARNING PLATFORM.
- We need to plan our lesson procedures and their TIMINGS (how long each lesson stage will take). How will the lesson start? What happens next? How will it end? etc.
- We will want to say whether the students will be working as INDIVIDUALS or in PAIRS or GROUPS →67.
- We need to plan for DIFFERENTIATION →42. We should think of how we can meet the demands of students at different levels and with different learning styles.
- When we plan, we will think of what the students already know and what they will do after the lesson. What links to other parts of the CURRICULUM can we build into our lesson? Where can we send them to find out more about our topic?

We show examples of different LESSON PLANS in Appendix C on pages 250–256.

110

Assessing CLIL

Types of assessment

As with all assessment, we can talk about SUMMATIVE ASSESSMENT (where we find out what students know or have learnt) and FORMATIVE ASSESSMENT (where we discover or diagnose how the students are getting on so that we can help them do even better in the future) →88.

What is special about assessing CLIL?

We discuss issues of assessment and TESTING in general in →88–90, and we look at assessing young learners in →101. However, CLIL is different in some respects.

- When assessing CLIL learners we need to be clear about whether we are testing the students' knowledge of the language or the content. For example, if we ask them to label the bones in a skeleton, are we going to take marks off for spelling if they can identify where the *cervical vertebrae* are but cannot spell them correctly?
- In CLIL evaluation, we may decide that if the students can explain (or demonstrate an understanding of) the content adequately, then we will not assess the accuracy of their language. On the other hand, we might decide that knowledge of content-obligatory language (or particular CONTENT-COMPATIBLE language such as LANGUAGE FUNCTIONS →30, etc.) is crucial and, as a result, give priority to that.
- We can use ASSESSMENT SCALES →90 to make the goal of our assessment clear. For example, if we are assessing an oral presentation in a CLIL class (rather than a general English class) we might have columns for content, organisation and language. But we might also assess the students in terms of the use of presentation software or the use of visuals and diagrams to back up the presentation.
- The most important thing (especially with formative assessment) is that the students should know exactly how and why they will be assessed. This will tell them what the point of the teaching and learning is, and help them to achieve their learning outcomes successfully.

Supporting students in CLIL assessment

If we want our students to get the most out of *formative* assessment, we can use a variety of SUPPORT STRATEGIES.

- We can simplify instructions, or re-phrase them, so that the students know exactly what to do. We can read the instructions aloud, using gestures to make them more comprehensible.
- We will give examples →89 so that the students understand the task.
- We can add visual support (picture, diagrams, drawings, etc.) to help the students perform the assessment task. We can make some of our tests OPEN-BOOK EXAMS so that they can consult notes, etc. rather than doing everything from memory.
- We can sometimes allow the students to work in PAIRS to help each other complete assessment tasks.
- We can help the students to REVIEW and EDIT their work →57 before keeping it in a folder (or on a LEARNING PLATFORM →76) for use in PORTFOLIO ASSESSMENT →88.

Support strategies like this are usually not appropriate for *summative* assessment.

Some CLIL test types

CLIL test item types should have VALIDITY →88: they should reflect the kinds of tasks that the students have done in their lessons. Although the number of possible test types for CLIL is almost limitless, here are a few examples:

- We can get the students to transfer written information into VISUAL ORGANISERS →105, such as graphs, tables, etc.
- We can get the students to label diagrams or name the stages in a life cycle, for example.
- We can ask the students to do MATCHING →48 exercises which test their understanding (but not their production) of language.
- We can ask the students to complete a summarising FILL IN about something that they have read or seen. We can give them words to choose from when they fill in the blanks.
- We can show the students pictures of animals and ask them to classify them according to whether they are vertebrates or invertebrates. Younger learners can do this by putting pictures on a chart, or by telling us which kind an animal is.
- We can keep a LEARNER LANGUAGE PROFILE (LLP) in which we record what individual students can do in various content and learning areas, for example, *… can explain things to his/her peers* (COMMUNICATION SKILLS), *… can calculate percentages from raw data about food consumption* (COGNITIVE SKILLS) or *… can take notes in a way that is appropriate for him/her* (ATTITUDES TO LEARNING).

Students assessing themselves and each other

- We can give our students checklists which they can use to evaluate their own performance, or the performance of others. For example (writing up a domestic science procedure):

Tick the stages that you (or your colleague) completed.

I listed the ingredients that were needed and the amounts that were needed.	
I listed the equipment that was necessary to complete the task.	
I explained what I did stage by stage.	
I wrote a conclusion in which I said what the result was. I included what went well and what the problems were (if any).	
I said what improvements I would make in the future.	

- Young learners who don't yet write well can tick pictures which show what they have been doing and put smiley/frowny faces on the picture to say whether they have done well or not.
- Older children can use self-evaluation sheets in which they complete sentences/prompts such as *I am good at …*, *Today we learnt …*, *I found … easy/difficult*, *I am best at …*, *I need to get better at …* . They can fill in charts which say things like *Good at …*, *Not very good at …*, *What I am going to do to get better …* .
- Students can complete their own CAN-DO STATEMENTS →41 in which they say *yes*, *no* or *not sure* to statements such as *I can describe the human digestive system* or *I can make simple multiplication and division calculations.*

Appendix A: Going further

As we said in Unit 78 (*Teacher development*), teachers can (re-)engage with their own development in a number of ways:

Journals

If you want to keep up to date with what is happening (and what people are saying) in the world of English language teaching, you may want to read one of the following journals:

- *English Teaching Professional.* This magazine offers very readable short, practical articles on all aspects of English language teaching. It has a special section on teaching young learners. *www.etprofessional.com*
- *Modern English Teacher.* This magazine offers articles on many aspects of language teaching and contains 'about language' and 'practical ideas' sections. *www.onlinemet.com*
- *ELT Journal.* This journal contains a variety of mostly theoretical articles based on the contributors' teaching experiences around the world. *eltj.oxfordjournals.org*
- *TESOL Quarterly*. This is a largely theoretical journal with a strong emphasis on US-based teaching. *www.tesol.org*
- All these journals have a reviews section which look at the latest publications.

Going online

Teachers can learn and interact with colleagues on many online sites:

- Teachers can go to the *ETK* website (*www.pearsonELT.com/ETK*) for activities, updates and information. We also list some of the many individual teacher blogs and sites.
- The *ETK* website also has news of webinars and other online meetings and discussion groups.
- Teachers can go to *www.eltcommunity.com* for discussions with other professionals from around the world about any topic that interests them.
- Many teachers use social networking sites such as *Twitter*, *Facebook*, *Google+*, etc. to stay in touch with their PLN (personal learning network).

Face-to-face networking

The best (and most enjoyable) way of going further is to attend workshops, meetings, seminars and conferences with other colleagues and teachers.

Many countries and regions have teachers' associations. When teachers join these, they get newsletters, journals, etc. – and they can attend regional and national conferences. There is a list of teachers' associations and conferences on the *ETK* website (*www.pearsonELT.com/ETK*).

Recommended reading

There are many, many books about teaching available from different publishers around the world. The following lists give a small taste (only) of what is available.

The *How to* series

The *How to Teach* … series, published by Pearson ELT, offers clear practical guidance with appropriate background theory:

How to Teach English by Jeremy Harmer

How to Teach English with Technology by Gavin Dudeney and Nicky Hockly

How to Teach for Exams by Sally Burgess and Katie Head

How to Teach Grammar by Scott Thornbury

How to Teach Listening by JJ Wilson

How to Teach Pronunciation by Gerard Kelly

How to Teach Speaking by Scott Thornbury

How to Teach Vocabulary by Scott Thornbury

How to Teach Writing by Jeremy Harmer

General methodology

There are a number of books which provide guides to many aspects of language teaching – including, for example, background theories of language learning, language system and skill teaching, classroom management, assessment and testing, etc.

The Practice of English Language Teaching by Jeremy Harmer (Pearson ELT 2007). This book takes a comprehensive look at the field of English language teaching.

Learning Teaching by Jim Scrivener (Macmillan 2010). A good practical guide to success in the classroom

An A-Z of ELT by Scott Thornbury (Macmillan 2006). A bit like an encyclopaedia, this book lists many important English language teaching topics in alphabetical order.

The TKT Course Modules 1, 2 and 3 by Mary Spratt, Alan Pulverness and Melanie Williams (Cambridge University Press 2011). This is the official TKT handbook which is entirely – and only – focused on the exam itself.

Dealing with Difficulties by Luke Prodromou and Lindsay Clandfield (DELTA Publishing 2007). Ideas for large classes, classes with discipline problems, mixed-ability classes, etc.

Teaching Unplugged by Luke Meddings and Scott Thornbury (DELTA Publishing 2010). This book gives ideas about teaching without materials (coursebooks, etc.).

CLIL

Teaching Other Subjects Through English by Sheelagh Deller and Christine Price (Oxford University Press 2007). This has a great range of activities for teaching core subjects together with English.

Content and Language Integrated Learning by Do Coyle, Philip Hood and David Marsh (Cambridge University Press 2010). This book explains much of the thinking (and practice) on which CLIL is based.

The TKT course: CLIL Module by Kay Bentley (Cambridge University Press 2011). This is part of the official TKT handbook which is entirely focused on the exam itself.

Young learners

The Primary English Teacher's Guide by Jean Brewster and Gail Ellis with Denis Girard (Penguin 2002). This book has sound practical advice for most aspects of primary teaching.

Teaching English in the Primary Classroom by Susan Halliwell (Pearson ELT 1992). Although published many years ago, this book has many practical examples, and insights into how to manage young learner classrooms.

500 Activities for the Primary Classroom by Carol Read (Macmillan 2007). As its name suggests, this book contains a range of activities for primary school English, divided into sections such as storytelling and drama, ICT, grammar, listening, etc.

Children Learning English by Jayne Moon (Macmillan 2005). This book looks at issues to do with teaching young learners.

Teaching Languages to Young Learners by Lynne Cameron (Cambridge University Press 2001). A slightly more theoretical look at young learner teaching.

Teaching English to Children by Wendy A Scott and Lisbeth H Ytreberg (Pearson ELT 1990). A book which is still widely read today.

Appendix B: Language for managing classrooms

These pages include some of the language which teachers often use to manage the students in lessons. Where a name or other word is in *italics*, this means that other words can be substituted. For example, in the question 'Does anyone know where *Reza* is?' we could substitute another name for *Reza*.

Greeting and starting

General greetings

- Good *morning* everyone.
- How are you all today?
- Did you have a good weekend?

Taking the register/calling the roll

- OK, I'm going to take the register/call the roll.
- Please say 'present' or 'here' when I call your name.
- Does anyone know where *Reza* is?

Remembering the last lesson

- Who can remember what we were doing/did last week?
- Let's go over it again.

Talking about today's lesson

- This is the plan for today's lesson …
- By the end of the lesson you will …
- There are three things we can do in this lesson. Which one shall we start with?

Dealing with latecomers

- You're late.
- Can you explain why you are late?
- That's the third time this week.
- That's not a very good excuse.
- Try to get here on time in future, OK?
- OK, well never mind. You can sit next to *Mario*. *Mario*, will you explain/tell *Emilia* what we are doing?

Stages of the lesson

Finishing a lesson stage

- Can I have your attention, please?
- OK, I'd like you to stop what you are doing (and pay attention to me).
- OK, could you finish off what you are doing now, please?
- What we are going to do next is …
- The next thing we are going to do is …
- Now we're going to do something different.

Deciding what to do next (with the students' help)

- Let's do something different.
- We can either do *a dialogue* or *some more work on pronunciation*; which would you prefer?
- Hands up if you would like to *read the text*. Hands up if you would like to *listen to a conversation*.

Homework

Setting homework

- For homework I'd like you to …
- Before next lesson (that's on *Thursday*) I'd like you to …
- I'd like you all to do some homework, please.
- You need to hand it in by next *Wednesday*.

Collecting homework in

- Have you done your homework?
- Could I have your homework, please?
- When will you be able to give me your homework?

Instructing students to do things

Books

- Open your books.
- Close your books.
- Look at the text on page 36.
- Who can give me the answer to question 3?
- Have you forgotten your book? Can you share with *Chen*?
- I'd like you to put away/close your books now. We're going to do something different.

Test instructions

- You need a pen and some paper, but you can leave your books behind.
- You have five minutes to finish what you are doing.
- You have one minute more.
- I'd like you all to stop writing.
- Could you all pass your papers to the front, please?

Putting students into groups/re-arranging the classroom

Groups and teams

- Could you all stand up (and come into the middle of the room)?
- I'd like you to form two groups.
- *Gloria*, will you join Group A, and *Miguel*, could you join Group B, please?
- OK, let's have three teams. You people here, you are Team A. You (yes that includes you *Carmen*) are Team B, and the rest of you are in Team C.
- I'd like you to arrange the chairs in groups of five.
- Could you all pick up your chairs before you move them, please?
- Could you all go back to your seats, please?
- Can I have one person from Group A, one person from Group B, one person from Group C? Come here, please.
- I'd like you all to make a line in the order of your birthdays.

Organising pairs

- OK, so you are going to/I'd like you to work in pairs.
- That's you and you, and you and you, and you and you …
- *Yumiko*, could you come here, please and work with *Keiko*?
- Can the people in row 1 turn back to face the people in row two? That's right. Now the people in row 3 turn back to the people in row 4, and the people in row 5 turn back to the people in row six, and so on.

Controlling the class

Stopping things

- Will you stop what you are doing and pay attention?
- Could you please stop talking?
- Please will you stop doing that?
- Could you please be quiet?
- Stop that right now.

Quietening students down

- I'm going to wait until there is complete silence.
- I'm going to count backwards from ten. When I have finished I want complete quiet.
- Let's see how long it takes to be quiet.
- Stop what you are doing and listen.

Suggesting consequences for actions

- If you don't stop what you are doing, I am going to …
- Listen carefully. If you do that again, you will have to see the head teacher / I will have to talk to your parents.

Follow up

- Could you come here, please?
- Could you see me at the end of the lesson?
- Could you stay here for a moment, please?
- You and I need a talk, so I'd like you to stay back at the end of the lesson.

Asking students to help

- Could you turn off/on the lights?
- Could someone please/open the window/close the window?
- Would someone (like to) clean the board?
- Could you collect everyone's homework, please?
- Could you pass the worksheets/books around, please?

Finishing and saying goodbye

Summing up

- Before we finish, I'd just like to sum up what we have been doing.
- What were the most important things you learnt today?
- Who can tell me ten new words that they learnt today?

Putting things back/taking things away

- Would you put all the books back in the cupboards, please?
- Before you leave, could you make sure that you have all your belongings?
- Before you leave, could you put all the tables and chairs back to where they were?
- Make sure you take everything with you. Don't leave anything behind.

Appendix C: Lesson planning

Many thanks for their lesson plans to Magdalena Custodio Espinar – Spain (CLIL young learner lesson), Cecilia Lemos – Brazil (Teenagers) and Kathy Simpson Davies – UK (Adults).

Checklist questions

When we start to plan lessons, there are a number of questions we need to ask ourselves: a kind of planning checklist. The following list of questions is in no significant order.

Questions	Planning area
• Who are my students? What do they know? What do they need? • How can I plan a lesson which is appropriate for the different individuals in the class?	CLASSROOM DESCRIPTION DIFFERENTIATION
• What should the whole lesson look/feel like? • What is the best way to start the lesson? • What is the most effective way of ending the lesson?	LESSON SHAPE LESSON 'FEEL'
• What topics/themes do I want to take into the classroom? • What topics and themes would be most appropriate for my students (based on their age, level, cultural background, etc.)?	CONTENT
• How does the lesson I am going to teach fit in with the overall syllabus? • What have we been doing in recent lessons – and how can that help me to decide what to do next? • What links can I make between the various topics and themes in past and future lessons and the topics and themes I am thinking of using in this one?	LESSON SEQUENCES TIMETABLE FIT
• When the lesson (or stage of the lesson) is finished, what will my students have achieved if everything goes according to plan? • How will I know if the students have achieved the aims that I set for them?	AIMS OBJECTIVES OUTCOMES
• What activities would be most appropriate for my students? • What materials, classroom technology, etc. (if any) do I need for the activities I am thinking of? • Exactly how can I make the activities work best? What procedure will I use? • What is the best sequence for the activities I want to use? • Who is going to be talking to/working with whom in the activities I have chosen? • Which is the best type of student grouping (pairwork, groupwork, individual, etc.) for the activity? • How long do I expect the activity to last (it will probably be longer than I think at first)?	ACTIVITIES MATERIALS PATTERNS OF INTERACTION PROCEDURES TIMINGS
• Based on my experience (and who my students are), what are they likely to find most difficult/complicated in the lesson I am planning? • How can I avoid the kinds of difficulties/problems that I am predicting? • What will I do if these problems arise?	ANTICIPATED PROBLEMS DIFFERENTIATION
• What extra activities/ideas can I take into the lesson in case we run out of things to do? • What extra ideas/activities can I take into the lesson in case what I have planned fails to engage the students? • What alternative ways of using my plan can I think of?	ADDITIONAL POSSIBILITIES
• What will I achieve with the lesson I am planning? • What new things might I try out/experiment with in the lesson I am planning?	PERSONAL AIMS

Lesson plan: **SOUND ENGINEERS**

Teacher: Magdalena Custodio Espinar

Subject: Conocimiento del Medio Natural, Social y Cultural

Level: Second level of primary (7–8 year olds)

Timing: Three sessions of 45 minutes

Aims: To introduce the concept of the unit and to show how to use *Audacity* (freeware)

CONTENT

Teaching objectives

- To introduce the concept of sound.
- To use ICT (computer and recording devices) as a means of learning about sound: tone, pitch, and loudness.
- To practise the structure of an interview.
- To model how to record the voice using *Audacity* software.
- To publish the interviews in a blog.

Learning outcomes

- The pupils will understand what sound is and the difference between pitch and tone.
- They will be able to change the pitch, tone and loudness of their voices using *Audacity*.
- They will play roles in an interview.
- They will record their interviews and save them in MP3 format on the computer.
- They will listen to their interviews on a blog.

COGNITION

Teaching objectives

- To provide the pupils with opportunities for:
  - relating the voice with a graph;
  - comparing changes in sound waves;
  - defining the concept of sound;
  - using freeware to apply knowledge for operating a recording device (play, pause, stop, rewind, fast forward);
  - recognising the structure of an interview.

Learning outcomes

- The pupils will infer the concept of sound from practice.
- They will understand the new vocabulary and concepts.
- They will extract the relevant information about the content.
- They will apply technological routines and skills.
- They will relate the use of *Audacity* with the content.
- They will predict the type of wave a sound will have depending on the tone or pitch of the voice.
- They will memorise an interview and roleplay it for recording.

CULTURE

Teaching objectives

- To raise awareness about the importance of using friendly language at the beginning and end of a formal meeting.
- To model intonation.

Learning outcomes

- The pupils will learn to emphasise the intonation of questions and exclamations in order to be polite.

COMMUNICATION

Language of learning

- Key words and concepts: *sound, pitch, tone, loudness.*
- ICT words: *record, save, play, stop, pause, rewind, fast forward.*
- Greetings:
  - *Hello! How are you?*
  - *Nice to meet you.*
  - *Thank you.*
  - *You are welcome.*
  - *It was a pleasure.*
  - *Goodbye.*

Language for learning

- Language to compare: *The wave is wider when … and narrower when …*
- Language to ask and answer questions: *What … ?*
- Language to give an order: *Say … , Repeat … , Play it again.*
- Language to ask for information: *What can you tell me about … ?*
- Language to ask for attention: *Look at this! Look!*
- Language to show surprise: *Wow! That is fantastic!*
- Language to give an opinion: *I think …*
- Classroom language.

Language through learning

- Language from manipulating the freeware.
- Language through peer interaction during the recordings.
- Language through memorising the interview.
- Language through activities and questions during the session.

Contribution to BASIC COMPETENCES

Learning strategies (basic competences)

- making use of prior knowledge
- following instructions
- recording new words
- critical thinking: observing and describing
- critical thinking: comparing and contrasting
- collaborative learning
- reflecting on learning and self-assessment
- using ICT resources to research, obtain, process and communicate information
- individual autonomous learning

Activities:

1 The pupils play with *Audacity* and discover, discuss and explain facts about sound while using these technological resources.
2 The pupils work on their booklets about sound (written activities for classifying, matching, drawing and word completion).
3 Pupils are given an interview worksheet to memorise.
4 One group practises with *Audacity* while the other rehearses the interview; then they swap round.
5 The 'journalists' visit the laboratory of the 'scientists' to conduct the interview and record it in pairs.
6 We publish our interviews in our blog!
7 We listen to the interviews from the blog to assess the results.

Resources:

- Computer with *Audacity* (freeware) and microphones
- Interview worksheets
- Sound booklets

Evaluation:

- **Of language:**
  - Teacher's oral language modelling on the spot.
  - Peer language modelling through feedback.
  - Group language assessment and individual assessment through listening to the interviews from the blog.
- **Of content:**
  - Teacher checks written activities.
  - Pupils answer oral and written questions about sound.
  - Pupils record and save sounds using *Audacity*.
  - Group correction of written activities.

Lesson plan: DREAMS

Name:	Class:	Level:	Length:
Cecilia Lemos	Teen 3	Elementary	60 minutes

Class description
There are 18 students in this group, 5 boys and 13 girls, all between 13 and 15 years old. They have English classes twice a week, for 1 hour and 15 minutes each time. Most of them have been studying English for about three years. It's an early group and they usually come to class still sleepy, so an active warm up, where they have to move, is always a good start.

Main aim(s)
By the end of the lesson the students will be able to use *will* to make predictions, based on the dreams they read about.

Subsidiary aim(s)
1 Review the use of the past progressive for describing an event in the past (in this case, a dream)
2 Introduce the topic (dreams) through the students' own writing

Personal aims
I will let the students work out for themselves that we use *will* for predictions – and see if this works better than giving them the information myself. I want to see how I feel about this.

Timetable fit
In the last three lessons, the students have reviewed the past tenses – simple and progressive – while talking about vacations and describing photos, saying what was happening when they were taken. In the next lesson we are going to study other uses of *will* (promises and offers).

Materials
1 Board and board markers
2 Big pieces of white paper with 'Dream' prompts on top
3 Sticky notes – enough to give each student a few

Anticipated problems
1 Some students may be left out during the forming of the groups.
2 Some groups may get stuck and may not be very creative.

Possible solutions
1 Teacher collects those students and puts them together in a group.
2 Teacher goes around asking questions that may spark an idea.

PROCEDURES

Stage/stage aim	Description	Interaction	Timing
Warm up / Have the students discover the theme of the class (dreams)	**1** Tell the students they have to guess what we'll talk about in class today – it's a word. **2** Explain I will write on the board words related to the word they're supposed to discover, one at a time, and each of them has one chance at guessing it. **3** Have the students stand in a semi-circle in the middle of the room. Tell them if they think they know the word they should run and touch the board. Only after I say his/her name should they say what they think the word is. **4** Write (pausing between words) the following words on the board: *bed*, *night*, *remember*, *nightmare*, *sleep*. If the students still can't guess the word, I'll draw it. When a student guesses it, write the word *DREAMS*, in large letters on the board.	T – SS	5 mins

Stage/stage aim	Description	Interaction	Timing
Lead in / Get the students talking about dreams	Ask the students if they usually remember what they dream about, what they think dreams are, if they usually have good or crazy dreams.	T – SS	5 mins
Writing / Have the students use the past progressive to create a dream	**1** Tell the students they will now create crazy dreams, writing what happens in the dream, starting from a prompt. They will have 15 minutes to do it. **2** Stick the six big white sheets of paper around the class. Each sheet of paper has the first sentence of the dream written on top (e.g. *Last night I dreamt I was flying over the city and then I saw … / Last night I dreamt I was watching a Lady Gaga concert and in the middle of the first song …*) **3** Ask the students to form trios. Give each trio a marker pen to write on the paper with. Ask the student who guessed the word during the warm up to stand up and get the sheet of paper/ prompt that his/her trio has chosen. That student should choose someone from one of the other trios to do the same, and so on, until each group has a piece of paper with a prompt. **4** Remind them that it's a good idea to brainstorm and think about the dream/what they are going to write before they start writing. **5** Give them 15 minutes to write their dreams. After they have finished, collect the papers and display them around the classroom. Go around the classroom, checking the students' work, helping when necessary and suggesting corrections.	SS – SS	20 mins
Reading comprehension / Have the students read what other students have written and predict what will happen to the person who had each dream	**1** Ask the students if they have ever heard about people who say they can predict the future based on other people's dreams. **2** Tell the students that they will be those fortune tellers today. They will say what will happen to each of the dreamers. Write: *What will happen to them?* on the board. **3** Read one of the texts aloud to the whole class and ask them to predict (saying out loud) what will happen to the dreamer. Recast if necessary, to suggest the use of the structure *He will / She will.* **4** Give each student a few sticky notes and tell them to go around the class, reading the dreams and predicting the future. Go around checking their work. **5** After 10–15 minutes, ask them if anybody wants to share a dream they read, together with what they predicted. Elicit the use of the structure. Use the board.	T – SS Individual	25 mins
Homework / Have the students continue using *will* for predictions	Tell the students that they have to write ten things they believe will happen in the next year. It can be about them or anything else (a sports team, a celebrity, etc.).		5 mins

Additional possibilities

- I can adapt this activity and have them write mystery stories without including the ending – have others predicting the end of each story.
- Get the students to record their dreams and have their classmates predict their future from these.
- Ask the students to predict what will happen in their favourite TV drama.

Lesson plan: LIFE EXPERIENCES

Name: Katy Simpson Davies
Class: B1 General English
Level: Lower-intermediate
Time: 120 minutes

Class description

A multilingual class of ten students from a variety of countries (Saudi Arabia, South Korea, Spain, Switzerland, Colombia). A mix of ages from early 20s to late 40s. The students are studying in the UK for different amounts of time, so some are new to the school and some have been here for months. There is a spread of levels, from those who have just moved up from pre-intermediate, to those who are nearly ready for upper-intermediate. Overall, this is an enthusiastic and chatty class, and they love games! They are generally confident, but not always very accurate. The lesson is aimed at improving their accuracy.

Main aim(s)

1. By the end of the lesson, the students will feel more confident using the present perfect to ask questions and to talk about their own life experiences.
2. By the end of the first stage of the lesson, the students will be able to use phrases to talk about life experiences in the past simple.
3. By the end of the second stage of the lesson, the students will have a better understanding of when they should use the past simple and when they should use the present perfect, and why.
4. By the end of the fourth stage of the lesson, the students will be able to use the past simple and present perfect to talk about their own experiences and the experiences of other people.

Subsidiary aim(s)

1. To revise collocations to do with life events (e.g. although the students know the word *married*, they often forget that the verb is *to get married*).
2. To revise time phrases.
3. To practise pronunciation.

Personal aims

I will use the board to give the students a useful model. I will check that my writing is big enough and clear enough by going to the back of the classroom to look at it, and I will use different colours to highlight words.

Timetable fit

In the last three lessons, the students have studied conditionals, so this is a new topic – although they will have covered the past simple and present perfect previously at other levels. In the next lesson, we are going to talk about the present perfect continuous for recent events (e.g. *I've just …*), and eventually move on to the present perfect continuous.

Materials

1. Photos from my life. Vocabulary cards to describe the pictures and cards with the years on.
2. A handout with the pictures matched to the correct vocabulary.
3. Six true or false sentences about myself, using both present perfect and past simple.
4. Pictures of my country and/or local area.
5. Small squares of paper to draw on.

Anticipated problems

1. The students might think that the present perfect is only used with been because of the frequency of *Have you ever been to …?*
2. If some students don't come to the lesson, there will be an odd number for the 'wheel'.
3. Students might feel that it's too easy, as they have almost certainly covered the present perfect and past simple before.

Possible solutions

1. I will make sure there are a variety of pictures for the mil drill which require the use of different verbs (e.g. *eaten*, *tried*, *drunk*, *played*, *watched*).
2. I will take part in the 'wheel' if necessary.
3. For the higher-level students I will monitor pronunciation carefully and encourage them to use contractions. I can also ask them whether they really feel confident using these forms, even though they've studied them before. The chances are that they 'know' the present perfect, but don't produce it very often. I'll try to keep the pace up, as a lot of this is not totally new (the vocabulary will be familiar to them, as well as the grammar), I might have to push them to keep them going, otherwise it could start to drag.

Procedures			
Stage/stage aim	**Description**	**Interaction**	**Timing**
Lead-in:	Tell the students there are pictures of me at different ages around the room.	T–SSS	5 mins
Demonstrate example	Write on the board the question *Can you guess what year it was?* Hold up one picture as an example, and write up the answer: *Katy was born in ______?* Ask the students to guess the year. Check pronunciation of years.	T–SSS–T	
Speaking to activate vocabulary about life events	In pairs, the students go around the room, talking about the pictures. Monitor for use of vocabulary – do they know collocations such as *get married*?	SS–SS	8 mins
Feedback to give the correct answers	The students sit down. Hand out smaller versions of the same photos to each pair. Hand out cards with years on them. The students match the pictures to the years.	T–SSS	2 mins
Feedback to find a winner	Check answers, and ask which pair guessed the most correct years.	T–SSS	2 mins
Vocabulary focus:	Hand out cards with vocabulary written on them (e.g. *to be born, to graduate from university, to become a teacher*). In pairs they match vocabulary to the pictures and years.	S–S	5 mins
To give the students the phrases they need to talk about life experiences, and focus on accuracy	When they have finished, give them a handout with the pictures matched to the correct vocabulary, and tell them to check their answers.	T–SSS	3 mins
To practise using the vocabulary	Elicit an example (e.g. *Katy was born in 1983*). Tell the students to stand up again. They go round the room looking at the pictures and say the sentences. Monitor and check that they are using the full phrase (e.g. *graduated* ***from*** *university*).	T–SSS S, S, S	5 mins
More practice	The students sit down. Hand out six cards with three true/three false sentences about me, with a mix or present perfect and past simple (e.g. *I've visited South Korea* – false / *I've visited Thailand* – true).	SS, SS	5 mins
Feedback	Check the correct answers. Is there a winner?	T–SSS	2 mins
Focus on difference in meaning and form between past simple and present perfect:	Write on the board one present perfect sentence and one past simple sentence. Ask the students to discuss the difference in pairs. Monitor. Get whole-class feedback. Highlight the difference in form on the board. Write up useful expressions the students use to describe the difference in meaning. Draw timelines for *I've been to Thailand* and *I went to Thailand in 2000*. The students decide which timeline fits which sentence.	T–SSS SS, SS T–SSS	10 mins
Discuss difference between present perfect and past simple	Write on the board the sentences I got married in 2008 and I've been married for three years. The students discuss differences in meaning and form and draw their own timelines. Monitor and ask those with good timelines to draw them on the board, and explain their timelines to the class.	SS, SS	
Writing stage:	The students write six sentences about themselves – three true and three false – using a mixture of past simple and present perfect.	S, S, S	5 mins
Speaking stage:	They bring chairs and papers into the middle in a wheel (two concentric circles). They tell their sentences to the person sitting opposite them who guesses if they are true or false. They get a point for each correct guess. The inner circle then moves round so the students work with different partners.	SS, SS, SS, SS, SS	5 mins
Feedback	Ask students who got the most points? What was the most surprising piece of information?	T–SSS	2 mins

Additional possibiliites

Homework: hand out squares of paper (preferably coloured paper). Tell the students to draw a picture of one thing from their country. Demonstrate an example on the board (e.g. stick figures playing football). Stress that it doesn't need to be a professional drawing.

Repeat the mill drill in class, but this time they use their own picture for the question, not the picture being shown to them. Then they exchange pictures and ask the new question to another person.

Ask the students to bring in photos of themselves to talk about their life experiences in the next lesson.

Glossdex

The *Glossdex* contains the technical terms that occur in *Essential Teacher Knowledge*, with definitions and unit references. The *Glossdex* gives the numbers of the units where the subjects appear. Where subjects appear in more than one unit, the most important unit for that subject is in **bold**.

Words in SMALL CAPITAL LETTERS appear as separate entries elsewhere in the *Glossdex*.

4Cs content, communication, cognition and culture →102, 108, 109

A-L – see AUDIO-LINGUAL METHODOLOGY

abbreviation a word or phrase that is shortened, often to its initial letters (e.g. BTW for 'by the way') →**31**, 32, 33

abstract thinking skills being able to reason, hypothesise or think *about* things →107

accurate, accuracy without mistakes; the ability to say or write something correctly →37, 49, 57, **73**, 92

achievement when we succeed at something →43

achievement test when we give a test to see if the students have learnt what they have been studying →88, 89

acknowledge, acknowledgement when we show that we have heard what a student has said or read what they have written →72

acquisition – see LANGUAGE ACQUISITION →**35**, 36, 38, 39, 60

action, do actions when we get YOUNG LEARNERS to move their arms or bodies →94, 95

action research when teachers try something out and study the results to see if it was a good idea →78, 79

action verb a VERB which describes an EVENT or action; sometime called a dynamic verb; opposite of a STATIVE VERB →4

activate – see also ESA when students try to use any/all of the language they know in communicative speaking and other TASKS →36, 39, 48, **80**

active voice – see also PASSIVE VOICE When we put the elements of a SENTENCE in the order SUBJECT + VERB + OBJECT (e.g. *Shakespeare wrote Hamlet*), we call the result an active sentence. →1

activity something we ask students to do to help them with their language learning →43, 69, 79, 80, 81, **83**, 85

activity book a book of activities which teachers use together with their COURSEBOOK →81

additional language any new language (English, Turkish, Japenese, etc.) that the students are learning →102

additional possibilities extra ideas that teachers put in their LESSON PLANS in case there is time left over in the lesson →79

adjective Adjectives (like *big*, *expensive*, *enjoyable*, *fair*, etc.) describe and modify NOUNS. We can create COMPARATIVE ADJECTIVES by, for example, adding *-er* (*bigger*, *fairer*) or *more* (*more expensive*, *more enjoyable*), and we can create SUPERLATIVE ADJECTIVES by, for example, adding *-est* (*biggest*, *fairest*) or *most* (*most expensive*, *most enjoyable*). →1, 9, 11, 12, **15**, 16, 17, 19, 20, 26, 35

adjective order When we use more than one adjective before a noun, we normally do so in a specific sequence. →**15**, 17

adolescent people between the stages of puberty and adulthood; see also TEENAGERS →38

adult (learners) students aged 18 and upwards; students aged 16–18 are often referred to as *young adults* →14, 16, 35, 38, **39**, 95

advanced level students who are above UPPER-INTERMEDIATE level; equivalent to CEFR levels C1–2 →**41**, 51

adverb	Adverbs (like *politely*, *enthusiastically* and *quickly*) describe VERBS. They are often, but not always, formed by adding *-ly* to adjectives (like *polite*, *enthusiastic*, *quick*). ADVERBS OF DEGREE say how much something is done, ADVERBS OF MANNER describe how something is done, ADVERBS OF PLACE say where something is done, ADVERBS OF TIME say when something is done and ADVERBS OF CERTAINTY say how sure it is that something is done. See also FREQUENCY ADVERB. →1, 3, 6, 9, **11**, 15, 20, 56, 82
adverb of certainty – see ADVERB	→11
adverb of degree – see ADVERB	→11
adverb of manner – see ADVERB	→**11**, 64
adverb of place – see ADVERB	→**11**, 34
adverb of time – see ADVERB	→**11**, 102
adverbial (phrase)	when two or more words join together and act as if they were a single ADVERB →1, 5, **11**
affect, affective	concerned with feelings →22, **26**, 43
affirmative sentence	a sentence that says that something is, was, will be or might be the case; the opposite of a NEGATIVE SENTENCE →3, 14
affix	a MORPHEME that we add to a word to modify its meaning; this can be a PREFIX (such as *un-* and *dis-*) which joins the beginning of a word (e.g. ***un****important*, ***dis****agree*) or a SUFFIX (such as *-ness* and *-ment*) which joins the end of the word (e.g. *happi**ness***, *amuse**ment***) →15, **19**
affricate	a CONSONANT sound which starts like a PLOSIVE and ends like a FRICATIVE, e.g. /tʃ/ and /dʒ/; see PALATO-ALVEOLAR FRICATIVE →24
agency	when students have some responsibility for (and control over) their learning →38, **39**, 43
aim (of a lesson, stage)	what we hope the OUTCOME of the lesson (or LESSON STAGE) will be →79, 109
alveolar fricative	the CONSONANT sounds /s/ and /z/ →24
alveolar nasal	the CONSONANT sound /n/ →24
alveolar plosive	the CONSONANT sounds /t/ and /d/ →24
alveolar ridge	the flat surface behind the top teeth →24
anaphoric reference	when we use PRONOUNS, etc. to refer to things we have previously mentioned; see also CATAPHORIC REFERENCE, EXOPHORIC REFERENCE →34
answer	the reply given to a question or a command →3
anticipate problems	when the teacher tries to predict what might go wrong (in their LESSON PLAN) →79
antonym	antonyms are words with opposite meanings (e.g. *hot* and *cold*, *big* and *small*); see also SYNONYM →**18**, 82
apostrophe	the punctuation mark which indicates contraction or possession, e.g. *I'm not sure*, *John's book* →31
appropriate language	language that is just right for a certain situation (not rude, too formal or informal, etc.) →33
approximant	the sounds /j/ and /w/ – CONSONANTS which sound almost like vowels →24
app, application	a program designed for use on SMARTPHONES and other MOBILE DEVICES →86, 106
aptitude	a natural ability for something →40
article	English has a DEFINITE ARTICLE (*the*) and an INDEFINITE ARTICLE (*a/an*). Some people refer to a ZERO ARTICLE as well when no article is used. →1, 14, 37, 104
aspect	a verb form that shows whether an action is continuing, is completed or happens again and again →5, **6**

assess, assessment	when we make a judgement about a students' English ability; we can use a variety of ways, e.g. CONTINUOUS ASSESSMENT, PORTFOLIO ASSESSMENT, INFORMAL ASSESSMENT, etc. to do this; we can also assess the effectiveness of something we (or the students) planned to achieve →**88**, 109
assessing CLIL	evaluating students of CLIL →102
assessment criteria	exactly what we are trying to test →88, 90
assessment scale	a way of grading something from, for example, 0 (= no good) to 5 (= excellent) →90, 110
assimilation	when we change a sound because of the sound we are going to use next →**25**, 28
attempt	a mistake students make when they try to say things that they don't yet know how to say →**37**, 84
attitude	the way teachers present themselves in front of the class →43
attitude to learning	how interested in (and responsible for) learning a student feels →110
audience	the people who will read what we are writing or hear what we are saying →**34**, 57
audio device	anything which allows us to record and play audio →60, 105
audio feedback	when teachers record comments about a student's work on an AUDIO DEVICE →75
audio recording	when we record our voices on an AUDIO DEVICE; see also RECORDED LISTENING →74, 76, 81, 85
audio-lingual methodology	a methodology most popular in the 1950s–1970s where students did a lot of REPETITION and DRILLING →36
audioscript	the words of an audio track written down exactly; see also TRANSCRIPT →85
auxiliary verb	a 'helping verb', such as *be*, *have*, *do*, etc. →3, **4**, 6, 8, 11, 25
avatar	a character that you create to be 'you' in a computer game, etc. →**87**, 93
back chaining	when we ask students to do CHORAL REPETITION, repeating bits of a sentence, starting at the end and working up to saying the whole thing →47
base form (of a verb)	the form of a verb with no inflections, e.g. *walk*, *sleep*, *learn* →**4**, 5, 6, 7, 16, 19
bar chart	a diagram using vertical bars to show different quantities →105
beginner	a student who is starting to learn English and knows almost nothing; similar to CEFR level A1; REAL BEGINNERS know no English at all; FALSE BEGINNERS have picked up a little bit of English →7, 26, 41, 44, 49, 51
behaviourism	a theory which suggests that people can be conditioned into behaving in a certain way if there is the appropriate STIMULUS- RESPONSE-REINFORCEMENT (if subjects respond to a stimulus in a certain way, their behaviour is rewarded/reinforced so that it becomes a habit) →36
BICS	basic interpersonal communication skills – a term used in CLIL to describe the everyday language that people use to talk to each other about their lives and what they are doing; different from CALP →103
bilabial	when we use both of our lips to make CONSONANT sounds such as /b/, /m/, etc. →24
bilabial plosive	the CONSONANT sounds /p/ and /b/ →24
bilingual dictionary	a DICTIONARY which shows the (meaning of the) same words in two different languages →82
bilingual learners' dictionary (BLD)	a BILINGUAL DICTIONARY written especially for language students →82
binary key	a diagram which divides information into two parts →105
blackboard	a BOARD at the front of a classroom for teachers and students to write on →85

Blackboard	a VIRTUAL LEARNING ENVIRONMENT (VLE) OR LEARNING PLATFORM where people can study online →66, 76, 87
blank	the space where students have to write a word or phrase in a FILL-IN exercise or GAP FILL test item →62, 63, 89
blend	when we mix two words together to make a new one, e.g. *smoke* + *fog* = *smog* →19
blended learning	when students use traditional learning aids, such as books, together with more modern technology such as WEBSITES and APPS →81, **87**
blog	short for *weblog*; a kind of diary on an internet WEBSITE →59, 66, 78, 87, 89
blog post	an individual text or entry written on a BLOG →59, 76
board	Boards are usually placed at the front of the classroom so that teachers and students can write or draw pictures on them. They can be different colours (e.g. WHITEBOARDS, BLACKBOARDS) and/or be connected to a computer (INTERACTIVE WHITEBOARD). →16, 62, **85**, 93, 99, 105, 106
bottom-up processing	when we try to understand a whole text, starting from finding the meaning of individual WORDS and PHRASES →54
brackets	punctuation marks used to separate out extra ideas in a sentence →**31**, 103
brainstorm	when students try to come up with ideas very quickly in DISCUSSION (often in BUZZ GROUPS) →63
burnout	when teachers get depressed or overtired and lose interest in (or have no enthusiasm for) teaching →**6**, 78
business English	when students study English because they want to use it in the world of business →41
buzz group	a small group where students have quick discussions about things →**52**, 55, 57, 59, 61, 63
CALP	cognitive academic language proficiency – a term used in CLIL to describe language that students need in order to hypothesise, give reasons and explain the topics they are studying; different from BICS →103
can-do statements	statements used in the CEFR to describe ability, e.g. *can understand short written messages* →**41**, 90, 101, 110
capital letter – see also PUNCTUATION	the big letter that we use at the beginning of a SENTENCE or a PROPER NOUN →1, **12**, 31
cards	small pieces of cardboard which we can write, draw or stick PICTURES on →83, 86, 93, 97, 98, 99
Carroll diagram	a diagram which groups information in a 'yes-no' format →105
cataphoric reference	when we use PRONOUNS, etc. to refer to things which we will mention later; see also ANAPHORIC REFERENCE and EXOPHORIC REFERENCE →34
cause and effect diagram	a diagram which shows reasons why something happens →105
CEFR	Common European Framework of Reference for Languages – a six-level description of language ability that can be used for any language →**41**, 54
centring diphthong	a DIPHTHONG which ends with the SCHWA sound →24
challenge – see LEVEL OF CHALLENGE	
chant	rhythmic speaking (like a SONG without music) →47, 93, **94**, 96
charades	a game where someone MIMES and acts out the title of a book, film or play and the others have to guess what it is →64
chart	a diagram with (space for) a lot of different information →49, 50, 55
chatbox	a place online where people can write messages to each other →87

check meaning – see also CONCEPT CHECKING	when we ask questions to see if the students have understood →44, **69**
checking instructions	when we try to discover if the students have understood our instructions →69
child development	the different stages of a child's physical and intellectual growth →91
choral repetition	when students all repeat the same word or phrase or sentence at the same time →42, 44, **47**
chorus	a group of students who all speak at the same time →95, 98
citizenship	understanding how we belong and should behave in the societies we live in →109
class description	when we say who our students are and what they are like in a lesson plan →79
class register	a list of students used to record attendance and absence; called a ROLL in American English →65, **66**, 70
classroom resource	anything that is in a classroom (including the teacher) which we can use to explain meaning, give the students exposure to language, etc. →68, 109
clause	a phrase with a subject and a verb – but part of a sentence, not the whole sentence →1, **2**, 16, 46
cliché	an IDIOM used so often that people get fed up with it →21
CLIL	content and language integrated learning; the STUDY of a SUBJECT together with the language that is necessary to study that subject →41, 81, 100, **102–110**
CLIL assessment	when we test students of CLIL →88
close vowel	the sounds /iː/, /ɪ/ /ʊ/ and /uː/ →24
closed information-gap activity	when an INFORMATION-GAP ACTIVITY has 'correct' answers which the students have to give →50
closed question – see YES/NO QUESTION	
closing diphthong	the sounds /eɪ/, /aɪ/, /ɔɪ/, /əʊ/ and /aʊ/ →24
cloze (test)	a test where texts have blanks which have been chosen at random, e.g. every sixth word →89
CLT – see COMMUNICATIVE LANGUAGE TEACHING	
co-hyponym – see also HYPONYM	*eagle*, *kite*, *marsh harrier*, *sparrow hawk* and *kestrel* are all co-hyponyms of the larger meaning category *birds of prey*: they are all at the same 'level' of meaning →18
code of conduct	a description of what is and is not allowed in class →70, **71**, 76, 107
cognition, cognitive skills	our ability to use our brains to work things out – to think effectively →102, 108, 109, 110
cognitive engagement	when students get involved in learning something (and remember it) because they have to use their brains to think about it →22
coherence, coherent	when something is comprehensible and ordered in a logical sequence →31, **34**, 57, 59, 69, 104
cohesion	when we use COHESIVE DEVICES to show how the parts of a text relate to each other →31, **34**, 59
cohesive device	any language which we use to show how the parts of a text relate to each other →34
collaborate	work with someone else to complete a TASK →102
collaborative writing	when students work together to complete a writing TASK →58
collective noun – see also NOUN	a noun which describes a group of things/people, e.g. *army* →12

collocate, collocation	the way in which words co-occur (are often found next to each other), e.g. *juvenile crime*, *fast asleep* →18, **20**, 37, 46, 82, 87, 103, 107
colloquial	language used in everyday CONVERSATION that is INFORMAL →31
colon	a punctuation mark used at the beginning of a list or before a definition or explanation →31
comma	a punctuation mark used to separate clauses and indicate a breathing space between ideas →15, **31**, 57
commenting	when we say what we think about a student's work (but don't grade it) →72
Common European Framework of Reference for Languages - see CEFR	
communication skills	the things we do which help us to communicate well →108, 110
communicative activity	an activity which makes students communicate with each other (usually by speaking) →22, 26, 48, 49, 77
communicative approach	an approach which says that communication in the classroom is the most important thing – and which also says that we should learn language *for* communication →36
communicative language teaching (CLT)	teaching which encourages students to communicate rather than just PRACTISING certain LANGUAGE ITEMS and which teaches language for communication (e.g. LANGUAGE FUNCTIONS) →**36**, 39
communicative speaking activity	an activity which makes students use speaking to communicate, rather than just PRACTISING different language items →**51**, 67, 73, 74
companion website	a WEBSITE which supports a COURSE or COURSEBOOK→81, **87**
comparative adjective - see also ADJECTIVE	Examples: *cleverer*, *more expensive*, *better* →15
complement	a word or phrase that follows a verb and describes the subject of the verb →1
compound noun	a NOUN which is constructed from two other nouns, e.g. *summertime*, *orange juice* →**12**, 19, 26
compound word	any word that is formed from two other words (whatever part of speech they are), e.g. *fair-haired*, *good looking*, *proper noun* →19
comprehensible input	language which students are exposed to and which they understand (comprehend) even if it is above their own production level →**35**, 54, 60, 65, 68, 77
comprehensible input provider	a TEACHER ROLE involving giving students COMPREHENSIBLE INPUT →65
computer	an electronic machine which stores information and allows us to access the internet and/or write programs/play games, etc. →57, 62, 63, 99
concept checking	trying to find out if the students have understood a concept →69
concept question	the questions which we use for CONCEPT CHECKING →69
concessive clause	a CLAUSE that is introduced with a phrase like *although*, *however*, *in spite of*, etc. →2
concordance, concordancer	a software program which allows us to get information about words in a language CORPUS →87
concrete thinking skills	when students process and order information in diagrams, etc. →107
conditional clause	a clause which states a condition, often starts with *if* and occurs in a CONDITIONAL SENTENCE →2
conditional sentence	a sentence which contains a conditional clause and its consequence; see also FIRST CONDITIONAL, SECOND CONDITIONAL, THIRD CONDITIONAL and ZERO CONDITIONAL →**2**, 46, 103
conjunction	a word used to join words, phrases, clauses or sentences →**1**, 2, 32

connotation	the idea or feeling that a word suggests: more than just its meaning →3, **18**
consensus	when everyone agrees about something →**51**, 82
consonant	a sound that we make when we stop (or nearly stop) the flow of air through the mouth; in the alphabet, letters like *b*, *c*, *d*, *f*, *g*, etc. different from VOWEL →13, **23**
contact clause	also known as a REDUCED RELATIVE CLAUSE; see RELATIVE CLAUSE →2
contact hours	the number of hours a teacher is in the classroom →78
content	the SUBJECT or TOPIC of something – what it is about →36, 57, 72, 74, 81, 84, 102, 106, 109
content word	a word which has CONTENT meaning, e.g. *dog*, *tree*, unlike function words such as *the* and *of*, which do not have content meaning →26
content and language integrated learning – see CLIL	
content-compatible language	language that is useful for a specific topic, but which is also common in everyday English →103, 110
content-obligatory language	language that we have to use when we are talking about a specific TOPIC →103, 106, 108
context	events, situations, circumstances, etc. which help us to understand something that happens in them →5
continuous assessment	when we assess students all the time during a course, perhaps using PORTFOLIOS →**88**, 101
continuous verbs	verbs which use the continuous ASPECT (PRESENT CONTINUOUS, PAST CONTINUOUS, PRESENT PERFECT CONTINUOUS, etc.) →6
contraction, contracted form	when we shorten sentences and phrases and elide words, e.g *He's talking. They're laughing.* →3, **25**, 31
contrastive stress	when we change the place of the STRESS in a PHRASE or SENTENCE so that the focus of what we want to say changes as a result →26
controlled practice	when students are involved in repetition and CUE-RESPONSE drills using specific (and restricted) language →44, 48, 72
controller	a TEACHER ROLE when we (usually) stand at the front of the class telling all the students what to do →**65**, 67, 92
conversation	talking to and with other people →84
conversational skills	the things we do to make CONVERSATION a success →83
copybook	a book where (usually) children copy new words that they have learnt in class →99
corpus, corpora	a large computerised collection of language examples taken from books, films, newspapers, etc. →46, 87
correct, correction	when we show students that they have made a mistake and help them to say or write something without that mistake →15, 36, 37, 39, 42, 46, 57, 65, 66, 72, **73**, **74**, **75**, 85, 88, 92
correcting written work	when we show students that they have made a mistake in their writing and help them to rewrite it without that mistake →72, **75**
correction symbols	marks which teachers use to show that a written MISTAKE has been made→72, **75**
count noun – see COUNTABLE NOUN	
countable noun – see also UNCOUNTABLE NOUN	a noun that we can count, e.g. *one apple*, *two apples*; different from an UNCOUNTABLE NOUN →**12**, 13, 14, 17, 73
course	a period of study (say, ten weeks) which usually follows a particular SYLLABUS →80

coursebook	a textbook that a teacher can use to base a COURSE on →**41**, 60, 62, 65, **81**, 83, 84, 85, 87, 90, 97, 102, 106
coursebook dialogue	a conversation between two people in a COURSEBOOK →60, 81
cross-curricular	when students study TOPICS from different subject areas together, e.g. English and geography →100
cue	the sign we give when we want our students to say something →47
cue-response drill	when we give the students a PROMPT to encourage them to respond by saying the SENTENCES or QUESTIONS which we want them to practise →44, **47**, 86
Cuisenaire rods	small pieces of wood of different lengths and colours which people use for language teaching →86
cultural elements	parts of a lesson which include references to (other) CULTURES →109
cultural identity	the idea we have of which social, geographical, linguistic, etc. group we belong to→109
culture	beliefs, way of life, arts, etc. that the members of a group share →102, 109
curriculum	the overall plan for a subject or for a school – more general than a SYLLABUS →41, 80, 109
cyber homework	homework which students do ONLINE →81, 87
cycle	a (usually) circular diagram to show a sequence of events →105
dashes	punctuation marks used to separate out extra ideas in a sentence →**31**, 103
data projector	a machine that projects what is on our computer screens →63, 85, 106
DEAR	'drop everything and read' →**54**, 69, 98
debate	When students have to argue different points of view (after they have prepared their arguments) →**52**, 56, 68, 76
deep-end strategy	another name for TEST-TEACH-TEST →45
defining relative clause – see RELATIVE CLAUSE	
definite article	*the* →1, **13**, 15
definition	the explanation of what something means (particularly in a DICTIONARY) →82
demonstrate, demonstration	when we show the students what we want them to do (instead of just telling them) →68, **69**, 85, 86
demonstrative pronoun	the pronouns *this*, *that*, *these* and *those* →12
demotivated, demotivation	when students lose their enthusiasm for learning →71, 75
dental fricative consonant	the sounds /θ/ and /ð/ →24
describe and draw	an ACTIVITY where one student has to tell another student what picture to draw →**50**, 69, 86, 96
developmental errors	the mistakes that most language learners make for a time as a result of the language they are learning →37
developmental stages (in children)	the different things that children can do and understand at different ages as they grow →35, 38, **91**, 100
diagnostic test	a test we give students in order to see what we should teach them next, and/or what level they should study at; see also PLACEMENT TEST →88
dialogue	(usually) two people talking together →30, **45**, 60, 62, 67, 74, 83, 86, 98
dictate, dictation	when the teacher (or a student) says something and the students have to write it down exactly, word for word; see also RUNNING DICTATION, SHOUTED DICTATION →**48**, 51, 89, 99

email	messages sent by COMPUTER, etc. →57, 58, 59
emerge, emergent language	language which the students start to understand or use when they are ready to do so, and which is part of their language development →84
emoticon	a little picture/diagram showing if people are happy or sad, sometimes called a *smiley* →31
engage, engagement – see also ESA	when students are emotionally involved, interested and motivated →36, 39, 55, 64, 65, 71, **80**, 81, 83, 84, 91, 92, 107
English for academic purposes (EAP)	when students study the English they need in order to attend an English-speaking university, college, etc.; EAP is one kind of ENGLISH FOR SPECIFIC PURPOSES →41
English for specific purposes (ESP)	when students study English for medicine, for physics, for tourism, etc. →**41**, 106
error	a formal word to describe MISTAKES and SLIPS →**37**, 85
ESA	ENGAGE, STUDY and ACTIVATE – three elements of a teaching sequence →80
evaluate, evaluation	when we make a judgement about how good something is →72, 99
event	a single thing that happens →4
evidence gatherer	a TEACHER ROLE when teachers listen to students to see what they are doing correctly and incorrectly →65
exam practice book	a book to help students PRACTISE the things they need to be successful in a future exam →83
exclamation mark	a punctuation mark used to show surprise, humour, etc. →29, **31**
exercise	something (usually written) that we ask students to do to PRACTISE their English, often for HOMEWORK →83
exophoric reference	when we use PRONOUNS, etc, to refer to things outside the text itself; see also ANAPHORIC REFERENCE and CATAPHORIC REFERENCE →34
experiment	when we try something out to see what will happen →86, 104
exposure (to language)	when we hear or see language being used →35
extensive listening	when students listen for pleasure and for meaning rather than for STUDY; different from INTENSIVE LISTENING →60, **62**
extensive reading	when students read for pleasure and for meaning, rather than for STUDY; different from INTENSIVE READING →43, **54**, 70, 83, 98
extrinsic motivation	MOTIVATION that comes from something outside the act of learning itself (such as a desire for a better job); see also INTRINSIC MOTIVATION →43
facial expression	when we show what we are feeling in our faces; some teachers use this for CORRECTION →73
facilitator (of learning)	someone who helps other people to learn by creating the appropriate conditions →65
falling tone – see also INTONATION	when the PITCH of the voice goes down in a TONIC SYLLABLE →**27**, 29
fall-rise tone – see also INTONATION	when the PITCH of the voice falls and then rises in a TONIC SYLLABLE →**27**, 29
false beginner – see also BEGINNER	a student who knows a little bit of English (but not much) →41
feedback	the way that teachers react when students have said or written something →14, 52, 65, **72**, 74, 107
feedback provider	a TEACHER ROLE involving giving FEEDBACK to students →65
field	what we are talking about (TOPIC) and why (purpose) →33
fill in – see also GAP FILL	when students have to write WORDS and PHRASES in BLANKS (in sentences, texts, etc.) →62, 101, 110

film clip – see also VIDEO CLIP	a (usually) short extract from a film →53, 62, 64
final assessment	when students are tested at the end of a semester, year or course →59
find the similarities/differences	an INFORMATION-GAP activity where students compare pictures (but they cannot both see both pictures) →**50**, 101
find someone who ...	a mingling activity to practise speaking – and which can be use to practise specific language →49, 68
first conditional	Example: *If it rains, you will get wet. If they don't leave soon they will be late.* →**2**, 49
fixed lexical phrase – see LEXICAL PHRASE	
flashcard	a CARD which we can show to the class as a CUE, etc. →86
flipchart	a board which has large pieces of paper on it that can be used to write on and which can be torn off to keep →85
flow diagram	a diagram which shows the process or direction of something, or the relationships between things →105
fluency	the ability to speak in reasonably long PHRASES, at a reasonable speed and without pausing in the middle of LEXICAL CHUNKS →37, **73**
follow-up question	a related question we can ask after someone has answered our first question →72
follow-up task	an additional task after students have completed a reading or listening task →42, 56
form, language form	the grammatical and PHONEMIC way that we express a language item →**36**, 44
formal debate – see DEBATE	
formal language	the language we use in serious, important or official situations →14, 30, **33**, 82, 104
formal operational stage	the stage at which children can start to think in abstract terms, according to Piaget →**91**, 95
formative assessment	when we use assessment in order to help students (after the assessment) to improve →**88**, 101, 110
fossilised, fossilisation	when a mistake becomes part of a student's language and won't go away →37
frequency – see also LOW FREQUENCY	the frequency of a word or phrase refers to how often people use it →**18**, 82
frequency adverb – see also ADVERB	an ADVERB that says how often something happens →11, 46
fricative	the sound of a CONSONANT caused by the friction of air between two parts of the mouth →24
full stop	the punctuation mark we put at the end of a sentence (called a PERIOD in American English) →29, **31**, 57
full verb – see LEXICAL VERB	
function – see LANGUAGE FUNCTION	
functional syllabus	a SYLLABUS that is a list of LANGUAGE FUNCTIONS →80
future	the time after now →5, 45
future perfect	Examples *I will have been here for three years; She will have been learning English for six months.* →6
game	a competitive and enjoyable ACTIVITY to help language learning →7, 49, 51, 70, 83, 93, 95
gap fill – see also FILL IN	an INDIRECT TEST ITEM or exercise where students have to fill blanks with words or phrases →89
general adjective – see also ADJECTIVE	an adjective that describes a general quality, e.g. *big*, *old*, etc. →15
general English	English studied for no special reason at schools, language institutes, etc. →22, 41, 104, 106, 108

genre	a particular type of writing or speaking (e.g. a letter, an advertisement, a lecture); see also SUB-GENRE →**32**, 55, 59, 60, 104, 107
genre analysis	when we study how and why a text in a certain genre has been written or spoken →59, 104
gerund	the *-ing* form used like a NOUN, e.g. ***Jogging** can be good for you.* →16
gesture	a movement of the arms and hands which expresses meaning →30, 45, 47, 73
gist	the general (not detailed) meaning of something →39, 54, 55, 60
giving instructions – see INSTRUCTIONS	
goal	something that we want to achieve, something that we are aiming for; see SHORT-TERM GOAL, LONG-TERM GOAL →43, 66, 71
***going to* future**	Example: *I am going to see my friend tomorrow.* →**5**, 101
good learner	a student who studies well →40
grade	the mark, such as A, B, 70%, 50%, etc., that teachers give when they mark student TESTS and HOMEWORK →70, 76, 87, 88, **90**
graded reader	books written at different levels to suit the level of different students; used for EXTENSIVE READING →**54**, 62, 83
grammar	the way in which WORDS change their forms and combine to make SENTENCES – and for which there are rules →1–17, 35, 37, 79, 81, 95, 109
grammar book	a book with explanations about GRAMMAR →46, 65
grammar syllabus	a sequence of grammar items in the order that we want students to learn them →80, 106
grammar-translation	a teaching method where students study grammar and translate from English to their HOME LANGUAGE and vice-versa →36, 77
group, groupwork	when we divide the class so that about 3–7 students work together to complete a TASK →22, 26, 39, 42, 46, 53, 56, 63, 66, **67**, 71, 74, 79, 89, 92, 93, 97, 101, 102, 107, 109
haiku	a type of poem with 17 syllables which connects emotions and the natural world →32, 63
half chorus	when we divide the class in half for CHORAL REPETITION with each half saying, for example, alternate lines of a dialogue →47
hard CLIL	when everything that the students do is organised for CONTENT AND LANGUAGE INTEGRATED INSTRUCTION (CLIL); see also SOFT CLIL →102
hard palate	the place at the top (and in the middle) of your mouth →24
headword	a WORD that has its own meaning explained in a dictionary →82
higher-order thinking skills (HOTS)	the skills students need (e.g. in CLIL lessons) in order to answer questions about why and how something is happening and what they think about it; different from LOTS →107, 108
home language	the language that people use at home; also called MOTHER TONGUE and L1 – the students' first language →28, 41, **77**, 92
homework	tasks and exercises that teachers ask students to do at home →42, 43, 54, 66, 75, **76**, 78, 87
homework record	when teachers and students keep a list of what HOMEWORK the students have to do and have done →76
homonym	a word that has the same spelling (and the same sound) as another word, but has a different meaning, e.g. *dear* (= expensive) and *dear* (= a greeting) →18
hot seat, the	when the class focus their questions on one student →51, 107

hyphen a small line which joins two words, e.g *good-looking* →12, 15, **31**

hyponym a word which is a specific type (part) of a larger (SUPERORDINATE) category, e.g. *dog*, *cat* and *hamster* are hyponyms of the word *pet* →18

hypothesise when we make an educated guess about something →104

hypothetical something that is not real, but which might happen (or might have happened) →2

icebreaker – see WARMER

idiom, idiomatic an idiom is a phrase that has a meaning which is different from the meaning of the individual words in it, e.g. *full of beans* = energetic, enthusiastic →4, 9, 18, **21**, 82

imperative the BASE FORM of the verb used for commands, e.g. *Be quiet!* →4

indefinite article *a* (or *an*) →1, 13, **14**

indirect object the person or thing that is involved in the result of an action →1

indirect speech when we tell someone what someone else said but we don't use their exact words, e.g. *She said she was happy*; also called REPORTED SPEECH →10

indirect test item a test item which tests grammar, vocabulary, etc., but doesn't ask the students to use the language realistically; see DIRECT TEST ITEM →**89**, 90

individual repetition when we ask the students to repeat something one by one →47

individual work when students work alone →60, 109

infinitive the base form of the verb, used in verb constructions like *I'm going to* ***travel*** →**4**, 5, 10, 40

inflection the way WORDS change their forms using different MORPHEMES, AFFIXES, etc. →19

informal language language used in relaxed or friendly situations →3, 8, 18, 30, 31, **33**, 82

informal assessment when we test students casually or informally →88

information-gap activity an activity where two or more students have different information about the same topic; they have to share the information to 'close the gap' →17, 42, 48, **50**, 55, 63, 68, 86, 89, 101

information technology any technology that we use to get or give information →81

inner voice the voice we hear (and use) silently in our own heads →51

input hypothesis, the Stephen Krashen's theory of language ACQUISITION →35

inseparable phrasal verb a phrasal verb where we can't put anything between the VERB and the PARTICLE →9

instructional scaffolding – see SCAFFOLDING

instructions the commands we give to students, such as *Work in pairs*, or *Open your books at page 63*; see also CHECKING INSTRUCTIONS →41, 65, **68**, 69, 92

instrumental motivation MOTIVATION that comes from a desire to achieve something specific, such as learning to do something because we think it will help us get a better job →43

integrative motivation MOTIVATION to learn a language because we like or want to be part of a TARGET-LANGUAGE community →43

integrative test item a test item which mixes different LANGUAGE SKILLS and different language items →88

intelligibility when people can understand us (even if we don't have 'perfect' pronunciation) →37

intensive listening when students listen to a RECORDED LISTENING or LIVE LISTENING mostly for language and meaning study; different from EXTENSIVE LISTENING →60

intensive reading when students read a (usually) short text, mostly for language and meaning study; different from EXTENSIVE READING →54

interaction when two or more people work together in class, usually by talking to each other about what they are doing →79

interactive whiteboard (IWB) a board which is connected to a COMPUTER so that we can play AUDIO, show VIDEO, display pictures, etc. →16, 60, 62, 85, 96, 105, 106

intercultural understanding when we compare (and try to understand) what people in our own culture do with what people from other cultures do →99

interference error a mistake that learners make because they try to use their L1 grammar and vocabulary in their L2 →37

interlanguage a language learner's own 'version' of the language they are learning (because they have not mastered it yet) →37

intermediate (level) the stage between ELEMENTARY and ADVANCED levels, equivalent to CEFR levels B1–2; see also PRE-INTERMEDIATE, LOWER-INTERMEDIATE, UPPER-INTERMEDIATE →17, 29, 41, 44, 46, 56, 59

internet the system which allows computers and mobile devices to 'talk' to each other →3, 16, 46, 53, 57, 86, 106

interview when one or more people ask someone questions, often to see if they can have a job or because they want to know more about their life →49, 51, 53, 56, 64, 87, 89

intonation the changes in pitch in someone's voice when they speak →3, 11, 26, **27**, 29, 30, 31, 37, 45, 46, 72, 73

intranet a computer network for a selected group of people (i.e. not available to everyone); different from INTERNET →59

intransitive verb – see also TRANSITIVE VERB a verb that doesn't have or take an object →**4**, 6

intrinsic motivation MOTIVATION which comes from the act of learning itself – and a desire to complete a learning task →43

inverted commas the punctuation marks we use to show direct speech; also called quotation marks →**31**, 57

irregular verb – see also REGULAR VERB a verb which doesn't use the *-ed* ending for the PAST TENSE or past participle →4, 6

isolate, isolation to get students to focus on a detail of a language MODEL →44

IWB – see INTERACTIVE WHITEBOARD

jigsaw listening when students hear different (separate) bits of a listening TEXT and have to tell each other about their extracts in order to understand the whole 'story' →60

jigsaw reading the same as JIGSAW LISTENING, but done with different bits of a reading TEXT →50, **55**, 77

journal, writing journal a place, sometimes a notebook, where students (or teachers) can write about things that they care about →**59**, 90, 99

jumbled sentences when sentences are all mixed up and students have to put them in a COHERENT sequence →1, 89

juncture the join between two PHONEMES; the juncture between *I scream* and *ice cream* is very slightly different and we can usually tell the difference →25

kinaesthetic activity an activity involving physical movement →4

kinaesthetic learner a student who learns best through movement and tactile sensation →92

L1 – see also MOTHER TONGUE, HOME LANGUAGE the language that children acquire at home; many children have more than one L1 →8, 41, 54, **77**, 107

labio-dental fricative consonant the sounds /f/ and /v/ →**24**, 25

language acquisition picking up a language without consciously learning it →**35**, 60

language corpus – see CORPUS

language exponent a PHRASE or sentence that we ask students to learn or STUDY because it demonstrates the construction of a piece of language →**30**, 79, 109

language function – language which does something, such as agreeing, offering, requesting suggesting, etc. →**30**, 35, 37, 80, 103, 104, 109, 110

language laboratory – a room where a group of students work with AUDIO DEVICES to (mostly) listen to and repeat language; very popular from about 1950–1990 →60

language level – We talk about students who have reached the advanced level or the intermediate level. We can also use CEFR (COMMON EUROPEAN FRAMEWORK OF REFERENCE) descriptions to say how good someone's language is. →35, **41**

language practice book – a book with exercises to practise grammar and vocabulary, etc. →83

language skill(s) – we generally talk about the four language skills; reading, writing, listening and speaking; we can also talk about SUB-SKILLS →40, 79, 80, 81, 83

large classes – classes with more than 30 students – sometimes as many as 150 or 200 →41, **42**

lateral consonant – the sound /l/ →24

learner autonomy – when students make decisions about their own learning →9, 40, 41, 43, 67, 76

learner characteristics – the identities that individual learners have which make them behave in the way they do →**40**, 42, 83

learner language profile (LLP) – a description of a student, saying how good they are at different areas of the language →101, 110

learner training – teaching students to identify and use techniques which will help them to be better learners →39, **40**, 42, 43

learner/learning styles – the way that different individuals like to learn and/or learn successfully →40, 76, 81, 92

learning – picking up a language by consciously studying it; different from subconscious ACQUISITION →**35**, 36, 39, 60

learning platform – see ONLINE LEARNING PLATFORM

lesson – a period of, for example, 45 minutes, an hour or 75 minutes in which students study a specific subject →79, 100

lesson outcome – see OUTCOME

lesson plan – see PLANNING

lesson shape – how the beginning, middle and ends of lessons are put together by the teacher →80

lesson stage – see STAGE (OF A LESSON)

level – see LANGUAGE LEVEL

level of challenge – how difficult a TASK will be for the students to accomplish →43

lexical approach – the idea that we should focus on VOCABULARY (LEXICAL PHRASES, etc.) more than GRAMMAR in our teaching →45

lexical chunk – see LEXICAL PHRASE →9, 18, **20**, 30

lexical cohesion – the use of a 'string' of words to help people understand a text →34

lexical field – see SEMANTIC FIELD

lexical phrase – a collection of words which are often found together and have a particular meaning, e.g. *break a leg* (said to an actor = have a successful performance), *see you later*; *break a leg* is a fixed lexical phrase (we can't change any of the words); *see you later* is a semi-fixed lexical phrase (we can also say *catch you later*) →18, **20**, 21, 30, 37, 45, 80

lexical verb – a verb which has a main meaning (different from an AUXILIARY verb) →**4**, 8, 11

line graph – a style of chart that is created by connecting a series of data points together with a line →105

linkers discourse markers which connect sentences and phrases →**34**, 80

linking sound when we put a new sound between two vowels to make the change from the first to the second easier, e.g. /j/ in /aɪjæm/ = *I am* →25

linking verb a verb (*be*, *get*, *feel*, *seem*, etc.) which links a SUBJECT with a COMPLEMENT →4

listening for general understanding when we listen for general (not detailed) ideas →60

listening for specific information when we listen because we only want to understand certain details →26, 60

literary concerned with literature or written in a style commonly found in literature →33

live listening when we listen to someone who is there in front of us (different from RECORDED LISTENING) →**60**, 61

live streaming when an event is broadcast over the INTERNET as it is happening →87

long-term goal what we want to achieve after a long time; opposite of SHORT-TERM GOAL →80

LOTE languages other than English →102

low frequency when a word is not used very often by speakers of the language →33

lower-intermediate the stage that students reach after the ELEMENTARY level and before they are at the UPPER-INTERMEDIATE level; equivalent to CEFR level B1 →17, 36, 41, 49

lower-order thinking skills (LOTS) the skills students need (e.g. in CLIL lessons) in order to answer simple questions or just classify information; different from HOTS →107, 108

lyrics – see SONG LYRICS

magic moment when something good happens in a lesson (such as a student story or discussion) which means we have to adjust or change our LESSON PLAN →52, 70, **79**, 84, 109

main clause a clause with a SUBJECT and a VERB that can exist on its own (without another clause) →2

main stress – see also STRESS the syllable which makes the loudest, strongest noise in a word or phrase →23, 26

main verb – see LEXICAL VERB

mandatory participation activities where all the students have to take part, like it or not →67

match, matching activities activities where students work out which bits of something are connected to other bits of the same thing →**48**, 70, 86, 89, 98, 110

materials-free teaching when teachers do not use books, recorded listening, etc. in their lessons →81, **84**

metacognitive skills ways of thinking which help us to become better at learning →102

metaphor when we describe something as if it were something else, e.g. *his legs turned to jelly* (= he was nervous) →**21**, 65, 79, 80, 109

MI – see MULTIPLE INTELLIGENCES

mid vowel the vowels /e/, /ə/, /ɜː/ and /ɔː/ →24

mime when people show meaning or tell a story silently, using only gesture, facial expression and actions →44, 45, 62, 64, 95, 96

mine texts when we get students to look at texts and extract any language that we/they think might be useful to study →46, 54, 56

minimal pair two words where only one sound is different, e.g *hot* and *hat* →28

mistake when students say or write something which is not correct; see also ATTEMPT, DEVELOPMENTAL ERROR, INTERFERENCE ERROR, SLIP →37, 57, 62, 75

mixed-ability class a class with students at different language levels →**42**, 83

mixed conditional – see also CONDITIONAL a conditional sentence which uses a variety of VERB TENSES →2

MLD – see MONOLINGUAL LEARNERS' DICTIONARY

mobile device any electronic device (such as a SMARTPHONE or TABLET COMPUTER) which can be carried around easily →57, 62, 76, 82, 85, **86**, 87

mobile phone a phone that does not need cables and can be carried around wherever we go →76

mock exam when students take an exam which is exactly like the real exam but is just done for practice →89

modal auxiliary verb the auxiliary verbs *can/could*, *may*, *might*, *will/would*, *shall/should*, *must* which tell us about the speaker's attitude, degree of certainty, etc. →4, 5, **8**, 10, 56, 103, 104

mode a word to describe the type/means of communication (EMAIL, letter, TWEET, etc.) →33

model when teachers say or write something clearly so that students can repeat it, they model it and we call it a language model; see also BACK CHAINING →**44**, 47, 104, 107

monitor (1) to watch and guide what our students are doing in GROUPWORK, PAIRWORK, etc. →65
(2) to try to evaluate what we ourselves are saying to see if it is correct →35

monolingual able to speak only one language →35, 77

monolingual dictionary a DICTIONARY written only in one language →82

monolingual learners' dictionary (MLD) a dictionary for students written only in the TARGET LANGUAGE →82

monologue speech where only one person is talking →33, 60

Moodle an ONLINE LEARNING PLATFORM →66, 76, 87

morpheme the smallest unit of grammatical meaning, e.g. the PAST TENSE *-ed* ending, the PLURAL *-s* ending →**4**, 6, 19, 28, 44, 98

mother tongue – see HOME LANGUAGE, L1

motivation, motivate a desire to do something; see also EXTRINSIC MOTIVATION, INTRINSIC MOTIVATION, INSTRUMENTAL MOTIVATION, INTEGRATIVE MOTIVATION →40, **43**, 64, 66, 74, 80, 81, 89

multilingual when people are multilingual they speak three or more languages →77

multiple-choice (questions) when students are asked to choose between answers marked a, b, c, d →55, **89**, 90

multiple intelligences (MI) Howard Gardner's theory that everyone has a number of intelligences (linguistic, musical, kinaesthetic, etc.) and that the strength of each one is different in different people →40

multi-syllabus a syllabus which includes GRAMMAR, VOCABULARY, language skills, LEARNER TRAINING, etc. →80

multi-word verb – see also PHRASAL VERB a verb which has more than one word, e.g. *get up*, *run out of* →4, **9**

mumble when we encourage students to speak (try things out) in a low voice →47, 63

music sounds made by voices or instruments to give pleasure, excite, provoke, etc. →58, **64**

nasal cavity the space inside the nose →24

nasal consonant the sounds /m/, /n/ and /ŋ/ →24

native speaker someone who speaks a language as their HOME LANGUAGE or L1 →**13**, 25, 82

native speaker teacher someone who is teaching their MOTHER TONGUE →**13**, 77

needs analysis an attempt to find out what students need their English for (using questionnaires, interviews, etc.) →41

negative sentence a sentence which is saying 'no' about something; the opposite of an AFFIRMATIVE SENTENCE →**3**, 14

neuro-linguistic programming — a model for management training which shows how people experience things (and succeed) differently →40

neutral (lips) — when our lips are not ROUNDED or STRETCHED →24

neutral language — language which is not especially FORMAL or INFORMAL →30, **33**

news broadcast — when people give the news on radio or television →61, 62

NLP – see NEURO-LINGUISTIC PROGRAMMING

nominate, nomination — when a teacher selects which student(s) should speak or do something →47

non-count noun – see UNCOUNTABLE NOUN

non-defining relative clause – see RELATIVE CLAUSE

notice, noticing — when we notice new language, we start to recognise what it looks like or sounds like →35

noughts and crosses — a game where students select different squares for question-answering; also called TIC-TAC-TOE →23

noun — a word (or group of words) that is the name of a person, place, thing, activity, quality or idea; nouns can be used as the subject or object of a verb; see also COLLECTIVE NOUN, COMPOUND NOUN, COUNTABLE NOUN, NOUN PHRASE, PLURAL NOUN →1, **12**, 14, 15, 16, 17, 18, 19, 26, 62, 82

noun phrase — a phrase in which every part refers to a noun, e.g. *the enthusiastic young **man** carrying an electric guitar* →1, **17**, 46

object — (in grammar) the thing (or person) that something is done to →**1**, 9

object pronoun – see also PRONOUN — a PRONOUN such as *me*, *it*, *them* which is the OBJECT of a VERB →12

object question — a question which asks about an OBJECT, e.g. *What did Shakespeare write?* see also SUBJECT QUESTION →3

objective (grading) — when we mark an exercise or a test and our own feelings and judgements are not involved; opposite of SUBJECTIVE →89

observation — when teachers are watched by their colleagues or by their director of studies, etc. →78

offer — when someone volunteers to do something for someone else, e.g. *Would you like a coffee? Shall I open the window?* →14

omit coursebook material — to make a decision not to use part of a COURSEBOOK →81

one-to-one classes — classes where the teacher is teaching only one student →41

online — TEXTS, exercises, DICTIONARIES, ONLINE LEARNING PLATFORMS, etc. available on/through the INTERNET →59, 78, 81, 82, 87, 105

online learning platform — a place on the INTERNET where students can learn with readings, DISCUSSION BOARDS, quizzes, and so on; see also VIRTUAL LEARNING ENVIRONMENT →59, 76, 99, 109, 110

open-book exam — when students can take books (such as dictionaries) into an exam to help them answer the questions →110

open (ended) question — a question which can have many different answers, e.g. *Why are you feeling sad?* The opposite of a CLOSED QUESTION →3, 107

open information-gap activity — an INFORMATION-GAP activity which is designed so that the students use a variety of language →50

open vowel — the vowels /æ/, /ʌ/, /ɑː/ and /ɒ/ →24

operational stage — when children start to be able to understand and work with abstract concepts →107

oral presentation — when a student explains something in a (probably short) speech →**53**, 65, 74, 76, 85, 87, 89, 90

organiser	a TEACHER ROLE when we explain what students have to do and then act to make it happen →65
outcome	what we hope the students will achieve/be able to do at the end of a TASK, LESSON or LESSON STAGE →39, 79, 80, 83, 109
over-generalisation	when a learner thinks a rule is more important than it is and applies it to too many things, e.g. ~~goeder~~, s~~heeps~~ →37
overhead projector (OHP)	a machine for projecting images →63, **85**
overhead transparency (OHT)	a transparent sheet that we can draw on (or photocopy onto), which can then be put on an OVERHEAD PROJECTOR →85
overlay	a sheet of paper (or a transparency) that we can put over a TEST paper and which tells us what the answers are →90
pair, pairwork	when two students work together →22, 26, 39, 42, 46, 56, 58, **67**, 79, 86, 89, 93, 102, 107, 109
palato-alveolar affricate	the CONSONANT sounds /tʃ/ and /dʒ/ →24
palato-alveolar fricative	the CONSONANT sounds /ʃ/ and /ʒ/ →24
paragraph construction	the way that people make paragraphs – often starting with a topic sentence to introduce the paragraph →75
part of speech	the grammatical category of a particular word, e.g. NOUN, VERB, SUBJECT, OBJECT, etc. →**1**, 82
participant	(1) people taking part in a CONVERSATION →33 (2) when teachers take part in an activity as if they themselves were students →52
participle	a VERB form that ends in *-ing* or *-ed* and can be used to make ADJECTIVES, e.g. *boring*, *bored* →10, 15, **16**
participle phrase	a phrase with a participle in it →16
passive voice – see also ACTIVE VOICE	When we put the elements of a sentence in the order object + verb + (by) subject (e.g. *Hamlet was written by Shakespeare*), we call it the passive voice. →**1**, 7, 32, 103
past	the time before now →5
past (tense)	a VERB form (e.g. *walked* – PAST SIMPLE, *was walking* – PAST CONTINUOUS, *had walked* – PAST PERFECT) which we use to talk about a time in the past →5, 28, 33, 34, 46, 103
past continuous	Examples: *I was eating. They were talking.* →**6**, 7, 80
past participle	the BASE FORM of a VERB with the addition of the *-ed* MORPHEME (e.g. *walk – walked*, *save – saved*) →**6**, 16, 37
past perfect	the AUXILIARY VERB *had* plus a PAST PARTICIPLE (e.g. *he had studied*, *they had run*) →2, **6**, 80
past simple	made by adding the *-ed* morpheme to the *base form* of the VERB (e.g. *he walked*, *they swam*, *she won*) →**6**, 80
past tense ending	*-ed* for REGULAR VERBS →37
peer	people who have equal status; classmates →39
peer approval	when our peers like what we do or have done →37
peer evaluation	when (one of) our peers says if our work has been good or not →90
peer observation	when two teachers who have equal status watch each other's lessons →20, 78
peer review	when one or more of our peers check our writing or speaking and make suggestions for improvement →57
perfect (verbs)	verbs referring to a time in the past which is still important in the time that the people are talking about →6

period — American English for the punctuation mark at the end of a sentence – called a FULL STOP in British English →57

personal aims — what the teacher hopes to achieve or understand in a lesson (and which they put in their LESSON PLAN) →79

personal pronoun – see also PRONOUN — a PRONOUN such as *I*, *you*, *he*, *she*, *it*, *us*, *they* which refers to a person or people →12

personalisation — when students use language to talk about themselves and things which interest them →**39**, 44, 84

phoneme — an individual unique sound →23

phonemic alphabet — an alphabet used to represent individual sounds; different from the written (A, B, C) alphabet →23

phonemic chart — a diagram which shows all the PHONEMES, and which we can use for teaching →23

phonemic script — the PHONEMIC ALPHABET, e.g. *photograph* is /fəʊtəgræf/ in phonemic script →23, 82

phonemic transcription — when we write down speech in PHONEMIC SCRIPT (instead of the written alphabet) →23

phrasal verb – see also MULTI-WORD VERB — a MULTI-WORD VERB with METAPHORICAL/IDIOMATIC meaning; phrasal verbs can be TRANSITIVE or INTRANSITIVE →4, **9**, 10, 20, 21, 70, 76, 82, 84

phrase — more than a word, less than a SENTENCE →15, 16, 26, 64, 74, 82, 102

picture — shapes, lines, colours, etc. to show what something or somebody looks like →45, 50, 51, 53, 55, 58, 61, 69, 84, 85, 86, 87, 93, 95, 96, 97, 98

pie chart — a chart which shows percentages, etc. in a circular shape – like slices in a pie →105

pilot — to try something out with one class before we use it with all our classes →81, 88

pitch — the pitch of the voice describes whether it is a high or a low tone →26, **27**

placement test — when we test students in order to decide what level they should study at; see also DIAGNOSTIC TEST →88

planning — when we make decisions about what we are going to do in a lesson *before* the lesson →43, 70, **79**, 80, 84, 88, 100, 103

planning CLIL — when we make decisions about what we are going to do in a CLIL lesson *before* the lesson →102

planning stage — the stage in the WRITING PROCESS where we think about what we are going to write →57

plateau effect — when students, often at about the INTERMEDIATE level, think that they are not making any progress and so feel DEMOTIVATED →41

play — a piece of writing designed to be acted out in a theatre →64

play extract — a part of a play →64

playacting — when we act things out for fun →97

plenary session — when everyone is listening/paying attention to the same thing, all together →107, 109

plosive — when the air from the lungs forces two parts of the mouth apart in a mini-explosion we call the result a plosive consonant (e.g. /p/ in *problem* or /d/ in *dog*) →24

plural — more than one of something →12

podcast — a recorded listening which can be downloaded from the internet on a regular basis →43, 60, 62, 87

poem — a style of writing which expresses feelings and emotions, often in a few short lines; the ends of each line may rhyme →**63**, 76, 86, 99, 100, 108

poetry — a NOUN to describe poems in general →28, 59, **63**, 99

poetry activity	an activity which uses poems →26, 58
poetry frame	outlines of poems given to students; they complete the different lines →63
poetry reordering activity	when we give students different lines from a poem and they have to work out what order they go in →**63**, 70
polite	respectful, not rude →33
portfolio	a collection of a student's work →59, 76, 99
portfolio assessment	when we give students a GRADE after looking at their PORTFOLIO →**88**, 101, 110
possessive adjective	*my*, *your*, *his*, *her*, *its*, *our* and *their* are ADJECTIVES which modify NOUNS →12
possessive pronoun	*mine*, *yours*, *his*, *hers*, *its*, *ours*, *theirs* and *whose* are pronouns which occur in sentences like *It's mine*, *the cat's theirs* →**12**, 45
possible solutions	when, in PLANNING, we think of how we might solve certain problems →79
poster presentation	when we make a poster with our ideas and then stand in front of it and explain it to people →53
PPP	a teaching procedure with three stages: PRESENTATION, PRACTICE and PRODUCTION →36, 39, 41, **44**, 45, 80, 81
practice activities	activities which are designed to get students to PRACTISE (usually) specific items of language →48, 51
practice/practise	when students get chances to repeat and use (usually) specific items of language; also the second stage of the PPP procedure →48–50, 83
praise	telling someone that their actions, appearance, etc. are good →14, 42, 66, 72, 91, 92
pre-intermediate – see INTERMEDIATE	→41
predict, prediction	when students try to guess what they will see or hear before they see or hear it →**55**, 61, 63, 85
prefix – see also AFFIX	a MORPHEME added to the beginning of a ROOT WORD, e.g. *happy* – ***un****happy*, *possible* – ***im****possible*) →**19**, 26
preposition	a word used before a NOUN, PRONOUN, etc. to show place, time, direction, etc. →1, 9, 15, **16**, 17, 104
preposition of movement	a preposition which shows the direction of something/someone →45
prepositional phrase	a phrase which starts with a PREPOSITION →1, **16**, 56
present	now →5
present continuous	Examples: *I am eating. They are sleeping.* →5, 103
present participle	made by adding the *-ing* MORPHEME to the BASE FORM of a VERB (e.g. *walk* – *walking*, *sail* – *sailing*); see also GERUND →**4**, 6, 16, 37
present perfect simple	Examples: *She has finished. They have just arrived.* →**6**, 7, 35, 49
present perfect continuous	Examples: *She has been swimming. We have been working.* →**6**, 7
present progressive – see PRESENT CONTINUOUS	
present simple	Examples: *He works in a factory. We live in Buenos Aires.* →5, **6**, 10, 28, 45, 101, 102, 103, 104
presentation, presentation software	explaining concepts, often using software programs such as *PowerPoint*, *Keynote*, *Prezi*, etc. to show images or play AUDIO or VIDEO to give examples of what we are saying →26, 53, 87, 105, 106
presentation, practice and production – see PPP	
pre-teach vocabulary	when we teach/explain the meaning of vocabulary that students will find in a text before they read it or listen to it →61

procedure a description (in lesson planning) of what we do and in what order →79

process writing an approach to teaching writing which focuses on the WRITING PROCESS as much as on the final product →72, 89

production the third stage of the PPP cycle, when students try to make their own sentences using new language →39

production dictionary a dictionary, like a THESAURUS, which helps us choose which words to use →82

proficiency test a test (often a PUBLIC EXAM) to see if students have reached a certain LEVEL →88, 89, 101

progress test when we give students a test during a term or semester to see whether they have learnt what they have been studying in the last week or month, etc. →88

prompt card a card which has words or pictures to suggest what students should do or say →52

prompter a TEACHER ROLE involving suggesting what a student should do or say →52, **65**

pronoun a word that is used in place of a noun or noun phrase; see also OBJECT PRONOUN, SUBJECT PRONOUN, REFLEXIVE PRONOUN →1, **12**, 14

pronunciation the way that people make and use the sounds of a language →23–29, 37, 62, 79, 82

proofreading (1) a test item where students have to find the mistake(s) in a sentence/paragraph (2) when we look at what we have written to see if it is correct →89

proper noun a noun which is usually the name of a person or place (or is one of a kind) and starts with a capital letter, e.g. *Mary*, *London* →12

proverb a saying or IDIOM which people use to give advice, e.g. *a stitch in time saves nine* or *where there's a will, there's a way* →21

public exam an exam which is open to anyone, whatever institution they are at →88

punctuation the marks that we use in writing (FULL STOPS, COMMAS, etc.) →1, **31**, 57, 103

puppet a model of an animal or person that you move with your hands →93, 95, 96, 97, 108

purpose clause a clause which says 'why' →2

pyramid discussion when student start a DISCUSSION in PAIRS, for example, but then those pairs join to form GROUPS of four and then of eight →52

quadrant a diagram in four parts which shows the relationships between things →105

quantifier a word or phrase which describes how much or many of something →1, 13, **14**, 17

question when we say (or write) something because we want some information or an answer →**3**, 14

question mark the punctuation mark we use in writing to show that something is a question →1, 29, **31**

question tag a phrase with (usually) an AUXILIARY VERB, used at the end of a sentence to make it a question or exclamation, e.g. *You're English aren't you? You shouldn't have done that, should you?* →**3**, 27, 46

question word a word which introduces a question, e.g. *how*, *what*, *when*, etc. →27

quiz a game with questions which contestants have to answer if they want to win →49

quotation marks another term for INVERTED COMMAS →57

rapport when teachers have a good professional relationship with their students →43, **66**, 77, 79

reading aloud when students are asked to read SENTENCES from a TEXT so that everyone in the class can hear →29, 39, 98

reading circle	when a teacher reads to YOUNG LEARNERS and they sit in a circle to listen →70, **96**, 97, 98, 108
reading for gist	when we read to get the general (not detailed) ideas; see also SKIMMING →54
reading for specific information	when we read to understand only the particular details which interest us →54
reading skills	what we do and use to make us effective readers →83
real beginner – see also BEGINNER	someone who know no English at all →41
realia	real objects that we take into our classes →**86**, 106
reason clause	a CLAUSE which explains 'why' →2
re-cast – see REFORMULATE	
recorded audio/listening	any listening text which is played through a machine →**60**, 61
recording device	any machine that we can use to record people's voices; see also AUDIO DEVICE →87
recycle, recycling	when we get students to experience and use language again that they have studied previously →39, 81, 84
reduced relative clause	also known as a CONTACT CLAUSE; see RELATIVE CLAUSE →2
reflective teacher	a teacher who experiments and thinks about what they do in lessons and how effective it is →43, 78
reflexive pronoun – see also PRONOUN	*myself, yourself, himself, herself, itself, ourselves, yourselves, themselves* →12
reformulate	when a student says something which has a mistake, and we say it again correctly, but don't ask the student to repeat it; also called RE-CASTING →**72**, 73, 74, 84
register	(1) the TONE (level of formality) and TOPIC vocabulary that we use in written and spoken texts →30, 31, **33**, 104 (2) see CLASS REGISTER
regular verb – see also IRREGULAR VERB	a verb which takes the *-ed* past tense ending →**4**, 6
relative clause	a clause which describes a noun and is introduced by a RELATIVE PRONOUN. DEFINING RELATIVE CLAUSES tell us which thing (NOUN) is being talked about. NON-DEFINING RELATIVE CLAUSES give us more information about the thing (noun). CONTACT CLAUSES (REDUCED RELATIVE CLAUSES) are defining relative clauses which do not need a relative pronoun. →**2**, 12, 16, 103
relative pronoun	pronouns like *who*, *whom*, *whose*, *where*, *which* and *that* used in RELATIVE CLAUSES →2, 12, **17**
reliable, reliability	a test is reliable when a student's paper gets the same grade from whoever has MARKED/GRADED it →90
reorder (activities)	to change the order of the activities in a coursebook →81
repeat – see REPETITION	
repetition	when students say the same thing again (and again) →**47**, 84
repetition of encounter	when students 'meet' the same language a number of times; see also RECYCLE, REVISE →**22**, 81
replace (activities)	to use our own ACTIVITIES instead of the ones in the COURSEBOOK →81
reported speech	a term teachers use to describe INDIRECT SPEECH →**10**, 103
reporting verb	verbs like *promise*, *agree*, *deny*, etc. which we use in INDIRECT SPEECH →10
request	when someone asks someone for something, e.g. *Could I have a coffee, please?* →14
research	looking for information; trying to discover new things →21, 45, 46
resource	a TEACHER ROLE when students can ask us for language information, advice, etc. →65

respond when the teacher makes helpful comments about a student's work (often their written work and done during the WRITING PROCESS to help them to write better); different from CORRECTING WRITTEN WORK →57, **72**, 75

retrieval and use when students have to try to find (in their brains) the language they have learnt and then use it →**22**, 51, 73, 84

review when students look again at what they have written to see if it needs EDITING →110

revise, revision when students look at (and use again) language which they have studied previously →39, 84

rewrite (coursebook material) when we write our own version of part of a coursebook →81

rhyme short poems where the lines end with words that have the same sound, e.g. *pet*, *get*; we can also say that *pet* rhymes with *get* →93, **94**, 96

rising tone – see also INTONATION when the PITCH of the voice goes up on the TONIC SYLLABLE →**27**, 29

role-card a card which has a role written on it for a student to play →**52**, 53

roleplay – see also SIMULATION when we get students to imagine they are in particular situations and we give them different ROLES to play →51, **53**, 56, 80, 86, 89, 97

role(s) of the teacher the different roles (ways of behaving) that teachers use in a lesson; see COMPREHENSIBLE INPUT PROVIDER, CONTROLLER, EDITOR, EVIDENCE GATHERER, FEEDBACK PROVIDER, ORGANISER, PROMPTER, RESOURCE, TUTOR →36, 52, **65**, 66

role when we ask students to pretend to be someone else – or pretend to feel something they may not themselves actually feel →52

root word the basic form of a WORD before it has had any AFFIXES, for example, added to it →19

roughly-tuned input simplified language that we use automatically to students (in the L2) or to children (in the L1) without consciously thinking about which items of language we can use →68, 92

rounded (lips) when we make our lips into an 'o' for certain vowel sounds →24

rubric the (usually) written instructions for an exercise or a test item →**81**, 88, 106

runner a member of a GROUP who comes to the front of the class to find out some information or collect something →92, 96

running dictation when students are in GROUPS and they have to send RUNNERS to the front to read something and then go back to their groups and DICTATE it →**48**, 58, 63, 70, 99

scaffold, scaffolding when teachers explain tasks in small logical stages and then help the students until they can do the task by themselves →36, **65**, 69, 74, 91, 97, 102, 107

scanning when we quickly read or listen for specific information →**54**, 60

scene an event in (an extract of) a film, play, etc. →64

schemata the knowledge about a TOPIC which we have in our heads and which we use when we read or listen to a text about that topic →61, 107

schwa the vowel sound /ə/ which is used in unstressed syllables, e.g. /ˈtiːtʃə/ →25, 26

Second Life a virtual reality software program where people can interact as AVATARS (not their real selves) →87

secondary stress the second most stressed SYLLABLE in a word or phrase; less prominent than MAIN STRESS →26

self-esteem feeling good about ourselves →39, 71, 91

semantic field words in a semantic field are related to each other and are used to talk about the same general TOPIC →34

semicolon a punctuation mark used to separate clauses when the pause required is longer than that suggested by a comma →**31**, 103

semi-fixed lexical phrase – see LEXICAL PHRASE

semi-modal auxiliary verb — *ought to, need to, used to* →8

sentence — a sequence of words with (at least) a subject and a verb, and which expresses an idea →**1**, 10, 74

sentence frame — part of a sentence which can be added to/completed in a number of ways, e.g. *I don't believe that …* (we can ask students to complete it with their own words) →20

sentence reordering — when student have to put words in correct sequences to make sentences →1, 88, 89

sentence stem — the beginning of a SENTENCE which students can use to make more sentences of their own →49, 51

sentence transformation — when we ask students to make a new SENTENCE using a word or words we give them so that the new sentence means exactly the same as the old one →89

separable phrasal verb — a PHRASAL VERB where we can put something between the VERB and the PARTICLE →9

sequence of lessons — lessons which follow each other, and which we plan to have connections with each other →79, 100, 101

shadow speaking — when students speak along with recorded audio material →63

short-term goal — something we want to achieve, but very quickly; opposite of LONG-TERM GOAL →80

shouted dictation — when students all shout different sentences (at the same time) for different partners sitting at a distance to write down →**48**, 58, 61

silent way, the — a method developed by Caleb Gattegno in which the teacher says as little as possible and the students rely on each other →36

simile — when we compare something to something else, e.g. *a voice like thunder* →21

simple — the simple ASPECT is used for actions which are complete; different from the CONTINUOUS aspect →6

simulation – see also ROLEPLAY — when we ask students to imagine that they are in different real-life situations – sometimes playing a role →51, **53**

since* and *for — ADVERBS often used with the PRESENT Perfect to say when something started or how long it has been going on for →49

singular — one of something →12

site – see WEBSITE

situation — what is happening at a particular time; sometimes used to introduce new language →**45**, 61

skill – see LANGUAGE SKILL — →40

skimming — when we look quickly through a text for GIST rather than reading it for detail →54

slip — a MISTAKE made because a student is not concentrating – and which they can easily correct themselves →37

smartboard – see INTERACTIVE WHITEBOARD

smartphone — a mobile phone which can access the INTERNET, make VIDEOS and AUDIO recordings and use APPS →16, 82, 86

social networking — when people interact and talk to each other, especially using programs such as *Facebook* and TWITTER →87

sociogram — a diagram which shows the relationships within a group of people →67

soft CLIL — when people teach some (parts of) lessons, but not all, using CLIL; see also HARD CLIL →102

soft palate — the soft skin at the back of the top of the mouth; also called the *velum* →24

solowork	when students work alone →67
song	music with words that people sing →**64**, 70, 93, 94, 100
song lyrics	the (lines of) words of a song →28, **64**, 87
speaking-like (writing)	writing that looks a bit like speaking, e.g. *Hey Dude! U OK?* →**31**, 32
special friend	puppets, cartoon characters, etc. that YOUNG LEARNERS can interact with →**93**, 95, 96, 97
specific adjective – see also ADJECTIVE	an ADJECTIVE which describes exactly what type of thing (NOUN) is being described →15
speech	when we talk (usually in a FORMAL way) to a group of people about a specific topic →76
spelling	the way we put letters together to make words →75, 76
spidergram	another word for a WORDMAP →59
spine poem	the title of a book is written vertically (as it would be on the spine); each line of the poem then starts with one word from that title →63
stage of a lesson	one of the different parts of a lesson →42, 68, 79, **80**
state	how people feel, what something seems like, how things are, etc. →**4**, 5
state of mind	how we feel at any certain time; we usually use SIMPLE verb forms to describe this →**4**, 27
stative verb	a verb that doesn't describe an action or an EVENT, but instead something that just 'is'; stative verbs are not usually CONTINUOUS; opposite of DYNAMIC VERB →6
stimulus-response-reinforcement	the stages which are used to condition people so that they always behave in the same way; see also BEHAVIOURISM →36
story	when we describe true or imaginary events to entertain people →39, 45, 53, 83, 94, 95, **96**, 97, 98, 99
story circle	an activity where students (in a circle) all participate one after another to complete written stories →42, **58**
story reconstruction	when different students are given different parts of a story, often shown in pictures, and they have to work out what the story is by talking to each other →**53**, 55, 67
storyboard	pictures which are used like notes to describe the scenes that people are going to film →62, 105
streaming	when students are put in groups according to their ability →42
stress	the force or loudness that we put on a syllable or word; see also MAIN STRESS, SECONDARY STRESS →11, 14, **26**, 27, 29, 31, 35, 37, 64, 95
stretched (lips)	when we pull our lips apart to make sounds like /iː/ →24
strip of paper	a long thin piece of paper →63, 83, **86**, 94
student talking time (STT)	the amount of time that students (not teachers) talk in a lesson →67, **68**
study (see also ESA**)**	to focus on the construction of language →35, 36, 39, **80**
sub-skill	Example: reading is a skill, READING FOR SPECIFIC PURPOSES is a sub-skill →40, 55, 83
sub-genre – see also GENRE	a business letter is a sub-genre of the GENRE letter →32
subject	(1) the person or thing that performs the action of a verb (or is described by the verb), and which comes before the verb →**1**, 3, 10 (2) the thing (topic, etc.) that you are talking about, reading about or studying →41, 80, 100, 102
subject pronoun – see also PRONOUN	a PRONOUN such as *I we*, *you* that is the SUBJECT of a VERB →12

subject question	a question about a SUBJECT, e.g. *Who wrote Hamlet?* see also OBJECT QUESTION →**3**, 49
subject-specific knowledge	(in CLIL) things students need to know for a specific TOPIC →88
subject-specific language	(in CLIL) language students need to know for a specific TOPIC →104
subject-specific sentences	(in CLIL) sentences which describe a particular TOPIC →107
subject-specific vocabulary	(in CLIL) vocabulary that is connected to a specific TOPIC →104, 107
subjective (grading)	when people use their own judgement to mark a TEST; opposite of OBJECTIVE →90
subordinate clause	a clause which depends on a MAIN CLAUSE →2
substitute teacher	a teacher who takes a lesson when the regular teacher cannot do it →10
substitution dialogue	a dialogue where students can change certain items to make new (but similar) dialogues →30
suffix – see also AFFIX	a MORPHEME added to the end of a ROOT WORD, e.g. *happy – happi**ness**, possible – possibil**ity***; see also PREFIX →**19**, 26
summative assessment	ACHIEVEMENT TESTS, PROFICIENCY TESTS, etc. which measure students' abilities at the end of a course or period of study; different from FORMATIVE ASSESSMENT →**88**, 101, 110
superlative adjective – see also ADJECTIVE	Examples: *cleverest, most expensive, best* →**15**, 49
superordinate	a word with a number of HYPONYMS, e.g *vehicle* (with hyponyms *car, truck, bus*, etc.) →18
supplementary material	any books or exercises that teachers use which are not their COURSEBOOK →81, **83**
support strategies	things that teachers can do to help students in informal evaluation →110
survey	a type of enquiry to find out how many people do something →108
syllable – see also TONIC SYLLABLE	(part of) a word which has only one vowel sound →**26**, 27, 29
syllabus	a list of items to be taught in a certain sequence; see also GRAMMAR SYLLABUS, VOCABULARY SYLLABUS →36, 79, **80**, 106
synonym	a word which means the same as another word →**18**, 82
syntax	the grammar 'rules' which say what order words should be in →88, 95
T-diagram	a chart that shows two aspects of a topic, such as advantages and disadvantages, for and against →105
table	a type of diagram which lists information in rows and columns →105, 107
tablet computer	a flat MOBILE DEVICE, like a computer but smaller →16, 76, 82, 85, **86**, 106, 109
taboo	not allowed; words we mustn't use because they are rude →82
tag question – see QUESTION TAG	
taking the register – see CLASS REGISTER	
target language	the language that students are learning or want to learn →36, 77, 82, 92
task	an activity for students which has an OUTCOME – a 'finish' →**36**, 39, 45
task-based learning (TBL)	when teachers ask students to use language to do TASKS rather than just learning GRAMMAR, VOCABULARY, etc. →**36**, 45, 87
task syllabus	a list of tasks in the order we want the students to do them →80
teacher development	how teachers continue to learn and grow during their years as teachers →26, 34, **78**, 79
teacher talking time (TTT)	the amount of time that a teacher (not the students) speaks in a lesson →68
teacher role – see ROLE OF THE TEACHER	

teacher's guide a book which explains how teachers can use their COURSEBOOK →81

teachers' resource books books which are full of ACTIVITIES for teachers to use →83

teaching aid anything (such as REALIA, the BOARD, CUISENAIRE RODS, etc.) which helps us to teach →79

teaching unplugged a name given to a style of teaching which does not use a lot of materials (e.g. COURSEBOOKS), technology, etc. →84

teenagers children aged 13–19 (though people usually mean 13–17 when they talk about teenagers in general); see also ADOLESCENT →35, **38**, 39, 95

tense, verb tense the form of a VERB which shows what time is being talked about →4, **5**, 6

tentative uncertain or hesitant →30, **33**

test, testing when we find out how much students know; see also ASSESSMENT, ACHIEVEMENT TEST, DIAGNOSTIC TEST, PLACEMENT TEST, PROFICIENCY TEST →29, 55, **88**–90, 70, 102, 110

test item – see DIRECT TEST ITEM, INDIRECT TEST ITEM

test-teach-test when we ask students to do something to see if they can, and then we teach it if they can't →45

text any piece of writing or speaking which is a collection of phrases or sentences →9, 16, 22, 29, 34, 42, 45, 46, 50, 55, 56, 81, 86, 89, 96

text and discourse how written and spoken texts are formed →80

text message, text a type of message which we can send on a mobile phone/cellphone; to send a message by mobile phone →33, 58, 86

theme (1) the main TOPIC or idea in a text →79, 80, 100
(2) topics/ideas which we use for PLANNING →100

thesaurus a type of PRODUCTION DICTIONARY which gives many different words for the same meanings →82

thinking skills the things we do to help us think effectively; see also COGNITIVE SKILLS →107

third conditional Example: *If I had woken up earlier I wouldn't have arrived late.* →**2**, 46, 56, 69

tic-tac-toe another name for NOUGHTS AND CROSSES →23

time adverbial a phrase which acts like an adverb and describes time (when), e.g. *all night* → 34, 102

time clause a clause which refers to time, e.g. *in two weeks, when we were young* →**2**, 3

timelines diagrams to explain verb tenses and when things happened or will happen →104

timetable fit (when we plan lessons) how the lesson follows on from previous lessons and fits into the SYLLABUS →79

timing (when we plan lessons) how long we think an activity will last →**79**, 109

tone the level of FORMALITY, COLLOQUIALISM, etc. in a TEXT – and which shows what REGISTER we are using →33

tonic syllable the SYLLABLE in a spoken PHRASE or utterance where the PITCH of the voice changes →27

top-down processing when we start by reading for GIST –trying to understand the general meaning of a TEXT before looking at details of language →54

topic a subject that people talk or write about →33, 61, 62, 79, 80, 81, 84, 87, 100

topic web a diagram (like a SPIDERGRAM) which shows how topics are related to each other; we can use this for PLANNING →100

topics and themes a way of organising a syllabus through CONTENT →80

total physical response (TPR) a methodology where students learn by performing actions →**4**, 45, 96

track an individual part of an AUDIO or VIDEO recording →60

transcript the written version of what people say in an AUDIO or VIDEO CLIP →62

transfer information to take information from a TEXT and put it in a DIAGRAM or some other form →55

transitive inseparable phrasal verb when the object of a PHRASAL VERB has to come after the particle, e.g. *look after* (someone), *look into* (something), *run into* (someone) →9

transitive verb – see also INTERANSITIVE VERB a verb that takes an OBJECT →**4**, 82

translanguage CLIL when a CLIL topic is taught in two (or more) languages →102

translanguage classroom a classroom where more than one language is being used, for example in CLIL lessons →103

translation (activities) activities which ask students to translate from L1 to L2 (and or vice versa) →39, **77**

transmission teaching when the teacher stands at the front and 'transmits' (= gives) the students information →65

tree diagram a diagram showing how things are connected in a hierarchy →105

true/false question when students are asked (in a TEST or EXERCISE) to say whether something is true or false →89

turn, turn-taking when people start and stop speaking in conversations →27, 52

tutor a TEACHER ROLE involving giving advice to (usually) individual students →65

tweet a message on TWITTER →32, 57

Twitter a social networking site where people can leave messages for everyone to read →32, 33, 58, 78, 87

two-particle transitive phrasal verb Examples: *He* ***gets along with*** *his brother. She* ***puts up with*** *his bad temper.* →9

uncountable noun a NOUN than cannot be plural, e.g. *furniture*; see also COUNTABLE NOUN →**12**, 13, 14, 17

unforeseen problems when something negative happens in a lesson that the teacher had not anticipated →70, **79**, 109

unintelligible – see INTELLIGIBILITY

unstressed when we don't emphasise sounds by making them louder, longer, etc. →26

unstressed syllable any SYLLABLE in a word or phrase apart from the stressed syllable(s) →25

upper-intermediate – see also INTERMEDIATE the level reached when students have (usually) done about 250 hours English study; equivalent to CEFR level B2 →29, 41, 42, 46 59, 75

utterance a PHRASE (or phrases) which make a spoken SENTENCE, QUESTION or EXCLAMATION →26

VAKOG an acronym used in NEURO-LINGUISTIC PROGRAMMING to describe different stimuli (visual, auditory, kinaesthetic, olfactory, gustatory) →40

validity, test validity TESTS which are designed (only) to test what they are supposed to test →88, 110

variety including a lot of different types of activity, etc. in a LESSON →80

variety of English the English spoken in a particular country, region, etc. →26

velar nasal the CONSONANT sound /ŋ/ →24

velar plosive the CONSONANT sounds /g/ and /k/ →**24**, 25

velum – see SOFT PALATE

venn diagram a diagram with overlapping circles to show differences and similarities between two or more things →105, 107, 108

verb a word or group of words that describes an ACTION, an EVENT or a STATE →1, **4**, 10, 18, 20, 26, 62, 93

very young learners learners aged from two to around four or five →91

video originally a film recording on tape; now also used to describe digital filmed recordings →60, **62**, 64, 66, 74, 85, 87, 106

video clip – see also FILM CLIP a (usually) short VIDEO RECORDING →62

video feedback when teachers make a VIDEO RECORDING of their comments about a student's work →75

video recording when things are filmed using a film/video camera →76, 78

visual learner a student who gets most benefit from seeing things →105

visual organiser a way of showing information with diagrams →89, 100, 104, **105**, 106, 110

VLE (virtual learning environment) any ONLINE site which students use to learn and interact; see also ONLINE LEARNING PLATFORM →3, 87

vocabulary the WORDS that we know or use →18–22, 35, 79, 80, 81, 109

vocabulary book a book where students write down new VOCABULARY →107

vocabulary syllabus a SYLLABUS which says what VOCABULARY should be learnt when →106

vocal cords the two strips of membrane (like muscle) in our throats behind the larynx →24

vocal folds – see VOCAL CORDS

voiced consonant a CONSONANT sound made with the VOCAL CORDS closed (so they vibrate as the air comes from the lungs) →24

voiceless consonant a CONSONANT sound made with the VOCAL CORDS open (so there is no vocal vibration) →24

vowel vowel sounds are made when there is no obstruction in the mouth for the flow of air from the lungs; in the alphabet, the letters *a*, *e*, *i*, *o*, *u*; different from CONSONANT →13, 15, 17, 28

wait time when teachers give students time to think before they speak →107

warmer an activity at the beginning of a lesson to get the students in a good mood; also called an ICEBREAKER →70, 109

washback when the form of an exam influences the way that teachers teach (because they want their students to pass the exam) →89

web 2.0 when the INTERNET changed so that people could interact with each other (and with the CONTENT) ONLINE →59

webinar an ONLINE seminar; people can watch and take part even when they are physically in different places →78, 87

webquest a type of project where students look for information on different WEBSITES →84, 87

website a place on the INTERNET where people place information, pictures, etc. →53, 76, 83, 86, 87

wh-question a question which starts with a word like *what*, *who*, *where*, *why*, *when*, *how*, etc. →**3**, 56

whiteboard – see also BOARD a classroom board that is white and can be written on with marker pens; see also INTERACTIVE WHITEBOARD →85

whole-class teaching when we teach all the students in a class at the same time →67

wiki a computer program which allows everyone to add to and change the content (like *Wikipedia*) →58, 59, 87

***will* future**	when we use the MODAL AUXILIARY VERB *will* to talk about the future, e.g. *I will see you tomorrow* →45
word	a single group of letters and sounds which, together, mean something →19
word family	all the different realisations (AFFIXES, etc.) of the BASE FORM of a word →19
word map - see also SPIDERGRAM	a diagram showing how words are related to each other →21, 22, 59, 85, 105, 107, 108
word order	the correct sequence of words in a PHRASE/SENTENCE →10
Wordle	a software program that produces a pictorial representation of the words in a text →63
workbook	a book which usually accompanies a COURSEBOOK, full of practice EXERCISES →76, 81
worksheet	a piece of paper (or document) with practice EXERCISES →42, 54, 62, 76, 82, 83
writing process	how people plan, review and edit their writing →**57**, 59, 75, 99
writing-like	when people speak as if they were writing, e.g. a FORMAL lecture →31
yes/no question	a question that needs a 'yes' or 'no' answer, e.g. *Have you read 'War and Peace?'* → **3**, 49, 107
young learners	usually students from about four years old to adolescence →14, 38, 91-101,108
zero article	when we do not use articles, e.g *war is terrible, life is beautiful* →13
zero conditional	a 'timeless' conditional clause, e.g. *if/when it rains, people get wet* →**2**, 46
zone of proximal development (ZPD)	when learners (especially children) are ready for the next learning stage – a concept suggested by Lev Vygotsky (1896–1934) →38, 91

Pearson Education Limited
Edinburgh Gate
Harlow
Essex CM20 2JE
England
and Associated Companies throughout the world.

www.pearsonELT.com/ETK

First published 2012

Ninth impression 2024

ISBN: 978-1-4082-6804-9

Set in Janson Text
Printed and bound by CPI Group (UK) Ltd, Croydon, CR0 4YY
CTPSC/01

Author's acknowledgements

I want to thank all those who have helped with *Essential Teacher Knowledge*.

People who read and commented on this book at various stages include Ricardo Fajardo Cortés, Nick Dawson, Jill Fortune, Nam Joon Kang, Cecilia Lemos, Carol Lethaby, Deniz Özdeniz and Damian Williams. It is difficult to thank them enough for their insights and wisdom.

Three teachers – Tom McDonnell, Emily Scrimshaw and Conor Short – let us film them teaching. They were fantastic to work with and did everything (and more) that we asked of them.

Finally, thanks to the many teachers whose voices are on the DVD and the website, and those who provided lesson plans. They demonstrate the wonderful and inspiring variety of ideas and techniques that make teaching such an exciting profession to be in.

Jeremy Harmer

Acknowledgements

The publisher would like to thank the following for their kind permission to reproduce their photographs:

(Key: b-bottom; c-centre; l-left; r-right; t-top)

Alamy Images: Associated Sports Photography 83br, Thomas Cockrem 18tr, 26tr, 78tl, Doug Houghton 103 (car), 108 (car), Mike Lane 18tc, Ilene MacDonald 102 (hospital), 108 (hospital), Pictorial Press Ltd 231r, Kirk Treakle 14tc; **Education Solutions Worldwide Inc**: 163l; **Fotolia.com**: 16tc, 32tr, 34tr, 42tr, 52tr, 56t, 62tr, 72r, 198l, jokatoons 209 (fireman), LeDav 209 (cauliflower), Lorelyn Medina 209 (watermelon), RRF 147tl, Wichittra Srisunon 209 (butter), Bernadett Szombat 76tr, Ivonne Wierink 103 (breakfast), 108 (breakfast); **Getty Images**: AFP 239c, Kris Connor 92bl, Tom Stoddart 115bl; **iStockphoto**: 12tr, 16tr, 20r, 28tr, 30tr, 74l; **Pearson Education Ltd**: 14tr, 22tr, 36tr, 38tr, 40tr, 40l, 46t, 48tr, 56tr, 58tr, 60t, 60tr, 64tr, 70tr, 70l, 72tr, 74r, 76bc, 116r, 117c, 133tr, 220r, 238tl, 238l, 239, 239t, 239tl, 239c (Above), 239c (Below), 239cl, 239bl; **Photolibrary.com**: Corbis 102 (doctor), 103 (doctor), 108 (doctor), 109 (doctor); **Rex Features**: Roger-Viollet 84br; **Shutterstock.com**: 12t, 20tr, 34t, 36cr (Below), 36r, 36r (Above), 46tr, 48l, 50t, 50tr, 76r, Senai Aksoy 32t; **SuperStock**: Westend61 76l (flight attendant)

All other images © Pearson Education

Every effort has been made to trace the copyright holders and we apologise in advance for any unintentional omissions. We would be pleased to insert the appropriate acknowledgement in any subsequent edition of this publication.